THE EARTH ONLY ENDURES

On Reconnecting with Nature
and Our Place in It

Jules Pretty

London • Sterling, VA

First published by Earthscan in the UK and USA in 2007

ISBN: 978-1-84407-432-7

Typeset by MapSet Ltd, Gateshead, UK
Printed and bound in the UK by Bath Press
Cover design by Andrew Corbett

For a full list of publications please contact:

Earthscan
8–12 Camden High Street
London, NW1 0JH, UK
Tel: +44 (0)20 7387 8558
Fax: +44 (0)20 7387 8998
Email: earthinfo@earthscan.co.uk
Web: **www.earthscan.co.uk**

22883 Quicksilver Drive, Sterling, VA 20166-2012, USA

Earthscan is an imprint of James and James (Science Publishers) Ltd and publishes in association with the International Institute for Environment and Development

A catalogue record for this book is available from the British Library

Library of Congress Cataloging-in-Publication Data
Pretty, Jules N.
  The Earth only endures / Jules Pretty.
    p. cm.
  Includes bibliographical references and index.
  ISBN-13: 978-1-84407-432-7 (hardback)
  ISBN-10: 1-84407-432-3 (hardback)
  1. Nature—Effect of human beings on. 2. Human ecology. 3. Animal-plant relationships.
I. Title.
  GF75.P74 2007
  304.2—dc22

                                                    2006101916

The paper used for this book is FSC-certified and totally chlorine-free. FSC (the Forest Stewardship Council) is an international network to promote responsible management of the world's forests.

Mixed Sources
Product group from well-managed
forests and other controlled sources
www.fsc.org Cert no. SGS-COC-2121
© 1996 Forest Stewardship Council
FSC

For Gill, Freya and Theo

Wi-ća-hća-la kiŋ he-ya
pe lo ma-ka kiŋ le-će-la te-haŋ yuŋ-ke-lo e-ha pe-lo
e-haŋ-ke-ćoŋ wi-ća-ya-ka pe-lo.

The old men

say

the Earth

only

endures.

You spoke

truly.

You are right.

Teton Sioux *ozuye olowan* (war path song) or *akicita olowan* (warrior song). Quoted in Dee Brown's *Bury My Heart at Wounded Knee* (1970, Holt, Rinehart & Winston).

Contents

Preface

Green Places,
Good Places

There is a blue sea between Africa, Asia and Europe known well to many millions of people. It has been the cradle of dozens of civilizations, and seen them go too, leaving behind mysterious stoneworks, epic myths and many undeciphered languages. Today, we might pause in the shade of lemon and olive groves on limestone slopes, or walk among the aromatic scrublands of thyme and rosemary, or linger by the deep cisterns of green water under contested hillsides, or bend into sandstorms while peering for the shadows of wild animals and humped cattle. We might find ourselves tripping over the remains of temples, pyramids, forts and agricultural terraces, or knee deep in wild grasses where Neanderthals and, later,

Homo sapiens made their ways out of Africa, and later, much later, began the business of agriculture. Camus's outsider, Patrice Mersault, contemplates a happy death overlooking a part of this azure sea, where the beauty of the place touches his heart, and the sky is brilliant and full of the rustling of wings and crying of birds. Thomas Hardy once wondered whether such scenes would go onward the same, though dynasties pass.

This book is about our relations with nature, animals and places. It centres on themes of connections and estrangement. For most of human history, we have lived our daily lives in close proximity to the land. Within the next few years, though, there will for the first time be more people worldwide living in urban than rural areas. Thus the estrangement grows. We lose nature and green places, and we forget the animals and birds that once were there. We eat anonymized foods that have no place-based stories, and put the fat of the land on ourselves. Even worse, convenient technologies do so much for us that we are considerably less physically active, and so excess calories do not get burned off. Bizarrely, we seem to buy into a comforting idea that all we do contributes to inevitable economic progress, and that this progress is always a good thing. We can no longer conceive of indigenous people living in old, uncivilized ways in the forests, tundras, deserts and polar regions, or of small-scale and inefficient farming communities, and so seek to convert them all to the benefits of modern life (and dispossess them of the old). Perhaps we are too frightened to think that they might have something useful to tell us, that their lives are not 'solitary, poore, nasty, brutish and short', as Thomas Hobbes believed.

At the same time, we are consuming the world to death. The modern lifestyles (and economies) put up as the most desirable in the world are precisely those that would need six to eight Earths to provision if all the world's population adopted them. Yet given the choice, this is what most people would want. On a pessimistic day, we moderns look to be joining one of those former civilizations that thought they would go on forever, but which then failed to endure for one forgotten reason or another. Optimistically, though, we can look forward a century and see that the world population will have begun to fall. The Malthusian expansion will be over, and lands will be returned to nature. Some settlements will have to be abandoned, especially by the sea, and green places and animals will have returned. But can we ourselves make it across this century?

Life made this planet as it is now, shaping and changing the conditions to make them more favourable to life. Individual organisms do the same thing by constructing their niches in ways to improve their likelihood of survival. As humans, we did the same over a few hundred thousand generations as highly successful hunter-gatherers. Today, we find ourselves in the remarkable position of being the first species to change our environment to make it less favourable to life. We are making our own world inhospitable, and so risk losing what it means to be human. Gaia will become Grendel, lurking beyond our great mead halls, silently creeping in with murderous intent when we are no longer observant. And as yet, we have no heroic Beowulf to come to the rescue.

The world is currently facing its sixth great extinction episode, and has now developed its fifth atmosphere. The last extinction pulse saw off the dinosaurs; the penultimate atmosphere was the pre-industrial unpolluted one. Arguments for saving nature have mainly centred on two themes – economic (nature provides many goods and services for our economies) and ethical (nature should be respected and saved because it is the right thing to do). Yet it is the emotional benefits that have tended to be neglected. How, then, does nature make us feel? Much, of course, will depend on what else is important in our lives. Is it a good day or a bad day? Irrespective of where we come from in the world, however, it seems that the presence of living things makes us feel good.

Nature, of course, is not always a good or even neutral place. We do terrible things to each other in the name of personal or collective gain. A woodland might be a site for a family picnic for some, but the location of a former war crime for others. A forest may be an ancestral home to people small in number, but they will be hurriedly forgotten when it is chopped down, burned and converted to productive farmland. Successful conservation efforts also mean there are now more predators on the land, and many communities are having to come to terms with what it means to be potential prey again.

Generally, though, green places are good places. They are where things happen to us, where memories are created, where identities are forged, where we can experience an elemental world and where today we say we appreciate the sense of escape. Take away these places and our knowledge of them begins to decline. Such ecological literacy falls with disconnections and estrangement, and once it goes, we are going to be less inclined to agitate when someone seeks to harm or take away another green place. Indeed, there are some who would celebrate this loss of knowledge, understanding and concern, as it enables them to strip away yet more of the world's heritage, turning it into money that provokes further consumption and drives us further towards doom.

It is now known that in the process of evolution, both environment and genes are equally important. We understand much more about the roles of individual genes, but also that they are switched on and off by both environmental signals and other genes. Fears over genetic determinism have abated (and certainly should be over). What we are is an emergent property of the world that we create and the world we live in. But there is much controversy. Many do not believe we descended from animals; others contest the sub-theories of evolution; others still feel discomfort over questions of our own free will, and how much genes or the environment intervene. What is clear, though, is that we should be seriously wondering about what kinds of natural and social environments we can now create. If we get it right, might we see a new and more humble and respectful phase of ecolution (where we choose appropriate natural and social environments that allow us to coevolve and survive)? Perhaps this is just wishful thinking.

The idea of progress deceives us into thinking we are at the summit, the best there is in the animal kingdom, with the best civilization there ever was. We also wrongly believe that we are happier than in the past, because we have so much more. Yet we aspire to levels and types of consumption that are destroying the world and have forgotten how to say enough is enough. The progress myth also distorts our views of ourselves in relation to animals. We are no more than animals, clever ones of course, yet our disconnections to wild and farmed animals are growing. Pets are popular, and forms of animal iconography are prevalent in every culture, from children's book characters to pub names and mythical beasts. But the estrangement grows, and as a result we forget how ecosystems work.

The hunting of animals is a noisy controversy, but then so is raising animals for food. Many of us conveniently forget that livestock have to be killed if we are to eat them (all twenty billion a year worldwide). There are many conflicts over wild animal management – from hedgehogs to kangaroos, wild boar to badgers, and tigers to wolves. Some of the largest of these even have their eyes on us as prey in some places. Supermarkets also make us forgetful of the land. In industrialized countries, the food shortages of all but the last two generations have long since disappeared, replaced by an abundance of saturated fats and sugary foods and drinks. Obesity is common in adults and children, and in many developing countries there are now more people overweight than hungry. Can the world food system ever change? It seems highly unlikely at the moment, though ecological and economic landscapes populated with small farmers in many developing countries are now showing that food production can be both environmentally sustainable and make links directly to consumers. There is a good story to tell. A major new challenge for all agriculture is rewilding. Sustainable agricultural systems make better use of nature's services within fields, on the rest of farms and in whole landscapes. We could begin to see the reintroduction of iconic animals and birds into distinctive landscapes. Some farmers are already doing revolutionary things to rewild their farms, and still find a way to stay in business.

Another feature of progress and estrangement is the growing incidence of physical inactivity. Hunter-gatherers and farmers expend energy to catch and grow their food; the rest of us rely on cars and are gradually losing the ability to walk. Physical inactivity (and junk food) is killing us, and our kids. It also reduces the chance of accidental or designed engagement with nature. We know that the natural environment positively affects our mental states. Is it any surprise to learn that mental ill-health is on the increase just as environments and biodiversity come under serious threat, just as we seem to stop going there? The World Health Organization predicts that depression and mental ill-health will be the greatest source of ill-health worldwide by 2020. Yet green places are good places – from the small patches in cities to the wide open wildernesses, and there are many ways to engage in green exercise, from gardening to forest schools to country walks. All these are good for health, but for many adults are no more than temporary remedial measures, as we dash back to the rat race. Maybe it is too late for some of us. We have forgotten, and will never reconnect enough. The real challenge is to get to today's young children, connect them with nature and its mysteries early, and prevent the extinction of eco-logical literacy that will dog us to our graves.

The landscape is full of stories and subtle meanings. It is where we can be anchored to places, where identities can be created. It is where we can experience the elemental world. You might ask, how often does the weather now intervene in our lives? Central heating and air conditioning increase our comfort, but decrease connections yet further. In the name of progress, we remove the small farmers, nomads and hunter-gatherers from the land, and then strangely find ourselves dreaming about these very lifestyles. What is so very wrong about a life connected to animals and the land, in which respect for the world is central, and in which time is not seen to be linear, and so progressing inevitably to something better? In T S Eliot's *Four Quartets*, the circularity of time forms a central theme. At the centre of time and space is the 'still point of a turning world', where we find peace and meaning. There are now very few social settings where precise timing is no longer the norm. Nearly all of us wear watches, and get jumpy when someone is late by a minute or two. By the time we stop to draw breath, we are again nearly in our graves. Time past and time future are all tied together, but then this is another thing we have forgotten.

Should we be optimistic or pessimistic? Do you think things will get better or worse? What are the prospects for getting our civilization across this century? The options for liberation probably centre on re-establishing the age-old reciprocity with the land, on engaging in ecological restoration and technological innovation, on eating food that comes from known places, on imagining the world as a different kind of place, and then going there. If we imagine nothing can change, then we can expect to be in deep trouble.

The sixteen essays in this book are organized into five parts. There is a logic to the structure, but they can be read in any order. The first essay, 'Becoming green', opens with a brief account of how the world evolved, and how life then changed the world, making it more hospitable to life. 'Birch bark and blue sky' investigates the way consumption patterns are threatening our modern civilization, and how we simply do not know how to say enough is enough. 'A room with a green view' sets the scene for how the view from the window actually does improve well-being, and the final essay in the first part of this book, 'Unhealthy places', describes evidence for how places can be malign or improve our health. Nature, it seems, is good for us, though we seem to be acting as if it is not.

The second part of the book, 'Animals and us', describes our often confused and contradictory relations with animals. The great species extinction brought on by us, and in which we are losing so much, is discussed in 'Where the wild things were'. At the same time, there are conservation successes, and the numbers of some animals are increasing. Some of these we hunt, as we once did for millennia, though there is controversy over what constitutes ethical behaviour towards animals. These debates are the subject of 'Hunters and the hunted'. The best fishermen and hunters become the fish and the prey, an intimate bonding. Thus the landscape may be inhabited by imagination alone, which changes the land as it appears to us. 'Animal magic' centres on our relations with animals and the land, our depictions of animals, our links with pets, and the emergence of big cats in the imagined and real British landscapes.

The third part, 'Food and the land', begins with 'The fatta the lan'', a reference to John Steinbeck's *Of Mice and Men*, in which Lennie and George dream of having their own farm, where they imagine they will be able to live off the fat of the land. Today the obesity crisis is now fully upon us, and health problems are growing, and the prospects for radical changes in the world food system seem very dim. Thomas Jefferson celebrated the idea of small farmers on the land, though recent agricultural development has adopted an economic model that now drives away these small farmers. 'Little houses on the prairie' describes the remarkable changes in southern Brazil, Thailand, Sri Lanka, and even in the Mid-west US prairies too. The drylands are tough, and likely to get harder in the face of climate change, and 'The shadow of the rain' tells the story of farmers who are connecting up and working together to make improvements in India, Kenya and West Africa. In the final essay, 'Rewilding agriculture', the prospects for a closer relationship between nature and agriculture are explored.

In the fourth part, 'People and the land', the first essay discusses the legibility of landscapes. Ecological literacy and knowledge about the land was once high, but is now falling. As it disappears, will we forget what it is to be human? 'Exclusion zones' describes the surprising transformation of a large area of Ukraine, Belarus and Russia after the Chernobyl accident. The removal of people (most, but not all) has created a 3500km^2 exclusion zone, which has been reinvaded by animals, birds and fish. The old people who remain are now entering their own end times. Similar reinvasions occurred after other civilizations disappeared, such as the Mayans in central America, and after the centuries of forced removal of villagers in mediaeval England and the creation of some 3000 lost villages. The final essay, 'Life and land on the North Atlantic fringe', links the lands of the Scottish Highlands and Islands to those in Labrador. Scotland suffered its own dispossessions in the clearances, as people were removed by hard-hearted landlords. In Labrador, the Innu are the latest group of native Americans to be removed from their hunter-gatherer and nomadic lifestyles and settled into modern villages. These disconnections are not just painful, they destroy lives and communities.

The final part looks to the future. In the first essay, 'Ecolution', the roles of genes and the environment in moulding us are discussed. Any lingering ideas of determinism should now be thoroughly discredited, as we now much better understand how we emerge from a continuous engagement with both genes and the environment. Unfortunately, we are now making a world inhospitable to life and cannot predict what will result. The final essay, 'Liberation', offers some thoughts on what next. Should we wait for wide-scale policy, institutional and market change to solve these problems? If so, then the prospects are probably not good. Environmental contrarians will continue to contest whether we have a problem at all. If their voices prevail, then this spells the end of the world as we know it. Or shall we instead try to live our own lives differently? To create time and space for contemplation, for re-engagement in the dance with nature, for meaning and stories.

We need to get inside the country, be a part of the land, engage with the land as a dance, where endless places may encourage new revelations. This will, of course, be increasingly difficult for those billions of people living in megacities. Wallace Stegner says the prairie taught him identity. Now we need to go out and find a new identity. As André Gide writes, 'the country only comes into existence as our approach gives it form'. Then, speaking to Nathaniel in *Fruits of the Earth*, he says, 'And when you have read me, throw this book away – and go out.' Set out, as Simon Barnes suggests, with high hopes and low expectations.

It does not sound like much. But maybe that is all we can do today and tomorrow. For the longer term, though, we will need very much more. There are exemplars, generally localized and somewhat small scale, throughout the world that point towards how to create more sustainable societies. It is possible to develop economies, up to a point, without harming the environment. But to transform the world, and prevent Gaia from becoming Grendel, it is going to need some radically different thinking and doing. I hope these essays will help, in some small way, to show that we can nurture our planet into a state that offers all living things hope for the future.

Jules Pretty
University of Essex
November 2006

Acknowledgements

I am very grateful to many people for their direct and indirect advice, help, insight and accompaniment during the research and writing of this book. They are Mike Bell, Nigel Bell, Dima Bondarkov, Mikhail Bondarkov, Perry and Silvia Broad, Ronald Blythe, Andora Carver, Igor Chizhevsky, Chris Cooper, Kathleen Delate, John Devavaram, Amadou Diop, Peter Ennis, Howie Frumkin, Sergey Gachuk, Murray Griffin, Julia Guivant, Vardan Haykazyan, Richard Hayward, Jilly Hall, John Hall, Jenny Harpur, Tommy Hepburn, Rachel Hine, Mark Iley, Ned Iveagh, Ray Jensen, Anthony Jenkinson, Karen Jones, J K Kiara, David Kline, Afonso Kloppel, Shushep (Joseph) Mark, Andy May, Philip Merricks, Rick Minter, David Orr, Ruth Ostin, Basile Panashue, Avi Perevolotsky, Sergio Pinheiro, Etienne Pone, Chris Pollock, Jo Roberts, Sawaeng Ruaysoongnern, Jim Rudderham, Colin Samson, Marcus Sangster, No'am Seligman, Martin Sellens, Nigel South, Rachel Steward, Hugh van Cutsem, Ray Tabor, Ronnie Theisz, Keith and Linda Turner, Marina Warner, Nancy Wells and Arnold Wilkins.

I am particularly grateful to Bill Adams, Neil Baker, Peggy Barlett, Nigel Bell, Ted Benton, Ronald Blythe, Kathleen Delate, John Devavaram, Tom Dobbs, Cornelia Butler Flora, Julia Guivant, Vardan Haykazyan, Hans Herren, Jim Hunter, Wes Jackson, Karen Jones, J K Kiara, Amanda Kiessel, Kevin Laland, Rob Macfarlane, Bill McKibben, Phil Mullineaux, Harsha Newaratne, David Orr, Jo Peacock, Sarah Pilgrim, Jim Rudderham, Colin Samson, David Smith, Hugh Warwick, Piran White, and Jan Kees Vis for their helpful comments and suggestions on earlier drafts of this book.

The perspectives and opinions offered here are, of course, all my own responsibility, as are the mistakes. I am very grateful to Jonathan Sinclair Wilson and Rob West of Earthscan for their continuing support and sage advice. The paintings that illustrate the start of some of the chapters are by my father, John Pretty, and the photographs are mine.

Part 1

Green Places

1

Becoming Green

At the centre of our sun, the extreme temperature of 10 to 20 million degrees causes protons to crash into one another, so converting some of their mass to energy. A cascade of reactions then produces energy-rich gamma photons, each of which eventually divides into a thousand photons during the several million years they take to reach the sun's surface. These photons then depart the sun at 300,000 kilometres a second and take about eight and a half minutes to travel the 154 million kilometres to our planet, the third nearest to the sun.

   This light has a wavelength of between 100 and 1000 nanometres, and when the Earth was stabilizing into a solid planet about 4.7 billion years ago, it would have struck first a primary atmosphere of hydrogen and helium. This early air, though, soon bled away to space, and came to be replaced by a secondary atmosphere formed by outgassing from volcanic activities. This new atmosphere would have been toxic to us, as it was mainly water vapour, methane, ammonia and hydrogen. The seas were highly acidic, readily eroding rocks, and of course quite dead. Some of the arriving light split water molecules to give off oxygen, but this was immediately sucked up by iron hydrides and sulphides in the Earth's rocks. At this time, the surface of the Earth was no more than grey, black and brown, though the seas were blue.

More than a billion years pass before macromolecules begin to be formed in what we like to call the primaeval soup, probably in rock pools by the seashore. Later, combinations of these macromolecules known as eobionts start to metabolize, grow in size and take up other compounds. In a series of steps that still remain utterly mysterious, the larger molecules become self-organized, resulting in the production of proteins and enzymes, and the formation of nucleic acids organized into a helix that could pass on stored information. Life had emerged.

At this time, the atmosphere is still a reducing one, and there is no free oxygen. An astonishing amount of time passes. The first organisms were single-celled and simple bacteria, appearing 1.5 billion years after the Earth was formed. Now another billion years pass before simple algae appear, and another 500 million years go by before even the first multicellular algae emerge. We are still 1.5 billion years away from the present.

These first organisms all relied on other chemical compounds for their energy, but there was a revolutionary breakthrough with the cyanobacteria (formerly known as blue-green algae). Some organisms began to use light as an additional source of energy. This created huge advantages for them, as chemical compounds in the soup were limiting, but light was inexhaustible. This sunlight, though, is harsh and unfriendly, as it contains ultraviolet at frequencies and intensities that would be lethal to life today. Organisms increasingly turned to light, transferring electrons and driving many chemical reactions. One of these involved the use of abundant water and the hitherto unused source of carbon bound up in carbon dioxide, in a process we now call photosynthesis, to make carbohydrates.

The remarkable innovation is the emergence of a molecule with a magnesium atom at the heart of five small pyrrole rings, and with a long tail of carbon atoms. It marks the beginning of a change in the whole of the Earth forever – land, sea and atmosphere. This molecule is chlorophyll, and it can capture and make use of the energy contained in light, eventually to make carbohydrates. The flat square containing the magnesium atom is about 1.5 nanometres across, and the 2-nanometre tail is used to stick the molecule to membranes inside the chloroplast. You could line three million of them up on your fingertip.

The mutation that enables some cells in the soup to make their own resources from water and carbon dioxide has great survival value, and these cells begin to proliferate. In the blue-green algae, the chlorophyll is distributed along membranes and is able to absorb a range of wavelengths of light. The later multi-celled organisms contain their chlorophyll completely within highly organized chloroplasts, typically 2 by 2 by 5 micrometres in size.

No one is quite sure if the process of photosynthesis first arose inside or outside cells. It ends up, though, located in one of a number of complex organelles in cells. These chloroplasts and mitochondria might owe their presence to bacteria or algae that were somehow taken up to become part of plant cells. No one knows, but both mitochondria and chloroplasts do have their own inheritable equipment for protein production, their DNA, RNA and ribosomes. Chloroplasts have much more DNA, but still not enough to produce all their proteins. The presence of the DNA does suggest, though, that they may have originally been independent organisms, and many chloroplasts and blue-green algae are today strikingly similar.

Though there are now many different pigments in plants capable of using light as an energy source, including bluish or red phycobilins in algae, yellow and orange carotenoids, and brown fucoxanthins in seaweed, it is chlorophyll that is the most common. It absorbs light at the blue and red ends of the spectrum, but rather poorly absorbs green at about 520–580nm and far-red above 700nm. As our eyes are not sensitive to far red, the organisms containing chlorophyll will appear green to us when we later appear.

As these new organisms begin to spread across the world, so the amount of oxygen released as a by-product of photosynthesis increases. For a very long time, though, any free oxygen is immediately absorbed by iron compounds in rocks, which turn rusty red-brown. Now the Earth begins to lose its grey-black colour. The sun is orange, like a permanent sunset, the sky pink and the sea no longer blue, but various shades of murky brown. But there comes a point, probably about two billion years ago at the end of the Archaean period, when oxygen begins to accumulate in the air, and the third atmosphere of the Earth is born. And, remarkably, the world changes path again. Plants begin to colonize the seas. A world once grey, and for a while red and brown, begins to change colour and become green (though not for a few years yet).

What is now clear is that life on Earth changed the chemical composition of the Earth by producing an atmosphere that remains in a state far from equilibrium. Earth without life was very much like Mars and Venus are today, with atmospheres containing 95–98 per cent carbon dioxide, 2–3 per cent nitrogen, trace amounts of oxygen and no methane, with extreme surface temperatures (ranging from -53°C on Mars through 240°C on Earth without life to 459°C on Venus). Earth with life today is quite placid, with the atmosphere containing tiny amounts of carbon dioxide (0.03 per cent), 79 per cent nitrogen, 21 per cent oxygen and 1.7 parts per million of methane. It has an average temperature of 13°C. The emergence of life changed the Earth to make it more favourable to the survival of life. It didn't intend to. It just did.

As the oxygen is produced by early plants, the atmosphere reaches about a fifth oxygen, which, with its associated high-altitude ozone layer, plays a new and critical role. It intercepts short-wave ultraviolet light and so allows life to survive out of water. Nucleic acids are lethally damaged when they absorb ultraviolet light. Life in the seas thus creates the conditions for life on land to succeed by producing enough oxygen to stop the UV light from reaching the Earth. There are some losers, though, with Archaean bacteria now unable to survive the presence of the toxic oxygen; they only live on today in our stomachs and in swamps, mudflats and other anoxic places.

More time passes. Soft-bodied animals do not appear on Earth until some 680 million years before today. They need large amounts of oxygen in the atmosphere to grow and survive. Over the next 300 million years, hard-shelled animals, and jawless and jawed fishes evolve to colonize the seas. Roughly 400 million years before present sees the appearance of the first land plants and amphibians. Now at last the land turns green, some 4.3 billion years after the Earth formed. Where there is light, on land and in water to certain depths, and where it is not too cold or dry, life forms succeed in dominating every single landscape. Some remain single-celled, such as plankton and diatoms in the seas. Others combine to form giant trees that can stretch back towards the sun for fifty metres or more. Others still end up as the longest-surviving individual organisms on the planet – the gnarled bristlecone pines of the high Sierra Nevada and upside-down baobabs of the savannahs. Evolution appears to pick up its pace: reptiles appear 50 million years later, and as dinosaurs are incredibly successful. During the Devonian period, vast forests come to dominate the Earth and are joined by lycopods, horsetails and ferns some 300 million years before today. Mammals and flowering plants make their appearance after 95 per cent of the Earth's lifetime, at about 225 million years before present.

Much, much later, we humans appear on the scene. Mammals get their chance to dominate after the savage obliteration of the cold-blooded dinosaurs 65 million years ago, and some 60 million years later, distinctive hominids appear on the savannahs of what is now East Africa. We are pretty recent animals at the party. But one colour continues to dominate the landscapes in which there is usable food – and this is the green of chlorophyll, still capturing light and fusing water and carbon dioxide. In the dry seasons or droughts, plants die and turn yellow and brown. In the periods of cold, whether winters or ice ages, the green plants become dormant or fail to survive. Seeds carry forward their DNA to future generations. But where there is green, there is life, and there will be energy and food.[1]

Today, of course, the harvest needs to ripen to glorious golds before the cereals that comprise three-quarters of the human population's diet can be consumed. But these are recent technological inventions. For all but 600 of some 300,000 generations, hominids relied for their survival on plants and animals that lived in green places. We evolved and grew up in a green world. To this point, the species on this planet and their environments have been tightly coupled, having evolved effectively as a single system. Life made its own home, terraforming the Earth, in a process called ecopoiesis by James Lovelock, and so transforming an otherwise uninhabitable environment into a place fit for life to evolve.

Now, though, human hubris is creating a new atmosphere that is likely to be hostile to many forms of life, especially humans and our apparently essential trappings of modern civilization. We are adding carbon dioxide to the air by burning fossil fuels (formerly buried carbon), and also destroying forests that could mop it up. Huge amounts of oxygen, more than a billion tonnes annually, are pumped into the atmosphere by plants. Without this, the oxygen and methane in the atmosphere would be readily converted by sunlight into carbon dioxide and water, and the planet would become more like Venus and Mars. Venus once had more water than Earth, but lost it when solar ultraviolet light split water into oxygen and hydrogen, and with this oxygen then captured by iron and sulphur, the hydrogen bled away to space. Without life to regulate these processes, Venus continued to heat up to its current hell of nearly 460°C. Life saved the oceans on Earth, and saved itself.

Organisms can and nearly always do change their environments, as well as then adapting to the new conditions. James Lovelock calls this a biocybernetic universal system tendency, or the self-regulating planetary control that has come to be called Gaia.[2] What of us now? Do we discover our mistakes soon enough, or do we carry on pushing the planet towards another quite unpredictable position? 'To survive', says Lovelock, 'we must also take care of the Earth.' Of course, the Earth is quite indifferent to our survival, but if our modern experiment in inadvertent terraforming does not fail soon, and we take with us many other species and habitats, then the Earth may well have changed irreversibly again. It will endure, but we may well not.

After the age of humans, the green will probably reinvade the concrete, brick, tarmac and metal, and our legacy will gradually disappear. One day, very much later, the sun will have swollen to become a red giant, swallowing up all the vast empty space as far as the Earth. Then the green itself will have disappeared forever, and the probably rather rare experiment of life on Earth will boil away.

Birch Bark and Blue Sky

On a crisp winter morning, when a dazzling white sun hangs just above the tree line, and the sky to the north is eggshell blue, I slip through deep sunken lanes, worn away over centuries by generations of carts and oxen, to come upon a thicket of silver birch standing by a patch of ancient heathland. The air is damp and resinous from nearby pines, but as the lane rises up into the sun, there comes a warmth with the light, even though we are only a few days into January. And as the hill climbs up past oaks still brown with autumn's clinging leaves, away from a pair of pheasants that leap and clutch at the air with a rattle of wings, here are the birch. The sunlight sparkles on the bark, and the white paper against the blue sky brings an elemental simplicity unlike anything else in the landscape.

Later, on a day when steel-grey clouds hang menacingly low, the light flat and easterly wind harsh, I take the same route, and, turning the corner, the world stops. I blink; there is a long silence in the air. Instead of trees there are beheaded white stumps, no more than chest high. There was no indication that this would happen. It just did. Here, then, is another wasteland becoming. Instead of the cracked white bark, it seems there will be off-road parking for cars. The chainsaw and its operator will brook no argument. The trees are gone. Apparently, this is an improvement for the owners, or at the very least only a tolerable loss. But it ought to be a message. If you enjoy nature, it may not be for long, for we also appear to be bent on dismantling this world. All that will remain will be ghosts and fading memories if we cannot find a way to take more care.

Until fairly recently in human history, our daily lives were intertwined with living things, from wild animals to green plants, from ancient bacteria to blood-sucking insects. We have chased animals, caught them, eaten them, revered them, and have been chased and eaten in return. Yet in the blink of an eye, a few generations at the end of several million years of hominid history, modern humans have provoked a sixth great species extinction. The fifth saw off the dinosaurs at the end of the Mesozoic period, and it took ten million years of evolution to restore biological diversity. The sixth is now putting at risk of extinction one in four mammal species, one in eight birds, one in eleven trees and one in eight plants.

Species are disappearing at a rate 100 to 1000 times faster than ever before in human history, and more than 16,000 face the imminent prospect of extinction. We need these species to survive. Yet in the decade after 1995, some 1.6 to 2.4 million hectares of Amazon rainforest were cleared annually as the cattle herd of the region increased from 20 to 60 million head. In 2004, 2.6 million hectares were felled, an area the size of Maryland or Belgium. Is this simply the real price we must pay for remarkable economic and technological progress, or is it symptomatic of some deeper problem? What we are at risk of losing, says E O Wilson, is 'most of the rest of life, and part of what it means to be a human being'. If we want to be thoroughly pessimistic, the consequences of coming upon our own end times would be upon us before we even can reflect on what has driven us to the edge.[1]

Ever since the earliest hominids crept through the tall savannah grasses of East Africa, we have survived in a world rich with biological diversity. We have, of course, been part of this diversity, shaping it and being shaped in return. We have burned grasslands to encourage grass growth and seed production, hunted some animals to extinction and looked after others, channelled water for the drylands, planted trees to aid forest regeneration, and harvested fish continuously from the same seas and rivers for tens of thousands of years. Over this period, nature has never been a fixed and unchanging entity. We have amended it, and it in return helped to choose which of us was to survive. What are the longer prospects, then, as we increasingly harm the very resources that have sustained us? Can we survive in a world that we are making increasingly uninhabitable, or are we instead about to break free from the shackles of history?

Our current crisis, for that is where we find ourselves, is not just a problem of loss of biodiversity and all nature's valuable ecosystem services, but a crisis arising from an idea so pervasive that we rarely think about it. The danger comes from assuming that we moderns are history's most successful society, and that we will be able to think and invent our way out of any difficulty, bending the world to our intentionality, thus making problems no more than temporary concerns. Put simply, our troubles centre on a myth of progress. We all too readily want to believe in the inevitable benefits of economic and technological progress, including new freedoms. There may be some costs, to be sure: a species lost, a sea stripped of oxygen, a forest clear-felled, a warm winter without snow, but these pale alongside all that we have achieved, and indeed promise to go on to achieve in the future.

For most of our history, evolution and natural selection have shaped our progress. Lately, though, culture and the economy have come to dominate the choices about who does or does not survive to pass on their genes. Looking back, it is all too easy to be deceived into thinking that there is a linear direction to the path we have walked. But evolution has no *a priori* direction, even though the now iconic images of crouched simians evolving through early hominids to tall modern humans regrettably suggest otherwise. Evolution is not about progress, nor about good or bad; it is about adapting to changing circumstances. Yet we have a hope that progress will 'solve, inspire, transform us and the world into a better place', as David Rothenberg and Wandee Pryor have put it. Today, we believe that we can build a better world than ever before. But John Gray of the London School of Economics asks, 'Why do we believe we are so much better? Why do we believe we will go on evermore?' What of other hominids that lived for much longer than *Homo sapiens* has so far managed, but then disappeared too? What of those later civilizations that knew so much, but then also disappeared?[2]

Neanderthals dominated Europe and Asia for at least 100,000 years, and then mysteriously disappeared about 28,000 years ago. They had larger brains than *Homo sapiens*, were capable of language, and probably were of similar intelligence to us today. They had many forms of advanced culture. They made tools, and their ritual burials are evidence that they had their own ideas about life and death. Buried Neanderthals have been found with flint tools, fragments of bones, Ibex horns, red ochre, necklace beads and ivory, musical instruments, flowers and medicinal herbs. Yet today Neanderthal has become synonymous with backward, something we like to think we are no longer. They are seen to be so inferior, perhaps because of their early extinction. Neanderthals and *Homo sapiens* coexisted for tens of thousands of years. We survived, and so must be the better. Or do we believe this myth of their backwardness because it makes us feel so much more advanced, and thus likely to carry on forever?[3]

The term civilization is derived from *civitas*, the Latin for city, and has come to be used to refer to distinctive cultures with complex social organization, settlements in cities, specialization of labour, state institutions, monumental public works, and writing, arithmetic and astronomy. Civilization implies permanence, yet has also been used to separate people – those who are civilized from the barbarians on the edge of the known map. Yet many of these other groups have been very good at permanence themselves, from the Innu and Inuit of the boreal north to the Ba'Mbuti, Ba'Twa and Ba'Yaka pygmy peoples of the tropical rainforests.[4]

Since the establishment of the first cities at Uruk, Tell Brak and Catalhöyük some 6000 years ago, there have been forty major civilizations recorded worldwide, on average surviving for 900 years each. Like the Neanderthals, they have come and gone too, leaving alarmingly little evidence about their people's hopes and desires, or their unique world views, scientific knowledge and values. All we are left with is mysteries – giant carved heads on Rapa Nui (Easter Island) and by the Olmec, the mud and stone pyramids and ziggurats of the Mayans, Moche, Toltec, Egyptians, Sumerians and Cambodians, enigmatic animals scraped into desert patinas by the Nazca, the spectacular mountain ruins of the Inca and Anasazi, the mounds and megaliths of the Bell Beaker, Celts and Hopewell, the temples of the Vedics and Mauryans, and the palaces of the Minoans and Mycenae. Some remains, though, seem still to belong to no known civilization, such as the 250 monumental stone Qiang towers of Sichuan and Tibet.

Of course, a great deal is known from many of these remains, inferred from generations of detailed archaeological, historical and linguistic study. But mysteries remain. Many languages and scripts remain undeciphered, such as those of the Hittites, Indus, Minoan and Rapa Nui civilizations. Some of these civilizations were tolerant and benign, such as the Achaemenids of Persia, and others grotesque to their people, such as the Assyrians. Some derived wealth from cattle rearing and trade, such as Great Zimbabwe, other from sea-faring, such as the Peleset (Philistines) and Phoenicians. All, though, at some point stopped what they were doing and abandoned cities, palaces and temples. In truth, we can only make informed guesses from that which happens to remain.

Walk through the towering rainforest of the Petèn in central America and you are brought to an awed silence by the Mayan temples and pyramids of Tikal. Jutting out beyond giant buttress trees, now occupied with vocal bands of howler monkeys, the tallest temple of the Giant Jaguar looks across a carpet of green to Mexico in one direction and to Belize in another. At one time, Tikal was a bustling city of tens of thousands of people, not long after the Domesday Survey of 1086 recorded just five settlements in Britain of more than a thousand people. Yet the Mayan empire fell after 1800 years of permanence, taking with it sophisticated knowledge of mathematics and astronomy.

The Minoans, long believed to be only the stuff of legend created by later Greek authors, lived on Crete from 2000–1450 BC. They had fine art, vaulted tombs, decorated pottery, a pantheon of gods, complex social arrangements and were expert sea-farers. The height of their prosperity was about 1800–1600 BC, but they later comprehensively disappeared, perhaps because of a combination of earthquakes, volcanic eruptions, fires and conflict. Excavations around 1890 discovered the palaces of Knossos (with 1500 rooms), Phaestos, Mallia and Khania, but their hieroglyphic Linear A script and language has still not been translated, and so written texts remain a profound mystery.

Perhaps some civilizations brought doom upon themselves. 'What', asks Jared Diamond in *Collapse*, 'were the Easter Islanders thinking as they cut down the last tree on the island?' Rapa Nui works a little like a metaphor for the Earth, owing to its extraordinary remoteness. It is 5000km from neighbouring Tahiti, 7500km from Samoa and Tonga, and 8000km from New Zealand. Recent archaeological evidence suggests they persisted with complex agriculture long after the last tree, but still we may never know the reason for the abandonment of their way of life around AD 1500. It took 20 worker years to make each of the 1000 *moai* heads, yet because we cannot read their Rongorongo hieroglyphs, we have no real idea why they were constructed. Perhaps, as for pyramids and temples, we wish to construct symbols of permanence to make us feel better.

I suspect a common symptom in all these civilizations is denial. Surely it cannot be that bad, we say. Look at what we have achieved, look at how far we have come. Many societies seem to have collapsed after acquiring great power and wealth. Perhaps they saw the end coming, or perhaps not. How do we measure up today? David Ehrenfeld points out that today 'globalization is creating an environment that will prove hostile to its own survival'. We think we have control too (another delusion), but this is a chimera:

> *our ability to manage global systems, which depends on our being able to predict the results of the things we do, or even to understand the systems we have created, has been greatly exaggerated. Much of our alleged control is science fiction.*

The crisis is, as he says, here now.[5]

David Orr of Oberlin College further states that 'no broadly informed scientist can be optimistic about the long-term future of human-kind without assuming we will soon recalibrate human numbers, wants, needs and actions [...] within a finite biosphere'. He goes on to say, 'the time for reason and reasonableness is running short'. Curiously, if we do see a collapse, it will be the rural citizens of many developing countries who will be best placed to survive, as they are comparatively self-sufficient and the least dependent on the technologies and interconnected markets and institutions of the industrialized world.[6]

More than two decades ago, the World Commission on Environment and Development began deliberating on the links between environment and economy. Chaired by Gro Harlem Brundtland, it came up with an enduring and compelling definition for sustainable development (at the time, a relatively new term): 'meeting the needs of the present without compromising the ability of future generations to meet their own needs'. Since then, there have been at least a couple of hundred further definitions of sustainability, and the term has now entered our common language, yet few better capture the core ideas of equity and justice set in a context of long-term care for the world's resources. But where are we now with this sustainability idea? Has it offered some new hope for the world, or has it effectively been some sort of a grand hoax?

In the 1960s, a single novel photographic image captured the world's imagination. Apollo astronauts returning from the moon were able to photograph our Earth in the middle of dark, empty space. Here was a lonely blue-green planet, just the one of them, with a clear boundary. If something went wrong, there could be no external solutions, no rescue by the cavalry riding over the hill. We would have to solve our own problems. This world, though, is now home to some six and a half billion people, and is so complex and intertwined as to appear almost impossible to comprehend. How would it look if we shrunk it down to a single village of 100 people?

Our global village would have 20 people in the north, 15 of whom would have 81 per cent of all the income; of the 80 in the south, 22 would have less than $1 a day. The village has 25 hectares of cropland, remarkably feeding four people for every hectare, but a third of the cropland is now degraded in one way or another. There are 57 hectares of pasture and, perhaps surprisingly, still nearly 70 hectares of forest. Food production in the village has increased enormously in the past four to five decades, and there is now enough to feed everyone plentifully if we all had the purchasing power to access it and if we did not feed so much of the cereal to animals. But 13 of the 100 people are permanently hungry and alarmingly 10 are now overweight and obese. The consumption figures are worrying. Villagers in the North American section consume 430 litres of water per day; in the south, 23 have no water. In the North American section, 308kg of paper is consumed by each person annually, in Europe 125kg, China 34kg, and India and Africa just 4kg.[7]

In North America, there are 750 motor vehicles per 1000 people, in Japan 570, in Europe 240, and in China, India and Africa just 6 to 9 (see table overleaf). Worldwide, some 400,000 hectares of cropland are paved per year for roads and parking lots (the US's 16 million hectares of land under asphalt will soon match the total area under wheat). The world motor vehicle fleet grows alarmingly, as the nearly wealthy look to other parts of our village for guidance as to what to buy. The largest 4×4s weigh three tonnes and fuel consumption is so bad it is almost into gallons per mile territory. By almost every measure of resource consumption or proxy for waste production, the US and Europe lead the way. And what do people in the south now want to do? What model is being held up as the one to follow? There are now few in the world who do not now aspire to the same levels of consumption as North America. And why shouldn't they? After all, that is what we all imply is the pinnacle of economic achievement.

This consumer boom is already happening. The new consumers, as Norman Myers calls them, have already entered the global economy and are aspiring to the lifestyles currently enjoyed by the richest. A number of formerly poor countries are seeing the growing influence of affluence, as the middle classes of China, India, Indonesia, Pakistan, Philippines, South Korea, Thailand, Argentina, Brazil, Colombia and Mexico engage in greater conspicuous consumption. The side effects are already

Indicators of consumption and population in different regions of the world (for 2004–2005)

	USA	Europe	China	India	Asia	Africa	Latin & Central America	World
Passenger cars per 1000 people	750	240	7	6	20	9	56	91
Annual petrol and diesel consumption (litres per person)	1624	286	33	9	47	36	169	174
Annual energy consumption per person (kg oil equivalent)	8520	3546	896	515	892	580	1190	1640
Annual carbon dioxide emissions (tonnes per person)	20.3	8–12	2.7	0.99	<1	<1	<1	3.85
Annual paper consumption (kg per person)	308	125	34	4	29	4	38	52
Annual meat consumption (kg per person)	125	74	52	5	28	13	58	40
Daily water consumption (litres per person)	430	159	135	174	172	47	147	173
Population (millions, 2005)	293	730	1306	1080	3667	887	518	6500
Children born per woman	2.08	1.56	1.72	2.78	3.1	4.82	2.75	2.55

being felt – the average car in Bangkok spends 44 days a year stuck in traffic. But there is still a long way to go. The car fleet of the whole of India is still smaller than that of Chicago, that of China half that of greater Los Angeles.[8]

This is now the concern: the idea of sustainable economic development seems to imply that the world can be improved, or even saved, by bringing everyone up to the same levels of consumption as those in the industrialized countries of the North. We can, it is said, grow out of many kinds of economic trouble. But this is grand larceny. It is stealing the truth. It cannot be done, as we would need six worlds at European and eight to nine at North American levels and patterns of consumption. And we simply do not have six to eight Earths. There is only the one, green and blue, and all alone in deep, dark space. Yet the drivers of consumption are powerful, and few are asking, how much would be enough? Or will we all charge ahead until we too join the list of civilizations that mysteriously ended?

What, then, should we make of the current drivers of consumption? There is a simple and stark problem. If everyone consumed at the levels and patterns of the world's gold medallists, then our modern civilization is seriously threatened. Yet our conspicuous consumption behaviour, as Thorstein Veblen first called it in 1899[9], is making things worse day by day. Most people think that having more money will make them happier. But the more we have, the more we seem to want. It is of course true that the poorest, who lack basic resources of food, water and security and the human dignity they bring, are certainly made happier as they get wealthier, but after a certain threshold is passed, well-being becomes independent of consumption. The problem, it seems, is that we appear to be somewhat hard-wired to assess our position relative to that of others, and if others are getting more, we want more too. We are, for example, much more satisfied with £40k of income if last year it was £35k than if it had fallen from £45k. We also prefer a lower salary if it is higher than other people rather than a higher one that is below the average. We have bigger houses and larger cars, spend less time with family and friends, work harder to get more money, take shorter holidays, and all for what? To have something larger or brighter or newer than someone else. It is true that we can choose what we spend, and so appear to have free will, but we cannot choose what someone else spends, and that makes a difference to our own behaviour.

Barry Schwartz of Swarthmore College has pointed to this new paradox of choice. No choice is bad, yet too many choices do not make us more liberated. Indeed they tend to overwhelm us. Advertisers are clever. They tell us about top of the range expensive watches, barbecues and cars not to encourage us to buy those, but to make us accept that something less expensive (but still more than we intended to spend) is appropriately frugal. In the US, there are now more shopping malls than high schools, and the average person sees several hundred television advertisements daily. To permit this, the average half-hour TV programme is four minutes shorter than a generation ago. The television also used to contribute to daytime social discourse, but now few people watch the same programmes at the same time, so it is less common for people to be able to talk about them together later.

The problem, it seems, is that we hominids are remarkably good at adaptation. We get used to things and then take them for granted. Adaptation is very useful in a world of misery – it allows people to cope – but as Schwartz says, 'if you live in a world of plenty then adaptation defeats your attempts to enjoy good fortune'. A year after winning the lottery or becoming paraplegic in an accident people are apparently equally happy. Yet if we could choose, everyone would think that winning the lottery was clearly the better option. Robert Frank of Cornell University points out that we do get a rush of satisfaction when we get a new TV, fridge or mobile phone, but unfortunately it soon wears off. He writes that 'the US remains by far the richest nation on Earth. Yet we are currently squandering much of our wealth on fruitless mine-is-bigger consumption arms races.' A seemingly inevitable outcome is that, when faced with a huge array of options, we end up regretting the fact that our choice might have been the wrong one. And these regrets are horribly corrosive. Bronze medallists are happier than silver medallists as they dwell on how close they were to getting nothing, while silvers tend to deeply regret not having won. Losing £100 induces more intense feelings than those acquired from a gain of £100.[10]

What have we won and lost in these consumption stakes? The average American house now has 190 square metres of floor space, up by 90 per cent since the 1950s. Yet because individuals now move fourteen times in a lifetime, there are fewer opportunities to accrue memories. As David Suzuki says, 'memories do not add a dollar to the value of your house, yet these are the very things that comprise real value.'[11] In just twenty years, the annual time spent commuting has increased over fourfold (to nearly 12 billion vehicle hours per year). Since the 1960s, rates of clinical depression and teenage suicide in the US have tripled, violent crime increased fourfold, the prison population fivefold. People are working longer, taking fewer holidays, have 800 hours of leisure time per year compared with 1000 in the 1970s, spend 40 per cent less time with their children than in the 1960s, feel more stress, and all so that we can stay ahead of someone else. At one time, this was a good plan. When a tiger runs towards you, asks Frank, what should you do? Sing a song? Admire its colours? No – you run immediately. You have no chance of outrunning the tiger, but you may be able to outrun one of the other people you are with, and so survive when it is they who are eaten.

If failure to consume is a mark of inferiority, what hope is there for the world? With the explosion in telecoms and media, there are now many more opportunities for people to see how both the wealthy and celebrities appear to live, and so to aspire after them. Niels Röling of Wageningen University writes of being in a group meeting an elderly Chinese farm worker. She appeared part of a traditional cultural scene, with conical hat and distant mist-covered mountains, and was digging night soil into her vegetable patch. But when approached, she said she was 'fed up with the stupid and dirty job. She was unhappy that her children were doomed to do the same. She would also like to visit Paris.' It turned out that a local TV station was showing a popular series about a young couple on holiday in Paris. And why indeed should she not go? That is the whole point behind the globalized media.[12]

Today, we think we have so much, yet our great deceit is a belief that our modern civilization as it is currently configured will go on forever. We also believe that we will never forget anything. But what of those floppy disks and videos of the 1980s and 1990s that are already becoming obsolete; what too of your current hard drives, CDs and DVDs, many of which will become incompatible as new generations of hardware emerge with terabytes of memory, but distinctly new software? Will we really so meticulously transfer all our memories, or will they simply fill drawers and shelves, mocking our descendants, who will wonder what was on them? Forgetting is something we do well. Prior civilizations were full of ideas that took centuries to reinvent somewhere else. The seventh-century Armenian scientist, Anania Shiratataksi, wrote that the Earth was a sphere, and that the moon reflected sunlight, but it took another 900 years before Copernicus would come up with the same idea and thus cement his name in the history books.

But this dominant idea about the inevitable benefits of progress would appear to be something of a modern invention. Indigenous peoples do not believe that their current community is any better than those in the past. To them, past and future are the same as current time. Their ancestors, and those of animals too, constantly remind them to be humble as they move about their landscapes. But our myth of progress permits the losses of both species and special places, as we believe we can offset any losses by doing something else that is better. The myth permits us to believe in techno-logical fixes, which are indeed effective in many ways, but rarely seem to make us happier in the long term. Our environmental problems are, after all, human problems. And this myth is built on memory loss too – those people before us surely could not have been as happy, as they had less material wealth, and anyway, they did not survive to this day, so must have been less clever too.

New technologies will make improvements, but possibly not fast enough to save us. They also bring some new risks, possibly rendering society more vulnerable. Soon to come will be fabulous electronic memory, a genomics revolution, renewable energy and human brains augmented by computers, though as Martin Rees puts it, 'a super-intelligent machine could be the last invention humans ever make'. Arthur C Clarke once pointed out that advanced technologies are indistinguishable from magic – they change us and the world, but we are very bad at predicting their effects. Rees recounts the 1937 efforts by the US National Academy of Sciences to predict breakthroughs for the rest of the last century. They made a good stab at agriculture, rubber and oil, but completely missed nuclear energy, antibiotics, jet aircraft, space travel and computers.[13]

Making predictions based on current trends is a hazardous business. To believe that all advances will lead to improvements is folly (though, equally, to believe none of them will is folly too). We simply have no idea what could happen next, again, because our idea of progress suggests that we are at the top already. Bill McKibben describes how our sensory world is changed by modern technologies by painting a picture of a tranquil lake local to his home in the Adirondacks. One day, motor boats arrive for water skiing, a not unpleasant pastime for many. Though they threaten the swimmers, he writes:

> it is not the danger, or even the blue smoke on the lake. It is that the motor boats get in your mind. You're forced to think, not feel – to think of human society and of people. The lake is utterly different on these days.

He indicates that we may be living at the end of nature: 'the moment when the essen-tial character of the world we've known [...] is changing'.[14]

To believe in the inevitability of progress is also to believe in a freedom from the constraints of the world. It is to have faith in an idea that we are masters of our own destiny. John Gray writes, 'we have inherited the faith that as the world becomes more modern, it will become more reasonable, more enlightened and more balanced. But such faith is not more than superstition.' We can and will, of course, do so much with intentionality – think of the advances in medical technology made in recent years. None of us would want to give these up. But will these advances be enough to make us more happy? Those people in the richer parts of the world have fabulous material goods that entertain and reward them for all the hard work spent in obtaining them. Yet, extraordinarily, they have not made us any happier.[15]

It is now clear from a variety of studies of people in the US and Europe that on aggregate people were happier in the 1950s compared with today (though there are many groups who were clearly worse off in the 1950s, such as those living in extreme poverty or in apartheid conditions). We can only guess about earlier times, as the data does not exist in comparable form. But it does seem that our programmed happiness is about striving for, not actually increasing, happiness. There is always a nagging gap, as Daniel Nettle has put it, between present levels of contentment and how it could be. We believe we will be more happy in the future, but seldom are. We also are constantly worrying about how future life events will affect our happiness. As Mike Bell has pointed out, we could work four hours per day, or for six months a year, if we consumed at 1940s levels, yet be equally happy. But would anyone choose this option if we could?[16]

Our time for leisure, too, has gone down. We appear, at least in industrialized countries, to be working harder so that we can earn more money to buy goods and services that are not making us content. In fact, we like to stay busy, even during leisure time. 'Being busy', as Jay Gershuny has put it, 'is a badge of honour.' Prepared meals and microwaves now mean that the average evening meal in the UK takes less than ten minutes to prepare, compared with some two and a half hours fifty years ago. At first sight, this has to be a clear candidate for progress. So much extra time, so much emancipation from the kitchen. But what has been lost? An intimate understanding of food and cuisines, the opportunities to develop good food habits in children. And the gains? More time, especially for women. But what do we moderns do with all this extra time? Sit in front of the television watching soap operas, or discover a special place in the country or local park? What looks at first glance to be all progress may be an illusion or, even worse, something that leaves us with the time to feel more guilt about not doing more. John Gray further points out that 'progress condemns idleness [...] nothing is more alien to the present age than idleness. If we think of resting from our labours, it is only in order to return to them'.[17]

Contrast this situation again with that of hunter-gatherer communities, the way of life for all but one fifth of a per cent of our time on this Earth. Marshall Sahlins famously called hunter-gatherers the original affluent society, and they typically do spend long periods resting, talking, telling stories and eating, with short periods of intense activity for hunting or gathering. They work two to five hours per day, live well and happily, while the rest of us are given a life sentence of hard labour. If the weather is bad – too hot, cold, windy or wet – then they think nothing of sitting all day to wait for it to pass. For those of we moderns brought up to believe we must not waste a minute, this feels like anathema. But it can be a release. Once I sat all day with a friend and two Innu hunters in a tent on Lake Melville's boreal shore as the rain lashed down on a cold and grey day that never really seemed to get light. We dozed and talked, told stories and listened well, made tea, and scorched bread on the glowing stove. Outside the clouds of blackfly swarmed; inside we moved a little here or there to miss the dripping leaks. The carpet of interwoven spruce boughs filled the tent with a resinous aroma. On another occasion, in the depths of icy winter, another group of us huddled around a similar stove for a day, watching a porcupine slowly stew, as our tent was battered by gale force winds, only venturing outside to pile more snow around the tent walls.[18]

Years earlier, I sat with a group of village elders in a raised wooden house in the sticky mangroves of Fiji. There was a ceremony marking the beginning of some work in the village and centred on the sharing of kava, a drink made from the root of *Piper methysticum*. For many hours we sat cross-legged, in quiet contemplation and discussion, punctuated by periods of drinking the cloudy liquid from half-coconuts marked by shared rhythmic clapping. Time passes in a different way when trust needs to be built. The ceremony says we are here, we are important, we respect you, and you respect us. Whole days pass, no more than still points in a turning world. Contrast this with the way that modern societies tend to work. How much, in the busy and stressed lives that so many of us now live, do we search for such moments, without giving ourselves the opportunity to find them? We have meetings at fixed times, rushing from one to the next to ensure highest efficiency. Yet without time to appreciate places and people, these efficiency gains are in truth zero-sum games. Something is lost as something else appears to have been gained.

In T S Eliot's epic poem about the circularity of time and the myth of progress, *Four Quartets*,[19] written between 1934 and 1942, all time is seen to be unredeemable: 'go, go, go', says the bird, for 'human kind cannot bear very much reality'. In the Burnt Norton quartet, Eliot states that time past and time future allow but a little consciousness, as:

> *At the still point of the turning world. Neither flesh nor fleshless,*
> *Neither from nor towards; at the still point, there the dance is,*
> *But neither arrest nor movement. And do not call it fixity,*
> *Where past and future are gathered.*

Things at one time are not more important than those at another, and so past and future coexist. The East Coker quartet begins:

> *In my beginning is my end. In succession*
> *Houses rise and fall, crumble, are extended,*
> *Are removed, destroyed, restored, or in their place*
> *Is an open field, or a factory, or a by-pass.*

Later, Eliot says, 'the only wisdom we can hope to acquire is the wisdom of humility', for:

The houses are all gone under the sea
The dancers are all gone under the hill.

The dance for Eliot is the unmoving motion of the timeless, the movement around a still point. But what of our modern dance, where the idea of circular time has disintegrated into linearity? The Neanderthal, Sumerian, Minoan, Longshan, Mayan and Rapa Nui dancers are all under the hill, and we may soon condemn many more coastal cities than New Orleans to a watery grave as sea levels sharply rise with climate change. Towns on the permafrost are falling apart, and may have to be abandoned too. How quickly might we forget that there were ever settlements there at all? How sharply will things change if events subvert the global food system and force us within countries to become wholly self-sufficient? How readily will we be forced to change if oil and gas supplies fail? Perhaps these things will never come to pass. We will again dream up a way to fix these emerging problems, say the sceptics. There are no limits, they say, to our technological potential. On the other hand, economics will drive decisions. A year after hurricane Katrina struck New Orleans, only a half of the residents had returned. Congress awarded billions of dollars for recovery, but it may not be enough to rebuild an economy too (even if the money were well spent).

A psychological problem we are yet to face is the consequence of future population decline. In 1798 Thomas Malthus argued that human population growth would always outstrip resources:

> *Population, when unchecked, increases in a geometrical ratio. Subsistence increases only in an arithmetic ratio. A slight acquaint-ance with numbers will shew the immensity of the first power in comparison with the second.*

Since then, most policies and practice regarding natural resources and food have been shaped by concerns about our growing numbers. We are, after all, an extraordinarily successful species. When agriculture emerged, some 10,000 years ago, there were probably five million people worldwide. To the mid-19th century, world population then doubled eight times. Since then it has doubled four more times and will continue to grow to probably eight and a half billion people by the middle of the 21st century. It will then stabilize for a while, and subsequently fall. Not because of wars, climate change or infectious diseases (though they may contribute to greater declines), but because of changing fertility patterns. More choices about contraception and decreasing poverty reduces the need to have so many children, and changing lifestyles among the rich delay childbearing ages. When one generation produces fewer daughters, and fewer daughters are produced by them, then the replacement rate soon falls below the 2.1 needed to maintain population stability.[20]

Today, the average woman in industrialized countries has fewer than 1.6 children, in the least developed countries 5 children and in the other developing countries 2.6. The lowest fertility rates are now in southern Europe, at 1.1 children per woman. In the mid-1970s the average Bangladeshi woman had six children; today she has about three. In Iran, fertility has fallen from more than five children in the late 1980s to just over two today. The worldwide annual gain is still 76 million people (down from 100 million in 1990), but this is expected to fall to zero by 2050 as the number of children falls from today's average of 2.55 to 2.0. Life expectancy at birth was 47 years in 1950–1955, rose to 65 years by 2000–2005, and will rise again to 75 years worldwide by 2045–2050. By then, the number of people over 60 will have tripled to 1.9 billion, and the number over 80 will have risen from today's 86 million to 395 million. Of course, these changes will not be evenly spread. Some countries are predicted to triple their numbers by 2050; these include Afganistan, Burkina Faso, Burundi, Chad, Congo, DR Congo, DR Timor-Leste, Guinea-Bissau, Liberia, Mali, Niger and Uganda. But the populations of at least 51 countries will fall, including Germany, Italy, Japan and most of the former USSR.

What will happen after this peak, less than two generations away from us now? The United Nations has made heroic population predictions for the next 300 years, and, uncertain though these must be, the medium fertility estimates suggest at least a levelling of world population for 250 more years at 8.5 to 9 billion. With low fertility (at the kind of levels we are already seeing today – after all, 93 out of 222 countries already have fewer than 2.1 children per women and 37 have less than 1.5), world population declines to 5.5 billion by the end of this century, to 3.9 billion by 2150 and down to 2.3 billion by 2300. Which track we end up on depends entirely on early changes in fertility. Demographers cannot, of course, agree on the probability of stability or decline. But any kind of fall will bring huge changes. In 2000 people on average retired two weeks before mean life expectancy (65 years); by 2300 people will retire more than 30 years short of life expectancy (unless age of retirement changes), when on average women will live to 97 and men to 95. And this does not take account of potentially revolutionary changes to human longevity that new medical technologies might bring.

John Caldwell, of the Australian National University, writes that 'the low scenario is by no means implausible', and that the low projections 'would probably portend to many the fear of human extinction'. Governments would try to raise fertility levels, but it could be very difficult to achieve, as people do not always do the bidding of their governments. What, then, will happen to all those settlements we do not need? What of the fields and farms that become surplus to requirements? What of the wild animals – will we see their return to places from which they had long been eliminated (not the extinct species, of course, as they are gone forever)? Or might the vision be quite different – of spreading urban wastelands, of forgotten linkages to nature, of the nightmare of decivilization?[21]

The progress myth also shapes how we humans now think of ourselves in relation to animals. Evolutionary biology indicates that we are no more than animals, though clearly the last few thousand years have seen us escape the dominance of natural selection to allow culture, wealth and power to help choose who is most likely to survive. The inherent belief that we are the culmination of evolution, or indeed the sole choice of one god or another, leads us to look on all the rest of the animal kingdom (and earlier hominids) as not quite so clever and resourceful. Indeed, to build the plinth on which we stand, we have had to differentiate ourselves from the rest of nature. But this insistence on the difference between humans and animals is another recent idea. For most of history, once again, we have not seen ourselves as different, and animals have been treated as equals – and especially respected, as we had to catch and eat them to survive, and so needed their cooperation.

Hunter-gatherers today still see animals as equals, and feel a belonging to the rest of nature. It is highly likely that the same feelings were common among all our ancestors. Such connectivity to living things may indeed be hard-wired into our genes, and not just a result of cultural learning. This is the basis for E O Wilson's 'biophilia hypothesis',[22] which suggests that we have 'an innate sensitivity to and need for living things, as we have co-existed with them for thousands of generations'. While this remains a hypothesis, as no mechanisms have yet been clearly identified or proven, connectivity to plants and animals is known to bring many emotional and psycho-logical benefits even to modern humans. It is known that exposure to green places, whether deep immersion in the country or via views through a window, has a signif-icant impact on mental well-being. We also know that our relationships with animals, whether wild or domestic or indeed pets, also have a significant effect on self-esteem and our feelings of personal identity.

It is for these reasons that animal iconography is still so very important in many cultures. For hunter-gatherers, animal spirits populate the forests, savannahs and seas around them. They are daily visitors to human life. To we moderns, animals still play a very visible role. Many of our stories use animals as the main characters – and they seem to be more convincing when the characters are foxes or bears, wolves or seagulls. Look on the shelves of your local bookshop, or in a young child's bedroom, and count the number of characters in children's books that are animals. By my reckoning, the dogs, bears, elephants, foxes and hedgehogs thoroughly outnumber the humans. The fables of Aesop and tales of the Grimm brothers, of course, did this so well that these characters have become part of many cultures.

We also remain fascinated by mythical beasts. On mediaeval maps, which always had the unknown and unconquered regions distributed around the edges of the civilized areas, it was in these remote regions that the vampires, griffons, giants, unicorns, yetis and wildmen were depicted. A subliminal message, according to Felipe Fernández-Armesto, was that expansion into these areas would mean a reduction in potential harm as well as expansion of what was clearly human and civilized.[23]

You could draw a map of many modern countries rather like these mediaeval beasteries. In today's UK, it still would have mermaids, loch monsters, master otters, winged snakes, owlmen, black dogs and, above all, big cats. But the last of these may actually be real. More than 1000 sightings of big cats are now reported each year, and yet most photographs and videos always seem to be fuzzy, paw prints somewhat indeterminate, and attacks on livestock rarely confirmed by human witnesses. The

British Big Cat Society believes that up to a hundred big cats could now be roaming Britain; others believe that people are overtaken by hysteria and are seeing nothing more than muntjac deer or domestic pets, though this is a bit harsh on respected naturalists. The truth is, we like to believe in such myths, as they carry a deep fascination. All landscapes, of course, exist partly as ecological and physical truths, and partly in our imaginations. If these reports had no resonance, then they reports would be dismissed out of hand, and the myths would dwindle. If there are big cats hidden in the landscape, perhaps one day they will be joined by beavers, lynx, wolves and bears as direct efforts to rewild the landscape come to fruition.[24]

On the one hand, we wish to remain connected; on the other, we seem to be trying to escape. Both the transhumanists and monotheists seek to escape human nature and the cloying effects of our genes, which are still determining so many of these interests in animals and nature. Their views are thoroughly modern. Through progress we can shed the restrictive and parochial practices of particular places and culture, and so create a new vision and future for humankind. In an increasingly globalized world, there will be harmonization and homogenization as we come to believe the same things. Inequality, slavery, drudgery and terror will be overcome as our dreams of being set free come to pass. Such freedom, we are told, will come when we escape the contingencies of place and the layers of history. But all this is surely so much nonsense. Globalization will certainly mean greater direct and indirect understanding of other cultures, but it will also bring with it a loss of languages (half of the world's languages are already under threat of extinction), and a sharing of bad habits, such as junk food, sedentary lifestyles, Prozac to control stress and depression, and CCTV to monitor behaviour. And as for escaping from the influence of our genes, research is increasingly showing us just how important genes are in interacting with the environment to produce who and what we are.[25]

And what evidence is there that progress will inevitably result in a reduction of practices that still terrorize so many people in this world? The 20th century was probably the worst in human history for tyranny and mass murder. More people were killed by other people in deliberate, cold acts of cruelty than ever before. Is this really a sign of advanced progress, or that we are actually less able to cope? In the 20th century, some 187 million people perished in wars, massacres and persecutions. If these people held hands, they would stretch around the world fifteen times. Between 1917 and 1959, some 60 million of their own people were killed in the Soviet Union. In his remarkable *Straw Dogs*, John Gray states, 'these mass murders were not concealed; they were public policy'. Add to this the nightmares of Nazi extermination of six million Jews, the killing fields of Cambodia, Rwanda and Bosnia, and recent deliberate attempts to eliminate the many pygmy groups in Congo and the western Sudanese in Darfur. In the Congo, four million people died between 1998 and 2004 from the broader effects of civil war, yet such suffering almost appears to be explicitly ignored by the rest of the world. And there are many other places where killings were premeditated for the sake of what were defined as improvements. These crimes are committed by both religious states and atheist ones. As Gray pointedly says, 'as the hope for a better world has grown, so has mass murder'.[26]

The hope for a better world was also brought by settlers to North America, yet they managed to exterminate many native American groups in the name of progress. A Cheyenne death song acknowledges that 'nothing lives long, only the Earth and the mountains', and because of particular events in history (and their representation in modern film), we remember a little of the Sioux, Arapaho, Commanche and Cheyenne. But rarely the rest. As Dee Brown puts it:

> no one remembers the Chilulas, Chimarikou, Urebures, Nipewas, Alonas or a hundred other bands whose bones have been sealed under a million miles of freeways, parking lots and slabs of tract housing.[27]

The dream of progress goes on. In *Dead Cities*, Mike Davis tells the story of Las Vegas, which he calls the 'terminus of western history', but which still attracts 1000 new visitors every week and has a population now of 1.6 million. Las Vegas cultivates images of infinite opportunity for all, yet consumes 1600 litres of water per person daily. Houses are hermetically sealed from the elements, and from other people, and authorities feel the need to provide only half a hectare of open space per 1000 residents. Even worse, notes Davis, the desert is no longer a special place, but something to be conquered: 'the desert has lost all positive presence as a landscape habitat; it is merely the dark, brooding backdrop for the new Babel'.[28]

We should be prompted to think: what horrors are being enacted today, both on people and environments, as we sit back and pretend an inability to do anything, as these other places seem so remote? Yet these actions are part of our progressive modern world. Not something committed by barbarians who are somehow clearly different. These losses are a consequence of who we are and what we currently try to do. The future was not supposed to be like this. And these undercurrents of chaos appear to be getting worse as the rich get richer and the poorest seem to have little or no prospect of ever acquiring a decent standard of living. If the world is to survive, will the rich accept that they will simply have to become more frugal, or at least discover a whole raft of new environmentally sensitive technologies so that the world can be saved?

What should we do? First, we could take time to find the still point, as T S Eliot says in *Four Quartets*, where 'words move, music moves' and 'dawn points, and another day prepares for heat and silence'. We might be more humble about our faith in linear progress and our capacity to undo the problems we are creating. Why should everyone be encouraged to join the modern world? What is wrong with staying in the forests or deserts? What is wrong too with developing other models, or inventing a post-industrialized world that has a light touch on the Earth? Can we survive on an abundance of less, or will our psychologies never permit a shift to lower and more sensible consumption patterns?

Should we be pessimistic or optimistic? James Lovelock said of his recent book, *The Revenge of Gaia*, 'I am usually a cheerful sod, so I'm not happy writing doom books. But I don't see any easy way out.' At the global level, I too am pessimistic. It is looking pretty bad.[29] Yet at the local level, there are considerable grounds for optimism. There is so much innovation and good practice in local communities worldwide, so much evidence of sensible thinking and novel practice. But can we scale these ideas up to a seemingly indifferent world? Perhaps we should reflect on what former civilizations might have been thinking towards the ends of each of their average 900 years of success, when many had some of the largest and most sophisticated settlements in the world. They probably thought they would go on forever, that their progress represented the pinnacle of human endeavour, that they were somehow untouchable. Yet many disappeared, leaving only ruins and indecipherable glyphs, and many long-standing mysteries for today's archaeologists.

Is this a lesson for our current civilization, or just a series of historical accidents? If it is a lesson, we should be asking, as David Suzuki puts it, how much is enough. How would we like to shape this world, if it too will shape us in return? The Earth will certainly endure for millennia. What is much less certain is whether our civilization as currently configured can endure across the next century.

3

A Room with a Green View

The first scene of E M Forster's *A Room with a View* centres on Miss Bartlett's emotional lament over the room she and her cousin Lucy have been given by the pension's signora on their arrival in Florence: 'She promised us south rooms with a view close together, instead of which here are north rooms [...] looking into a court-yard.' Lucy says, 'it might be London', and Miss Bartlett continues, even more animated, 'Oh, it is a shame! Any nook will do for me, but it does seem hard that you shouldn't have a view.' But that evening they meet with good fortune as, in their first exchange before dinner, a Mr Emerson and his son, George, offer to swap, as they have rooms with a view. They turn the offer down, but later after intervention by Mr Beebe they accept, even though there is some sneering about the lowly status of the Emersons and their presumed political views. But late that night, Lucy can open the window in her new room, and she 'breathed in the clean air, thinking of the kind old man who had enabled her to see the lights dancing in the Arno and the cypresses of San Miniato, and the foothills of the Apennines, black against the rising moon'. In the morning, the view is fresh and sparkling, and she now flings open the windows 'to lean into the sunshine with beautiful hills and trees and marble churches opposite, and, close below, the Arno, gurgling against the embankment of the road'.

This is why the view from the window means so much to Lucy and her indignant cousin. It relaxes them, and it takes them into something special and distinctive about this place, the very reason why they had travelled there. Much later, Lucy and George come back to the same room in the Pension Bertolini and gaze through the open window and reflect on how far they had come, and how little, in fact, Charlotte (Miss Bartlett) seemed to have won. The tale ends with the two of them listening to the river, bearing down the snows of winter towards the Mediterranean. Pause now a moment, and look out of your nearest window. What do you see? Rolling corn fields, trees on a skyline, sheep on a meadow? Or the blur of cars speeding down a grey street; maybe a solitary patch of grass by a skyscraper? Or perhaps a garden with glorious flowers? Worst of all, a plain brick wall, the concrete of an elevated highway, or perhaps just an empty courtyard or car park like the one that so at first disappoints Lucy and Charlotte in northern Italy?

More than a century has passed since Forster wrote his story, and yet the emotional importance of the nature of the view from our windows is only just being properly understood. We ought to be surprised that it has taken so long. After all, when we go on holiday, do we prefer a hotel room that looks onto the car park, or one with the view of the hills or beach? Why should it matter? We are going to spend much more time on the beach than sitting in the room, and when in the room probably more time looking at the television than out of the window. It seems that even short periods of time spent looking out on green and blue scenes makes us feel good. As a result, we will also expect to pay more for a house that overlooks green or water scenes, or the sweeping vistas of city lights.

It has become increasingly clear that many features of the natural and built environment affect our behaviour and actual mental states. The environment can, therefore, be seen to be therapeutic, neutral or potentially harmful. Though there are many reasons for preserving nature – after all, the future of the world depends on it – relatively little attention has been paid to the potential personal health benefits. What, then, makes many people care about nature, and why are so many of us distressed about its loss? Why does nature still seem to have a positive effect on people, despite our increasing preferences for urbanization in modern societies? Evidence is beginning to show that exposure to nature can make positive contributions to our health, help us recover from pre-existing stresses, have an immunizing effect by protecting us from future problems, and even help us to concentrate and think more clearly.[1]

We could hypothesize that there are some evolutionary reasons for all this, as we have lived close to the land and nature on a daily basis for most of human history, while having industrialized, and increasingly urbanized, for only the past six to ten generations. Today, almost half the world's population lives in urban areas. Nonetheless, many of us still spend a great deal of time engaging with nature in many different ways. In the UK, more than one billion day visits are made to the countryside each year, with five billion visits to urban parks; five million people are regular anglers and some fifteen million garden regularly; six of every ten households have a pet; and many millions of others are birdwatchers, wildfowlers, pigeon-racers, dog-walkers, ramblers, runners, horseriders, cyclists and game-shooters. Why do we do all these things? What possesses us to take the trouble to be in the presence of green nature and living things, when we now can easily stay at home and watch it on the television? Why do we say that we feel great after green activities? And if we feel so good doing it, why do we still put up with such urbanized lives and stressful jobs?

Green places are, in short, good places. From research involving more than 3000 people, we have discerned five reasons for engaging with nature and green space: the sensory stimulation, the natural and social connections, the physical activity, the livelihood services, and the escape.[2] Here the term green space is used to include any natural areas, which may not actually be green (such as beaches, seas, deserts, high mountains and snowscapes), as all these places seem to have a similar range of effects on people. Human-made landscapes without nature not only do not have the same effect, they are often felt to be malign.

The first reason for seeking this engagement is sensory stimulation. We are affected by colours and sounds, fresh air and excitement. We appreciate the green and other diverse colours of nature and landscapes, the beauty and scenery, the birdsong and cries of other animals, the quality of the light (especially at sunset and sunrise: who on this planet owns a camera and does not have at least one photograph of a sunset?), and the aesthetics of landscapes. We commonly talk of the pleasure of fresh air, as a contrast to indoor and city life (especially urban pollution), and of being exposed to all types of weather and the unpredictable nature of the changing of the seasons. We also often engage with nature for some excitement – the adrenalin rush and exhilaration of some physical activity that may be risky (such as mountain climbing, sailing, cycling or shooting) or of some outcome achieved, such as catching a particular type or size of fish.

The second reason centres on the felt value of connectivity both to nature and to groups of other people. Many of us value the direct bonding with companion animals (such as dogs or horses) and with wild animals, both by hunting and observing, and feel something special about exposure to the mystery and otherness of wild birds and animals. We often feel a spiritual connection to something elemental about nature, to a larger cosmology and the scale and longevity of nature, which can be humbling. We also have positive affective sentiments for places where things happened to us in the past, where memories and ghosts now reside in the landscape.

These memories coalesce into stories and help to shape our personal and cultural identities. Many of us also engage with nature and green places in order to establish social bonds with friends and family. Common experiences can strengthen existing links, especially with families, help people establish new friends, or just expose us to new cultures and ways of thinking.

Another reason for engagement is to express ourselves through some activity. This may comprise manual tasks, such as building a fire, chopping a tree or carving wood, that are a challenge and can lead to a sense of achievement. Physical activity is known to improve self-esteem and mood as well as lower blood pressure, and the burning of calories brings further health benefits. A fourth reason for engagement is the long-standing livelihood services we derive from nature – the harvesting and gathering of wild foods, the shelter and fuel, medicines and water that have kept us alive for millennia. In industrialized society, this has come to be much less important for most people, though the value probably survives in today's many millions of gardeners. Finally, there is a new and increasingly common modern reason for engagement with nature. We value it as an escape from modern life. We commonly say we need to 'get away from it all' (rather than go to it all) or to have time alone or with the family. We value opportunities to think and clear the head, to find tranquillity and freedom, where time will pass slowly, to find peace and quiet, recharge our batteries, and escape from relentless pressure and stress that is now so commonly felt in modern life. The idea of escape has to be a modern one. Did early hominids feel a need to escape? Perhaps they did, and that is why they spread across the world.

The idea that nature is somehow an essential part of human existence was captured by E O Wilson's 'biophilia hypothesis'. This states that the desire for contact with nature is something we partly inherit and act on instinctively without necessarily appreciating the underlying evolutionary reasons. The theory proposes that this natural instinct is affiliated with our genetic fitness and contributes to intensifying our well-being, mental development and personal fulfilment. It also underpins the reasons for a human ethic of care and the growing importance of conservation of the natural environment.

These ideas are, of course, not new. Hildegard of Bingen (1098–1179) developed her own philosophy of *viriditas* to capture the spiritual centrality of nature. William Cowper later observed that 'man immured in cities still retains his in-born inextinguishable thirst for rural scenes'. Francis Bacon's view was localized: 'nothing is more pleasant to the eyes than the green grass kept finely shorn', and Wordsworth said, 'a wilderness is rich with liberty', which he then went on to express by walking and walking (he is said to have walked 175,000 miles in his lifetime over the Lake District hills). And in 1848 John Stuart Mill said that:

> *solitude in the presence of mutual beauty and grandeur is the cradle of thoughts and aspiration, which are not only good for life for the individuals, but which society could ill do without.*[3]

These comments suggest some differences in types of engagement with nature, all of which, however, seem to bring some form of well-being. We can view nature, as through a window, or see it represented in a painting. We can be in the presence of nearby nature, which may be incidental to some other activity, such as walking or cycling to work, reading on a garden seat or talking to friends in a park. Or we can actively participate with nature, such as by gardening, farming, trekking, camping, cross-country running or horseriding. The evidence shows that there are positive outcomes from all these levels of activity.

The benefits of window views have been shown not just in Forster's Florence, but in many workplaces, hospitals and homes and during travelling to work.[4] Windows in the workplace buffer stresses, and over long periods people working in workplaces with windows have been shown to have fewer illnesses, feel less frustrated and more patient, and express greater enthusiasm for work. People are also able to think better with green views, and those in offices without windows often compensate by putting up more pictures of landscapes or by keeping indoor plants. Those who cannot compensate, however, often respond by becoming more stressed and aggressive. One long-term study of Alzheimer's patients in care homes found that those with gardens had significantly lower levels of aggression and violence than those of homes with no gardens. Roger Ulrich also reports on a Swedish psychiatric hospital in which patients over a fifteen-year period often complained about and damaged paintings on the walls. Damage, though, was only ever done to abstract paintings, and there was no recorded attack on any depicting nature and landscapes.

At home, the view is equally important. Frances Kuo has found that small amounts of green in the urban environment of Chicago make a large difference to people's well-being.[5] Green views from home, plus nearby nature in which to play, also have a positive effect on the cognitive functioning of children. Residents in very poor neighbourhoods like trees and grass near their blocks and say the greener the view the better. Buildings with plentiful nearby vegetation also have half as many property and violent crimes than those with none. Interestingly, there is a greater difference between non-green and moderately green locations than between moderately and very green, suggesting more of a benefit would come from a light-greening of all urban spaces rather than a dark-greening of just a few. Indeed, well-maintained vegetation may be an additional cue to care, as it signifies to outsiders that local people already care for their environment and so are more vigilant and ecoliterate.

Good views from the window also increase the economic value of hotels and housing.[6] Green space alters room pricing policy in hotels in Zurich and increases by a quarter the value of homes with gardens looking onto lakes and parks in the Netherlands. Street trees in Berlin increase real estate value by a sixth, and the value of housing near to water is greater in Merseyside. A recent study of ten urban settings in England found that properties with a park view had a 12 per cent higher value than those in the same locality with no view. Again, this should not be a surprise. After all, why have so many urban planners in the past planted trees to create boulevards and avenues? And the drive to work matters too. People on an urban drive dominated by human artefacts are more stressed than those driving through the nature-dominated scenes of forests or golf courses. These nature drives also seem to have an immunizing effect against future stresses that might arise during the day. However, civic and park authorities often seem to act as if none of this is true. Green spaces are often removed to keep down maintenance costs, and there are often fears that well-vegetated places offer opportunities for criminals and drug-dealers to hide, echoing old fears of thieves and highwaymen in the forests. Rachel Kaplan, one of the first to recognize the health value of green space, notes that 'considering the vital role played by the view from the window, it is surprising that this aspect of housing has not received greater empirical attention'.

The evidence does indeed suggest that nearby nature should be seen as part of a fundamental health resource. Two classic studies from the 1980s confirm this. The first found that prisoners in Michigan whose cells faced farmland and trees had a quarter lower frequency of sick-cell visits than those in cells facing the prison yard. The second was a ten-year comparison of post-operative patients in Pennsylvania, in which it was found that patients with tree views from their rooms stayed in hospital for significantly less time than those with brick wall views, needed less medication and had fewer negative comments in the nurses' notes.

Interestingly, these effects occur even if the view is a landscape picture by your hospital bed. A recent study of patients at Johns Hopkins hospital split bronchoscopy patients (in which a fibre-optic tube is inserted into the lungs) into two groups: one control and the other with a large landscape picture hung by their bedside, listening to the sounds of birdsong and a babbling brook prior to the operation. The second group had a 50 per cent higher level of very good or excellent pain control than those who did not have the picture or sounds, thus substantially reducing expenditure on painkilling drugs. If you were of a suspicious mind, you might wonder why this kind of research has not been widely tested (especially if it were to confirm a reduced need for drugs). We might also ask why most hospitals are now built upwards with little regard for the views from wards, or even for the quality of the grounds and gardens. Howie Frumkin, formerly of Emory University and now at the Centers for Disease Control and Prevention, points out that 'hospitals have traditionally had gardens as an adjunct to recuperation and healing', and almost all people living in retirement communities say windows facing green landscapes are essential to well-being.

So what is it in these various views of real and photographed nature that seems to have a positive effect on us? First, the structure of a scene matters irrespective of content. Arnold Wilkins of the University of Essex has shown that highly abstract pictures with a high density of lines and patterns are more aversive than simpler pictures with less density and more space. And urban scenes are more structured in this way than rural, and so are more aversive to the average person. We are hardwired, it seems, to prefer certain kinds of scenes that are more likely to be rural than urban.

What, then, is important about the content? Jo Peacock, also at the University of Essex, showed people of different ages nearly 300 photographs of rural and urban scenes to find out which they thought were pleasant or unpleasant.[7] Everyone agrees on what constitutes a 'rural pleasant' scene. These are diverse landscapes with a variety of habitats, containing trees, water, blue sky and clouds. The presence of livestock, such as lambs and calves, can substitute for sky and water. Viewers tend, however, to dislike dark skies and thundery clouds, and always prefer greens over browns in the landscape. Viewers also commonly put themselves inside pictures, saying they would like to visit or even live in the scene. Most, though, struggle to say that any rural scene is unpleasant. All agree that a pile of rubbish or an abandoned car make a rural scene unpleasant, but they tend to assume that these problems are temporary. Again, green trees and other vegetation combined with blue skies or water seem to override anything unpleasant. Broken machinery, damaged trees, abandoned buildings, billboards, and pipes carrying effluents are all unpleasant elements.

Both 'urban unpleasant' and 'urban pleasant' are relatively straightforward to categorize. Damaged, degraded buildings and environments are unpleasant, as is graffiti, scaffolding, concrete blocks, rubbish and broken windows. Where places appear abandoned or deserted, they are unpleasant. However, skyscrapers and distant cityscapes are consistently seen as pleasant, though many people comment they would be more pleasant to visit rather than live in. Tall buildings become urban pleasant if there is water in the foreground, particularly if reflected blue from the sky. In general, urban scenes with green, whether urban parks, allotments or private gardens, together with water and blue sky, are consistently said to be pleasant.

These pictures were then used to assess what effect they had on people's well-being while they engaged in physical activity. We know that exposure to green nature is good for us; we also know that physical activity improves self-esteem as well as a range of other physiological measures. Putting the two together into what we call green exercise could, we supposed, lead to further benefits for health. In a laboratory study, the effects of exercise were tested for five groups of twenty subjects on a treadmill while observing a sequence of pictures projected on the wall. The four categories of scenes were tested: rural pleasant, rural unpleasant, urban pleasant and urban unpleasant; the fifth was a control without exposure to any images. Blood pressure and two psychological measures, self-esteem and mood, were measured before and after the intervention.

The blood pressure differences were startling between groups. For those in the rural pleasant group, blood pressure fell by nearly 8mm of mercury, while in the rural unpleasant and control (no pictures), blood pressure fell by 2mm. The urban pleasant group was unchanged (which is effectively an increase in blood pressure relative to the control), and those in the urban unpleasant group had a significant increase in blood pressure by 3mm of mercury. It appears that exercise in green places has a hypotensive effect (reduces blood pressure), whereas in cities it is hypertensive (increases blood pressure). There were also significant effects on self-esteem and mood. The rural pleasant and urban pleasant scenes produced large improvements of self-esteem over the control group, which in turn ended with higher self-esteem levels than both unpleasant groups. Both types of unpleasant scenes thus have a depressive effect on self-esteem. For those people starting with low self-esteem, a larger proportion had significant increases in the rural pleasant group. Mood is measured in six ways, and these again showed that rural and urban pleasant scenes had the greatest positive effect. Unexpectedly, rural unpleasant scenes were worse for mood than urban unpleasant, appearing to suggest that views embodying threats to the countryside had a greater negative effect on mood than already unpleasant urban scenes.

Lucy and George would surely have approved, and perhaps also Miss Barlett and the generous Mr Emerson.

So much for the effects of nature through a window or in a picture. What of the next level of engagement, where we are exposed incidentally while engaged in some other activity? This may be nearby nature in the neighbourhoods of homes or work, or in the grounds of hospitals and care homes. Nancy Wells and Gary Evans of Cornell University have found that eight- to ten-year-old children in upstate New York communities exposed to both indoor and outdoor vegetation are less stressed and more able to recover from stressful events than those in greenless homes and backyards. This confirms earlier work on younger children in day-care facilities either surrounded by orchards, pasture and forests or by tall buildings in the city – those in the all-weather facilities with regular outdoor exposure to nature had much better attention capacity and motor coordination. Nancy Wells also found that children in families moving to houses with more nearby nature had higher levels of cognitive functioning, though it could have been that these families were more able to select certain types of preferred homes. Cause and effect can be difficult to disentangle. In New York City, for example, children in poor neighbourhoods have access to 17 square metres of park per person, while those in better-off districts each have access to 40 square metres.[8]

Terry Hartig of Uppsala University has been continuing the pioneering work of Stephen and Rachel Kaplan which indicates that nature can restore deficits in attention arising from overwork or over-concentration, making people both feel and think better. He has found that sitting in a room with tree views promotes more rapid blood pressure decline than sitting in a windowless room, and also that walking in a nature reserve reduces blood pressure more than a walk along an urban and non-green street. In both contexts, the green room and green walk, people recover more rapidly from attention-demanding tasks. The long-term effects may be important. Another five-year study of older people found that access to green space in which they could walk was an accurate predictor for longevity, as those who walked in green places lived longer.[9]

Plants in offices are also important. In one study, all the plants were removed from two office floors for three months. At this point, one office floor was professionally landscaped, and to maintain a sense of environmental change, the other floor was given artwork on the walls. After a further six months, it was found that employees enjoyed the environment with plants more, and also derived pleasure from looking after the plants themselves. Nearly half of the employees situated on the plantless floor found themselves regularly visiting the other floor to view the plants. Another experiment measured the effect of indoor plants on productivity, attitude toward the workplace and overall mood in the office environment. Offices were randomly transformed to incorporate no plants, a moderate number of plants and a high number of plants. In situations where plants were present, participants perceived the office to be more attractive, were more comfortable and reported enhanced mood status.[10]

Plants outside are good for us too. The health benefits of gardens appear to have begun to be appreciated at Babylon, where Nebuchadnezzar built the hanging gardens in about 600 BC. Later, in the Middle Ages, garden cloisters and vegetable gardens were used as part of the healing process. In the Victorian period, gardens were routinely set out in hospital grounds for the benefit of patients, and hospitals themselves located in pleasant surroundings. It could be that modern health systems, with a focus on treatment of diseases rather than patient comfort and care, have abandoned some useful principles regarding connections with nature and place. There is again evidence that patients and hospital staff with windows overlooking gardens have lower levels of stress, and patients regularly report positive changes in mood when visiting gardens. Gardens and nature in hospital environments enhance mood, reduce stress and improve the overall appreciation of the health care provider and quality of care.

Some gardens are specifically designed as healing gardens, and these can work well for both the patients and staff of hospitals. One healing garden at a children's hospital in California was found to have positive effects on users, with more than half reporting they were more relaxed and less stressed, a quarter refreshed and rejuvenated, and a fifth more positive and able to cope; only a tenth experiencing no effect. Even very short visits were beneficial, as nearly half of all observed visitors spent less than five minutes at a time in the garden. Those who did go to the garden went 'to escape the stresses of the hospital and enjoy the relaxing and restorative elements of nature'. The problem, however, was that a quarter of staff and almost all visiting families and patients had never been to the garden, and did not realize what benefits it could bring. Some of these green principles are being applied in the Eden Alternative nursing homes in Texas, where healing gardens, greenhouses, atriums and plants have been recently deployed. After conversion, there were half the number of bedsores, and a significant reduction in patients restrained, in behavioural incidents and in staff absenteeism. The costs of such nature-based treatments are much less than expenditure on drugs and surgery to achieve the same outcomes.[11]

All of this suggests that short or occasional exposures to nature can improve our well-being. However, we do not know whether cumulative short exposures, such as looking out of the window or short walks, equate to longer, less frequent exposures to nature, such as a weekend away in the country. It also does not tell us whether there is an enhanced effect of exposure to places that are special because they have memories and stories associated with them. In other words, some environments may be green and beneficial, but anonymous, whereas others may also be evoking pleasant memories as well. An oak tree could just be a tree, or it could remind us of a picnic on some past summer's day. But memories cannot be created unless people have engaged with nature at some prior point.

The third level of engagement with nature comprises direct participation in some activity in green spaces, which could include gardening, trekking, walking, mountaineering, running, camping, cycling or boating. This could be exposure to nearby nature, such as in gardens or nature reserves, or to distant ecosystems, such as national parks and wildernesses. Private and community gardens provide a direct link to nature for many people and are particularly valuable in urban settings. In the UK, there are 15 million gardens covering 800,000 hectares, together with some 300,000 occupied allotments on 12,000 hectares of land. Allotments were first set up following the Captain Swing riots of 1830 and rose in number to 600,000 by 1914. Though today's allotments yield 215,000 tonnes of fresh food each year, they more importantly provide an opportunity for regular contact with nature. Some 70 per cent of 600 allotment gardeners surveyed in the 1990s said that enjoyment and satisfaction were their primary reasons for having an allotment. They wanted fresh produce, but they also liked the fresh air and exercise, as well as having something fulfilling to do with their time. Our love for gardening may be extending people's lives by giving meaning as well as improving well-being.

In the US, 35 million people are engaged in growing their own food in back gardens and allotments (about 75 million households have gardens). Their contribution to the informal economy is estimated to be about $12–14 billion per year. Private gardeners cultivate to produce better tasting and more nutritious food, but also to save money, take exercise and for therapy. In short, gardening makes them feel better too. This is again true of community gardens and farms which, by contrast, seek to enhance both food production and social benefits. Many of the recently established Community Supported Agriculture farms, with direct links to their consumers, not only provide weekly food boxes but also run horticultural therapy and educational sessions. One survey of community gardens in upstate New York found that people participated primarily to access fresh foods, to enjoy nature and for mental and physical health benefits. In more than half the cases, the gardens had changed the attitudes of residents about their neighbourhood, and in a third had led to collective action to address local issues.[12]

Based on these experiences of the value of gardening for mental health, a tradition of horticulture therapy has emerged in recent years. This is defined as 'the process by which individuals may develop well-being using plants and horticulture. This is achieved by active or passive involvement.' Many people have benefited, including patients recovering from major illness or injury, physical or learning disabilities or mental ill-health, the elderly, offenders, and drug or alcohol abusers. The benefits gained include 'increased self-esteem and self-confidence, the development of horticultural, social and work skills, literacy and numeracy skills, an increased sense of general well-being and the opportunity for social interaction and the development of independence'. Inclusion in social and therapeutic horticultural programmes has also been known to lead to employment opportunities or aid individuals in training or education progression.[13]

Forest Schools are a new idea to involve children in activities in green places. The idea came from Denmark as a way of teaching about the natural world, having become an integral part of pre-school education from the 1980s. Children who had attended Forest Schools were found to be arriving at formal school with strong social skills, high confidence and self-esteem and could work well in groups. In the UK, the Forest Education Initiative has taken on the idea and has developed a country-wide initiative.[14] Participation has already been seen to improve children's confidence, well-being and self-esteem, and perhaps more importantly gives them pride and ownership of their local environment. Each time children leave the woods, they are encouraged to take something with them so that they can continue discussion and engagement with parents and friends. Many arrive, though, with a quite astonishing lack of knowledge of nature. One leader, Sian Jones, said, 'at first, some of them cry at the thought of going into the woods [...] some of them can't even walk on uneven ground; they've only ever been on pavements and carpets'.

Beyond nearby nature are what have been long called wildernesses. Even though the term is problematic (wilderness seems to imply a lack of people, but there are very few environments in the world that are not an emergent property of active shaping by people), it is still widely used to mean places physically and/or mentally far from the influence of modern, urbanized environments. It was the testimony of 19th-century writers such as John Muir and Henry David Thoreau that helped to draw attention to the benefits of experiences of the wild. Muir's writing on the Sierra Nevada, and the importance of wild areas for well-being, was instrumental in the establishment of the world's first national park at Yellowstone in 1872. Since then, many studies have shown that people both seek and derive a variety of values when they visit wildernesses, in particular a desire for tranquillity and natural beauty, escape from the stresses of urban life, and the potential for dramatic peak experiences or transcendental moments. But despite this long history, Thomas Herzog of Grand Valley State University in Michigan suggests that 'the restorative potential of natural settings is probably underappreciated', as many urban and sedentary people still appear not to appreciate the full benefits of such settings, particularly in the face of competition from multiple other leisure and entertainment opportunities. Rather depressingly, many are now only exposed to plastic nature in indoor atriums.

What happens when urban people are first exposed to real wild nature? Laura Fredrickson and Dorothy Anderson examined the effects of deep immersion wilderness experiences on two groups of women during and after trips to Minnesota and Arizona. Participants stated that benefits came from both individual contact with nature and from connections with the rest of the group. Personal testimonies show that the experience left a lasting impression, particularly as these experiences were so different to those of their daily lives at home. Many spoke of renewed hope, a reawakening of emotions and a new sense of identity. One said, 'It was so incredible being able to hear the birds [...] the sounds of the forest, the snapping of twigs, hearing the tiny sigh of the wind through the treetops at night.' Another stated, 'I noticed more, I felt more. I felt more connected to myself and even to other people on the trip.' And another said, 'I can't even fully capture in words what happened to me when I was out there. [...] It's like the spirit is burning deep inside me again, and I'm looking at my life a little differently.'

But it is important to note that person-to-person interactions are just as important as person-to-place connections: 'the affective appeal of a particular place setting has as much to do with the social interactions that occur there, as with the overall visual appeal of the landscape itself', say the authors, who conclude that wildernesses contribute substantially to participants' well-being. Similar experiences have been noted in the forests of Australia, where transcendent experiences provoke a sense of harmony, freedom and well-being that can be sufficiently long-lasting to change long-term attitudes to the environment. Several other studies have noted the value of natural and wilderness experiences and their therapeutic potential and the additional role that physical hardship and risk can play in triggering more profound experiences.[15]

The evidence appears to be strong. Green places are good for us, and if we engage in physical activities too, then we derive further cardiovascular health benefits. Green exercise therefore has important implications for public and environmental health. A fitter and emotionally more content population would cost the economy less as well as reducing individual human suffering. Obesity and related conditions already cost more in public health terms than smoking and will soon overtake smoking as industrialized countries' biggest killer. Support for a wide range of green exercise activities could include the provision and promotion of healthy walks projects, exercise on prescription, green school environments, travel to school projects, green views in hospitals, city farms and community gardens, urban green space, outdoor leisure activities in the countryside, and wilderness programmes. However, there is a distinct tension between these proposals and the existing drivers of economic development in both rural and urban regions. In urban areas, green spaces are undervalued and often ignored. In rural areas, modern land management methods continue to put pressure on habitats and places where people could be enjoying nature too.

And what of Lucy, Miss Bartlett and the long-term effect of the views from their rooms? The women later return to the forested countryside of Sussex, but their friendship falters as they both end up pursuing the same husband. Lucy wins that contest, but all we learn about the effect of the view in Florence is that it still seems to work some magic when she returns with George.

4

Unhealthy Places

In the face of widespread and growing threats to the natural environment, two arguments about the need for biodiversity and nature conservation are commonly used: the environment should be conserved for ethical and for economic reasons. The whales or rainforests are to be saved because it is the right thing to do, or because they provide valuable economic services. Relatively little attention, though, has been paid to the potential emotional benefits. How does nature make us feel? Much, of course, will depend on what else is important in our lives at the time. Is it, anyway, a good day or a bad day? Irrespective of where we come from in the world, it seems that the presence of living things makes us feel good. They help us when we feel stressed, and if there is green vegetation, blue sky and water in a scene, then we like it even more. This idea that the quality of nature in our home neighbourhood affects our mental health is not a new one, but strangely it has not greatly affected the recent planning of our urban and rural environments. Time spent observing or experiencing natural environments contributes to psychological well-being. This ought not to be surprising if we take an evolutionary perspective. We appear to function better in environments that offered us a good chance of survival in the past.

Yet since the advent of the industrial revolution, a growing number of people have found themselves living in wholly urban settings. Indeed, within the next decade, the number of people worldwide in urban areas will exceed those in rural contexts for the first time in human history. In 1960 the world population was three billion; by 2010 there will be more than three billion people dwelling in urban settlements. A century ago, only a tenth of the world's population lived in cities; very soon it will be more than half. Some of this will be by choice – some cities offer the best, or even only, opportunities for employment. There are more services concentrated together, implying better access to schools, hospitals, theatres and sports clubs. But one thing is quite clear: an urban setting has by definition less nature than a rural one. And less green nature regrettably means reduced mental well-being – or at least less opportunity to recover from mental stresses. And this seems to be very unfortunate. As our green environments have increasingly come under pressure from industrial and housing development, so it seems we ourselves have suffered more.

There are many different ideas about what constitutes mental health. For a long time, it has been taken to mean the absence of a recognizable illness. Yet this type of deficit model does not explain how mental health and psychological well-being also positively influence us – helping to shape how we think and feel, how we learn and communicate, how we form and sustain relationships, and, critically, how we cope with shocks and stresses. Thus everyone has mental health needs, not just those with an illness. However, this is not widely accepted, and mental ill-health is still commonly assumed to be the fault of the sufferer. For centuries, the policy response has been to lock up the sufferers, and so protect the rest of society from them. In most health care systems, the predominant focus for both treatment and expenditure has come to be on people who are ill. This is also true for our environments. We tend only to become concerned when something important is harmed. Yet the best approach, and in the end the cheapest, is to focus efforts upstream, and try to create healthy environments in which people can flourish rather than flounder. We ought to be concerned not just with preventing mental ill-health, but with creating places where we can be healthy.

Yet today, stress and mental ill-health are becoming more common in all parts of the world, and the associated public health costs are rising steeply. The World Health Organization estimates that depression and depression-related illness will become the greatest source of ill-health by 2020.[1] This is partly because other behaviours, such as smoking, over-eating and high alcohol consumption, act as coping mechanisms for stress and mental ill-health, and have their own serious consequences. Depression is known to be a risk factor for a range of chronic physical illness, including asthma, arthritis, diabetes, strokes and heart disease. Stress, now a major problem for working people in modern societies, is also a strong predictor of mortality, with industrialized countries increasingly having to raise expenditure for the provision of care, lost outputs and costs to individuals. Today, a fifth of people in work in the UK say they are very or extremely stressed, and mental ill-health costs some £77 billion per year (more than the £60 billion cost of crime). Each year, a tenth of UK gross national product is lost due to stress, and three in ten employees will have a mental health problem. The easy option is drugs, such as the widely prescribed selective serotonin reuptake inhibitors (SSRIs) such as Prozac (fluoxetine). SSRIs can be a lifeline for those suffering clinical depression, but for many other people, as Daniel Nettle has put it, they have become a convenient 'shelter from the normal pains of being human'. In both the US and UK, 3 per cent of the population is now taking SSRIs (some ten million people), while in the US, some four million young adults and children are prescribed amphetamine-like stimulants to treat what is now called attention deficit hyperactivity disorder. Chemical intervention is rapidly becoming a norm.[2]

Yet many of today's urgent mental and physical health challenges, including obesity and coronary heart disease, are closely connected to the sedentary and indoor lifestyles we have adopted through choice. Physically active people have a lower risk of dying from coronary heart disease, type II diabetes, hypertension and colon cancer. Activity also enhances mental health, fosters healthy muscles and bones, and helps maintain health and independence in older adults.[3] The UK Chief Medical Officer, Liam Donaldson, has formally said:

> *physical activity helps people feel better, as reflected in improved mood and decreased state and trait anxiety. It helps people feel better about themselves through improved physical self-perceptions, improved self-esteem, decreased physiological reactions to stress [and] improved sleep.*

The design of the built and natural environment thus matters for mental and physical health. People seem to prefer natural environments, yet live in unhealthy places. Stephen and Rachel Kaplan indicate that such natural settings need not be remote wildlands and emphasize the value of 'the everyday, often unspectacular natural environment that is, or ideally would be, nearby' – parks and open spaces, street trees, vacant lots and backyard gardens, as well as fields and forests.[4]

There have not been many cross-cultural studies, but it seems that there might be some universal truths. Peter Kahn has studied communities in the US, Brazil and Portugal, and people at all three locations said that animals, plants and open spaces played an important part in their lives. People's reasoning was 'virtually identical across locations', and everyday nature seemed to be a psychological necessity for most, not a luxury of the few. Steve Brechin of Syracuse University studied attitudes in twelve wealthy and twelve poor countries and found no differences within or between groups on environmental problems. All groups seemed to have biocentric concerns for living things.[5]

The value of such open space is because it is both green and a place where people can be active. An urban park can enhance local people's lives and provide communal benefits by encouraging social interaction. Green space is important for mental well-being, and levels of use have been linked with longevity and decreased risk of mental ill-health in Japan, Scandinavia and the Netherlands.[6] Open space is particularly important for children. Childhood play experiences in the form of memories and imaginings have been shown to have an influence on their later mental well-being as adults. It is also known that children's social play, concentration and motor ability are all positively influenced after playing in nature. Yet the opportunities for children resident in both urban and rural neighbourhoods to join in safe play are rapidly diminishing, mainly because of parental fear of crime and road traffic. Children now wander less, and discover less, and perhaps are losing some important connections to nature and place.[7] And when children come to accept this as normal, they no longer know what they are missing. Peter Kahn calls this problem environmental generational amnesia and cites examples of poor communities in Houston, Texas, where children know about air, water and garbage pollution, but only a third believed that these environmental problems affected them directly. They had reset their environmental barometers, coming to assume that bad was neutral, or even than bad was good.

Further problems arising from physical features of the built environment include sick building syndrome caused by some construction materials and ill-designed air-conditioning systems, long-distance commutes to work, and suburban communities with self-contained homes that encourage little contact with neighbours or the local environment. But some of the most dramatic effects have been observed when whole environments are transformed, especially when in the name of improvement. After slum clearances, for example, people gain from changes in physical assets and services, but lose out when social networks deteriorate and break down. As Hugh Freeman puts it, such clearances often involve:

> the demolition of a neighbourhood and not just the destruction of buildings, but also that of a functioning social system, with a characteristic culture of its own and important social networks that could never be reproduced artificially.

One study of social change in the 1920s among the 20,000 people originally resettled to Dagenham from inner-city east London found that there were wide variations in sociability according to the make-up of the new streets. People who came to live in small, narrow streets and cul-de-sacs had more social connections and reciprocal arrangements than those in wider, busy streets, where few people could get to know their neighbours. When housing was replaced by large modern high-rise estates, social support networks based on geographic proximity entirely broke down, leading to an atomized community less able to buffer against stress.[8]

Another study of a massive 43-block housing project in St Louis, Missouri, built in the mid-1950s to house 12,000 people, found that although residents had a similar number of friends as non-project dwellers, these relationships 'bore little or no relation to the physical proximity of families to each other'. Neighbours became more hostile, and the quality of life fell, even though individuals were generally satisfied with their own apartments. The problem was that the project offered no natural, or, as Oscar Newman calls it, defensible space or common facilities around which neighbourly relationships could develop. The open space between the blocks that was supposed to do this was soon called 'wasted space' by residents. In 1972, only 18 years after the project had been opened, all the blocks were demolished after years of vacancy rates exceeding 70 per cent. Like many such projects, the design had earlier won architectural praise, but only before the people had moved in.

Bizarrely, the same kinds of mistakes are being made today as cities now spread outwards rather than upwards, again with significant consequences for public health.[9] As urban regions diffuse into former rural areas, they produce settlements with low density, a heavy reliance on motor cars for transport and increasing segregation of communities from one another. Urban sprawl also influences air pollution, produces heat islands, changes physical activity patterns, increases motor vehicle crashes, makes pedestrian behaviour difficult, and eventually shapes mental health and social capital. All this leads to significant health and identity consequences which are rarely acknowledged by urban planners.

Frances Kuo of the University of Illinois has found that 'greener neighbourhood common spaces give rise to stronger neighbourhood social ties'. Residents in urban areas with more local green space had 'more social activities and more visitors, knew more of their neighbours, reported their neighbours were more concerned with helping and supporting one another and had stronger feelings of belonging'. This indicates that regular contact with nature is indispensable, as residents prefer areas with trees and grass and negatively respond to barren areas without vegetation. The mere presence of trees encourages more frequent use of the outdoor space and experiencing nature reduces mental fatigue, diminishes sensations of stress and has positive effects on mood.[10] So why do we not do this routinely in the planning of our settlements?

There appears to be a dose–response relationship, too, with a significant relationship between the number of times an urban open green space is visited and the level of self-reported stress experienced. A recent study of eight European cities found that in places with more greenery and less graffiti people were more likely to take exercise and thus reduce obesity. Residential environments with high levels of local green space had people three times more likely to be physically active and 40 per cent less likely to be overweight.[11] The amount of time spent per week in urban green areas is also influenced by the distance to home or work. People who live 50 metres or less from the nearest green area visit them three to four times per week. If this distance is increased to 300 metres, then the number of visits falls to two and a half, and if the distance is 1000 metres, then visits occur only once a week. If residents have few green environments within their local area, they do not recompense for this by visiting more distant public parks or urban forests more frequently.

Thus the built environment can be therapeutic or harmful. Hugh Freeman writes, 'there is a need to restore in human settlements the benefits of [...] a social matrix in which a worthwhile quality of life and work can grow'. This sense of the particularities of place is important, as many of us have positive affective sentiments for specific places – things happened there and we remember them. Places are not just anonymous geographic locations, but are full of stories and meaning. Gary Snyder uses the term 'reinhabitation' to describe the need to dwell in a place in a balanced way, with respect for the stories of the other inhabitants, and author Wallace Stegner writes, 'no place is a place until things that have happened in it are remembered in history, ballads, yarns, legends or monuments'. An important part of our personal identity is created through interactions with specific places and the attachments we then develop. Take away the green and common space, and these opportunities diminish.[12]

What do we know about these attachments? Laura Fredrickson and Dorothy Anderson note that:

> *past research on place and place attachment has typically focused in a one-way direction, that of individual to place, often overlooking the relationship of place to individual, that is, the affective appeal that place impresses upon the individual.*

Thus we are partly shaped by the environment and by our attachments developed during specific experiences and interactions. The personal benefits include psychological well-being, self-image and self-esteem, and the social ones include family stability, community pride and cultural identity. So, is contact with nature and place a fundamental part of the way we establish self-identity? Identity is a relationship in which something is shared, and linkage with nature and communities partially helps to do this. Such a sense of identity emerges out of regular contacts, whereby self is formed in relation to the other. If we break the connections, the sense of identity is broken, so increasing the likelihood of ill-health. To a certain extent, then, who and what we are is constructed through relationships with people and with nature. Thus if we lack these relationships and connections, it would mean that we must also lose a sense of personal identity and self-esteem.[13]

Abraham Maslow famously showed in 1950 how context directly shapes how we see the world and act in it. He designed three rooms with different aesthetics, which he called beautiful, average and ugly, and then put volunteers in each of the rooms to study the same set of photographs of people's faces, and to judge whether they showed energy and well-being. They were supervised by three examiners, two of whom did not know the real reason for the experiment. In the beautiful room, people saw more energy and well-being in the faces; in the ugly room, the same faces were seen to be tired and sick. The examiners themselves also rushed the experiments when in the ugly room, wanting to get them over with as soon as possible.[14]

An important distinction to make here is between space and place. Space is anonymous and lacks stories, whereas place has meaning and memories. Yi-Fu Tuan writes, 'place is security, space is freedom: we are attracted to one and long for the other'. Spaces become places because we know that events of significance happened there.

Tuan tells of the famous visit by physicists Niels Bohr and Werner Heisenberg to Kronberg castle in Denmark, just any old fort until we imagine Hamlet's dark brooding presence: 'Isn't it strange how this castle changes as soon as we imagine that Hamlet lived here?' says Bohr. All places are similarly full of ghosts that help to give meaning to our daily lives. They help shape our identities and allow us to develop preferences for one thing over another. Stories and memories convert anonymous things and space from commodity to culture. Michael Bell asks if you would give up your wedding ring for another that is identical. Most people would not, even with a hundred dollars thrown in, as the original carries memories with it (almost no one would know by looking at it). A problem we face today is that as interactions with nature and green places diminish, so our knowledge of places also declines, thus tending to turn them into anonymous commodities with only abstract economic value.[15]

But perhaps attachments to nature are actually deeper and not so easy to destroy. Most of us still turn to flowers to send at times of celebration and death. More than ten million hectares of lawns are regularly cared for by American families, presumably because this constant transformation creates places of value for them, as well as the green itself making them feel well. There is, in addition, a constant tension between our desire for variety and diverse experiences and the need for places we know well. We want some mystery, but also some comfort. Places, therefore, are created by us. They are where time happens, where things of significance occurred, and will occur in the future. Since the Neanderthals, all hominids have marked their mortality with graves for their dead. 'The surest way to takes possession of a place and secure it as one's own is bury one's dead in it,' states Robert Harrison. If we had no affective sentiment for ghosts and memories, we would not waste valuable land by filling it with the deceased and then prevent any change over centuries. There is little worse in many cultures than to dig up a graveyard or to deface graves. But again, things are changing in our crowded modernized worlds. Most of us now do not know where we will be buried. Harrison says, 'this is astounding. Uncertainty as to one's post-humous abode would have been unthinkable to the vast majority of people a few generations ago.' Will this increasing anonymity about place lead to a further crisis of identity? Unless we connect with nature, we will not develop knowledge and deep understanding, and nor will things happen. We may never even recognize that identity and mental well-being are slipping away.[16]

Though it is clear that contact with the natural world can benefit mental and physical health, there is also a dark side to nature and people. Not all green places are always seen as good; not all social interactions leave good memories. In some cultures, the forests are seen as friendly and welcoming. In Romania, people say 'the forest is our brother', as for many centuries it was a place to hide from marauding armies. In mediaeval Britain, however, the forests were seen by many as dreadful, gloomy, unpeopled, beast-haunted and dangerous. Forests clearly did provide some shelter for thieves and highwaymen, but they were also home for many people dispossessed from their common lands (and so not so dreadful for them). In Thomas Hardy's *Return of the Native*, Edgon Heath was portrayed as a dark and destructive place for local people. Mountains were seen for centuries as places harbouring wild beasts and mythical mountain men, but then by the 19th century had become transformed into places to escape to for privacy and contemplation of nature. Robert Macfarlane's lyrical and perceptive *Mountains of the Mind* shows how these real external landscapes change at the same time as our imaginations of them. Mountains, once feared, are now places where people go to be frightened and awed. More than 1000 people have died on Mont Blanc, 500 on the Matterhorn and 170 on Everest. As Macfarlane puts it, mountaineering is unique as 'it demands of some of its participants that they die'. Nonetheless, many now like to go to mountains when once they were feared.

For most of our history, we have also led lives under the constant threat of attack by predators. We were potential prey and had to live with this knowledge. But today, nature is no longer a daily threat for most people in industrialized settings. In Africa, hippos trample many people to death each year, and agitated chimpanzees have attacked and taken children. In India, tigers and leopards have long been a source of constant worry for families resident in or near national parks. In North America, mountain lions and bears occasionally attack joggers and walkers, and wherever there are wolves, people have been fearful (even though their record of attacks is minimal). A greater danger is invisible, and arises from pathogenic microorganisms that transfer to humans, such as Ebola virus and bird flu, and from parasites, such as malaria and bilharzia. Contemporary environmental risks include toxic waste dumps, slag heaps and landfill sites. Yet the greatest top predator today is none of these. It is other people and the many malign urbanized environments we have constructed in the pursuit of progress.

Worse still is our behaviour to one another in the name of this progress. It seems there always were conflicts and struggles, or at least for as long as post ice-age memory can recall. Mostly, these have been relatively localized, lacking the global reach that modern technology brings. Are we really so much more civilized today that we can record so many effortless genocides? Compared with what we would now deem clearly backward mediaeval villagers, who drowned or burned people as witches, have we got the higher moral ground when so many millions of Rwandans, Bosnians, Sudanese, Congolese and Cambodians are permitted to be killed in the last two to three decades of the 20th century alone? What of the systematic destruction of the many pygmy peoples of the forests of central Africa? One of the last remaining regions of intact tropical rainforests in the world, this is a vast area the size of Europe inhabited by small numbers of people who have a light touch on the landscape. For thousands of years, possibly much more, these people have lived in a way that causes no harm to others, and no particular harm to the forests. The pygmy groups are small in number, on a stage of apparently little geopolitical importance, so the international community does not intervene as their habitats are destroyed. It has happened before, and, pessimistically, will probably happen again.

This is how we turn a good place into a bad place – through indifference driven by a deeper belief that this is, ultimately, some kind of cost we have to pay for progress. It is not. It is just another way to allow people to suffer further. Again, our problem is one of forgetfulness. Our lives and cultures are built on memories that link histories together. As survivors, we rewrite those histories with selective memory. But these stories do bind us together, and link us to places, making things no longer anonymous and meaningless. How is it, though, that we are so good at storytelling, yet so bad at remembering the bad bits? Those who do suffer do not forget, of course. But the perpetrators seem easily to forget and then move on.

One of the most notorious episodes in recent human history was the extermination of several million Cambodians by their own leaders in the late 1970s. The Khmer Rouge believed in their own form of progress, an agrarian and anti-intellectual politics that led them to conclude that they should torture and kill their political opponents during a four year reign of terror. The film, *The Killing Fields*, dramatized the discovery of their grisly and genocidal regime. Lest we forget – there were eleven million Cambodians when they came to power, and only eight million by the end. I once spent an afternoon at the former school, Tuol Sleng, which had been used as a killing camp in Phnom Penh. It remains as it was in 1979. It is an utterly chilling place. Here the Khmer Rouge tortured and killed thousands of people. Some 20,000 entered Tuol Sleng; six were known to have survived. The captors took pictures of everyone they killed, and these photographs of men, women and children line room after room. The torture chambers are enough to make you feel physically sick. Why did they do this, you wonder? After they were ousted by the Vietnamese, the Khmer Rouge continued the war in remote regions until the formal ceasefire in 1998. These dense remote forests, though, still contain pockets of resistance and many mines, and so remain no-go zones for visitors. Through all these actions, places that could have been good remain painfully haunted.

Resettlement is clearly a lesser evil, but it too disrupts people's lives by disconnecting them forever from home places and families. The World Bank's expert on resettlement, Michael Cernea, estimates that ten million people were forcibly resettled in each of the last twenty years of the 20th century.[17] These 200 million people, one in thirty of the world's population, were moved for new industries, irrigation projects, highways, power plants and dams, hospitals, schools, and protected areas. The world's biggest resettlers are the Chinese government, where agencies in the latter half of the 20th century moved people both to establish new industrial cities, such as Baotaou in Inner Mongolia and Taiguan in Shanxi, and developed a multitude of water projects that have together displaced some 30 million people since 1980. The massive Three Gorges project continues the theme, with its 182 metre megadam, and two cities, ten county towns, 116 markets, 1600 factories and 800km of roads now submerged under the new reservoir, and more than one million people having been removed. Will they have better lives? That is always the promise from authorities, but rarely the outcome. Lin Zhibin estimates that 2.6 million people were also voluntarily resettled in China in the 1980s and 1990s. There is nothing necessarily wrong with moving voluntarily to somewhere new – after all, the average American is said to move 14 times in a lifetime.[18] But what does all this moving do to people's identity and connection to places? Do they feel less or more committed to caring for where they currently live? Do they miss their old place and its drowned memories? How long will it take to call the new one home?

Resettlement can feel like a form of bereavement for people. Bereavements rob us of attachments to people and place, leaving us with a sense of grief. Grieving is often evoked when our adaptive abilities are threatened, and we no longer know what to do. The same seems to happen with places too. During slum clearances, developers and planners are often surprised to find people grieving for their lost homes, even though they have improved material benefits in their new locations. Of course, we know about the grief that comes with death, yet we are rarely prepared. The same goes for communities who are resettled from their homes, histories and memories, and put somewhere else that someone believes is an improvement. People may overcome their sense of grief in new places, but they will need strong attachments to other people and to re-establish links to local nature if they are to do so. The problem for whole resettled communities is that everyone is undergoing the same experience, and so there is no one in a position to help overcome the grief.

Control and choice are critical. As David Halpern writes:

the negative impact of environmental stresses is greatly reduced when people feel they have control over them. Similarly, the impact and quality of people's relationships with their neighbours is critically mediated by the extent to which they are able to regulate their interactions with them.

Acute forms of deprivation arising from a lack of control have been noted after some environmental disasters. Terrence Lee has coined the term 'chronic environmental stress disorder' to describe the effect of stress arising from environmental harm, either directly experienced or arising over the long term from simply knowing that a problem may be having an effect. Such stress is manifested through headaches, demoralization, upset, perceived threats, declining quality of life and distrust of authorities. It is known that stress causes psychological effects, especially on both the autonomous nervous system and the endocrinological system. Thus stress has a negative feedback on the well-being of individuals. Stress can be alleviated if the stressor is removed, if people are provided with a sense of control, and if the ways in which they perceive the source of the stress can be changed.[19]

But if places can be bad, then they can also be made better. If formerly degraded places are restored, they can be good for people as well as for the environment. Many small-scale urban ecological restoration projects have been successful in recent years. In Detroit, formerly known as a city of trees, a quarter of the population deserted the city in the last quarter of the 20th century, leaving behind 65,000 vacant housing lots. These soon became overgrown and used for illegal dumping and other criminal activity. The more unsafe they became, the less likely it was that nearby people wanted to stay. Now, though, people are replanting trees and clearing away the tall weeds, with the result that both place and people are transformed. Said one resident, 'when you feel good about where you are, you do more'. Robert Sommer says of these urban tree planting projects, 'we don't know if we're organizing communities to plant trees, or planting trees to organize communities'. Trees in urban streets also moderate temperatures and the heat island effect, increase property prices and create stress-reducing environments. But traffic engineers will have none of it. They still call trees FHOs – fixed hazardous objects. In France, many mature roadside trees have been cut down in recent years because of the number of fatal traffic accidents, as if it were the trees at fault rather than fallible drivers.[20]

In Michigan and Wisconsin, some 70,000 volunteers spend a million hours on service to city parks and gardens each year. These volunteers have helped to transform environments, but they, in turn, have been personally transformed. They gain self-respect as they feel valued, and also develop strong personal attachments to their sites. One said, 'it has made me more aware, and both happier and sadder for my new knowledge of the environment and its condition'. Another said, 'it was really good exercise and a great stress reliever'. Barbara Lynch's study of Latino gardens and *casitas* found that gardens create a territory for people, helping to shape them and their identity. The logic of gardening is mainly nostalgic and therapeutic rather than economic:

> *these seemingly single rustic dwellings and adjacent gardens are meant to be places for leisure – safe places in which neighbours can celebrate, relax, share a meal, watch their children play, escape the heat of their apartments, drink a few beers and connect to a carefully chosen set of companion plant and animal species.*[21]

There is also a long experience of the use of adventure therapy for many groups of people, particularly in Australia, South Africa and the US. In the US, there are some 500 wilderness therapy programmes, taking 12,000 people out each year, including bereaved children, mental health patients, children with renal disease, emotionally disturbed adolescents, addiction recoverers, children with learning difficulties and urban adults. These programmes mostly involve deep immersion in natural and wild areas far from urban development, with participants camping and taking part in a range of physical activities, such as rock climbing, swimming, canoeing and hiking.[22]

It is evident that the lives of many of the individuals in these wilderness adventure and eco-therapy programmes are significantly changed.[23] Engaging in these challenges often leads to a transformation in at least one feature of their lives. Nature provides a number of things: experience of continuity and stability (the world still turns and the birds still sing, despite our very human problems); opportunities to develop new social relationships; a rejuvenation effect in a non-institutionalized environment; improvement in self-worth; the opportunity for close observation of non-judgemental nature; and finally the opportunity to take risks. The longer the time that people spend, or the more often they return, the more fond they grow of those places. An important unanswered question, though, is to what extent do the benefits of such wilderness experiences continue off site? Do they provoke long-term changes in thinking, which could lead to deep social and political transforma-tions? Is there an immunization effect, or even a pre-immunization effect on people, who come to know what the benefits of a trip are and then to think about trips in advance? It may well be that the future of the planet depends partly on our ability to engage with nature in new and better ways.

In our research, we have found that small ecological restoration projects in urban parks, by canals and along the coast carried out by the Environment Agency in south London, Welshpool and Durham have not only made the places more green, but have changed people's behaviour towards them. Local people visit more often, and stay a third longer each time, thus deriving both physical and mental health benefits. A quarter of people only started visiting after the improvements, and all said that they care for the wildlife and the scenery. In the urban settings, one visitor said, 'it feels you are somewhere else other than inner London'. Another said, 'it is more tranquil, much more peaceful'. Another said, 'it is a transformation. It has the poten-tial to become a special place'. Those at the canal expressed similar sentiments: 'I enjoy the walking', 'it is relaxing and peaceful with lots of nature' and 'it is nice to be close to nature'.

Large restoration projects are having significant effects on people too. One of the largest in the UK is the designation of the new National Forest on 500 square kilometres of the Midlands containing a population of some 200,000 people. Huge numbers of trees are being planted, and of course it will take many years before former fields become mature forest. But, as one local resident said, 'it was amazing how quickly the wildlife moved in after the tree planting [...] skylarks, buzzards, deer'. Many visitors also seem to appreciate the value of social interactions in the forest, and it is possible that some social networks are being reconfigured. A visitor commented, 'we've been soaking up the atmosphere [...] it's been such a great day, and we'll have lots of special memories', and a local farmer said, 'I love the wildlife that's coming onto the farm [...] and it's great that other people can come and have a walk about. We're going to farm people too.' In this radical alteration of the landscape, property prices are rising, and local businesses are beginning to use the forest as part of their branding. Much can change on the back of such ecological restoration, and this is without the ideas for large rewilding that could mean reintro-duction of iconic predators to the landscape.[24]

Green care is defined as the utilization of farms as a base for promoting mental and physical health. On such farms, animals, plants, gardens, fields and woodlands are used to provide recreational and/or work-related activities for psychiatric patients, people with learning disabilities, people with a history of drug abuse, disaf-fected youth, elderly people and social service clients.[25] There are now several hundred green care farms in Norway, the Netherlands, Italy, Germany, Austria, Belgium and Slovenia. Such green care farms are formally tied to local social services and hospitals and provide a new component of care in the community. Farmers receive payments for taking patients, receive free labour and are still able to sell the food they produce. There is great potential for the use of farms, as well as forests, canals and nature reserves, to provide programmes of green care, which could bring greater connections between people and the land (both farmed and non-farmed) and thus greater understanding of the environment. Green care involving green exercise could link policy priorities for farming, conservation, countryside and health agencies, and help create healthy places for us all.

But these are still rather functional arguments for green places being made into healthy places. The key question is how to make these favourite places too. Something has to happen to create a memory for us, so that we can feel some affective sentiment for somewhere and then remember it. These memories help to make us what we are, and they give individual value to landscapes, places and things. These memories, and the ethic of care that comes with them, come from direct personal experiences. Perhaps we should all be making greater efforts to escape the progress treadmill and find just a few moments to let the land change us, and a few more to contemplate what we can do to make the land more healthy for us all. As the poet Gary Snyder reminds us, 'nature is not a place to visit, it is home'.[26]

Part 2

Animals and Us

Where the Wild Things Were

In Maurice Sendak's remarkably popular children's book *Where the Wild Things Are*, written more than forty years ago, the hero Max, grounded in his bedroom for a series of misdemeanours, watches in his wolf suit as the bare walls and ceiling sprout leaves and turn to a jungle overlooked by a silvery moon. He sails across an ocean, in and out of weeks and over a year, to a land where the wild things are. They gnash their terrible teeth and show their terrible claws, but he says, 'be still' and tames them with a stare. They become frightened and, perceptively, call him the most wild thing of all. After being crowned king of all wild things, the fun begins. But as time passes, he becomes homesick. Leaving the wild things, who gnash their terrible teeth in dismay, he sails back home to his bedroom and finds his hot supper waiting for him.

Though we have lived with wild things for a long time, many are now extinct or on the edge of extinction. *Homo erectus* walked out of Africa one million years ago and was later followed by *Homo sapiens* (80,000–90,000 years ago), who followed the coastline to reach Australia 10,000 years later. Another band swung into Europe at about 50,000 before present (BP), during the time of the last great ice age. At this time, ice covered half of the Earth's surface and the sea level was 100 metres lower than today. Within 10,000 years of their arrival in Europe, *Homo sapiens* had completely replaced the Neanderthals, formerly dominant for 300,000 years in Europe, and were about to leave their signs of advanced culture in the form of cave paintings, intricate carvings, tools, bird bone flutes, beads and ceremonial burials in what is now central France. As the glaciers retreated further, so the modern hominids continued to press northwards, establishing their first permanent settlements in Britain by about 12,000 BP.[1]

At this time, all our ancestors were still hunter-gatherers. They were not, as popular history would have it, short and rather dim cave men and women, but long-legged, tall, broad-shouldered, with long, narrow heads. They shared Europe with the auroch, the giant Irish elk and the woolly mammoth, though the scimitar-toothed cat, wrongly known as the sabre-toothed tiger, had long since become extinct, along with the woolly rhinoceros, hyena and hippopotamus (between 40,000 and 32,000 BP). The first signs of domesticated animals date to about 7000 BP, and the first farming to 6000 BP, some 4000 years before the Romans ventured across Europe to establish their empire.

After the last ice age, domesticated food culture spread rapidly throughout the world. The first crop cultivations occurred in the Fertile Crescent, where wild wheat and barley seeds were collected and then deliberately planted, and goats and sheep domesticated. Agriculture then independently appeared in several locations in the following millennia: in Mesoamerica by 9000 BP, with maize, beans and squash; in China and Southeast Asia by 8000 BP, with rice, millet, water buffalo, pigs and cattle; in South America by 7000 BP, with potato and llamas; and in sub-Saharan Africa by 4000 BP, with sorghum and millet. Domestication of animals almost certainly began with the wolf's evolution to dogs, which dates to at least 14,000–15,000 BP in Iran, and possibly tens of thousands of years earlier.[2]

These domestications marked the beginnings of a new type of utilitarian relationship with animals that extends to today. We can assume from today's hunter-gatherers that the relationship for thousands of generations had been an intimate one based on respect. Humans are unlikely to have seen themselves as somehow in a different category to animals. Domestication, though, began to change this, with some animals being raised for their meat, milk, hides and power, and others kept simply as companions or pets. To raise animals for these specific purposes requires a degree of control and management, with our choices as humans fundamentally affecting the lives of many animals.

As agriculture and human settlements expanded, and forests and other wild lands converted, so some species gradually disappeared. In Britain, the brown bear survived certainly until AD 750, and possibly to the time of the Domesday Book. The last beavers were recorded in the 1300s, wild boar were common to the late middle ages, but then disappeared until their recent re-establishment, and the last wolf probably died in the 1600s. Today, we are left with 44 species of land-breeding mammals, the most common of which are voles, shrews, rabbits, rats, mice and moles. In North America, the losses of species have been much more dramatic. Since the arrivals at Plymouth on the east coast in the 17th century, some 500 species of animals, fish and plants have disappeared, at a rate of between one and two species per year.[3]

Now domestic animals across the world have increased dramatically in numbers, and the wild ones have diminished. Worldwide, there are more than four billion cattle, pigs, sheep and goats, together with 16 billion chickens, alive at any given time.[4] This now makes the chicken the most successful animal species worldwide, though the cramped lives of many broilers might not be seen by all as a great success. At the same time as domestic animals have increased in numbers, so those in the wild have shrunk back, forced into ever smaller habitats, pockets of wildness in landscapes largely now manipulated for the production of food for our six and a half billion people. Worldwide, one in four mammal species is at risk of extinction, as is one in eight birds. We do regret these losses, yet collectively also seem to do very little about it.

The problem is that we moderns have become increasingly disconnected from the real lives of most animals (except pets, of course), thus strengthening the notion that animals are in a separate category, the alien other. 'Do you really believe you are an animal?' asks Gary Snyder.[5] In truth, we like to believe we are better than animals. Wild animals live out there, somewhere far away. At the same time, domestic livestock have become increasingly elusive to many people in industrialized countries, most of whom do still eat meat. Most of us no longer keep animals, say a pig or chickens in the backyard, and so we do not need to engage in the business of slaughter, of turning an animal into meat. As a result, this distasteful business can be neatly forgotten, or at least parked in a distant corner of our consciousness. In a similar way, we do not find the need to confront inhumane factory conditions under which many animals are now reared, tethered as they are in hog-barns, or packed into broiler sheds with beaks clipped, or standing shoulder to shoulder in muddy feedlots. The wild ancestors of all three of these animals – pig, chicken and cattle – are all forest-dwellers, yet their modern lives now resemble the urban ghettos of many humans.

Defining differences between humans and animals allows us to domesticate, hunt, eat and experiment on animals, as well as keep them as pets. Other peoples are often seen in the same way, with certain groups portrayed as monkeys, for example. In the not so distant past, to be beast-like was to be non-human. Keith Thomas summarizes the range of relationships: animals and birds can be eaten, hunted and used as medicine, observed for signals about the weather, seen as evil or good, eaten for special occasions, or not eaten at all, given magical properties, invented where they did not exist, and kept as companions and pets. Animals, in short, do lots of different things in their relations with humans.[6] In a famous paper, Harold Herzog reflected on the number of different types of mouse. There are good laboratory mice, which are the subject of research and would not survive in the wild. There are bad mice, which are the former good ones that have escaped, and whose status quickly changes to prey that must be caught. There are feeders, raised as food for reptiles and other carnivores. There are vermin, too, that eat the food in kitchens and leave their droppings, and which are again poisoned and killed in traps. Finally, there are wild mice, some of which are very rare and have protected status, with large amounts of money spent for their conservation. One type, the harvest mouse, remains a symbol of the success of the corn harvest.[5]

Similar kinds of differentiation occur in other animals. Horses, for example, can be raised for work in agriculture, forestry, mines and armies and might be eaten at the end of their lives. Others are bred for racing or are kept for a weekend ride; these are certainly not eaten. Others, still, are imbued with a romantic image as they roam the wild – the mustangs on the range – or carved into hillsides as enduring landscape icons. Pigeons, too, have many personalities, including the brave wartime homing birds, the feral city pigeon, the wild dove of the coasts, the semi-domesticated dove of dovecotes, the racing pigeon, and the carriers of blood samples from city hospital rooftop to rooftop.

Racing pigeons are quite remarkable and are kept by tens of thousands of fanciers today. Some have names as they are so famous. Red Daniel, raised by Keith and Linda Turner, won 20 of 23 races and was stolen from their loft with a number of other birds. He arrived back three months later, having somehow escaped captivity and probably flown some 500km to get home. He is now 17 years old, still a sleek and graceful bird with rufous breast, more purple than red. In races, the birds will fly for hours at an average of 50–60 miles per hour, and we still do not know how they navigate so accurately. Keith has been keeping birds for 42 years and worries that young people are no longer entering pigeon racing. He has a kind of pigeon-literacy – the management and skill to bring the best out of a breeding programme and to spot winning behaviour. But, of course, pigeons have their predators, and some are lost. Once, a hooded falcon came into the garden by the lofts, and Keith caught it, and was ready to dispatch it when its owner popped his head over the fence, saying he'd been trying to catch his bird for hours, and begged for its release. Birdman to birdman, says Keith, he handed it over with agreement that the falcon club would relocate. Pigeon keeping gives great pleasure, meaning and identity to many, but is probably seen as a quirky activity by most people, something that is not really part of today's modern world.

A key category today is the rare animal or bird, and these have attained a special status because they are rare. We spend more on trying to protect them and save them, but only when they are designated as rare. In *Wild Echoes*, Charles Bergman points to a paradox: 'I have begun to think that we actually want creatures endangered, paradoxical as that sounds.' Rare animals and birds have prestige and are thus political. There is always great controversy over their numbers too. Some interests will want to say they are few, in order to provoke action; other interests will want to say they are many, in order to maintain the status quo. Why the controversy? Because as numbers get smaller, so the likelihood of action increases – until a species enters a shadowland, as Bergman calls it, where we think they might exist, but can no longer find them. They might be extinct, but might not be. When it is too late, then we stop worrying (and spending).[7]

Charles Bergman also recounts the sad tale of the dusky seaside sparrow, the last one of which ironically died in Disney World in Florida. It was a creature that never seemed to matter. Who, after all, has heard of it, or since mourned its demise? Did it ever really exist? At the end, in the late 1980s, there were only two males left in a cage. The sparrow's home was the Spartina marshes of the Florida coast, but as these were squeezed out of existence by a new road between Orlando and Cape Canaveral, so the dusky sparrow stopped being seen. Five were caught in a desperate attempt at captive breeding, but all were males. You can drive the Beehive Expressway to see the space programme, all geared at grand gestures to escape the gravity well that keeps us on Earth. But you would never know that the dusky sparrow was lost, extinct since 1989. So much, though, depends on classification decisions. Until 1973, the dusky was seen as a separate species, but then was reclassified as a subspecies. It then no longer qualified for federal financial support, and its fate was sealed. Who would want to campaign for a subspecies?

The dusky sparrow never received iconic status, unlike the thylacine, or Tasmanian Tiger, another poor creature that no one wanted (or at least, none of the newcomers to Tasmania) until it was too late. The thylacine was the world's largest marsupial carnivore, some two metres in length and 60cm at the shoulder. Not long after sheep were introduced in 1803 to what was then called Van Diemen's Land, bounties were declared for predators, and the thylacine was rigorously hunted. By 1933, the last one was captured. It died in 1936, leaving as a legacy only one brief piece of grainy film, showing it pacing an enclosure. Many official searches have since found no trace (though there were reports of footprints in the 1950s), and it was officially declared extinct in 1986. The thylacine lived throughout Australia and New Guinea for some two million years; it was wiped out in a hundred.

Will our impacts on animals always be so dramatic? Perhaps not, as there have been some recent changes in attitudes. I rather doubt that anyone would now countenance the slaughter of the buffalo that occurred on the Great Plains in the 19th century, when hunters killed some 75 million animals in the thirty years after 1850. In some parts of the world, wild animals are recovering, as a result of positive management and human intentionality. These are welcome efforts, though, as we shall see, not without controversy, particularly where recovering animals, such as wolves and tigers, can consume people's livestock and even people themselves. In this rather packed world, with its disrupted ecosystems, it is clear that some kind of management of many animals is required for them to coexist with humans. But this word management can mean several things: from managing environments to make them more habitable for the animals in question to active removal of other animals that may be keeping their numbers down, or even active culling of the animals themselves (particularly if there are no predators left to do it).

One culling controversy occurs in Australia. Each year, millions of kangaroos are killed to limit their effects on forests, grasslands and crops. Mostly, the public seems content that this has to occur to maintain some kind of ecological balance. But when the koala bears of Kangaroo Island off South Australia, the 30,000 of which are now eating every eucalypt present, were targeted for culling to protect the island's unique habitat, a sentimental backlash was provoked. The authorities had tried sterilization (ineffective) and relocation (too stressful for the koalas), but had to conclude that removal of 20,000 koalas was the only option. Why should we moderns care about koalas and not kangaroos? Is it because they are apparently cuddly and resemble children's teddy bears, which are false constructions of bears anyway? Why should a rather unsocial tree-dweller deserve more attention and concern than the equally destructive kangaroo? In the severe drought of 2004, kangaroos entered many Australian towns and cities in search of food, which brought them into close contact with many people, bringing in its wake even more controversy about feeding, management and culling.

Another good example of how our relationships with animals change over time is that of the coypu, also known as the nutria. These were first imported into the UK in 1929 for their fur. Some escaped captivity, and soon came to be serious pests of waterways and farmland, particularly in Norfolk, where they could live in the network of rivers and shallow lakes that make up the Broads. By the 1960s, the wild population had reached 200,000, and an extermination campaign was launched by government. It then took nearly three decades before they were entirely eliminated, the last individual being caught in 1987. Meanwhile, the coypu had entered popular culture of the region, and there were many who were saddened by its final demise, as this was seen as a loss to regional distinctiveness and identity.

A major controversy has emerged in recent years in the Western Isles of Scotland regarding hedgehogs and their predation of wild birds' eggs.[8] Hedgehogs were first released by a gardener on South Uist in 1974 and later spread to Benbecula and the southern tip of North Uist, with a population of some 7000 giving birth to 10,000 young per year. Typical densities are 15–50 per square kilometre. These hedgehogs are lucky, as there are no natural predators on the islands (such as badgers and foxes), and only a few cars on the roads. However, these islands also support some of the most important populations of ground-nesting birds in Europe, such as lapwing, dunlin, ringed plover and redshank. A study in 1983, a couple of years after hedgehogs were first found in the wild of the Uists, counted 17,000 of these nesting waders. Twenty years later, the numbers of breeding snipe, dunlin and ringed plover had fallen by 60 per cent and redshank and lapwing by 40 per cent. On North Uist, where there are no hedgehogs, numbers also declined, but only by a small amount. Oystercatchers were unaffected, as their eggs are too large for hedgehogs to eat. The

finger was therefore pointed at egg predation by hedgehogs in early 2003, and authorities were faced with a challenge – how to reduce hedgehog numbers humanely?

They could catch and hold in captivity, catch and release on the mainland, or
catch and kill. They concluded that the last option was best for hedgehogs, as mortality can be very high after catch, translocation and release. Whether they show signs
of disturbed behaviour, as suggested by some as a further reason for culling, is
contested by others. However, hedgehog and other animal welfare organizations did
not accept that culling was best, and a national campaign was launched with spectacular effect. Hedgehogs, often represented as Mrs Tiggywinkles, were featured on
the national news, and many offers of homes made. A coalition of animal groups –
including the British Hedgehog Preservation Society and Advocates for Animals –
called Uist Hedgehog Rescue set up to counter the cull. Each spring volunteers have
come to the islands to try and find hedgehogs to rescue. At the same time UHR
have also put up a bounty of £20 for each hedgehog rescued by an islander. Money
for this has come from all over the UK, including many celebrities. *The Scotsman*
newspaper reported one islander earning £1000 in one month in 2004 from rescu-
ing 50 hedgehogs. In 2005 some 140 hedgehogs were caught and killed by the
authorities, though there is some dispute as to whether this rate of capture could
ever have an effect on the whole population (between 2003 and 2006, 756 hedgehogs were rescued and 658 culled). Some said hedgehogs were endangered, even
though there are 1.5 million across the whole of the Britain, others that their
numbers were indeed falling, but only in some places. It is another case where the
contradictions cannot be resolved. Either we are for the waders or we are for the
hedgehogs – but we cannot unequivocally be for both, unless we accept some losses
on both sides.[9] As the hedgehogs are recent alien introductions into small island
habitats that do not have predators to keep them in check, it would appear that their
removal is a sensible course of action. But it may be too late already. When it comes
to the raw fact that one thing eats another, then it is inevitable that contradictions
will persist.

Badgers are a public favourite too, yet on Kew Gardens' 120 hectares there are
no hedgehogs, as they are all eaten by badgers. In general, large predators suppress
the numbers of smaller ones, such as hyenas over wild dogs, lions over cheetah and
coyotes over foxes. As David Macdonald has noted, conservationists have to make
choices, and it is too easy for the politics of the environment to find victims and
villains. Such binary categories tend to be unhelpful. Practical wildlife organizations
have to make other tough decisions, such as shooting foxes to ensure they maintain
good relations with neighbouring farmers, shooting crows and mink to increase the
survivability of rare waders, and waxing goose eggs to control numbers.

As the numbers of some animals are increasing, owing to changes in rural and
coastal management, so invasions into urban areas are on the increase. In Britain,
the most noted, and now accepted, is the urban fox. These first began to be noticed
in London in the 1970s, and there are now some 30,000 urban foxes out of a UK
population of some 220,000–240,000 animals. At first they were secretive, creeping

along the networks of green corridors by railway lines, but now they seem to be content to live side-by-side with urban people, who do not want to cause them harm. But in Germany, urban racoons have become an urban menace. These were introduced in 1934 from the US for their fur and now number more than a million. They have no predators and are omnivorous, so can find many sources of waste food in cities. In Kassel, north of Frankfurt, there are estimated to be 100 racoons per hectare. It is no longer possible to contemplate their removal, and so the public are going to have to learn to live with them.

Something rather similar has occurred with wild boars in Berlin. About 8000 individuals now live within the city boundaries, though 2000 did have to be shot in 2002 to reduce the pressure on the city's 28,000 hectares of forests and parks. These animals are adaptive and opportunistic and seem to survive well in urban areas. Females can be seen with their families of piglets in some neighbourhoods, though as interactions with people increase, so attitudes may change. Some have been stranded in swimming pools, or found digging up football pitches, or have broken into houses or crashed into food shops. Adults are typically 100kg in weight, but large males can reach 1.5 metres in length and 300kg in weight and could certainly be conceived as a threat to some people's safety.

The wild boar has been absent from Britain for some 400 years, but following escape from farms, and possibly some deliberate releases, some 500 animals have now become established in at least four herds in forested parts of Kent and Sussex, Dorset, Herefordshire and Wales. But are they pest or welcome wildlife? Most public seem to think they are a good thing, though they can cause damage to crops, transmit disease to livestock, and could threaten people and their dogs. How might we feel if these herds grew to thousands in number? Boar are secretive, but we have become so used to a landscape devoid of large wild animals that they could be a great surprise to anyone encountering them.

In the UK, a strange new threat in urban areas has emerged in the form of what many of us would still call seagulls. There are now 130,000 breeding pairs of gulls in urban UK, and another 130,000 non-breeding birds. They are increasingly deserting their sea cliffs and invading new urban cliffs and rooftops, where there are no predators and where the throwaway society and remains of junk food provide a ready source of food. They are mostly lesser black-backed gulls and herring gulls, which in the UK appear to be separate species, but which show a circumpolar curiosity in that they grade into a single species around the polar regions and then regrade back to two apparently different species. The concern of some urban people, though, is over the increasing reports of gulls attacking people, an echo of life imitating the art of Hitchcock's film *The Birds*.

For most moderns, the idea that animals could actively be a direct threat seems to have long passed. We were predators and prey for several hundred generations, but now the feeling of being prey has largely departed. But not for everyone. There are now only about 5000 tigers in 162 populations across 13 countries of Asia, though some people are very gloomy and think there are far fewer. No one is quite sure as they are so elusive. A century ago, there were perhaps 100,000 across lands ranging from Siberia to Indonesia and India to China. Some species are now extremely rare, and large numbers are still being lost to poachers each year. A skeleton weighs 10–12kg, and 1kg of tiger bone can fetch $2000 on the black market for medicine, a skin $4500.

I once looked for what seemed an age into the eyes of a tiger in Cambodia. Rescued from wildlife traders, bent on selling it for medicine, it padded around the large teak forest enclosure and stopped and gazed. What does it know, you wonder? The keeper passes inside, and, rearing up on its hind legs, the tiger towers over him for a moment. One swipe would be enough to finish me, if I were foolish enough to try this. That much we know. But all the rest cannot be understood. It is, after all, a wild animal, and it would not reward us for saving its life. But the reason why it is endangered is because of its symbolism. A strong and powerful beast must also be strong medicine, and so they are caught and killed, until there are so few left that they need special attention and huge amounts of money to protect them.

But in some parts of Asia, tiger conservation has been something of a success. National parks have been set up to improve their numbers. In the long grasses and deep gullies of a number of Indian and Nepalese national parks, tigers are making some remarkable recoveries. This is a wonderful success for conservation. One example is in the 900km^2 Chitwin National Park in Nepal, another is the 400km^2 Kanha Park in Rajasthan, India. Yet how would you feel if you were to swap places with villagers living in the buffer zones around these parks? Since 1979, 19 people have been killed by tigers around Chitwin, a mix of walkers in the park, children taken from the verandas of their houses and herdsmen. Around Kanha, two women, three men and a young girl were taken by tigers between September 2003 and April 2004. In Greater Mumbai, around the Sanjay Gandhi national park, 14 people were killed by leopards between 1986 and 1996. Humans are not the natural prey of tigers or leopards, but they are attacking for two reasons – their habitats are being invaded, and they are trying to disperse as existing animals push them out. Female tiger territories are 20 square kilometres in size, a male's up to 50 square kilometres. When India's 28 tiger reserves were set up, 80 whole villages were moved, but another 1500 remain in the reserves. In all, some 100 people were killed or injured by tigers in the first five years of the 21st century, and it would appear that attacks are increasing. This is, of course, inevitable. Save the tigers and, as predators, some of them will kill livestock owned by humans and some attack their owners too, particularly if their habitats are restricted in size.[10]

For long periods in our history, the loss of a predator would surely have been the cause for celebration. When the scimitar-toothed cat was finally exterminated, there must have been many hominid communities who breathed easier at night. They were not, I suspect, concerned with maintaining biodiversity, nor the ethical problems of species extinctions. Today, there may be as many as 5000 tigers privately owned in the US. No one is quite clear why, but it seems to be partly because people can afford them, partly because laws are lax, and partly because some people want to own dangerous animals. Some, though, are kept for canned hunting in small enclosures, giving some people who call themselves hunters a thrill.

For most of us, chimpanzees are accepted as the closest relatives to humans and so deserve special protection in the natural environment. Uganda has the fourth largest number of chimps of any country (some 5000) but is also the location for an increasing number of attacks recorded on people. As deforestation is reducing both habitat and sources of food in the forest, so chimps seem to be more likely to attack people, mainly children. Some fifteen attacks have been recorded in recent years in western Uganda, half of which were fatal. In some cases, children have been snatched from inside their homes. Villagers recall very few such attacks from earlier decades, but now some live in fear that they could lose a child. But then some studies have shown that a quarter of chimps in Uganda are carrying injuries inflicted by human snares, which are intended for bush pigs or duiker but harm the chimps too. Is it any wonder that they should strike back?

We all know about sharks, and our fear of them has been exploited by popular modern culture. Yet this fear of sharks is out of all proportion to the number of people who are harmed by them each year. And those harmed are, ironically, generally not fearful. In the 2000s there were 60–80 unprovoked attacks recorded each year worldwide, more than a third of which were in Florida. Of these attacks, three to seven per year were fatal, and there is no evidence to suggest that these are increasing or decreasing. But also in Florida, attacks by alligators seem to be on the increase, with 2006 seeing three deaths in a single week, following five decades of an average of only one every three years. It seems likely that the humans are losing their fear of alligators, perhaps feeding them or encouraging them in other ways, and alligators are in turn losing their fear of humans. It is also true that housing with a water view has a higher price, and so more properties are being built close to alligator habitat. Predators are real and harmful, but many of us have now forgotten this. In *Monster of God*, David Quammen quotes one Australian crocodile expert, who says, 'some people would say, look, crocodiles, they're not that bad. But they *are* that bad.' Environmental philosopher Val Plumwood knows this to be true; she wrote a famous article called 'Being prey' after being attacked and rolled several times by a crocodile in 1985.[11]

Despite the modern disconnections and gradual reinvasions, there is an enduring fascination with the wild, and especially with imagined exotic creatures. We have believed for centuries that unicorns, griffons and dragons existed, and these beliefs have changed the way we think and act. Some myths persist – there can surely be no one in Britain that has not wondered about the Loch Ness monster. Despite organized searches, high technology monitoring and a sensible conclusion that dinosaur-like creatures simply could not have persisted when the ice ages covered Scotland, even in a lake so deep as this, the grainy pictures continue to feed the myth. In truth, we mostly like to believe it because it is a good story that deserves not to be disproved.

Very few people have ever seen a wild wolf, yet they remain remarkably strong in the imagination of many people. They were, of course, the ancestor of the domestic dog, some 14,000–40,000 years ago, but their ancient association continues to divide people. At one level, they are simply another predator that can take domestic livestock; at another, they are mythical beasts symbolic of so much more. Many people today love wolves, and many viscerally hate them. They are written into children's stories, such as *Little Red Riding Hood* and *The Three Little Pigs*, and are part of common idiom – we say, for example, we are as hungry as a wolf, or want to keep the wolf from the door, or even describe some attack as coming down like a wolf on the fold. For centuries in Europe, they were systematically hunted; in Britain, the last one was supposedly seen in 1743, but the final reliable records probably date to one hundred or more years earlier. The early settlers to North America took practices of wolf extermination with them, and worked at it for hundreds more years. In Montana, for example, 80,000 wolves were killed by bounty hunters in just a 35-year period over the end of the 19th and beginning of the 20th centuries. The wolf bounty was not repealed in Ontario until 1972. Many of these wolves were called outlaws, as if subject to the same laws as people. Many attained legendary status too, thus increasing their mystical power, such as Old Lefty of Colorado, Three Toes (who took 13 years to catch in South Dakota), Ghost Wolf of Montana, Old Aguila of Arizona (who eluded hunters for a decade) and White Lobo of Texas.

There are estimated to be some 15,000–18,000 wolves in Europe, mostly in Romania and Poland, 60,000 in Canada and 4800 in the lower states of the US, and another 7500–10,000 in Alaska. In France, their presence has become very controversial, as some wolves migrated from central Italy to arrive in a national park and two regional parks in 1990. Their presence has caused two opposing groups to coalesce – on one side farmers and land managers concerned about potential losses of livestock; on another, ecologists, town-dwellers and tourist organizations. Both have different government ministries in support, but it is the conservation groups who are most numerous and have the wider support. Who has the greater legitimacy to speak for the wolf? Do their small numbers (perhaps only 20 or so in France) really mean a high risk and cost for livestock owners; and even if they did, is there not a way to develop a fair compensatory mechanism?

In Norway, the wolf problem has also become a social problem, with the emergence of a strong anti-carnivore movement. The environmental movement finds itself portrayed as part of an evil external conglomerate that tramples over the views of local people, in a rather similar way to the portrayal of multi-national corporations. Two wolf packs have entered southeast Norway from Sweden and have provoked sheep owners to join big game hunters to oppose their presence. The fear of wolves has been used to suggest a danger to children and the elderly, even though none have been known to have caused any humans harm.

Part of the problem is the recurring controversy over numbers of particular wild animals. When does a particular species become endangered and so deserve special attention? When do its numbers, if it is a predator, increase to a level that constitutes a cost or risk to particular groups of people? If there are accurate and objective estimates of population numbers, then there still remains the question of what such numbers mean. Does a given number of wolves in North America mean that moose, deer or caribou numbers will fall into a predator pit? Or are they at a level that will permit stable coexistence? Will there be sufficient moose for the hunters too? In short, do we have more right to a wolf or a moose?

Karen Jones takes some of these ideas further in her book *Wolf Mountains*. She describes the reintroduction of wolves to four national parks of the US and Canada (Yellowstone, Glacier, Banff and Jasper), together with the many ecological and social tensions that have arisen. Here, too, the wolf is both a real and mythological beast. It is popularly depicted as a formidable foe of humans, yet it is a social animal with many of the same potential ties to humans that dogs now have. Through the centuries, wolves have been hunted and exterminated, even though, as Jones says, 'no attack on a human by a healthy wolf has ever been authenticated in North America'. The wolf is thus something that has been 'consistently imagined', as Barry Lopez has put it. In the history of human–wolf interactions in both Europe and North America, wolves were long economic enemies too, preying not only on wild deer but also cattle and sheep. Having eradicated wolves in all but the remote mountains of Europe, settlers to North America labelled the wolf as the shark of the plains. Yet these frontier myths have been replaced by another story of cultural resonance, with citizens now subscribing to a new environmental folklore in which the wolf is friendly, useful, charismatic and above all to be protected. Wolves were shot by national park authorities through the early 20th century as part of predator control, but then became the subject of vociferous and embattled efforts for their reintroduction at the end of the century.

Yellowstone National Park saw a long period of wolf extermination after the park was established in 1872. Reintroduction was then proposed a hundred years later, in 1980, and begun in 1994, and by the early 2000s, there were more than a hundred animals. As Karen Jones has put it, 'it took longer to discuss bringing the wolves back to Yellowstone than it did to extirpate them'. It also cost more – some $6.7 million to reintroduce them, but only $0.3 million in bounty payments to get rid of them. Some 160,000 public comments were collated during the 1980s, testament to the widespread interest in the wolf. One Montana senator stated that 'there'll be a dead child within a year'. But these new wolves have also attained a different status. They are wild, but they are also actively managed. They are shot if they kill sheep, they can be relocated to new places and their health is closely monitored. Can truly wild animals really be managed, though? Or are all our landscapes doomed to be managed in some way? Can we even know enough about wild animals to manage them? Barry Lopez observed this about native American views of the wolf:

> the animal is observed as part of the universe. Some things are known, other things are hidden. Some of the wolf is known, some is not. But it is not a thing to be anxious over.

In Wisconsin, wolf numbers have risen from 25 to 250 animals between 1980 and the early 2000s, with a resulting increase in attacks on livestock, pets and hunting dogs. But social groups in the state have very different views of the wolves. Most citizens seem to support carnivore conservation. Yet the costs fall on only a few people. As wolves have been reintroduced, or at least managed, by government agencies, for some rural people wolves have themselves become a symbol for unwelcome government interference. People who had interacted directly with wolves held the strongest views, either for, or against if they had lost domestic animals and pets. In Minnesota, there are 2000 wolves, yet of the 7000 farms in the northern part of the state, only 25 per year suffer livestock losses to wolves. The last wolf in Yellowstone was killed in 1943 by rancher Leo Cottemoir, who said 'it was kind of sad to think he was the only one that I'd ever seen, and I'd killed him'. Contrast this knowing and unknowing with Charles Bergman's encounters with a panther in the swamps of Florida. This is the state mammal of Florida, but only 20–30 are left and they are under such threat that they have to be captured and given medicinal and vitamin treatments by vets. Some are given radio collars to track their last few movements before urban sprawl and habitat destruction finally finishes them off. Now there are plans to move them to another state.[12]

A more realistic worry for many people is the loss of livestock to predators, and objections to reintroductions of bears, wolves and vultures to parts of Europe have centred on these concerns. In the Pyrenees, for example, griffon vultures have recovered from 20 pairs in 1970 to 500 in 2004 because of bans on hunting and the use of poisons. With their three-metre wingspans, many sheep farmers believe they take live prey (even though they have no talons and their beaks are unsuited to killing). Their concerns, though, are linked to the recent presence of wolves and the reintroduction of brown bears from the early 1990s. As agriculture changes, and becomes more wildlife-friendly, so it is likely that we will see more of these controversies.

Perhaps there is more than meets the eye to our relationships with animals and wild places. Perhaps, too, they influence more of us than we might think in this modern world. Might we, therefore, now think about moving towards a wilder Britain, where the wild things once were? In the short term, this will be unlikely, as we need our land to produce food. However, in the very long term, over a 50–100-year timescale, our views may change. After 2050, world population becomes greyer, and then falls in number. There will be fewer children, and a larger proportion of people will be over 65 years of age. The United Nations predicts that the world population might then fall to three to four billion. With the kinds of productive and increasingly environmentally sensitive agricultural systems that we already have, and may be expected to develop, then perhaps we will not need so much of our land for food production, and can devote some more to the wild.

Despite great economic progress, and apparently growing nature–human disconnections, wild animals and nature are still enormously significant to us. We celebrate the return of the sea eagles, Europe's largest birds of prey, to Scotland (up from zero to 32 pairs), the remarkable recovery of bitterns and hen harriers in lowland wetlands, and the thus far successful reintroduction of the great bustard to the remotest parts of Salisbury Plain.[13] For all these, though, nests still have to be kept secret to protect against illegal egg collectors. Ecological restoration is increasingly bringing back the missing animals and birds, but it remains to be seen whether we will still be able to find enough green nature nearby, or have to travel far, as Max did, over a year and in and out of weeks. Or will the sixth great species extinction episode come to diminish us too, as other species of great significance continue to disappear from the Earth?

6

Hunters and
the Hunted

A steady grey rain patters in the forest as we tread silently, eyes slowly ranging from one side to the other, listening intently to every sound. We hear the distant crump of hooves, the warning call of a circling buzzard, a muted roe bark. The sleek black gun dog walks at heel, and then freezes, pointing and sniffing at the air. We stop and wait patiently, and then walk on. The plaintive fawn call is used to cry to the does; the bucks are indifferent, but during the rut they will follow the does in. The pine, sweet chestnut and oak forest is carpeted with a dense under-storey of butcher's broom, foxgloves, brambles and nettles, and a still deer can hide here with ease. This sodden evening, they are mostly silent. The rain dampens everything. In the open glades, the deer can be seen from a distance, brown against the grey gloaming of a July dusk. But in the forest, there is alchemy at work. A deer appears as if from thin air, bounding, thumping and then freezing, and then melting away even though you think you have all the angles covered.

A buck stands tall between two forest-edge trees on the skyline, turns, looks directly at us, appearing to know we are too far away to shoot. The stubby muntjacs are abundant. They step into the rides and peer, and would be an easy shot, except we are not after them tonight. They too seem to know. We walk on, the rain now heavier, although the forest floor is still mostly dry. In the glades, though, the grass and bracken are wet and heavy. We stop at fairy rings of churned soil, where bucks have chased does in tight circles. But all is silent now. In the open, a buck and doe graze on a hillside, but beyond them is a house hidden in the trees, and an attempted shot would be inadvisable. The deer nearer housing seem to know they are less likely to be shot, and take to the open confidently. Deer learn quickly. Jim Rudderham tells a story about his time with a forest agency, where almost identical vehicles were used by both rangers and game control officers. A drive in the rangers' vehicle would elicit many observations of deer, but a drive in the slightly different sounding game vehicle would result in not one deer being seen. Author Richard Prior believes that deer have a sixth sense, that there is some kind of communication between stalker and deer. Deer seem to know if people are out simply for a walk, or whether they are stalking.

At one level, then, this is simply a walk in the wood. But the stalk itself changes our behaviour, increasing our intensity and concentration. You look for signs, a bent branch or hoof print, listen to the birds, walk in one direction, and then circle back in front of the wind. The deer are canny. They will not be beaten unless you are quieter, and cleverer, and lucky. This night, we do not take a single shot. This does not seem to matter. Yet deer numbers do need to be limited, otherwise they would cause too much damage to the forest and to nearby crops. But this is no failure. You have to be quiet, centred, still and observant. You have to be ready at any moment to take a shot, and yet know it may never happen. When you do line up a shot, the world stops for a moment. You breathe slowly, and then slower still. The pressure grows, and you understand only too well the concept of buck fever – the inability to squeeze the trigger when a deer is finally in the sights.

Today, in industrialized countries, the idea of hunting, whether for food, ecological management or pleasure, elicits great controversy. It is seen by some as the ultimate in cruelty to animals, and by others as a direct link to thousands of generations of human history. Some point to the contradictions inherent in those who happily consume domestic meat or animal products, yet at the same time object to the hunting of wild animals. Others raise questions about power and the gun, and how some groups appear to use hunting as a means to control the land. Some are more anti-hunter than anti-hunting. Another perspective focuses on the needs of indigenous hunting peoples and their moral relations with the animals they hunt for food. Yet another might draw attention to the visceral worries of families with small children living near national parks where predatory cat numbers have so increased that they threaten personal safety. Some say hunting is a tradition; others say so was slavery. It does not take long to see that the issue of hunting and being hunted raises fundamental questions about human relations with animals, and ultimately where we see our place on this small planet. It also suggests that the issues are so complex and contested, and so rooted in the particularities of place and culture, that it would be wrong to generalize about whether hunting is good or bad. Hunting is not one thing. It is many things, and judgements must account for the many social contexts and motivations, and the many ecosystems and types of animals.

Despite the ten-thousand-year advance of agriculture, it is only relatively recently that wild animals and plants have become unimportant in the lives of people in industrialized countries. In many developing countries, wild foods still make up a substantial proportion of people's diets, and even in industrialized countries, older generations can generally still recall a time when the wild harvest had a critical cultural as well as nutritional value, from autumn berries and nuts to rabbits, wildfowl and birds' eggs.[1] Today, modern food systems have encouraged a forgetfulness about the land, such that 'most of us are only dimly conscious of our own personal ecology', as author Richard Nelson puts it. But this is not true for the remaining indigenous groups across the world, whose relations with animals and the land are consistent reminders of hominid pasts common to all our ancestors. Their voices, rare today, demonstrate the widespread intimate connectivity that people can have with nature, and natural respect and understanding.[2]

In his perceptive commentary *Make Prayers to the Raven*, Richard Nelson describes the lives of the Koyukon, a northern Athabascan group resident above 62°N in central Alaska. The world to them is watchful, and all things in nature have a unique and special life. To the Koyukon, 'the surroundings are aware, sensate, personified. They feel. They can be offended. And they must, at every moment, be treated with utmost respect.' Thus there is a strong moral code that defines and continually shapes interactions with all of the environment. At the time that Nelson was writing, the Koyukon relied almost entirely on wild animals, fish and birds for their food, supplemented by some berries and flour. They made 'strong emotional and psychological investments in the food they eat'. Perhaps, therefore, we should not be surprised to find that, although large predators and herbivores have diminished and often disappeared across large parts of the North American continent, these animals are still abundant where people rely on them for food. Their conservation ethic is strong. One Koyukon hunter said:

> *I trapped there all my life. But if you go there now, it's still good ground – still lots of beaver, plenty of mink, otter, marten; good beaver country. I took care of it, see. You have to do that; don't take too much out of it right now or you'll get nothing later on.*[3]

For thousands of years, people in these northern areas have eaten moose, caribou, bear, wolverine, porcupine, otter, beaver and hundreds of types of fish and birds. All these species are still abundant. But the Koyukon, like other indigenous groups, are not accidental managers. They watch the world carefully, continually gathering evidence; they seek to alter the relative abundance of animals they favour through niche manipulation. They are aware of interdependencies and dynamics between predators and prey, and how change is a norm in an uncertain world. Yet there is still a kind of balance that results in sufficient animals for them. They say, we do not kill animals for fun, and 'each animal knows way more than you do'.[4]

They have evolved a range of practices that would today be called by wildlife biologists sustainable yield policies. They intentionally limit harvests, do not take waterfowl or geese during the mating season in spring, avoid young plants, animals and fish, leave new beaver lodges untrapped and whole regions fallow, and let deer alone at certain seasons. In short, they are aware of the consequences of their own actions, and their stories provide a context for the rules and norms that govern behaviour towards both animals and non-living things in the environment. Like other northern sub-Arctic groups, such as the Innu and the Cree, they believe it is the animals that control the hunt, and such a belief brings a respect and a desire to behave properly. This respect is again common to indigenous groups worldwide, they do not boast about a successful hunt, they do not make uncomplimentary comments about animals. One hunter said to Nelson:

> the country knows. If you do wrong things to it, the whole country knows. It feels what's happening to it. I guess everything is connected together somehow.[5]

One example of how these ethical positions emerged and were coded into stories is the Navajo's 'Deer Huntingway' and 'Deer Stalkingway' stories. These describe how the first people were taught by deer to hunt and act properly towards animals. The deer themselves supplied the first hunters with the knowledge that was necessary to hunt them, and also the moral codes for the interaction: no talking badly, always leave some deer, do not be greedy, remember to give thanks, the deer control the hunt, not the hunters, who will be punished if they break the rules. After a successful kill, the Navajo recite a prayer to the deer:

> To the home of the dawn you are starting to return
> With jet black hooves you are starting to return
> By means of zigzag lightening you are starting to return
> By the evening twilight your legs are yellow
> That way you are starting to return [...]
>
> Pleasantly may you have arrived home
> Pleasantly may you and I both continue to live.

It is clear, then, why indigenous people of the sub-Arctic and Arctic still hunt and fish, but why do people elsewhere still hunt, and why is there now such an opposition to hunting among large sections of society in industrialized countries? After all, the supermarkets are full of food, and modern economic development has taken away habitats and put many animal populations and some whole species at risk. Yet hunting in urbanized societies polarizes opinion in a way that would be utterly alien to indigenous groups. And this polarity is a recent phenomenon, rising at the same time as increasing numbers of people became concerned for the conservation and preservation of wildernesses, habitats and particular species.[6]

In the UK, the growth of government action against cruelty to animals occurred from the early part of the 19th century. Jeremy Bentham had earlier famously suggested in 1789 that the only moral question with respect to animals was 'can they suffer?' In the 1820s, the Society for the Prevention of Cruelty to Animals (SPCA – later the RSPCA) was established, together with the first Act of Parliament against cruelty to horses and cattle. This was followed by bull-baiting and cockpits being declared illegal in 1835, with more acts against cruelty to dogs in 1839 and 1854, and the banning of cockfighting in 1849. But it was never exactly clear whether animal sports were disliked because of cruelty alone, or because of their association with gambling and disorder, or with the pleasures of an audience drawn from particular social groups (the earliest animal sports to be banned were those with the greater following from the labouring classes). Foxes and their hunting never received the same attention, mainly because they were seen as agricultural pests; indeed they were even managed locally in some places in order to be hunted. The legislature finally caught up with fox-hunting in the early 21st century, when first Scotland and then the rest of Britain controversially banned hunting with dogs.

This is not the place to discuss the many different views on animal rights now held by moderns. Some take a utilitarian approach that seeks to maximize pleasure and minimize pain, in which animals are seen as equals. Others hold that it is moral to be vegetarian, and others still hold that animal rights are only for animals like us. But how do we define 'like us' and 'not like us'? Paradoxically, animal rights are not applied to all animals equally. Others, like Paul Tester, believe that animals are a blank paper on which can be written any message – that they are only socially constructed. Conveniently, many animal rights writers avoid having to comment on whether indigenous groups are right or wrong to hunt, kill and eat meat.[7]

In the US, there were 4.5 million hunters in 1955, 10.7 million in 1985, and 13 million in 2005. Hunters spent $21 billion in 2001, of which $500 million was on licences, which through the Pittman-Robertson provisions are used for wildlife restoration and hunter training. By contrast, there were 66 million wildlife watchers in the early 2000s, spending $38 billion per year. In the UK, there are no aggregate estimates of hunter numbers, but there are several hundred thousand members of shooting and wildfowling organizations. People who hunt and fish seem to have a number of reasons for doing so. They talk of the escape, freedom and renewal that comes from getting away from urban and stressed lives and out into the country. They appreciate the direct connection with nature, the opportunity to be intimate with the woods, to find the reconnection that remains central to the lives of indigenous hunters. They also recognize the value of companionship and the opportunity for storytelling. In an increasingly atomized modern world, this value of social capital creation, being with people you trust and who hold similar norms, is often forgotten. A further reason for hunting centres on the exercise of technology and control – the incursion of modern life and its technological sophistication into what some see as a traditional activity. Finally, there are biological reasons for hunting, whereby certain populations of animals may need to be reduced in number, usually to limit damage to habitats or to other wild or domestic animals.

People who oppose hunting do so for several important reasons too. The most common is welfare concerns for animals, which usually centres on the cruelty of the hunt and the mode of dispatch of an animal. Many are anti-hunting because they see it as a sport or leisure activity, and so are concerned about the moral position of killing for pleasure. Others still see hunting simply as a primitive activity, something that belongs to pre-moderns only, and so should be eliminated from today's so-called civilized society. Finally, many of those against hunting are also anti-hunter. They oppose or simply do not like the people who hunt, and perhaps see the opportunity to ban or limit hunting as a way to limit the activities of certain social groups.

Where do these wildly differing views leave us? Mostly, it appears, with a war of words, very little common ground, and policies that make everyone unhappy. The late writer and philosopher Edward Abbey said, 'hunting is one of the hardest things even to think about. Such a storm of conflicting emotions.'[8] Yet any close examination of particular contexts, animals and people suggests that to generalize is to adopt an absurd position. All hunting and anti-hunting is full of contradictions and dilemmas, and to take one position that all types of hunting are all good or all bad is to engage in a largely belief-based rather than evidence-based view of the world. What should the anti-hunter say to an Indian villager who just lost his daughter to a tiger successfully conserved in a nearby national park? Equally, what does the ethical hunter say to the city-dweller who considers canned hunting and tower shoots as an appropriate way to behave towards animals and birds?

At the centre of the hunting debates is the issue of death. If we are to eat, we must kill something else. If we are prey, then something else kills us. Even vegetarians who eschew the consumption of meat have to come to terms with the fact that their plant produce comes from agricultural systems that raise domestic livestock and directly affect wild animal populations. Let us start with some biological facts. Before the advent of agriculture some ten thousand years ago, hominids survived for thousands of generations as hunters and gatherers. We must have been good at these activities, or we would never have made it to here. The domestication of crops and livestock brought the need for different knowledge and skills, and different relations with land and nature, and later came to dominate modes of food acquisition for humans. Today, we consume more than four billion tonnes of cereals and roots each year, together with some twenty billion chickens, cattle, pigs, sheep and goats. We now treat food as a commodity and have largely forgotten the story about its production. George Wallace said this of an elk shot on the Wyoming–Colorado border:

> *should I be sad? He lived better than most.... He didn't stand corralled and knee-deep in snow and his own dung waiting to be fed, ear-marked, dehorned and injected, only to be herded, prodded, trucked and knocked on the head at the end of two years.*[9]

Supermarkets have made us forgetful. Animals are mostly just cuts of meat made ready for the stove, and no longer (somewhat) sentient beings that have lives, and then bloody deaths. There was a time, a couple of generations ago, when many rural families in the UK, and some in towns too, would keep a backyard pig. It was fed on scraps and food wastes and would become an important part of the family. One day, the pig would have to be slaughtered, and all the family would know it. Today, the bacon comes wrapped in plastic, and you do not need to think of the pig. As Ruth Rudner says:

> *what has the ease of buying food done to our awe of the animals that feed us? How awed is anyone by a cow? How many people, for that matter, cutting into a piece of cow, remember its life or have much interest in ingesting its spirit? How many ask its forgiveness?*[10]

Yet this is far from true for those indigenous groups who still hunt and fish for their livelihoods. Their needs are different, and their relations to animals are different – so very different that many moderns and agriculturalists have come to see their ways of life as not just ancient, but primitive and thus coming before civilization. And this makes it easier to complain about them for their actions. It is strange that the 57,000 people of Greenland are castigated for killing harp seals or for catching whales, when those who are against it are often from countries which had been engaged in commercial whaling for centuries. Subsistence hunting is not the same as commercial, and ethically must be treated differently if we are to have any regard for other cultures. Under Home Rule in Greenland, the Inuit have more rights to hunt and fish than many other indigenous peoples elsewhere in the world. Seals, whales, other sea mammals, birds and fish are important sources of food, but also have powerful ideological and symbolic value. These products are sold at small markets on quays and also often appear in supermarket freezers, which might appear to be commercializing wild foods. Yet, as Mark Nuttall says, 'many people do not have the time, means or ability to hunt, yet value and rely on Greenland's meat and fish production as the basis for their diet'. Each hunting settlement has its own *piniarfik*, its personalized hunting place, and these are framed by local people, understood by them and cared for.[11]

The greatest contemporary controversy in the UK, though, has been over the tradition of fox-hunting with dogs. To some, this is a legitimate and long-standing countryside tradition necessary for control of predators of lambs and poultry. To others, it remains an uncivilized way to eliminate unwanted animals, which only have a negligible effect on agricultural production. There is no obvious solution. Hunting is a part of our history, and killing of many millions of animals, for those of us who eat meat, still occurs on a daily basis – though mainly behind the closed doors of abattoirs. This we seem to accept, but not the hunting. Is this fair or consistent? Yet without some sensitivities to animal welfare, we might still widely condone bear-baiting and cock-fighting because they, too, could be said to be traditional activities.

Few people today would condone the idea of otter-hunting, particularly as otter numbers went through a disastrous decline from the mid-20th century, due mainly to the effects of pollutants on fish stocks, loss of riverside habitats, traffic accidents, drowning in eel nets and hunting itself. Yet organized otter hunts were not banned until 1978. Having disappeared from most English rivers by the 1970s, otters are now a compelling story of successful recovery. They remain mysterious to all but the most patient and observant, yet their numbers are increasing. In the east of England, otters started to reappear in the early 1990s, and their presence has now been recorded in most rivers. We can now imagine otters in our rivers, and most people like that.

Hunting and shooting also brings money and people into the countryside. Grouse moors in the uplands are carefully managed so that the glorious twelfth of August and the following weeks can be a great success. Many of the marshes on the east coast estuaries are owned and managed by wildfowling groups so that they can shoot ducks in the autumn. Each year, some 20 million pheasants and 400,000 mallards are raised and released for shooting in and around our woodlands and wetlands. Who can say categorically whether these activities are wrong? And what would happen to the land if it were no longer looked after for these purposes? It might be changed to intensive crop production. A recent study found that landowners who both hunt and maintain game-bird stocks conserve some seven per cent of their farms as woodland, whereas those who do neither keep less than one per cent as woodland.[12]

But what if wild animals or birds are hunted for food rather than for sport? Might some of our views be different? On the Isle of Lewis, men from the fishing village of Ness have for generations travelled 60 kilometres every August to the uninhabited rocky island of Sula Sgeir to gather young gannets. In the Second World War, the gannet was called the Highland goose and was a major source of food in northern industrial cities. Some 2000 of these *guga* are collected from nests on the rock faces and killed, to be salted and stored for local consumption. The meat is an acquired taste, said to be rather oily and fishy, yet is a highly valued delicacy – not just for its nutrient value, but also because of the associated tradition and its long history, dating back at least to the 14th century. Yet this tradition is challenged by some animal welfare groups and bird conservationists, who see it as being cruel and are campaigning for the practice to be banned. There is, however, no evidence that the gathering has any adverse effect on the overall population of the gannet colony.

Is it so very different to the harvesting of domestic chickens and turkeys, about which people are considerably less exercised?

How, then, do hunters today feel about death? Author Bruce Woods says:

> *I hunt, despite the killing, because it puts me in the outdoors during the most beautiful seasons and in its most lovely environments [...] Sure, the killing bothers me. It's supposed to.*

Woods indicates that many animals are passed up by hunters – maybe because the shot is difficult, but more often because the hunter is not ready. Thomas McGuane recalls talking to an old government hunter, Alvin Close, who had been engaged for half a century in predator control. Like Aldo Leopold in earlier times, his target was wolves, and he shot the last stock-killing wolf in Montana. 'How did you feel about that?' asked McGuane. 'How do you think I felt?' 'I don't know.' 'It felt like hell.' In the early part of the 20th century, wolves were hunted to destruction as they were seen as pests; now they are being reintroduced into many parks.[13]

What, then, is ethical hunting? Most would agree that indigenous groups are ethical hunters. They understand their ecosystems, they have respect for animals, they have extensive codes of practice, and they eat to survive. But what constitutes ethical hunting in industrialized societies? This is hard to say, as it is probably easier to define what is ethically indefensible. David Petersen suggests the following as a start: baiting to encourage bears or deer to come to a particular place to be shot; using hounds to force bears and mountain lions into trees so that they can be easily shot; globetrotting trophy hunters; canned hunts on fenced game ranches; all-terrain vehicle abuse of environments and the chase; road hunting (shooting from cars); and using space-age technology to minimize the challenge. Ethics would suggest asking, is it right, rather than is it legal?

There are more than 3000 commercial shooting preserves in the US, many of which use tower shoots. Columnist Ted Williams describes how these work: captive bred birds are released from a 15-metre tower and shot at as they fly away. Typically, some 100–300 birds are thrown out, and at the end the ducks and pheasants can be exchanged for ready frozen birds; 'how fresh the air, how pleasant the uncluttered countryside,' say the shooters. But how genuine an experience is this hunt, where the visitors add little to their nature literacy, as Gary Snyder puts it, and certainly do not develop any intimate relationship with the land and its animals? They say, 'it's a lot of fun, isn't it?' But is this activity moral, along with raising animals in captivity and shooting them in pens, or shooting at wolves from the air? As Jim Harrison says, 'it is a silly mistake, I've found, to assume that the rules of fair play are shared'. What is the logic of those who put out chocolate bars for bears or apples and salt-licks for deer, and then set up to shoot them when they arrive?

A more complex story is told by Jim Fergus about road hunters, who infuriate traditional grouse hunters by their actions. Fergus hitches a ride early in the morning with two road hunters, crawling along with beer in one hand and gun in the other.

They are car mechanics, and they say this is their tradition. This is how they and their fathers have always hunted, and they hate the rich city people who come to the woods with their ten-thousand-dollar shotguns to shoot the local partridges. The road hunters shoot for the pot, and kill twenty birds a season: 'What's so wrong with that?' they say. All hunting teaches people things, and these may be more important than just the food for the pot. Essayist Stephen Bodio writes:

> *falconry taught me to be polite to an animal, to have manners towards the wild, to listen and move slowly, to watch and keep my mouth shut [...] Hawks have moulded me more than I have ever influenced hawks.*

What is clear is that pro- and anti-hunters often speak completely different languages. Some speak about the need for hunting to control populations and maintain habitats, while others are thinking about the ethics of killing. Ann Causey suggests that 'neither side has a monopoly on hypocrisy, zealotry, narrow-mindedness or irrationalism'. Some people display, as she puts it, 'a shocking irreverence, arrogance and hubris' by taking great pleasure in inflicting careless and casual death on animals, or in considering success only when the largest antlers have been downed. Others, though, are equally extreme. The founder of the Fund for Animals, Cleveland Amory, has described his perfect world in this way:

> *all animals will not only be not shot, they will be protected — not only from people but as much as possible from each other. Prey will be separated from predator, and there will be no overpopulation or starvation because all will be controlled by sterilization or implant.*

However, lambs only lie down with lions in myths. The real world of ecosystems shaped by ecology, and latterly by human interaction, requires a thoroughly different and rather more sensible approach.[14]

Despite all this disagreement, there remains a necessity for ecological management in many landscapes that have been heavily shaped and restricted by modern society. Another biological fact centres on the need to manage herbivore populations in environments where top predators have been removed. In Europe and North America, we have long been engaged in the elimination of predators so that domestic livestock can be safe. In the last two decades, with the abandonment of farming in many places, and the deliberate conversion of fields to woodlands elsewhere, the numbers of wild deer have increased spectacularly.

At the time of Columbus, there were several million people in North America, speaking some 175 languages and sustaining their livelihoods, at least in part, by hunting, gathering, fishing and trapping. New arrivals to the continent then eliminated many animal populations, and some species, with the period of greatest hunting pressure in the later 19th century. Between 1850 and 1900, American farmers cleared 23 square kilometres of forest, prairie and wetland every day. The fall in wildlife numbers was in part a reason for the emergence and support for the conservation movement and the establishment of the world's first national park in 1872. Since that time, the numbers of herbivores have dramatically increased, though predators remain mostly in enclaves. There are five species of deer in North America: moose, elk, caribou, white-tailed deer and mule deer (with black-tailed a subspecies). The deer population today stands at between 15 and 25 million, with densities in southern Wisconsin at 27–30 per square kilometre and in central Texas at 120 per square kilometre. In general, wildlife biologists have found it impossible to stabilize deer populations unless hunters are allowed to take females. There is also evidence to suggest that deer are often healthier in the presence of animal and human predation than they are in its absence.

The example of New York State illustrates how rapidly ecosystems and populations have changed. In the 17th and 18th centuries, deer were abundant, but by 1887, less than a dozen deer were said to exist in the whole of the Catskills. But by the early 1900s, marginal farms began to be abandoned, and forest cover began to increase. By the 1940s, many farmers were stating that deer were now a nuisance. By the late 1970s there was a population of some 450,000 and by the 1990s more than a million, thus creating many conflicts with farmers, owners of gardens, park wardens and car drivers. Now a completely false situation has been created. The deer are no longer hunted by people (as they had been by Native Americans), and they are no longer consumed by predators (as these have been eliminated). The abundance of deer is a human creation arising out of changing policies and practice. And something has to be done in return.

Many people value these deer. They enjoy seeing them and appreciate the presence of wildlife in their local ecosystems. On the narrow Fire Island, off Long Island, there are now 30 deer per square kilometre, up tenfold on the 1970s. The habitat is severely damaged, and many birds and small animals have disappeared. But most local people still oppose hunting, and when the deer are starving, they feed them by hand. As Richard Nelson says, 'now they are no longer wild; they are like city pets'. Fed deer spend less time foraging and so can devote more energy to offspring. Many first-time visitors are thrilled to see deer. But if local people and visitors favour the deer, they cannot also have other valued elements of ecosystems.

And here is the dilemma. People like deer, yet increasing numbers have brought disarray to many protected areas and created conflict and disagreement about how to control them. Some suggest trapping and transfer, capture and euthanasia, and sterilization. Yet biologists still conclude that the best method is hunting – a quick death being better than the torture of transfer or the slow death of starvation. In the 1990s, there were more deer in the city limits of Philadelphia than lived in the whole of Pennsylvania a century earlier. Once they overcome their fear of humans, deer colonize urban areas. People try all sorts of repellents, but still do not want them killed. Yet in Wisconsin and California, relocated deer have been shown to survive poorly – they do not know their new environments. More deer also means more traffic accidents. In 1961, 400 deer were killed on the roads of Wisconsin; in the 1990s, some 35,000–50,000 were killed annually on the roads, with 800 people injured. Another example is moose in Newfoundland, which were introduced there in 1904. Now they are so numerous, some 150,000 on the island, that they are a road hazard, particularly at dawn and dusk.[15]

At the core of the decisions that must be taken about population control are some important biological imperatives. Richard Nelson describes the conflict around deer on another island, the 300-hectare Angel Island in San Francisco Bay. After hunting had eliminated deer by 1900, 12 animals were reintroduced in 1915. In 1955 the island was closed to hunting, and black-tail deer numbers increased to 300. The island's vegetation collapsed, the forest floor was stripped and deer starved to death. Park officials shot some deer, but the public disapproved. The Society for the Prevention of Cruelty to Animals (SPCA) took court action to prevent culling, in which they were successful, but this only provoked another starvation crash. The constantly hungry deer pleased visitors, as they readily came to be fed from the hand. One suggestion to release six coyotes was greeted with horror. A trap and release project captured 200 animals and released them on the mainland, but nine out of ten were dead within the year as they had no understanding of motor vehicles or predators. At the same time, the surviving deer on the island grew fat and healthy as there was little competition for food, and the does started producing twins. The numbers soared. A sterilization campaign by the SPCA resulted in only a quarter of females being captured, and the programme failed. In the end, culling was the only sensible option, and the most welfare-friendly. There are now 80 deer on the island.

In the UK, deer numbers are also increasing, and they too have to be controlled. In the past twenty years, the area of woodland has increased by 600,000 hectares to some 2.6 million hectares, and there are now thought to be 500,000 roe deer, 360,000 red deer, 100,000 fallow deer, and some 50,000 muntjac, sika and Chinese water deer, though numbers are notoriously hard to estimate. Deer remain mysterious and largely invisible, even in our dense and managed landscape. Total numbers, though, are accepted to be greater than at any time in the past 1000 years. Numbers are increasing because of more woodland cover, warmer winters, improved urban habitat management and more golf courses. Their natural enemies – wolf, boar, lynx and bear – have long been eliminated, though domestic dogs still kill many fawns. On our crowded island, increasing numbers of deer are seen by most people as a good thing, as they show that not all is lost with policies and practice towards nature. Deer are now seen regularly in urban centres, such as Leeds, London, Northampton, Oxford, Sheffield and Southampton, echoing the invasion of foxes 30 years ago. But as in the US, more deer means more conflict with other land users. In Scotland, numbers of red deer are rising rapidly, despite an annual cull of some 70,000 animals, and are preventing woodland regeneration at some locations. There are some 20,000–50,000 traffic collisions annually, and though few result in serious injury to the public, their economic impact is substantial. Unless something changes, farmers, woodland owners and gardeners will have to give up some of their hard-won plant productivity to these herbivores. There are many possible approaches to the problem, which in itself is likely to mean an increasing number of conflicts.

Some other animals have seen spectacular changes in their numbers in the 20th century, none more so than the humble rabbit following the release of myxomatosis in 1953. Raised as a source of food in earlier centuries, they had become an agricultural pest, and this highly contagious virus was deliberately released to control numbers. Numbers fell from 100 million in the early 1950s to a million by the end of the decade, since when they have risen steadily to 37 million. I recall as a young boy walking with a friend through a dark Yorkshire forest and coming upon an abandoned country house in a bright clearing. Before us was the grey and forbidding building, with unseeing windows boarded with planks of wood and surrounded by the fading glory of formal gardens gone wild. And everywhere, thousands of unmoving, lonely rabbits. They sat in groups or singly on the grass, silently awaiting their end, eyes weeping with pus, blind like the house, stumbling occasionally into one another. It was a sad and desolate scene brought about by the need to control a population that no longer had its own predators. We systematically removed the predators in earlier centuries and then feel sad when we have to control the increasing numbers of their prey.

Is this conflict over hunting, then, actually a symptom of modern society's increasing estrangement from the wild? Is it the lack of ecological, land or nature literacy that reduces the understanding, and allows us to take sides and not to see the greys rather than the black and white in the arguments? This estrangement is a recent phenomenon, but it appears set to increase as urban populations grow over rural, and food systems become increasingly disconnected from the places of production.

One problem is that many who hunt keep quiet about their activities. It is almost too complex an issue to engage in public deliberation. Yet this is itself increasing the likelihood of hard positions being taken by both sides. Perhaps this is partly because the ethical hunter's eyes are often turned inwards. They value deep personal bonds with nature, in a similar way to indigenous people. Such a view is not easy to express in a technology-led society. The late John Madson said a genuine hunter is 'someone with a deep personal bond to the game hunted and the habitats in which it is hunted'. He said he searched for 'that flash of insight again, trying to close the magic circle between man, wilderness and animals'. Admitting to the shaping and being shaped is to take a different ethical, and possibly also spiritual, view of the world:

> *When you go into the woods, your presence makes a splash and the ripples of your arrival spread like circles in water [...] You can always feel it when those circles stop widening; you can feel it on the back of your neck and in your gut, and in the awareness of other presences.*[16]

Some of these views may be echoes of the past, but one thing has changed in recent human history – we have become more tolerant of predators. This is quite a remarkable shift. For thousands of generations, hominid survival depended in part on avoiding being prey for larger and more dangerous animals.[17] Put yourself in a remote African savannah as dusk falls, and the sky flames from orange and red to purple, and then quickly darkens to a deep black, and you can begin to imagine the challenges that bands of early humans faced. We cannot run very fast, our teeth are small, our eyes are feeble in the dark. And the predators that today we so enjoy seeing are better in all these attributes. It is a bit of a mystery that we made it at all, or perhaps, more accurately, a testament to our capacity to work together in groups and out-think our predators. In short, for most of our history predators were enemies, and we were potential prey. Yet we now recognize that we have been so successful, such emphatic winners in this war, that large predators have been comprehensively eliminated from many ecosystems. And now we want them back. Wolves for North America, Scandinavia and the Alps, snow leopards for the high mountains, lions for savannahs, and tigers for the Asian forests.

The Carpathians remains one of the few habitats in Europe where all the top predators are still present, with some 3000 or more wolves and lynx, and perhaps twice as many brown bears. Recent years have, however, seen the growth of trophy hunting for bear. Hunters pay some $7000 for a large bear, and overall bear-hunting brings in over $20 million for Romania each year. But this commoditization of the bear has led to conflicts over numbers – government figures say there are 6300 individuals left, and so the issuing of a quota for 2004 of 658 bears was acceptable. But wildlife groups believe there are only some 2500 bears left. Protagonists say that hunting gives forest managers an incentive to look after the bears; others say it encourages their slaughter as an economic value has been attached to their deaths. Like most predators, though, these bears are elusive in the landscape. As David Quammen says, 'you can walk for many days, through the woodlands and high meadows of the Carpathians, as I've done, without even chancing on a bear. This is normal.'

The mountain lion, also known as the puma, cougar or panther, was once ubiquitous in North America, until it was eradicated from the eastern US from the early 1800s. It is North America's largest cat, at some 30kg, and despite its now restricted territory is still hunted in some regions. In Utah, for example, ranchers argue that they are a pest and regularly shoot them (the hunting licences generate more than $4 million a year for the state). California banned hunting of pumas in 1990, but pro-hunting groups have regularly sought to overturn this decision. Mountain lions make several fatal attacks on humans a year – and each time that they do, calls for their eradication resurface.[18]

One of the most famous predatory cats was the man-eating leopard of Rudraprayag in Himalayan India. It became notorious because of its extraordinary consumption – 126 people were killed over an eight year period between 1918 and 1926 – and also because the legendary tiger-hunter, Jim Corbett, was called in to dispatch the leopard. For three years, the leopard took victims from inside their own houses, but it was eventually shot by Corbett. You would think you could see a large carnivore in the bushes, that we would be good enough to spot them. But we are not. Corbett's descriptions of the leopard removing people without sleeping family members hearing are echoed by David Barron's reports from Boulder about recent attacks by pumas. People simply did not know or hear. Said one women of an attack on her five-year-old daughter:

> *I was standing next to her, then the next second there was total silence. I didn't hear any growling, Laura didn't scream, I didn't hear any dragging. They were gone [...] there were no marks on the ground. There was nothing.*

The woman did find her daughter, locked in the jaws of the cat, and a stranger with a stick managed to persuade the puma to drop the girl. In the same year, a six-year-old boy was snatched whilst on a family hike, again in complete silence.[19]

Hominids have been engaged in a long struggle to outwit predators. Being prey may indeed have helped to make us human. The hunted had to work together, value trust and friendship, and think their way through the landscape. The hunters had to work together too, and maintain a deep respect for their prey. The core dilemma, as Barry Lopez put it in *Arctic Dreams*, is 'How can we find a way to live moral and compassionate lives when we are aware of the blood and horror inherent in all life?'[20] How peculiar too that so many of us now are concerned at the killing of some animals, but not, apparently, of domestic livestock in abattoirs. How sad that through our modern estrangement from nature, we seem to have forgotten so much about how ecosystems work.

Animal Magic

The chalk downs of southern England are famous for their sweeping hills and grass swards kept flower-rich by sheep and rabbits. They are also stalked by white horses, great beasts created by filling trenches cut in the grassland with blocks of white chalk. There are twenty-four known white horses in the UK, thirteen of which are in Wiltshire. Most date from the period between 1700 and the late 1800s, though the most striking was created by Bronze Age Britons around 3000 years ago. All, though, carry power and mystery as they prance, canter or race across the landscape. Like the Nazca's geoglyph animals of the high Andes, these are designed to be seen from far away, and each one attracts myths and stories.

The most famous is the oldest of British chalk figures, a horse which races across a steep scarp near the village of Uffington. It crosses the Ridgeway, an ancient 135-kilometre trade route that winds across hilltops from east of Oxford to Avebury's ring of standing stones. Nearby is a 5000-year-old Neolithic long barrow, and on the main hilltop are the vast earthworks of the Iron Age Uffington castle, expansive and empty now, but indicative of the value the ancients held for this site. You approach the horse across a wide and closely cropped hillside that seems to hover like a space station above the patchwork plains below, once thick forests, and now a spectacular mosaic of fields and farms. A flock of rooks swirls up, a commentary of *kraa* calls to join the evening song of skylarks. Below a train streaks from east to west and joins other distant echoes of modern life down on the surface of the planet.

Dropping down from the path, you come first upon the horse's five-metre head, and then the whole figure become apparent, stretching more than one hundred and fifteen metres to its tail and trailing hind leg. The design looks to be special; it also appears on some celtic coins, but is not used on other chalk figures. A long thin body with neck and shoulders almost as long; forelegs stretched out in front as if ready to jump an obstacle; hind legs tense and sprung, one in a stylized reverse curve. It gives the impression of being a particular individual horse, like Barry Lopez's stone desert horse, not a generalized one. As you walk around the trenches, it is difficult to make out that it is an animal. It appears to have been carved from a distance, as if by a great god in the sky. What is clear, though, is that without regular maintenance, the chalk would quickly disappear under invading grasses. Generation after generation has thought it important enough to look after, but you still wonder what prompted people to carve a great horse on this hillside 3000 years ago. Why not a cow, or a bear or wolf? And why this horse in particular?

Below me, a pair of swallows dive and twist, and below them in the valley is a conical mound where George is supposed to have slain the dragon and where its blood spilled on the flat top, so preventing any grass from growing. This is other significance in these chalk figures. They attract stories, which become tied to the place. Here the dragon, there the burial site for King Arthur's father. It is said that the Uffington horse will animate and dance on the dragon hill when King Arthur himself awakes. Every one hundred years, the horse is supposed to gallop across the sky to the long barrow to be reshod by Wayland the smithy. The horse, a mare, also comes down at night with her invisible foal to drink in a nearby stream. Standing in the eye of the horse is supposed to bring wishes granted. The horse is not only important as a landscape icon, but also as a source of stories that make the place somehow more special. How many other places were once full of stories like this, but about which we have collectively forgotten?

The first white horse of the modern era was cut at Westbury around 1700, followed by others at Cherhill in 1780 and Pewsey in 1785. Most of the remainder were cut in the 1800s, though the recent millennium celebrations brought new designs at Devizes, Heeley and Folkestone between 1999 and 2002. White horses have also been cut in South Africa and New Zealand. Again, all are horses, and the designs are more realistic figures than Uffington's gaunt mare.[1]

A prominent one overlooks the village of Alton Barnes from a south-facing slope some six kilometres south of Avebury. Cut in 1812, this horse is again part of an ancient landscape, as on every hill are tumuli, earthwork enclosures, long barrows, kitchen barrows or strip lynchet field marks. This horse carries less of the glamour of Uffington and is more difficult to approach. Late on a windblown summer evening, I walk from the north, up and over a series of burial mounds, past black cattle chewing curiously on thistles rather than grass, and perched 120 metres above Pewsey Vale look down to see another iconic symbol of today's England. For here is a crop circle in a barley field, a spinning series of geometric shapes again designed to be seen from afar. Two people walk in silence through the flattened corn. And up here is the giant prancing horse, four legs of equal length with a deep body and short stubby tail. Two weasels streak across the chalk of the body, and disappear in the grass. Apart from the cattle, this hillside appears to be mostly deserted.

Below, a field of blackened rape awaits harvest; another of barley is in, and old-style square bales are piled in tottering towers. Again, as you approach the horse, it becomes more difficult to recognize. It is made to be magic from the valley floor settlements. At the figure, enclosed each way by 80 metres of rusty barbed wire to keep off the cattle, the grass is longer and unkempt. Here, then, is another animal sign on the land, newer than the Uffington ancient, but again an enduring symbol of our relationships with animals and the land. When we forget who made them, then the myths can begin.

Many mysteries remain in our mostly modernized British landscapes, despite its 24 million hectares containing nearly 60 million people. This, it seems to me, is a good thing. Our lives are not so controlled and managed as we might think. Things can happen beyond our understanding. The landscape is ever changing, and the stories associated with it also change. It exists as one form of reality; it also exists in our imagination. One good example relates to the apparent emergence of big cats. Could this land of ours, seemingly so dense and known and described by art and science, contain sufficient numbers of pumas, leopards, panthers or lynx that they could breed and persist? If they do exist, surely we would have seen them more often, or at least more regular signs of their presence?

But it does seem as though more of us have indeed seen them. The British Big Cats Society receives more than a thousand reports of sightings per year, with some video footage and still pictures, details of sheep kills and paw prints. Scotland is the most common location for sightings (more than 200), followed by Devon, Kent, Wales, Leicestershire, Gloucestershire, Norfolk and Essex (between 50 and 100 each). Individual testimonies seem convincing, even though some people may be mistaken, but, as for the Loch Ness monster, the pictures mostly are blurred and confusing. Could there really be such wild animals out there in our crowded land? And, if so, are they escapees from zoos or circuses, or deliberate releases by pet owners or welfare activists; and if they are present, are they breeding? The lack of hard evidence is strange. Is it because they genuinely do not exist, or are they really so elusive that we cannot locate them in the landscape? It may be that some of our desires to see them are so great that domestic cats grow to become two-metre beasts of the wild, or possibly it is muntjac deer that are being mistaken. On the other hand, our powers of observation may have so diminished that we no longer notice the real signs of their presence, or indeed know how to look at the land properly.[2]

Once there have been a number of sightings at one location, the animals inevitably receive a popular moniker – the Beast of Bodmin, the Fen Tiger, the Surrey Puma, the Bungay Black Dog, and lately the Beasts of Bennachie, Bont and Ballymena. In this way, they enter popular mythology, and increase the likelihood of people seeing something that may not really be present. We are, however, still left with sheep and dog kills and horse mutilations that seem to point only to big cats, although officials with night sights have searched at some locations for weeks with little success, though many have found large paw prints. Down on the marshes of the Essex coast, we recently came upon some huge paw prints in the mud after heavy summer rain within a mile of where a policeman had recorded a large black cat crossing a road. You stand and wonder when such things are difficult to explain. Farmers in Norfolk, Wales and Devon have observed sheep depradations that are strongly suggestive of predators rather than of dogs or even people. Cats lick flesh, and typically leave clean skeletons. Domestic dogs attack sheep at the shoulder, and never consume whole carcasses. Farmer Robert Harding from Winford said of his sheep:

> this was not a dog, fox or badger. We are talking about throats, shoulders and ribs being ripped open. One of the ewes had her face skinned from her nose right across her head. It would have to be a powerful animal to do that.

Perry and Silvia Broad have been recording cat sightings in Suffolk and Essex for some time. They first saw a black cat at Nacton, which appeared at first to be a large dog, but the body and legs were longer and the front shoulders higher than the head. They saw another black one chasing a deer, a sandy one with two cubs in central Suffolk, and various blacks on and around Dunwich and Walberswick heaths and marshes. One gamekeeper friend also thought he saw a black Labrador one evening, until it climbed a tree. Perry, like many others, says that he is 'a bit careful who you mention these cats to'. Yet he is a good naturalist, like many others who have spotted these cats.

Attacks on people are very rare. One farm worker in East Sussex was attacked in October 2002 by a large cat with tufted ears. One notable conservationist says of his local reserve in Gloucestershire that there are so many sightings that he has taught his children to stay together when they visit. He is not being alarmist, just careful. Elsewhere, there are reports of big cats attracted to abattoirs, and of fox hunts flushing up others, and of sheep and deer carcasses found in trees and horses with distinctive claw marks. Clearly, the strongest evidence would be of actual bodies, or of DNA analyses of fur or clear video footage. There is one excellent piece of CCTV footage from September 2005, though, showing a cat walking by a zebra crossing in

Cirencester. It is clearly not a garden tabby. But for the moment much remains the subject of lively conjecture and mostly in the territory of myth. And whatever the reality, there is nothing wrong with a good story. It shows we are interested and still care.

Or maybe there is something more subtle in all of this? Perhaps we simply would like to sustain some mysteries and stories that are not resolved to a final truth of presence or absence. To those who have seen a big cat, there is no question. They believe their own eyes. But how is it that these observers cannot persuade a sceptical public, especially government departments, who completely dismiss the idea of big cats in the UK? Are we in UFO territory here, with people wishing to believe their own eyes? On the other hand, people may not be reporting all sightings for fear of being mocked. Or perhaps we should believe people who know a great deal about the behaviour of animals and feel that they should be trusted for their observations. They know what constitutes unusual behaviour, and what this might mean. I believe this evidence suggests that something is out there in the British countryside, but whether it is breeding populations of big cats, or small numbers supplemented by zoo escapes and deliberate releases, no one yet knows. Big cats continue to occupy real places in ecosystems and imagined places in our minds. And if they do convincingly appear in real landscapes, then how soon will it be before there are calls for their elimination (on public safety grounds)?

Of course, our main relationships with other animals on a daily basis are no longer with wild animals, but with domestic pets and companion animals. Half of all households in Britain keep a mammal, bird or fish. There are 6.5 million dogs, 9 million cats, 27 million fish, 1 million caged birds, 4.5 million rabbits, and 1.7 million guinea pigs and hamsters. In the US, nearly six in ten households keep pets – 62 million dogs, 69 million cats, 31 million caged birds. In Europe, the proportion of households with pets ranges from 37 per cent in Germany to 70 per cent in Ireland and Belgium. Why so many? It appears that at least part of the reason is that these companion animals bring physical and mental health benefits to their owners (though not for all – the RSPCA records in the UK some 70,000 cases of animals not being given food, water or shelter). Large numbers of people believe that owning pets is good for their health and well-bring. Pet owners have been found to have lower blood pressure and cholesterol levels than non-pet owners in Australia and to make fewer visits to doctors in the US. Dog owners suffering from heart trauma are six times more likely to survive a year after the trauma than those with no dogs, though, as there is no effect for cat owners, it is probably the physical exercise that is critical. There have also been recorded positive effects of animals on depressed and asocial patients, in which unresponsive patients start interacting with animals by holding, stroking and hugging, smiling and laughing, and also talking to the animals and the people who care for them.

The idea that animals could assist in therapy began in the 1960s, when child psychologist Boris Levinson found that when his dog happened to be present in the consulting room, some formerly uncommunicative children were able to establish rapport through the dog. A variety of companion zoo programmes for children with disorders have since been developed, and companion animals have been widely used as they give unconditional support to people. The therapeutic value of horses has long been known, particularly when as working animals they were a common part of the landscape.

Yet there is a dark side to companion animals too. In the US alone, some eight to ten million cats and dogs are abandoned and then rescued by shelters each year, about half of which then have to be killed humanely. Domestic cats are also predators, and each individual is estimated to kill more than 100 songbirds and 50 small mammals per year. These cats also consume more than 1.5 million tonnes of meat each year, and the total pet food market in the UK is worth £1.5 billion per year. In the US, owners spend $85 billion a year on dog and cat food and another $7 billion on veterinary care. Dog wastes are a health hazard in many places (one million kilograms are deposited by dogs every day in the UK), with many green spaces in urban settings no longer clean enough for children to play. Each year, more than 100,000 people receive treatment for dog bites in the UK, 600,000 in the US (costing $120 million to treat). Dogs also injure or kill 10,000 head of livestock a year in the UK.

Pets appear to have been kept by most societies throughout human history. They are rarely killed and eaten and so come to occupy an ambiguous territory between humans and domestic livestock. Pets have little practical use, but are nurtured and cared for, whereas livestock have utilitarian value, yet are often treated inhumanely. As James Serpell says about animals, 'we seem to harbour two totally contradictory and incompatible sets of moral values'. People allow themselves to get close to pets, and these in turn have a marked effect on our well-being. But today we employ a number of detachment and concealing devices to distance ourselves from livestock and meat.[3]

There are also taboos about eating some animals. Few people, I suspect, would contemplate eating their pet after it dies. But it was not always so. Keith Thomas records a Dorset farmer in 1698 who wrote, 'my old dog Quorn was killed, and baked for his grease, of which he yielded 11 pounds'. Eating any dog in Europe and North America today would be taken by most people to be quite unacceptable. But why should the dog be any different to the pig, which is known to be intelligent and yet happily consumed by the billion every year? Would you eat your dog if you had no other food? Would you if it was a dog raised for food in a modern factory farm? What if dog meat was very cheap at the supermarket, or if it was said to have excellent nutritional qualities? Would you eat one if a politician said it was your duty to do so, or if a friend served it up on a special occasion, and waited for you to go first?

Why are some of us content to eat cows but not dogs and kangaroos? And why was there such a media furore in the UK at the time of the 2002 football World Cup about the host South Koreans, who consume dogs on special occasions? In Britain, we do not eat guinea pigs (but if you go to Ecuador you will be expected to do so), but are entirely content to consume (and first have killed) five million 'normal' pigs a year. These preferences also shape the politics of food and environmental organizations. Some Japanese like to eat whale meat; others are concerned that such choices may lead to the extinction of whales. In Australia, many kangaroos are shot each year to control their numbers, and some are eaten; other people campaign against such practices.

So what is it about eating that provokes such strong reactions to certain foods and not to others? And why is it that many of us seem no longer to care about its effect on our health, nor of the production and long-distance transport of food from farmed landscapes to our plates? It could be said that one of the most political acts we engage in on a daily basis is to eat. We vote only every few years, but we eat every day, and our food choices make a difference to farms, animals, communities and landscapes somewhere near or far. But these choices are not freely made, as they are guided by cultural norms and, increasingly, by today's corporate advertising. They are also shaped by the regular use of animal analogy and metaphor in daily speech, suggesting that animals and humans still occupy the similar moral space for many people. In the past, many birds were given Christian names in English, such as robin redbreast, tom tit, polly parrot, jackdaw, jenny wren and the generic dicky bird. Today pets are almost always named, as are race horses and some domestic cattle, but generally not sheep and pigs. Even bears used for baiting in the 19th century were named as if they were people, such as Harry Hunks, George Stone and Ned of Canterbury. And, of course, a very large number of pubs contain the names of animals or birds. Other nature-based sources of important iconography in our lives include flowers, which still have great symbolic value. They are used at funerals and marriages, put on graves, given for holidays and valentines; poppies are used to remember the fallen in wars.[4]

In our increasingly urbanized lives, we still remain fascinated by animals and wild places. A recent survey of 20,000 people in Britain to find the top fifty things they wanted to do before they died discovered overwhelming interest in wild places and animals. Twenty-nine choices were wholly nature based, including swimming with dolphins, watching whales, polar bears, elephants and orang utangs, going on safari, or visiting spectacular places such as the Grand Canyon, Uluru, Kilimanjaro or the rainforests. Six of the top fifty involved visiting a significant human artefact in a nature setting, including camel-riding at the Pyramids and visiting the Great Wall of China, Machu Picchu and Sydney Harbour Bridge. Nine involved travelling through nature, such as journeys on the trans-Siberian railway and Orient Express, wing-walking, paragliding and riding a motorbike on the open road. Only six of the fifty were entirely non-nature based, such as gambling at Las Vegas or visiting Disneyworld.[5]

Zoos remain very popular today, even though there are many other attractions and leisure activities now available and many people have concerns over the restricted area over which animals can range, whether in cages or more open spaces. In Britain, the largest 60 of the country's 300 licensed zoos are members of the British Federation of Zoos, and in the early 2000s, there were 12 million visitors annually to these zoos, up from an average of just under 10 million visitors per year in the late 1990s. Each year, about the same number of people visit zoos as attend Premier

League football matches, which of course receive rather more media attention. The situation is similar in the US, where the 210 members of the American Zoo and Aquarium Association recorded 137 million visitors in each of 2000 to 2002. This is up from an average of 91 million per year in the 1980s and 117 million in the 1990s and again compares favourably with the high profile professional sports in the country. The major football, baseball, hockey and basketball leagues had an average of 127 million spectators in each of 1999–2001, some 10 million less than those still happy to spend money to see animals, birds and fish in a zoo.

One danger with this interest is that certain animals and their habitats can become seen as another commodity in our modern world. Tourism now accounts for about 10 per cent of world trade, employs 110 million people and has annual revenues of some $3 trillion. About one in five tourists worldwide can now be classi-fied as ecotourists, and nature-based activities are on the increase. Whale and dolphin watching, for example, now attracts ten million people annually in 87 nations, up from half a million in 1980, and is worth $2 billion a year. The Great Barrier Reef in Australia is now worth $700 million each year for tourism, and only $300 million for fishing. In Austin, Texas, the Congress Bridge was restored in 1980, and it now provides shelter for some 1.5 million Mexican free-tailed bats from March to November. Each year, some $8 million is spent in the city by the 100,000 people who visit the bridge to witness their emergence at dusk.[6]

Is ecotourism, then, an opportunity for people to engage in authentic experi-ences and reconnect with the natural world, or does it bring a set of new problems? Tourism can affect local animals by transmitting disease (in Africa, gorillas have picked up intestinal parasites from humans and meerkats have been infected with tuberculosis), increasing stress (such as for dolphins) and reducing rest periods (such as for bears). The mountain gorilla was only scientifically discovered in 1902 and there are now less than 900 left in the wild. Ecotourism is vital to bring money to their national parks, but a tenth of this population is now said to be habituated to humans. And once they lose their fear of humans, so they become more susceptible to poachers and diseases. Tour operators also cannot guarantee an encounter with animals, which is not a problem faced by those people who visit gardens and landscapes for their flowers and trees. But the whales and dolphins may not show up, even though the boat's captain says that this is first time, ever, that they have not appeared. As a result, interactions can be staged, involving, for example, the throw-ing of fish blood off boats to encourage shark encounters. Such staged authenticity is becoming increasingly common and can go hand-in-hand with efforts to redesign and commodify landscapes and their animals.[7]

One problem is that many people do not feel that they have had a genuine encounter if the animals ignore them. In this way, zoos in the past have suffered from visitors provoking animals into a reaction in their cages or compounds. In the 19th century, some visitors to zoos in the UK took their own pets to feed to zoo animals. Today, visitors like to purchase food to feed animals if they can, or prefer to see them fed with anonymous meat (but certainly not whole animals, such as sheep and goats). I was once in one old zoo in an Asian country in which the animals were cramped into small cages, and where the visitors rattled cages and bars, threw food and other materials, all to provoke a response. An animal making no response is apparently not what people have paid their money for. In some zoos, in India and the US, for example, listless animals have been maimed or even killed by people throwing stones.[8]

Perhaps it is partly because we do not understand animals, and wish to. Animals remain a source of magic and mystery in many contexts. Hares, for example, have long had associations with witchcraft. People used to be afraid to meet one in the street, fearing it might be a witch or bad fairy, or that it presaged a house fire. Hares were never mentioned by name at sea, and their boxing behaviour in March has become associated with madness. In Alice in Wonderland, Lewis Caroll's Mad March Hare was a major character, since entering popular culture. But these ideas seem distant superstitions when you see them flash across a stubble field in winter, or when with sadness you see another early morning roadside kill.

Strange behaviour among animals is often seen as a sign that something deeper may be wrong with the world. Like other Native Americans, the Innu of Labrador in eastern Canada believe that animals control the hunt, so that when they are successful they thank the animals by hanging their bones from trees. When an animal behaves strangely, though, they believe it is a sign that the fabric that connects them to animals and collectively to the land is disturbed. Basile Panashue told me how he had once been driving home at night, when the headlights picked out an owl walking around in a circle in the middle of the road. The owl has special significance, as indeed it does in many other societies, and this behaviour was seen to be highly unusual. When he arrived home, an ambulance was at his neighbour's house. A child had died.

Horses were domesticated 6000 years ago, and, Stephen Budiansky suggests, 'have been enveloped in human dreams, myths, ambitions and sentiments for so long'. They were easy to domesticate, having no horns or antlers, requiring only a simple grass diet and not needing to rest after eating, and were able to run at 70km per hour. The working horse has always attracted stories about magic. Horses were the source of power on farms, and so the focus of much folklore too, almost all of which concerned how the horsemen were able to shape their behaviour. Drawing oils were common – these were jading substances or oils used to stop a horse. They were painted on gateposts and often used while horsemen were in the pub. The toad bone was even more powerful magic. The bones of a frog or toad were thrown into a river at midnight: one of the bones would float upstream, and this was kept as it exerted a magical control over a horse. Sometimes a donkey was put in a field with horses, as this prevented them from trying to escape – they would not leave without the stubborn donkey. A horse hair was sometimes tied around the leg at a joint to cause the horse to limp.

But it is horse whispering that has recently become famous as a practice. Horsemen always talked to their horses, sometimes even putting something in the horse's ear to maintain control. Horse whisperers are people with the apparent capacity to cure horses of illnesses, yet no one knows how. Some horse owners are convinced that something inexplicable has happened when the horses become well. Clearly, they might have recovered without the whisperer's help, but individual testimonies on serious injuries cannot easily be dismissed. It is a mystery, and cannot be explained by our current knowledge. One day, that might change. Alternatively, it might turn out to have been just a good story.

One of the rarest animals in the world persists in patches of modern farmed landscapes. This is the Suffolk Punch, the giant horse first bred in the 16th century to work the heavy Suffolk clays of eastern England. Suffolks are tall, often with a white star or blaze on the face, and have long been admired for their calm temperament and ease of care. But in the modern era, such shire horses could not compete with machinery, and from the 1950s were rapidly replaced with tractors and mechanized combines. Farms, of course, became more efficient. More land was cultivated in less time with less labour. But when these horses and their horsemen disappeared from farms, something else was lost too. For the horsemen had an intimate relationship not just with their horses, but with the whole farm landscape. They were expert botanists, using up to forty species of wild plants for horse care. Today, having forgotten this knowledge, we call these once useful plants weeds, and the Suffolk only survives through the efforts of dedicated societies and individuals, one or two of whom still farm with shire horses.

From generation to generation, horsemen passed on knowledge about the value of certain plants for treating illness and disease, shining the coat or improving appetite. George Ewart Evans, eloquent observer of English agricultural change, wrote in *The Horse and the Furrow* of fevers treated with agrimony or with apples sliced and stored until infested with antibiotic-carrying fungi, and of colds and coughs cured with feverfew, belladonna, meadow rue and horehound. For deworming, the horsemen used celandine, yellow-flowered indicator of spring, and to encourage appetite put gentian, elecampane, horehound and felwort into food. They used box to keep down sweat and burdock, saffron, rosemary, fennel, juniper, tansy and mandrake for coat conditioning. Hazel, holly and willow were fashioned into withies and traces for harnesses. This example shows that there is a simple principle for our modern era of agricultural progress. As food efficiency increases, so landscape diversity is lost, and so too goes an intimate knowledge of nature and a duty of care. The Hollesley Bay open prison long had one of the last groups of Suffolk Punches, and these were kept precisely for their therapeutic value. John Bromley, the estate manager, said in the 1970s:

> we make a big play of the therapeutic value of the heavy horses with the boys [...] that is why we keep horses. We attach one boy to the horse; and the boy's character changes: he has now got responsibility, direct responsibility. [...] And their attitude changes.

Regrettably, the prison service has now closed the farm, arguing that cost cutting was necessary and the horses were only a luxury.[9]

These growing disconnections must be a concern. Our countrysides have lost many of their animals, including almost all the threatening ones. Now, however, some are increasing in numbers, the deer and otters and possibly big cats, and others are being reintroduced. There is even some discussion about reintroducing wolves. Perhaps these will help to bring back some more mystery to the countryside and its wild places. If we allow it, the land will include us.[10]

Part 3

Food and the Land

The Fatta the Lan'

When the first Europeans caught an onshore breeze and drifted from the Pacific into the bays of what is now central California in 1542, they found a land inhabited by forty different groups of hunter-gatherers. It was one of the densest populations of Native Americans on the continent, with some ten thousand people speaking some one hundred languages. Wild foods were well managed and abundant, with people making use of marine, seashore, river, grassland and forest resources during different seasons of the year. They had long learned how to leach the bitter tannins out of acorns and horse chestnuts, which were an important source of carbohydrates and fat, alongside pinion nuts and salmon. Local people sometimes collectively called themselves the Ohlone, and through bonds of trade and marriage had peacefully coexisted for thousands of years. There was no personal land ownership, though individuals did have their own tools, clothing and hunting weapons.[1]

But the arrival of Juan Rodriguez Cabrillo and his Spanish expedition at Monterrey spelled the beginning of the end of hunting and gathering in this productive region. They and later arrivals saw the non-farming cultures of the Native Americans as simplistic and backward. Over time, local people were evicted and pressed into reserves, and within a few centuries California had been turned into one of the world's most productive agricultural regions. Today, there are no hunter-gatherers left, yet somehow this lush productivity has turned sour in the growing recognition that modern foods are now a major source of ill-health. How did it all come to this?

The Salinas River rises in the coastal mountains half way between Los Angeles and San Francisco and flows to Cabrillo's footsteps in Monterrey Bay, now a national marine sanctuary. The river valley is also the location for John Steinbeck's 1930s tragedy about people and the land, *Of Mice and Men*.[2] It begins in an apparently empty land, where:

> on sand banks, the rabbits sit as quietly as little grey, sculptured stones. And then from the direction of the state highway come the sound of footsteps on crisp sycamore leaves. The rabbits hurried noiselessly for cover. A stilted heron laboured up into the air and pounded down the river. For a moment, the place was lifeless, and then two men emerged from the path and come into the opening by the green pool.

They are George and Lennie, one small and sharp, the other large and lumbering, both wearing black shapeless hats, and they make some sort of living as itinerant farm hands, harvesting barley, driving cultivators, filling grain sacks and living off the land as best they can.

But they have a secret dream, which always seems unlikely to be fulfilled. It is an idea about a quiet rural idyll centred on a small farm that threatens no one, but which seems to be the very essence of freedom itself – a freedom that the Ohlone had some 400 years earlier. Sitting by the fire of brushwood by the dark pools of the river, the sun long gone, Lennie begs George to 'tell about how it's gonna be', and George says, 'OK, someday, we're gonna get the jack together and we're gonna have a little house and a couple of acres an' a cow and some pigs and…' 'An' live off the fatta the lan',' Lennie shouts. Later, they expand on their dream at a ranch where they have temporary work, and all the listening farm hands want to join them. George again says:

> we could have a few pigs. I could build a small smoke house like the one gran'pa had, an' when we kill a pig we can smoke the bacon and the hams, and make sausage an' all like that. An' when the salmon run up river we could catch a hundred of 'em an' salt 'em down or smoke 'em [...] When the fruits come in we could can it – and tomatoes [...] We'd jus' live there. We'd belong there.

Lennie again whispers softly, 'we could live offa the fatta the lan'. In the flickering light in a corner of a large barn, they all wistfully agree, and one says, 'everybody wants a little piece of land, jus' something that was his'.

Later, though, Crooks the horse hand is scornful: 'I see hundreds of men come by on the road an' on the ranches [...] an' that same damn thing in their heads. Hunderds of them [...] an' every damn one of 'ems got a little piece of land in his head.' He concludes, 'An' never a God damn one of 'em ever gets it. Just like heaven.' Crooks is right, and it does all end in tragedy, which is what happens for the likes of these poor farm hands with no more than dreams. He says, 'ever'body wants a little piece of lan' [...] nobody never gets to heaven, and nobody gets no land'. And so it proves to be in this story. The fat of the land, with its peace and bounty, is no more than distant hope and a dream of freedom for these boys. It is a dream common to many, and we have long used the phrase, the fat of the land, to indicate what was good about the food acquired, raised or grown on our places in the land. And yet today so much has changed. We have lived off the fat of the land, but the land has now become thin, and we have become fat. Extraordinarily, in the short period of success of modern agriculture, those of us in industrialized countries now consume such an abundance of calories that dietary ill-health, combined with sedentary lifestyles, has become a leading cause of morbidity and mortality. How could we have taken so many steps backwards, and at the same time ruined George and Lennie's dream?

In the past two generations, the diets of most people in industrialized countries, and of an increasing number of those in developing countries, have changed enormously. We have undergone what Barry Popkin calls a nutrition transition – choosing diets high in refined cereals, sugars and saturated fats, and generally low in fruit, vegetables and fish.[3] Large numbers of people now consume more food calories than they burn, along with too many simple sugars, saturated fats and an excess of salt. Ironically, just as food shortages have been largely conquered in industrialized countries, so has come a recognition that ill-health arising from food is now a major public health cost. We seem to know that diet and physical activity are critical determinants of physical and mental well-being, and can substantially increase life expectancy, yet seem strangely unable to do anything about changing an inevitable slide into deep trouble.[4]

The average diet has changed substantially in the UK over the past half century. According to the National Food Survey, which has been recording weekly household consumption of food since the war years of the 1940s, the average Briton now consumes less milk/cream, eggs, vegetables, bread, direct sugar, fish and fats, and more cheese, fresh fruit, cereals and meat than in the 1940s and 1950s. Consumption of sugar, meat, eggs, milk/cream and fats rose until the 1970s, but has since fallen back. Of particular concern for public health is the 34 per cent fall in vegetables consumed over fifty years and the 60 per cent decline in fish consumption. On the other hand, the consumption of fresh fruit (mainly as juice) has increased by 129 per cent – though this still leaves the UK the third lowest in the EU (fruit consumption ranges from 400 grams per day in Greece to 100 grams in Iceland). Vegetable consumption in Europe ranges from 440 grams daily in Greece to 60 grams in Iceland, with the UK somewhere in the middle at 280 grams per day.[5]

At first sight, this data may not be as expected. We appear to be eating more fruit and less direct sugar and oils, more cereal and fewer eggs. In addition, total energy intake in the home increased to a peak in the 1970s, and then fell during a period in which obesity has substantially increased. Surely, then, things ought to be getting better. Two factors here are explanatory. Increases in energy intake outside the home have played a critical role (we now eat much less at home than we used to), particularly the consumption of fast food and soft drinks. At the same time, all types of physical activity have declined and this has had a substantial impact on body energy balance. Thus, although diets have shown some improvements over the past 25 years, we are still consuming too many fats and sugars, and not burning off these calories, to maintain physical well-being.

Let us pause for a visit to a fast food outlet, and see what is being eaten. You do not need to go far to find one. In every town in Europe and North America, and increasingly in developing countries, there are many choices in every high street or shopping mall. What will you get for your money? A large cheeseburger contains 1000kcal of energy (and 75g of fat), and large fries add another 590kcal (and 28g of fat). A soda adds 400kcal and a deluxe desert another 435kcal (and 18g of fat). This is one single meal, a max choice, but not the largest supersize (think of those monster thickburgers now becoming popular), and it gives 2400kcal and 120g of fat in one dose (the original McDonald's meals of the 1950s contained just 590kcal). And how do you feel two hours later – in need of another meal, or able to survive on an apple or two for the rest of the day? In one meal, you have all the calories you need for a whole day – for an adult male, daily guidelines are only 2500–3000kcal (with a maximum consumption of 90g of fat). Yet the average American diet now provides 3800kcal per day, up by 500kcal since 1970 (a typical thanksgiving meal can give some 7000kcal). This is well over the energy requirement for inactive women and men, and now is the cause of many health problems.[6]

Pause, too, for an evolutionary perspective on these modern diets. As hunter-gatherers, humans would have craved fat and sugar. These were difficult to obtain – ripened berries were available only at certain times of the year, and wild meat is very lean (which is why bones are cracked open for the fatty marrow). Among current hunter-gatherer communities, there is almost no evidence of obesity, heart disease, high blood pressure and type II diabetes. Wild meat is also less energy dense than modern meats: caribou, pheasant, beaver, rabbit, moose, duck, salmon and trout contain about half of the energy of domestic-reared meat products. They also contain a third more protein, a quarter of the total fat, a fifth of the saturated fat, twice the iron and three times the vitamin C. Only when the hunter-gatherers settle and change diets do the afflictions begin for them.[7]

We are designed to survive times of scarcity by gaining weight in the good times. People who did not fatten up after food was temporarily abundant, after the hunt or more recently after the harvest, could not survive when times became scarce. An important time seems to be during pregnancy, as the foetus appears to set its metabolism according to the prevailing nutrition conditions. During periods of food shortage, women have smaller babies, but these are more prone to heart disease and diabetes in adulthood if they live in environments with access to abundant food. But if these children who have been programmed to store energy as fat were to live in times of famine, then they would survive better.[8]

When there is famine, the body hoards calories as best it can, which is why dieting is so hard (scarcity results in the body slowing down its metabolic rate to save calories). When there is plenty, calories are stored as fat. And plenty there is – the three companies of Burger King, McDonald's and Tricon Global (owners of Taco Bell, Pizza Hut and KFC) have 60,000 restaurants worldwide, employing 3.7 million people. This junk food is a wonderful option in evolutionary terms (densely concentrated calories), but only if we do not eat another such meal soon after. In the boom and bust conditions of hunter-gatherers, calories are a luxury, especially sweet and fatty ones. In our modern lifestyles, they are the road to ruin.

But we do seem to love this ruin. The average American eats three hamburgers and four portions of fries per week, and some 90 per cent of children between three and nine years of age visit fast food restaurants and their enticing play areas at least once per month. On average, adults consume 600 cans of soda per year, more than 250 litres each (up from 35 litres in the early 1950s). Each 12 ounce (330ml) can contains ten teaspoons of sugar, and a teenager drinks two cans per day. The largest soda drink of the 1950s is now called child size. Yet all these sodas do is to deliver empty calories: they add to the sugar burden but do not reduce appetite. In 1970 Americans spent $6 billion on junk food; by 2000 the amount had risen to about $115 billion per year.[9]

The curious thing is that we do know what is the gold standard diet. It is the so-called Mediterranean diet identified by Ancel Keys in the 1960s. It is high in fruit, vegetables and carbohydrates, low in meat, with some fish, olive oil (an unsaturated fat) and some red wine for the protective anti-oxidants. Such a diet seems to make us well – or at least protect against ill-health. It is the source of the public health messages that encourage us to eat five fruit and vegetable portions a day. Again, we know about these targets, but cannot seem to do anything much about them (except put on weight). In the UK, one in five children eat no fruit or vegetables, and three in five no leafy vegetables. The WHO goal is 400 grams per day.[10]

Meat remains a controversy. Is its consumption a good or a bad thing? Vegetarians have concluded bad, and for a variety of ethical, animal welfare and energetic reasons eat none at all. For many people in developing countries, meat is a speciality food eaten once or twice a week. For some hunter-gatherer groups, particularly in the Arctic and sub-Arctic, on the other hand, wild meat is their mainstay. But in industrialized countries, domesticated meat is now consumed in huge quantities. Americans, again, lead the way at 100kg per person per year. The average Briton consumes 70kg, the average Chinese still less than 10kg. Some have argued that the adoption of meat-rich diets by increasingly wealthy populations in developing countries could put unbearable pressure on the world food system, but much depends on how the meat is raised. One kilogram of feedlot-raised beef requires seven kilograms of cereal and 100,000 litres of water, a kilogram of pork some four kilograms of cereal, and a kilogram of chicken two kilograms of cereal. Some 75 per cent of cereal in industrialized countries and 37 per cent in developing countries is now fed directly to animals. Such modern meat lacks many of the nutrients and vitamins of wild meat and is higher in saturated fats. Yet other meat, such as grass-land-raised beef, can have a quite different input and quality profile. So we eat more meat, but because it is now largely produced in intensive conditions to increase economic efficiency, it is less good for our health.[11]

Diet-related illness now has severe and costly public health consequences. According to the Eurodiet study published in 2001, in the second half of the 20th century, most of Europe saw:

> *a very substantial increase in a number of chronic diseases in adult life. These become worse with age and are multifactorial. The principal factors, however, are diet and inactivity in coronary heart disease, strokes, obesity, maturity onset diabetes mellitus, gall-stones, osteoporosis and several cancers.*

Worse still, it concluded that 'disabilities associated with high intakes of saturated fat and inadequate intakes of vegetable and fruit, together with a sedentary lifestyle, exceed the cost of tobacco use'. Some problems arise from nutritional deficiencies of iron, iodide, folic acid, vitamin D and omega-3 polyunsaturated fatty acids, but much more serious is the excess consumption of energy and fat (causing obesity), sodium as salt (high blood pressure), saturated and trans fats (heart disease) and refined sugars (diabetes and dental caries). Diet is also a factor in about a third of cancer cases in industrialized countries.[12]

Perhaps unsurprisingly, it is North America that leads the way in food over-consumption and its dire health consequences. Instead of a stringy, lean rabbit cooked over an open fire, Lennie and George would today be able to go supersize for another 79 cents at the local fast food takeaway. They might not have got into as much social trouble, but Lennie could well have died as early as he did in the story. Worryingly, it is not only North Americans and Europeans who have become overweight. In some developing countries, such as Brazil, Columbia, Costa Rica, Cuba, Chile, Ghana, Mexico, Peru and Tunisia, overweight people now outnumber the hungry. Across the world, there are thought to be about a billion people overweight, of whom 300 million are obese.[13]

The prevalence of overweight and obese people is measured by body mass index (BMI is calculated by dividing your weight in kilograms by the square of your height in metres). A score of 25 to 30 puts you into an overweight category, more than 30 is obese. Less than 20 is underweight. It is not a perfect measure, as some athletes with high muscle mass (muscles weigh more than fat) can appear in an obese category but are clearly not unwell. However, it is widely accepted as a good proxy for the whole population, as it closely correlates with body fat. By the early 2000s, 30 per cent of American adults (some 60 million people) had a BMI of 30 or more – up from 23 per cent in the early 1990s and from just 15 per cent in the late 1970s. Altogether, 65 per cent of adults are overweight, with a BMI of 25 or more (up from 47 per cent in the 1970s and 56 per cent in the late 1980s/early 1990s). Some 16 per cent of children (9 million) aged 6–19 are now overweight, up threefold since the 1980s. The US Centers for Disease Control and Prevention has published annual maps showing the proportion of obese people per state since the mid-1980s, and these echo all the patterns of the spread of an infectious disease. What is worrying is that there is no sign that the expansion is going to slow, let alone come to a halt. People are trying – some $33 billion is spent on diet products and weight-loss programmes each year – but all this expenditure cannot seem to reverse these trends.[14]

Europe is catching up quickly. Obesity now affects one to two in ten of the adult population of Europe, and excess weight (BMI greater than 25) affects a majority of middle-aged adults. In the UK, 6 per cent of the adult population was obese in the mid-1980s; in twenty years this rose to more than 22 per cent. Where do we go from here? Downwards it seems, for we are storing up problems for future generations. In the early 2000s, it was found that a third of boys and girls aged 2–15 in the UK were at least overweight, and a sixth obese. The likelihood of obesity is ten times greater for children if both parents are obese, and obesity during childhood tends to persist into adulthood. Childhood obesity also greatly increases the likelihood of acquiring type II diabetes in adulthood, and some have said that this generation of children may substantially pre-decease its parents. It is almost too much to bear. It is only half a century since fifteen continuous years of food rationing ended in the UK.

Americans spend more than $100 billion on fast food each year, and companies spend $34 billion on fast food advertising persuading the public to buy it. The costs of overweight and obesity (caused by both diets and physical inactivity) are estimated to be $117 billion per year. Each obese person costs the health system $1250 per year more than non-obese people. Obesity affects lifestyles and well-being and contributes to many additional causes of ill-health, particularly heart disease and type II diabetes. Yet, in a troubling echo of the controversies about smoking and the emergence of evidence on cause and effect, there has now emerged a contrarian movement. According to lawyer Paul Campos, author of *The Diet Myth*, obesity is all a conspiracy of doctors who run diet clinics, and he stated that 'the current war on fat is an irrational outburst of cultural hysteria, unsupported by sound science'.

Quoting figures that show life expectancy rose from 75 to 77 years in the 1990s (without taking account of how changes in infant mortality affect such statistics), Campos says, 'the medical literature simply does not support the claim that higher than average weight is a significant important health risk'. He is right in some ways – the war on fat may be creating social pariahs out of people who are overweight, and who are assailed with daily images of the thin and beautiful, but some statements are breathtaking: 'what we should not be doing is telling Americans that they will improve their health by trying to lose weight'. Nonetheless, the controversy continues, with one epidemiological study suggesting that being in the overweight category may protect against mortality, yet agreeing that being obese does increase mortality. These contrarian views, however, do not take into account certain medical treatments – drugs to combat hypertension and high cholesterol, for example, are increasingly keeping overweight people alive. Like many scientific controversies, the oxygen of publicity seems to burn more for those who believe in conspiracy, even thought the vast majority of scientific evidence points in the other direction.[15]

Another reason why it is difficult to attribute cause and effect to food consumption and health outcomes is that physical activity plays an equally important role in weight regulation. High food consumption is fine provided all the excess calories are burned off by activity. But just a small excess above requirements quickly leads to problems – 200 grams of fast food once per week above energy needs will lead to the putting on of 4 kilograms of weight in a year. Unfortunately, over the same period that modern foods have become abundant and available, there has been a catastrophic fall in physical activity. People in both industrialized countries and urban settlements in developing countries have become increasingly sedentary in all aspects of daily life, including during leisure time, in travelling to and from work, and during work itself. In Europe, the fall in physical activity over the past 50 years results in 2MJ (500kcal) less energy output per day in adults aged 20–60. According to the National Audit Office, an adult 50 years ago did the equivalent of a marathon each week more exercise than the average adult today.[16] Yet this problem has crept up, almost without anyone noticing, and the public health consequences have only recently begun to be widely accepted. As the Eurodiet study states, 'the importance of physical activity has been underestimated for many years by both doctors and policy-makers'.

Although similar trends have occurred across Europe and North America, the UK compares badly with many countries. Jobs themselves have become less physical, people are more likely to take the lift than walk the stairs, and adults and children are more likely to travel to work or school by car than to walk or cycle. In the mid-1980s, two-thirds of primary school children walked to school, but by 2000 this had fallen to just over a half, with car travel increasingly becoming the norm. In the UK, the distance walked per year by each adult has fallen from 410km in the mid-1970s to 298km in 2000. Walking has declined across the whole of the EU since 1970. Cycling varies from an annual low of 70km in Greece to a high of 900km in Denmark and the Netherlands, with the UK again well below the average at 200km per person. Our dependence on the car is further illustrated by the fact that the UK is one of only four EU countries in which bus and coach travel has declined since 1980 (the others are Germany, Finland and the Netherlands). The 20 per cent fall in the UK compares badly with a 40–80 per cent increase in Denmark, Italy, Spain and Portugal. Over the same period, car travel per person in the UK increased by 51 per cent, and the road system has lengthened by 34,000km since the early 1960s.[17]

In the US, the 1996 report of the Surgeon General was the first to document similar alarming declines in physical activity and consequent effects on ill-health. It found that six out of ten Americans are not regularly active, and a quarter are not active at all. Just 15 per cent of adults exercise vigorously at least three times per week for 20 minutes, and just one in five engage five times per week in 30 minutes or more of sustained physical activity of any type. In young people, physical activity is lowest during adolescence. Of those reporting regular physical activity, 44 per cent engaged in walking for exercise, 25–30 per cent in gardening, yard work or stretching exercises, 10–15 per cent in stair climbing, riding a bicycle or exercise bike, or weight lifting, 5–10 per cent in running, swimming or aerobic dancing or basketball, and less than 5 per cent in tennis, bowling, golf, baseball, squash, football or skiing.

Although there is no clear data to establish long-term trends, it is clear that lifestyles have changed fundamentally, and that it will already be difficult to change them. According to the Surgeon General:

> most Americans today are spared the burden of excessive physical labour. Indeed few occupations today require significant physical activity, and most people use motorized transportation to get to work and to perform routine errands and tasks. Even leisure time is increasingly filled with sedentary behaviour.

Echoing Barry Popkin's phrase, 'the nutrition transition', it is clear that modern societies have also gone through an 'activity transition' in the past two to three generations. And this transition has significant health consequences for whole populations. Physical activity is known to reduce the risk of dying from coronary heart disease, and also reduces the risk of developing diabetes, hypertension and colon cancer. It enhances mental health, fosters healthy muscles and bones, and helps maintain health and independence in older adults.[18]

Compared with active people, those who are sedentary have up to a twofold increased risk of dying early, with levels of cardiovascular fitness strongly associated with overall mortality. Adults reduce their risk of death by a third if they walk fifteen or more kilometres per week, by a quarter if they climb 55 or more flights of stairs a week, and by a half with three or more hours per week of moderate sports activity. There also appears to be a protective effect in later life – the effects of activity early in life persist into the 70s and 80s. Nonetheless, taking up activity later in life can also be protective, with men aged 45–84 who take up moderately intense sports adding on average 0.72 years to their lifespan. The Surgeon General's report concludes that 'regular physical activity and higher cardiovascular fitness decrease overall mortality rates in a dose–response fashion' – thus, the more exercise, the better for personal and public health.

The World Health Organization now indicates that in industrialized countries physical inactivity is one of the ten principal causes of death, leading to 1.9 million deaths worldwide annually. According to the Department of Health, physical inactivity levels account for the following disability-adjusted life years:

23 per cent of cardiovascular disease in men and 22 per cent in women, 16 per cent of colon cancer in men and 17 per cent in women, 15 per cent of type II diabetes, 12 per cent of strokes in men and 17 per cent in women, and 11 per cent of breast cancer.

The risk of developing type II diabetes (non-insulin-dependent diabetes) is increased by a third to a half in inactive people compared with physically active individuals. Regular exercise can reduce this risk by up to 64 per cent, therefore offering a preventive effect. Moderate intensity activity also facilitates improved blood glucose control in sufferers of type II diabetes. And more significant effects are observed with more intense physical activity. Consequently, the risk of all-cause mortality in patients with type II diabetes is diminished with moderate to high levels of physical fitness.[19]

But how do these declines in average activity square with the increase in provision of gyms and other opportunities for people to stay fit? Part of the problem is that home life has also become more sedentary, and though gym and fitness club membership has risen in the past twenty years, there are indications that people are becoming less likely to engage in organized sports. In the UK, there have also been falls in the provision of opportunities for physical exercise in schools, linked not least to sales of playing fields in the 1980s and 1990s. The proportion of young people spending two hours or more per week on physical exercise fell from 46 per cent in 1994 to 37 per cent in 1999. The average young person also spent 26 hours per week watching television in the 1990s compared with 13 hours in the 1960s. For children aged 3–12, the amount of time spent outdoors per day has halved from 86 to 42 minutes since the early 1980s.[20]

One long-term problem is that physically inactive children tend to become physically inactive adults, and in the UK only a third of adults take thirty minutes of moderate exercise five times a week, the minimum recommended to maintain optimal health. In almost all activities (except swimming and yoga), female participation is lower than male. In the group aged 16–24, 42 per cent of men and 68 per cent of women are inactive, and these proportions rise steadily as people age. But this trend is not the same everywhere – in Sweden and Finland, in particular, participation in organized sport increases among older people. One of the major concerns is that although eight out of ten people in the UK correctly believe that regular exercise is good for their health, a majority wrongly believe that they take enough exercise to stay fit and well.

But there is another benefit on top of physical health. An active lifestyle can also enhance psychological well-being. Regular physical activity is linked with four types of favourable psychological outcomes: enhanced mood, stress reduction, a more positive self-concept and higher quality of life. Specific groups, including the clinically depressed or anxious individuals, heart disease patients, and the elderly, may experience even more marked and distinct psychological benefits.

Interestingly, certain foods can also have a positive effect on mood, though poor mood can itself stimulate the choice of unhealthy food options. Recent years have seen the discovery of a range of signal compounds in the body that affect appetite. One of these, leptin, is secreted by fat cells, and the signal is read by the hypothalamus in the brain, which coordinates eating behaviour. Leptin levels thus tell the brain about the amount of fat reserves. However, people who gain weight develop a resistance to leptin, with the hypothalamus progressively interpreting high levels of leptin as normal. When levels fall, the brain thinks starvation is coming, and encourages food consumption. Omega-3 unsaturated fats, which are common in wild meat and fish, but rare in domestic livestock, are now known to affect neurotransmitters such as serotonin, and therefore can have a direct effect on mood. Omega-3 fats also appear to have marked effects on brain development in children (perhaps the reason why we were told as children to eat up our fish as it would make us clever), as well as having a positive effect on the immune system.[21]

One question that David Benton at the University of Wales has asked, then, is whether a good diet can keep you happy. A bad mood stimulates the eating of high carbohydrate and high fat foods that stimulate the release of endorphins. High carbohydrate diets can also stimulate the release of tryptophan, which is transformed in the brain to serotonin, which has a calming effect, as well as elevating self-esteem and feelings of optimism. A good balanced breakfast has been shown to improve memory and cognitive performance. Mental health is improved by foods high in omega-3 fats, vitamin B, zinc and magnesium, and proteins containing tryptophan.[22]

The level of weekly physical activity required to achieve general health benefits has led to the development of a universal recommendation by the UK Department of Health. We should participate in activity 'at least 30 minutes a day, of at least a moderate intensity, on five or more days of the week'. Accomplishing this target would enhance psychological well-being, reduce the risk of premature death from cardiovascular disease and certain cancers and significantly diminish the risk of developing type II diabetes. Appropriate activities include brisk walking, cycling, and certain garden and domestic activities, as well as more formal structured sports and leisure activities. Walking 10,000 steps a day is good for health; 20,000 can lead to weight loss (put your pedometer on now).[23]

But it will not be easy to reach these targets. A dramatic cultural modification is going to be needed. Many people wrongly believe they are already active enough, and there are many barriers relating not only to the costs of participating in terms of both time and expense but also from feeling that the activity does not belong in a particular environment. Walking may be a good thing, but how easy is it if you live in a neighbourhood with no pavements or sidewalks? Gyms and fitness centres also appear to be full of fit people, which decreases the attractiveness of these places for overweight or unfit people. The active are already fit, but the sofa-dwellers find it hard to get up and be active. This raises many questions about urban design, car use and transportation, and the use of labour-saving devices in the home. A pessimistic view would be that these are now so accepted as the norm that it will be extremely difficult to get whole populations to be at least reasonably active.[24]

Unfortunately, individuals with sedentary lifestyles also impose costs on others, as public money must be spent to care for them when ill. For policymakers, the irony is that if public money were to be spent to reduce ill-health and thus make people live longer, then this may well increase health care costs. However, only a perverse accounting approach would suggest that this was a cost rather than a benefit arising from longer lives. The costs of over-consumption of calories combined with sedentary lifestyles are staggering. In the UK, the costs of physical inactivity are roughly the same as the costs of obesity. Assuming a full range of effects of physical inactivity, including depression, the total cost is £8.2 billion per year (comprising £1.7 billion direct health care costs for the NHS, £5.4 billion in earnings lost due to sickness absence and £1 billion in earnings lost to premature mortality). Each day, 235 people die prematurely due to the effects of physical inactivity. Clearly, any increase in physical activity coupled with better diets could bring substantial public benefits through avoided costs, plus personal benefits for the people involved. For the US, the economic cost of diet- and exercise-related illness amounts to $137 billion per year, and compares with costs of alcohol abuse at $118 billion and of smoking at $90 billion. Diet and inactivity account for between 100,000 and 300,000 deaths per year, second only to tobacco.[25]

So where does nature come into all this? Did Lennie and George's lifestyle – one life cut short though it was – have anything going for it? They were physically active, ate moderately but apparently sufficiently, but could only dream of luxuries, which for them were pork, salmon and tomatoes. Today, we have access to all the luxuries, but can only dream of a lifestyle that would keep us well. We know that exposure to nature is good for us; perhaps we should emulate our hunter-gatherer forebears by undertaking physical activity in the presence of nature? Such green exercise brings mental and physical health benefits, as well as improving our knowledge of green places and associated biodiversity. This suggests that the countryside, from the grandest national parks to the most local reserves, together with urban parks and city gardens, should all be seen as part of a national health service. They are places where we can burn off excess calories and perhaps contemplate a little on food and where it comes from, since our food choices, shaped by advertising as well as appetites, affect our health and the health of environments where the food is grown. We just may have an opportunity to keep the fat on the land, and off ourselves.

But it may need some novel policies to help, one particularly good example of this coming from North Karelia in Finland. Dietary ill-health was recognized as a serious problem in the early 1970s, and a series of policies was put in place to encourage consumption of low fat diets, better labelling of foods and better quality foods in schools. These resulted in a threefold increase in vegetable intake by the late 1990s, a doubling of fish consumption and a large reduction in consumption of saturated fats. And one result of this has been a sharp fall in mortality from coronary heart disease.[26] The daily decisions are ultimately ours to make, but these are shaped in turn by the choices in the consumption environment around us. If we can access and afford distinctive foods that come from recognized landscapes, then there is a possibility of using food to link to memories and images of places. In such a way, food becomes less of a commodity and more something to celebrate. It becomes a broader responsibility. Whether this might begin to change the world food system is, however, quite another matter.

9

Little Houses on the Prairie

Thomas Jefferson's ideas about the fundamental value of family farms in rural communities are still fondly remembered today. His father was the one of the first settlers in Albermarle County in southwest Virginia. Thomas was born in 1743, and when his father died in 1757, he was left 2000 hectares of land, to which he later added another 2000 hectares. After being elected as representative of Albermarle at the age of 26, he then moved to Monticello, where he built a house on a wooded summit, which he said had a 'splendid panorama of nature, waves of forest, rolling hills and deep valleys, sharply edged to the west, against the noble background of the Blue Ridge'. He saw in the environment around him 'an immensity of land courting the industry of the husbandman', and believed farming was an essential part of a virtuous way of life, thus securing dignity and independence.

Sadly, Jefferson would not make money out of farming (though he did from land speculation). At the time, it was often cheaper to buy a new acre of land than improve an old one, and many parts of Virginia quickly became degraded. But Jefferson was concerned more with the moral values of agriculture than the economic and he is remembered for this agrarian legacy. He idealized those who tilled the land and believed the progress of agriculture was closely associated with an increase in human happiness. At his retirement, he declared 'no occupation is so delightful to me as the culture of the earth'.

It was his strong defence of small-scale land ownership that shaped generations of cultural values about the land. Some commentators have since argued that his agrarian views were no more than archaic and obsolete – they do not fit with many modern ideas of agricultural efficiency. He also advanced agriculture as superior to other forms of subsistence, such as hunting and gathering. But Jefferson wanted farming to promote fundamental values forged by human labour, moral imagination and continued engagement with nature, and he stated that 'these virtues that grow out of the agrarian life are concerned with care and cultivation of self, family and the land'. The life on the land and the varying seasons promoted for Jefferson a spirit of 'permanent improvement, quiet life and orderly conduct both in public and in private'.

He also linked these concepts about care for the land to civic independence and political free-thinking:

> *cultivators of the earth are the most valuable citizens. They are the most vigorous, the most independent, the most virtuous, and they are tied to the country and wedded to its liberty by the most lasting bonds.*[1]

In 1785 he said, 'small landholders are the most precious part of the state'. How things have changed. What would he now make of the closure of more than 200 US farms on every single day in the second half of the 20th century? After Jefferson's death, though, US farm numbers were still rising, and grew from one million in the 1850s to more than six million in the 1930s. They then fell dramatically to less than two million – all in the name of an idea about a particular kind of progress. And this fall has been echoed in most industrialized countries. Economic efficiency has to mean fewer and larger farms, and if some cultural values are lost as the small farms slip away, then that is simply the price to be paid for progress.

Jefferson's ideals were later perfectly captured for many thousands of families by Laura Ingalls Wilder in her series of *Little House on the Prairie* books. Written in the 1930s, they tell the story of Pa and Ma and their three girls, who leave the Big Woods of Wisconsin because they feel hemmed in by too many incomers arriving on wagons, 'slowly creaking by'. Wild animals would not stay in a country when there were so many people, according to Pa, so they decided to go west to 'Indian country', just as Wilder herself had done on a covered wagon. In the West, they understood that the 'land was level, and there were no trees. The grass grew thick and high, [and] the wild animals wandered'. The family put all their belongings on a wagon, and cross the wide states of Minnesota, Iowa, Missouri and Kansas, where 'day after day, they saw nothing but the rippling grass and enormous sky'. Wallace Stegner, in *Wolf Willow*, called this land 'an ocean of wind-troubled grass and grain [where the] drama of landscape is in the sky, pouring with light and always moving'.[2]

The landscape is full of gentle hills, open sunny places, rushing creeks and distant wild animals; of corncakes and sizzling pork frying on the open fire; and of this contented family heading west until they stop to build a house, where there is 'nothing but grassy prairie spreading to the edge of the sky'. They make a home of logs, and Pa plays his fiddle to a singing nightingale. Over time the prairie is ploughed, and the land transformed. The Indians, as they are called, end up peacefully riding away further to the west, when they are at first minded to take some revenge for losing their land. Later, the family leaves too, travelling onwards with wagon to resettle again on another part of the frontier.

What is striking is the discord between these tender cultural images (and some 30 million copies of Wilder's books were sold and read) and today's reality for many rural towns in the Mid-west. Wes Jackson set up the Land Institute in Salinas, Kansas, to create a new vision for these emptying prairies. They also have a presence in the small town of Matfield Green which is, he says:

> *typical of countless towns throughout the Midwest and Great Plains. People have left, people are leaving, buildings are falling down or burning down. Fourteen of the houses here that do still have people have only one person, usually a widow or widower.*

The aim of the Land Institute is to find ways to allow people to become native to their places, and in the Mid-west this means recreating the tall grass prairie in places and breathing life into rural towns.[3]

This will need stepwise changes in thinking, as past incrementalism has only worked to remove all sorts of people from the land. Sitting in his 75-year-old house, 'abandoned more times than anyone can recall', Jackson describes the sad decline of the town's life:

> *I can see the abandoned lumberyard across the street next to the abandoned hardware store. Out another window is the back of the old creamery that now stores junk [...] from a different window, I can see the bank, which closed in 1929 and paid off ten cents to the dollar. [...] Around the corner is an abandoned service station. There were once four! Across the street is the former barber shop. [...] This story can be repeated thousands of times across our land.*

Are we content to allow many rural communities in modern industrialized countries to die these kinds of slow death? It is not just happening in the US. In the Mediterranean countries, the emptying of rural settlements is called desertification:

several million farms have closed in France and in Japan over the past fifty years. Is there no hope, then, for family farms in the face of continuing global changes in our industrialized farm and food systems? Or perhaps there is, as the best signs of a new kind of progress are coming from developing countries, where many farmers have either avoided the great modernizing pressures or have found the space in their economic landscapes to innovate and create farming patterns that are friendly to both people and environments.

The three states of Paraná, Santa Catarina and Rio Grande do Sul comprise the most southern of Brazil's regions and produce a per capita economic output considerably greater than the national average. Most of this economic success is based on an agrarian structure that maintains small family farms on many parts of the land. The region is also home to traditional gauchos, cattle ranches with their sweeping South American prairies. Migrants first arrived on the coast of Santa Catarina in about 1700, from the Azores, and established what is now the capital city of Florianópolis, a settlement of pastel and stucco buildings sprawling by the vivid blue Atlantic and now dissected by modern highways. Later waves of farmer settlers came from Germany, Ukraine and Italy. Small farms still dominate the land, with just under a half of Santa Catarina's properties being less than ten hectares in size.

If you travel inland from the narrow subtropical coastal plain, you soon climb into the Sierra Geral range, which rises sharply up to rolling hills of up to 1000 metres above sea level. The coastal ecosystem is replaced by the planalto's long, sweeping valleys, which are cool, even cold, in winter, and tropical in summer. One hundred years ago, 85 per cent of the state was under forest; now less than a third is. But these new farms on the slopes brought their own problems. They lose water rapidly when rain falls, and soil erosion had become a serious statewide agricultural problem by the early 1990s. It was at this time that the state government's research and extension agency, EPAGRI, began its *microbacias* programme, working in more than 500 catchments to encourage all farmers to adopt conservation tillage methods to cut erosion and conserve water. They worked in 200 municipalities, and helped conservation tillage to spread from 100,000 to more than 1 million hectares by the early 2000s. The critical part of the process was the attempt to develop an explicitly participatory approach, working closely with farmers on technology development and innovation. As a result, more than 100,000 farmers have benefited, as their yields have increased while input costs have fallen. In this young farmed landscape, farmers have already moved away from ploughing, as if it were a short-term aberration rather than a fundamental agricultural practice of some ten thousand years. Adopting zero-tillage methods requires many innovations – new ways of direct seeding or rotary hoeing, roller-blades for cutting cover crops, mini-tractors and carts, some hand-pulled, some drawn by animals, others motorized. A variety of farmers' associations have emerged to help in technology development and sharing, and there are 6000 groups sharing machinery, thus enabling farmers to access technologies that would normally only be available to large operators.[4]

It is in one of these long valleys, Ituporanga, that groups of farmers are engaged in an ecological and social experiment. At the top end, where forests still crest the hills, is the 17-hectare property of Afonso Klöppel, just 10 hectares of which is farmed. In the mid-1990s, Afonso converted his farm to organic production, though more out of desperation than real hope. The land had become degraded, and his very basis for food production was under threat. He had been growing onions and tobacco, and then onions alone, but was no longer able to compete with larger growers elsewhere. He could well have gone the way of those many small farmers in North America, except that EPAGRI encouraged a group of farmers to travel to Rio Grande do Sul to see how farmers there had been able to cope. They heard about the value of working together, and this encouraged Afonso and his neighbours to set up an association of their own. Working together is critical when large changes in our lives are to be made. Having a friend or neighbour to share the experience, to provide moral support, to succeed and to fail as you do, is an essential prerequisite for most landscape transformations. The fear of failure is enormous. It keeps people awake at night, it gnaws and worries at the edge of consciousness. Crossing the mental frontier is not easy, and most of us need some help, even if the local associations do not last forever.

Afonso uses agroecological approaches on his farm and now grows more than fifty crops, including vegetables and herbs (radishes, onions, garlic, oregano, parsley, lettuce, squash, ginger, potatoes, tomatoes, sugar cane and brassicas), cereals and legumes (maize, oats, peas and various beans) and fruits (apples, oranges and grapes). He raises pigs and chickens and has plans for a fish pond. He remembers that 'this area was so bad, a lot of erosion; the land needed repairing'. His main method of repair is the nitrogen-fixing mucuna bean and crotolaria. Mucuna is widely grown in Brazil as a green manure and cover crop. It's a modern magic bean, fixing up to 150kg of nitrogen per hectare each year and producing huge amounts of leafy material, which is allowed to fall on the soil and become incorporated to improve soil structure. A healthy soil is the basis for a healthy farm.

Afonso smiles, 'after three years, the soil was very well, and there was no problem with insect pests'. The soil is now dark and rich in organic matter, in contrast to a neighbour's farm, where the farmer still maintains the old (so-called modern) ways. Afonso does not use herbicides for the zero-tillage, preferring 'just hard work'. We walk down through the farm, admiring the mixtures of crops sweeping around hillside's contours. The wind drives up the valley, chilling our bones, and rolling grey clouds bring new squalls of rain. We look over the fence, and see a different type of farm. This neighbour has reportedly said, 'yours is not a farm; how are you making money?' He thinks the cocktail of crops on the farm looks a mess. It does seem curious that an idea about what he thinks is best could stop the neighbour from seeing an important truth.

There are a number of farmers' associations in the valley with several hundred members. But even with all this organization and transformation, how can they possibly succeed on such small amounts of land? The trick comes in another sort of connectivity – that to consumers. These farms do not just produce many different crops and animals, they convert them into foods that people want, and try their best to sell direct to consumers. Under the brand name of *'cultivando o futuro'*, Afonso has his own on-farm agro-industry, producing molasses, tomato sauce, cheese, honey, pickles, jams and preserved fruits. He sells boxes of produce directly to twenty families, and there are a similar number on the waiting list. Each box is individually adapted for each consumer. He also sells to supermarkets in Ituporanga and Florianópolis and even into distant Rio de Janeiro. They seem to like the diversity and quality of his produce.

Farmers elsewhere in the world have much to learn from the sophistication of this marketing operation. Success lies in connectivity to the land, to fellow farmers and to consumers. Afonso uses the internet to stay in touch with customers and fellow farmers and says 'sometimes you learn more than you can teach in these associations'. But you suspect that he does have more to teach. Further down the valley, other farmers have got some of the message. Alidor and Nair Correa farm seven hectares of a twenty-hectare farm dominated by towering remnant forest. They are not part of an association, and cultivate mainly onions, with millet and sunflower as the summer cover crop and oats and mucuna as winter cover crops. They adopted zero-tillage methods eight years earlier, and Alidor smiles when he looks at the soil. Onion productivity has doubled, there is less work needed on the farm and so need for expensive soil conservation structures as the non-tilled soil no longer erodes. But damage by thrips has increased as more farmers have taken up onion growing in this part of the valley, and so they have had to increase insecticide and herbicide use. Some of these products are harmful. Nair says she warns him, but Alidor still does not use protective clothing for spraying or gloves during mixing.

In Brazil, the term agro-industry does not have some of the negative connotations now common in English-speaking countries. Farmers know they will not survive on ecological transformations alone. They have to grow plants and raise animals that can be sold to consumers, and sold at a price that will make them a living. And they have to do this while competing with increasingly dominant, and more international, corporations, which have been enormously successful at adding value to food commodities and getting them to consumers in forms they seem to like. The problem, though, centres on the desires that we may have for a certain sort of landscape supported by a certain type of community structure, and the linkages between the two. If farm operations have to get larger to compete on national and global markets, and if success is primarily measured on how costs can be driven down, then the small farmer is doomed the world over. They will be remembered only as a relic, a quirk of another distant Jeffersonian age.

For small farmers to succeed, they have to find ways of converting primary produce into added-value foodstuffs for consumers. And this is where the development of small-scale agro-industry in southern Brazil works so well. Chapecó is the main city of the west of Santa Caterina state, close to the border with Argentina and Paraguay. A city of one million people built on steep hills, it was established at the beginning of the 20th century, yet still feels like a dynamic frontier town. Like most settlements in the region, the economy is dominated by large agro-industrial complexes using pigs and poultry. Around Chapecó is the largest concentration of pigs in Brazil. Most farmers are engaged in contract farming for these companies – they raise the animal produce to order, and get the price offered.

Once again, however, some farmers in new associations using ecological approaches are crossing new frontiers. They seem unlikely to threaten the big operators, but who knows in the long run? The Lovera's farm is about ten hectares in size, mostly pasture, about one hour out of Chapecó down a dusty red track. They keep about 100 pigs, plus poultry and dairy cattle, and grow vegetables and fruit, all organically. The Loveras also have two pristine buildings for cheese and meat production, both of which fully meet tight hygiene standards (white hats, overshoes and showers before entry). Both are producing high-value produce for local and statewide markets. They said the biggest change over six years since conversion has been to their self-esteem – instead of being controlled by the agro-industries, they can choose what to raise and grow, when and how to market, and are fully linked to the internet and the outside world. They produce about 40kg of cheese per day, and this is vacuum-packed and labelled with their own brand name.

On the other side of the valley, the Malagutti's farm is based on both cheese and sweets, and involves the families of two brothers and a cousin. It is situated twenty minutes down a rough track from the tarmac road-head, overlooking a dramatic mosaic landscape dotted with orange groves. The families employ several local people in their cottage factory, and source milk from 72 local producers, all of whom receive a higher price as they all use organic practices. They produce 400kg of cheese each day. The women are confident and say they now have a stronger role in the household. They are members of the local women's group, which shares technical knowledge on farm and business improvements. And there are other signs of social change that could be significant. Young members of farm families are more willing to return to the farms to work and live, as the work is now varied and interesting. It is also linked directly to the outside world through marketing channels, and so families feel not only a part of their own place, but also members of a wider community. More importantly, they feel in control of their food chain, so know it is worth investing in making further improvements.

Some farmers have already taken their successes further than just farming and food. Agreco is an ecological farmers' association based in the eastern hillsides of Santa Catarina, closer to the coast. In seven years, they have already expanded their activities into ecotourism, school meals and links to wider economic development. The association was set up in the mid-1990s by a dozen families near Santa Rosa de Lima and began organic production of legumes, honey, grain and fruit. Though there are now 300 families involved in the network, Agreco does not intend to expand further (though some external advisers do want them to grow), preferring to help others to set up in the same way. Produce is now sold directly to urban consumers in mixed baskets, to selected supermarkets and to schools for children's dinners. Another innovation has been the emphasis on agritourism. They adopted the French *accueil paysan* approach, with accommodation in farm buildings, and families actively seeking to exchange and share life experiences with visitors. Agreco has gone on to form two regional forums – one to link public and private agencies, which has already had success with energy supply, rural transport and school meals, and another to link urban with rural development.

It is instructive to reflect on this alternative development model. An ecological approach to farming, organized small businesses, connections to food consumers and wider economic development. At first it was not easy, and it required vision to give it momentum. Sergio Pinheiro explains:

> *this initial resistance may be explained because individualism is normal for most people. The ability and enthusiasm to work in groups has increased among farmers, and participation and trust have grown too.*

This resistance is common elsewhere, as farmers who are not organized often feel that they will lose something by collaborating. This is odd, as such cooperation was of course fundamental to all agricultural and resource management systems throughout early history.

The Brazilian experience with farmers' associations and ecological land management arose partly because of enlightened people in government agencies, who were able both to help on the ground and to provide appropriate institutional support that created the social space for innovation. With better policy support, more might have been done. In northeast Thailand, by contrast, the organization of more than 100,000 farmers into networks also concerned with alternative land use has occurred precisely because the old (modern) agricultural approaches had abjectly failed. The northeast region has always seen itself as a little different to the rest of the country, with its Khmer influence to the east and Laotian to the north, both beyond the slow and mysterious flow of the Mekong River. It is a region of dry, sandy soils and erratic rainfall, dominated in the past by dipterocarp forest. The success elsewhere of the green revolution in raising rice productivity had only partially reached the northeast, and when the Asian economic collapse of the late 1990s occurred, many families found themselves saddled with debt for agricultural inputs that they could not pay off. In addition, the income sent by family members working in distant urban areas dried up, leaving rural families with no obvious place to turn. Sawaeng Ruaysoongnern, of Khon Kaen University, who has worked closely with these farmers networks, says that 'this extreme failure caused people to think differently'.

The first reaction from farmers was to step back from the monocultures that had become increasingly common since the 1960s and begin to recreate polycultures. They diversified with vegetables, herbs, animals, fruits and multi-purpose trees and started to organize into groups. These soon connected into networks across the region. They developed an active recruitment system – each farmer aims to recruit two more each year, and each group of ten farmers seeks to establish another group each year. The consequences have been remarkable. Farmers have become more self-sufficient, growing more of their own food, but also earning more from better links to consumers in local and regional markets. The aim is to have a million members one day – perhaps this is too ambitious, but then again, big thoughts are needed if whole regional landscapes and communities are to change for the better.

There is a great diversity in these local wisdom networks, as they are called. The Organic Rice Network in Yasothon is led by Vichit Buonsoong and has 2000 core members and more than 20,000 network members. All these farmers no longer use inorganic fertilizers and pesticides. Another network with 760 members focuses on agroforestry – though they translate this to mean more than just trees. Sawaeng explains that 'agroforestry is not about planting trees on agricultural land, but the development of new relationships between human and natural systems'. In a drier region, another network of 170 farmers in twenty villages is working to establish trees to reduce water tables and reclaim saline seeps that are threatening crops. And yet another is focusing on intensive polycultures, with the aim of producing enough food (other than rice) for an entire family from one rai of land (a sixth of a hectare) – the 'one rai per family' concept.

The average farm size for the region is less than two hectares, yet these very small farms have strength in numbers. The networks use modern technology to share knowledge, ideas and innovations where they can. They have created video profiles of individual farmers and put these on CDs to distribute across the region. These help to tell a story to consumers and policymakers too. And while these farmers' networks are beginning to influence local and national policies, many farmers say happiness is the most important thing for them – not maximizing production through debt accumulation, or sales of land for development speculation. Their model for development, therefore, is different and again instructive. Why make all this effort if you cannot be happy?

Sri Lanka is famed for its glorious tropical climate, rich culture and mostly fertile soils. Yet today many small farmers seem to struggle to make a living. As in most developing countries, policymakers are under pressure to encourage their domestic agricultural sectors to become export-focused, and if a few farmers disappear through inefficiency, then this is the price of such progress. But here there are also local organizations working with farmers to develop sustainable forms of agriculture that are both productive and diverse. One such is the Sewalanka Foundation. Sewalanka is working in the north with more than 4000 farmers organized into several hundred self-help groups. This is a region where the civil war caused severe disruption for two decades, and where since the 2002 ceasefire rural people are showing that they can create alternative futures for their communities. Head north for an hour from the ancient city of Anuradhapura, centre of a 1200-year-old Buddhist dynasty, and you come to Vavuniya, a bustling small town supported by some of the best examples of sustainable farming you can find.

We walk first across the farm of the Jayawardne family, abandoned when the conflict started. Now they have cleared two hectares of scrub and planted a complex mix of perennials and vegetables. The papaya and banana shade the chilli, onions and aubergines, and the 25 cattle provide manure for the soil. The family have a shop in the village and are proud that farmers' groups are brought from all over the country to see what can be achieved. They say, 'during the war, we didn't know whether we'd ever be able to start life again, and yet we've now achieved so much'. Their spirit of cooperation is infectious:

> It's important for us to work in groups. If we only develop ourselves, there will still be problems in the village. Our plan is to get everyone in the village working together.

In this way, small farmers can act like large farmers and sell to traders on their own terms.

A few kilometres away, Patrick Jeyabalan's family have effected another kind of transformation. They took on their one-hectare farm just two years earlier, and have already paid off the loan. At that time, only one crop was grown – it was not an unsuccessful piece of land, but certainly not a very productive one. As we walk around the farm, stooping beneath the bananas and other hanging fruit, stepping over carefully staked vegetables, listening to the chatter of distant monkeys, we count 38 types of crops. Here are limes, lemons, coconuts and guavas; over there are gourds, beans, tomatoes, chillies, capsicums, onions and cabbages. There is ground-nut and green gram, and manioc, sweet potato and maize for staples. Around the house are herbs and medicinal plants, and an enormous compost heap. Every corner of the farm is growing something useful. Who says small farmers are inefficient and unproductive?

What is also significant is that we are in Sri Lanka's dry zone, where farming is tough. But these farmers are showing that ingenuity, hard work and cooperation can transform the land. They can do this with low-cost and locally available methods, and they are improving their soils as they go. The diversity of crops is good for family diets and for pest control, and also helps with year-round marketing. These farmers are showing us that efficiency in farming does not have to be achieved through monocultures and ever-increasing farm sizes. More importantly, they are showing us that having people on the land is a good thing.

Some may say that these stories may offer hope for small farmers in tropical countries, but that their economies are so very different from those in industrialized countries that little can be transferred. But such a view is based on an idea about what is best for economic growth, not on evidence from the field. Some kinds of farming do increase the number of people on the land. One example is organic farming. We recently studied the use of labour on more than 1100 organic farms in the UK and Republic of Ireland. We found that organic farms employ 2.5 people per farm compared with 1.28 on conventional farms, which by area amounts to 4.33 people per 100 hectares (again about double that on conventional farms). In addition, small organic farms employ more people per unit area than larger ones, and indeed there is a striking linear relationship between area of farms and number of jobs per unit area. Interestingly, a quarter of all farms are involved in some on-farm process-ing of foods, and half are engaged in direct sales and marketing. They are adding value to commodities, telling a story and receiving a good proportion of the final price paid by consumers. It should be no surprise that they have developed success-ful farm models that require more labour, when the prevailing and dominant model of efficiency is to get big (or get out) and reduce labour costs.[5]

But what is the relevance for those prairies in North America that are increas-ingly being abandoned? Can the little houses return with the people? First, it is important to note that in some regions, they have never gone away. The principles of contentedness and balance are the fundamental tenets for the Amish communi-ties of Ohio and Pennsylvania. David Kline is a writer and farmer and a member of the Old Order Amish who have preserved profound connections between people and the land for generations. The Amish have kept themselves separate from much of the rest of the industrialized world, choosing not to use electricity or motorized vehicles. Their farms tell a very particular story. David has two chestnut work horses, and says of his central-Ohio farm, 'the year is a never-ending adventure'. The farm is diverse, and home to many wild birds and plants. The rhythm of the farm is the pattern of Amish life – by haymaking in June, the bird migrations are over, and meals are all strawberries, shortcakes and jams. September is for apples and sowing wheat. October is the time of the maize harvest and cider-making, and walking the woods for their spectacular colours. David was recently asked to write about the advantages and disadvantages of his way of life: 'that bothered me all summer. Quite honestly, I couldn't think of any disadvantages.' Walking around his farm, a mosaic of fields and habitats, the horses quietly chomping in the stable, you have to agree.[6]

It takes courage to maintain a strong culture in the face of so much rural change. It also takes strength to try to do something different. Head far south to North Carolina by following the migration routes of geese and butterflies, and you will come to Randolf County, where Steve Tate and his family run a 24-hectare farm called The Goat Lady Dairy. This is where cotton and tobacco once were dominant, and where farmers today struggle to make a living from these commodities. Steve, though, has a different kind of concept for his farm, some three-quarters of which is woodland. He says, 'we started by saying, what do we want to do every day when we wake up?' Their dairy produces a variety of distinctive hard and soft cheeses from the herd of thirty goats. They also run regular 'dinners-at-the-dairy', where all the served food is from the neighbourhood, and altogether 2000 people visit the farm each year. Steve says, 'we tell the story about the whole farm – never underestimate the desire of people to get in touch with the land'. Here is a tiny farm in a failing farmed landscape, and the family say happiness is the most important thing to them. What can possibly be wrong with that?

Swing north and west again into the rolling plains that once were all tall grass prairie and you might find yourself in Adair County of southwest Iowa, the home of another Jeffersonian farm leader. Born 145 years after Jefferson, Henry Wallace grew up in a small white-shingled farmhouse perched on a rise. At the side stands a great barn, a modern cathedral in this open land of huge skies. Wallace went on to become Secretary of Agriculture from 1933 to 1940, and then Vice President from 1941 to 1945. He had progressive ideas about people and the land, but left office perhaps when he was most needed – just as the post-war rural decline was about to set in.

Standing by this little house on the prairie, floating ship-like as Wallace Stegner describes, a patch of restored prairie stretches down to a limpid blue pond. The heavy air shimmers above the faded grasses, and an insect chorus drowns every other sound. In the 1850s, a third of Iowa's 14 million hectares was under tall grass prairie containing some 300 species of native plants. In the 1850s, the soil was 35cm deep, but 150 years of ploughing has reduced it to only 14cm. The county life centre that looks after the Wallace home now runs a community-supported agriculture unit (CSA) on just under a hectare of land. Kathleen Delate of Iowa State University and Ray Jensen, who manages the Prairie Harvest CSA, proudly walk across the farm. Nearly fifty families buy fruit and vegetables for twenty weeks from this tiny patch. The sheds are full of melons, squashes, and red and brown onions twisted on long strings, and the orchard is heavy with the fruit of apple, pear and peach trees, and currant and gooseberry bushes. And it is not just crops on this farm. Ray says, 'I see more and more bird species each year', and you know that both Jefferson and Wallace would have been proud. Recently, some CSAs in Iowa have been formed into wider collaborative CSAs, in which many producers are linked to consumers, and growers are helped with business development, workforce management and ideas for wider community participation.[7]

A sensitive, small farm, a patch of tall grass, a restored wetland and direct links to consumers. Is this a model? It is for some places. But drive the straight prairie roads, past acre upon acre of maize, through rural towns centred on ageing grain silos and boarded businesses around town greens, the long trains clanking through the late afternoon dust, and you wonder, are these small farmers of Brazil, Thailand, Sri Lanka and rural America some of the new pioneers for real sustainable futures? Or will they, too, still come to be lost and replaced by ever larger fields and farms?

10

The Shadow of the Rain

When the southwest monsoon sweeps up from the Indian Ocean in June, it brings welcome relief and renewal to communities across southern Asia. In India's southwestern state of Kerala, the abundant rain produces a region of canals, coconuts and rice fields of green. The weather fronts continue eastwards, but only just make it past the Western Ghats, a north–south range of hills stretching along the border of Tamil Nadu up through Karnataka. Beyond these hills, life on the same latitude is remarkably different. For here are some of the driest areas outside formal deserts on the continent. This is the land of the former Dravidian kingdoms with their ornate temples, and it centres on Madurai, which the Pandyas made their capital more than 2000 years ago. A thousand years later, it fell to the Chola emperors, was later regained by the Pandyas and was lost to a general from the Delhi Sultanate, who in turn was overthrown by the Hindu Vijayanagar kings. Finally, the Nayals overthrew them in 1585, and ruled for 216 years until the arrival of the British East India Company.

It was in the reign of Tirumalai Nayal in the mid-1600s, though, that the magnificent Meenakshi Temple was built on the site of the old Pandya capital. It sprawls across six hectares and comprises dozens of towers reaching up to 45 metres in height. Such is its importance that 10,000 visitors and pilgrims visit daily, making their way past the noisy bazaar at the outer walls, through the long, dark corridors, and eventually to the quiet square pool at the centre. The splash of water echoes across the steps, and back from the green, red and gold columns. The water, though, imparts a reassuring sense of permanence and settled silence after all the chatter and external drama. Here, after all, is the source of life for all those living in the drylands.

Walk from these cool and damp corridors out into the dusty bustle of Madurai itself, and then head to the south, and you will find yourself in the driest district of southern India. First you pass the rich green fields on the edge of the city, where urban sewage is turned into fodder for the backyard dairy cattle. Soon though, the land becomes drier, and rural people have to make a living mostly from rainfed rather than irrigated crops. At night, the road takes you past looming white-washed tree trunks; by day, groups of people stand aside at the last minute from beans and grain laid out on the road for vehicle tyres to do their threshing work. Virudhunagar District is so dry that it is the centre for the match and fireworks industries, where children with dextrous fingers work long hours in great warehouses, packing matches into tiny boxes. Later, you pass kilometre after kilometre of invasive *Prosopis juliflora* thickets, dense choking shrubs that are good for little except charcoal production.

Just before the road rises on a ramp over a single-track railway line that stretches to the distant horizon, you can swing right through the *Prosopis* to find a group of villages that are part of a land and water revolution that deserves some serious celebration. We worry about what happens in the drylands, where water is short. We worry when we hear that the numbers of people have increased, and that the pressure on local resources is growing. We worry about the likely effects of climate change. Yet, here, twenty years after desperation seemed set to stay, something special has occurred in the rainshadow. It began when a young man set up a group to encourage rural people to increase their literacy by learning about their own places and what they can do to change them. John Devavaram launched the Society for People's Education and Change (SPEECH) in 1987 and, together with Erskine Arunothayam and Nirmal Raja, began their work in 47 villages. Their approach is to help form self-help groups, or *sanghas*, and to build the social and human capital of the area so that environmental improvements can be made and then sustained. The effect on the landscape and community has been remarkable.

I first came upon the village and sub-village of Paraikulum and Kottam riding on the back of a straining motorbike rattling along the railway line, the only route to the village when the rains do come. It is one rural settlement among some half a million in India. The sixty houses are clustered together near the tank, the wide low-lying area that collects rainwater behind a bund. It is used for irrigating a small patch of paddy fields and as a source of drinking water. Above the railway line is the upper watershed, an area of sands, capped soils, sparse grasses and thorn bushes. When it does rain, the water simply rushes off the barren land to join distant rivers, and a valuable resource is wasted. People say this area was once farmland, but then there was a conflict with another village, some disturbance, a lack of cooperation; something, no one is quite sure what, led to the land being abandoned to free grazing for goats and cattle. Later, we will see these lands green to the horizon, with mango and neem trees swaying in the hot wind, and thirty types of vegetables and cereals being grown.

Ordinarily, this is a region of savage economic rules. Poverty is endemic. The daily labouring wage is just ten to twenty rupees. Dowries are still paid, and women have little power or choice. Adult literacy is low. Food is always short, and farmers struggle to raise their crops and obtain enough feed for their livestock. Class and caste differences are entrenched, and many people have taken out loans and cannot pay them back. Abandoned land is readily invaded by *Prosopis*, making it less likely ever to be used for food production again. SPEECH's approach is to begin with non-formal education, building a class of village animators, who in turn receive training in participatory learning methods, conflict resolution, songwriting and storytelling. The animators visit every house, raising awareness of the common problems faced by the village, and the need for effective organization and participation to resolve them. After a period, local people are helped to form a *sangha* or village committee. *Sangha* leaders, elected by their members, attend further training courses and meet key personnel from government organizations and banks who have been invited to the region. As the *sanghas* become more confident, they develop their own capacities and priorities, providing for health care, road upkeep, small-scale credit, tree nurseries and new farming methods. These *sanghas* are critical, as they become the only platform for poor families to change their whole communities.

At Paraikulum, the women's *sangha* plan first to work on the fifty hectares of degraded land in the upper watershed. It is hard work to clear the thorn trees and their roots, but eventually the land can be ploughed. A series of water conservation and harvesting measures are added so that rainwater can be channelled to percolation areas to feed the groundwater. The new field design includes stone bunds at the low slope corners to control water flow across the fields. When the rain does come, it will no longer be permitted to escape without doing useful work first. The land is divided up evenly, and trees from the village nursery planted along all the boundaries. SPEECH help with the digging of a new well, so that there will be some water in the dry seasons.

Now, when it rains, the water is channelled, collected and ponded and seeps into the ground to replenish the aquifer. This has produced a double benefit. First, the watershed turned green within three years, as crops could now be grown. Second, enough water was collected in the tank for the community to irrigate the tiny 12-hectare patch of wetland rice close by the village for an extra season each year. With existing resources (after all, the water had been there before), they now produce an extra 30–50 tonnes of rice each year. Increasing cropping intensity on small patches in this way offers great hope for farmers of drylands in many parts of the world. But it requires community organization and motivation.

The upper watershed is now unrecognizable. When I first walked across the dusty scrubland, it would have been difficult to imagine such a transformation. The soils were sandy and barely capable of sustaining grasses and shrubs, let alone crops. Today, there are tall fruit trees on the field boundaries, and fields full of finger millet, groundnut, maize and cotton. All of this came about through collective action, led in this case by the local women's group, who had in turn been helped by an active and enlightened local group. Put the farmers on the land, and it can become productive again. Valli is from the sub-village of Kottam, and she describes the change:

> *fifteen years back the land was a waste land where only shrubs and thorns grew, it was a cattle and goat grazing land for the villagers. Trees in the areas always wore a dried-up look. The entire land looked like a graveyard. We formed a sangha, with the help of SPEECH, and look at the change.*

Local people have a saying, *thaan vuzhu nilam thariso* – land without a farmer becomes barren.

A potential for transformation has been awakened. In villages across the region, *sanghas* have taken on a range of activities, including developing safe drinking water sources and better sanitation, street lights, marketing and children's education. In Paraikulum, the women's group have recently bought a patch of land from another village, allowing them to increase the numbers of dairy cattle they own. Their children now have more milk, and surpluses are sold for cash. As the connections to the outside develop, rural families become more aware of the potential to access resources. At the same time, local government has become more aware of the value of land rehabilitation and the capacities of rural people, who in turn say they have acquired a stronger identity of their own, giving them much needed power when it comes to external negotiations and trading, although there are, of course, new difficulties to face, such as continuing monsoon failures, unforeseen political rivalries within villages, and difficulties in priorities between landowners and labourers.

So, is this a special case, or are some of the ideas and processes generalizable? These people are among the poorest in the world, with the least number of opportunities coming from the outside. This is close to a desert, subject to extreme vagaries of the weather, something many are going to have to accept as part of post-climate change life. Importantly, they have changed their own world, and no one else would have done it for them. The poorest, when well organized, can build on their special knowledge of local environments and use new ideas and technologies from the outside, and then their worlds can change. What is it that has worked here, and why does it appear so simple, that degraded land can be turned green? After all, nothing particularly special happened, just some soil and water conservation methods, and some transformations in local beliefs and organization, and now the water works for them.

It is clear that new configurations of social and human relationships were a prerequisite for land improvements. Without such changes in thinking, and the appropriate trust in others to act differently too, there is little hope for long-term sustainability. It is true that natural capital can be improved in the short term with no explicit attention to social and human capital. Regulations and economic incentives are commonly used to encourage changes in behaviour, such as establishment of strictly protected areas, regulations for erosion control and economic incentives for habitat protection. But though these may change behaviour, they do not guarantee a change in attitudes: farmers commonly revert to old practices when the incentives end or regulations are no longer enforced.[1]

There can be quite different outcomes when social relations and human capacity are changed. External agencies or individuals can work with individuals to increase their knowledge and skills, their leadership capacity and their motivation to act. They can work with communities to create the conditions for the emergence of new local associations with appropriate rules and norms for resource management. If these succeed in leading to the desired improvements in natural resources, then this has a positive feedback on both social and human assets. When people are organized in groups, and their knowledge is sought, incorporated and built upon during planning and implementation, then they are more likely to sustain activities after project completion.

The term 'social capital' is now commonly used to describe the importance of social bonds, norms and collective action. Its value was identified by Ferdinand Tönnies and Petr Kropotkin in the late 19th century, shaped by Jane Jacobs and Pierre Bourdieu seventy to eighty years later, and given novel frameworks by sociologist James Coleman and political scientist Robert Putnam in the 1980s and 1990s. Coleman describes it as 'the structure of relations between actors and among actors' that encourages productive activities. These aspects of social structure and organization act as resources for individuals to use to realize their personal interests. As social capital lowers the costs of working together, it facilitates cooperation. People have the confidence to invest in collective activities, knowing that others will do so too. They are also less likely to engage in unfettered private actions that result in resource degradation. There are four central features of social capital: relations of trust; reciprocity and exchanges; common rules, norms and sanctions; and connectedness, networks and groups.[2]

Trust lubricates cooperation and so reduces the transaction costs between people. Instead of having to invest in monitoring others, individuals are able to trust them to act as expected. This saves money and time. It also creates a social obligation, as by trusting someone this also engenders reciprocal trust. There are different types of trust: the trust we have in individuals whom we know, and the trust we have in those we do not know, but which arises because of our confidence in a known social structure. Trust takes time to build, but is easily diminished, and when a society is pervaded by distrust, cooperative arrangements are very unlikely to emerge or persist. Reciprocity and regular exchanges increase trust, and so are also important for social capital. Reciprocity comes in two forms: specific reciprocity is the simultaneous exchanges of items of roughly equal value, while diffuse reciprocity refers to a continuing relationship of exchange that at any given time may be unrequited, but which over time is repaid and balanced. Again, both contribute to the development of long-term obligations between people, which is an important part of achieving positive sum gains for the environment.

Common rules, norms and sanctions are the mutually agreed or handed-down norms of behaviour that place group interests above those of individuals. They give individuals the confidence to invest in collective or group activities, knowing that others will do so too. Individuals can take responsibility and ensure their rights are not infringed. Mutually agreed sanctions ensure that those who break the rules know they will be punished. These rules of the game, also called the internal morality of a social system or the cement of society, reflect the degree to which individuals agree to mediate their own behaviour. Formal rules are those set out by authorities, such as laws and regulations, while informal ones shape our everyday actions. Norms, by contrast, indicate how we should act (when driving, norms determine when we let other drivers in the traffic queue; rules tell us which side of the road to drive on).

Connectedness, networks and groups are the fourth key feature of social capital. Connections are manifested in many different ways, such as trading of goods, exchange of information, mutual help, provision of loans, and common celebrations and rituals. They may be one way or two way, and may be long-established, and so not respond to current conditions, or subject to regular update. Connectedness is institutionalized in different types of groups at the local level, from guilds and mutual aid societies to sports clubs and credit groups, from forest, fishery or pest management groups to literary societies and mothers' groups. High social capital also implies a likelihood of multiple membership of organizations and good links between groups.

There is a danger, of course, of appearing too optimistic about local groups and their capacity to deliver economic and environmental benefits. There are always divisions and differences within and between groups and communities, and conflicts can result in environmental damage. Not all forms of social relations are necessarily good for everyone in a community. A society may be well organized, have strong institutions with embedded reciprocal mechanisms, but be based not on trust but on fear or power, such as in feudal, hierarchical, racist and unjust societies. Formal rules and norms can also trap people within harmful social arrangements. Again a system may appear to have high levels of social assets, with strong families and religious groups, but contain abused individuals or those in conditions of slavery or other forms of exploitation. Some associations can also act as obstacles to the emergence of sustainability, encouraging conformity, perpetuating adversity and inequity, and allowing some individuals to force others to act in ways that suit only them.

For farmers to invest in collective action and social relations, they must be convinced that the benefits derived from joint approaches will be greater than those from going it alone. External agencies, by contrast, must be convinced that the required investment of resources to help develop social and human capital, through participatory approaches or adult education, will produce sufficient benefits to exceed the costs. Elisabeth Ostrom puts it like this:

> *participating in solving collective-action problems is a costly and time consuming process. Enhancing the capabilities of local, public entrepreneurs is an investment activity that needs to be carried out over a long-term period.*

For initiatives to persist, the benefits must exceed both these costs and those imposed by any free-riders in collective systems. This is why it took SPEECH several years to develop the relations of trust with people in their villages.

One way to ensure the stability of social connectedness is for groups to work together by federating to influence district, regional or even national bodies. This can open up economies of scale to bring even greater economic and ecological benefits. The emergence of such federated groups with strong leadership also makes it easier for government and non-governmental organizations to develop direct links with poor and formerly excluded groups, though if these groups were dominated by the wealthy, the opposite would be true. This can result in greater empowerment of poor households, as they better draw on public services. Such interconnectedness between groups is more likely to lead to improvements in natural resources than regulatory schemes alone.

But this raises further questions. What will happen to state–community relations when social capital in the form of local associations and their federated bodies spreads to large numbers of people? Will states seek to colonize these groups, or will new broad-based forms of democratic governance emerge? Important questions also relate to the groups themselves. Good programmes may falter if individuals start to 'burn out', feeling that investments in social capital are no longer paying. There are also worries that the establishment of new community institutions may not always benefit the poor. There are also signs that they can all too easily become just a new rhetoric, but this is an inevitable part of any transformation process. The old guard adopts the new language, implies they were doing it all the time, and the momentum for change slows. But this is not a reason for abandoning the new. Just because some groups are captured by the wealthy, or are run by government staff with little real local participation, does not mean that all are fatally flawed. What it does show clearly is that the critical frontiers are inside us. Transformations must occur in the way we all think if there are to be real and large-scale transformations in the land and the lives of people, particularly those in the drylands who have struggled with the uncertainties of rainfall and whose challenges may be even greater in the immediate years to come. What, then, of the improvements being made in Africa, where the challenges for agricultural development also remain substantial?

In mid-summer, the skies over the East African Rift Valley are cloudless. During the day, the dust and heat leave you yearning for the cool of dusk. At night, the depth of the sky and the glittering stars encourage you to forget the heat of the landscape and the desires of its people for the still distant rains. On such a night, we rise early to relight the fire for breakfast, and watch the blue-black sky lighten to gold. The first sunlight catches the flat-topped acacia trees, then the taller grasses. Slowly, out of the shadows, we see that the whole of the valley floor is dotted with clumps of black dots. The mystery does not last long, as these dots can be seen moving away to the south. Perched on the dramatic scarp face, this is our view of one of the greatest coordinated animal movements in the world – the annual migration of wildebeest. Each year, the females in this region give birth to roughly half a million calves within a two-week period. The predators eat their fill, but the vast numbers of prey mean most survive. No one is quite sure how female wildebeest, spread over several hundred square kilometres, can come into oestrus at the same time some eight months before. Obviously, there are strong evolutionary pressures to swamp the predators with spindly young during a short period of time. Three minutes after birth, they are on their feet and ready to run with the herd.

The Rift Valley of East Africa is now thought to be the cradle of humankind, as it is the location for the discovery of extraordinary fossil remains of early hominids. The Leakeys' discoveries at Olduvai Gorge indicate that hominids emerged as distinct from other apes at least five million years ago, possibly as many as seven million years. Over some 300,000 generations, a variety of hominid species fanned out across the world. Animal and plant domestication brought opportunities for hunter-gatherers to develop pastoralist and farming lifestyles, and for the past ten thousand years they have further helped to shape this landscape, coevolving with the animal and plant communities around them. On the better lands, farming came to dominate, but in the drier regions the pastoralists survived by moving across their landscapes to make use of the patchy fodder, feed, tree and salt resources. In recent years, though, farmers have been pushed further into the drylands, as population pressure and policy exclusions have forced them across old frontiers. The conflicts between those who move and those who farm are long-standing, but are becoming ever more intense as land and water become increasingly scarce.

Some 200km east of the Masai Mara's wildebeest, communities have been forcibly resettled from the fertile soils of the uplands to the searing heat of the floor of another part of the Rift Valley. They know about the problems of wild animals, as they struggle in the dry heat between the increasingly uncertain short and long rains. Government soil conservation officials are seeking to build capacity for self-management in a community flung together with no history and so no local knowledge of relevance. Thigio is in Limuru Division, and comprises 200 families, each with about two hectares of stony land. There are no rivers, and the pump on the single borehole breaks down so repeatedly that the children spend most of their days walking to collect water. The lucky ones have donkey carts with drums. March and April are the hungry months. Most families grow maize, sweet potatoes, squash and beans, and try to raise a couple of cattle and some chickens. Many families have planted trees on their farms, and over time this former grazing land may come under the spell of these resourceful farmers, if they can beat the droughts and the rocky soils, lack of water and lack of fuelwood. And, of course, the wild animals.

For on top of all their other challenges, farmers have to cope with gazelles and elands coming to their farms to eat their crops. They come in great numbers at night, they say. This is hardly surprising – never have these stony soils yielded such plant productivity. And with the herbivores come the predators, and people say they do not like to be out at night. Here wild animals are not cute; they do not yield to human intention. They pose a continuing threat to the livelihoods and indeed lives of poor people who were forced to leave their former homes and settle here. Walking along one hilltop, one man says, 'it is nice that you are walking here, even though it is hot, so that you can understand us'. Well, we might try, but can we ever succeed? Here, in the most ancient of human landscapes, with modern people simply trying to survive, what can be done?

For too long, Africa has been dismissed as being somehow unable to engage in patterns of development that aid both people and environments. Food production lags well behind the rest of the world. On average it is 10 per cent lower per person than forty years ago. Yet such a view misses a critical truth. Despite the many political, institutional and infrastructure difficulties, there are many encouraging successes, if only we would listen. Some of these new thinkers are in governments, and their successes are even more remarkable. At the end of the 1980s, Ministry of Agriculture officials in Kenya realized that they needed a new way of protecting soils, water and communities. Kenya has a long history of state intervention in both soil and water conservation and land management. For five to six decades, farmers had been coerced or paid to adopt soil conservation methods. These require coordinated action at a catchment level, and state suspicion of local people's lack of knowledge meant that external decisions were simply imposed. In the long run, this approach did not work, as people do not maintain structures and practices over which they feel no ownership or control. By the end of the 1980s, it had become painfully clear that the conventional approach to soil and water conservation was not conserving soils.

But a group of soil conservation officials, led by J K Kiara, Maurice Mbegera and M Mbote, recognized that the only way to achieve widespread conservation coverage was to mobilize people to embrace soil and water conserving practices on their own terms. Financial subsidies were stopped, and resources allocated instead to participatory processes, good advice and training, farmer trips, and local institution building. The 'catchment approach' was adopted as a way of concentrating resources and efforts within an area of 200–500 hectares, so that all farms could be conserved with full community participation. Small adjustments and maintenance are then carried out by the community members themselves, with the support of extension agents. But these participatory methods imply shifts of initiative, responsibility and action to rural people themselves, and this is not easy for government officials formerly used to getting their own way. A catchment conservation committee of farmers is elected to be responsible for coordinating local activities. Quietly, and with little fuss, some 4500 committees were formed, and by the late 1990s about 100,000 farms were being conserved a year. This was more than double the rate, and with fewer resources, than in the 1980s. The process of implementation of the catchment approach itself has, of course, varied according to the resources available and differing interpretations of the degree of participation necessary to mobilize the catchment community. Some still feel farmers should simply be told what to do. Others do not invest enough time in developing relations of trust. But where there is genuine participation in planning and implementation, the impacts on food production, landscape diversity, groundwater levels and community well-being can be substantial.

The soil conservation programme ended in June 2000, but was then broadened in scope to form a National Agriculture and Livestock Extension Programme with the support of the Swedish Government. This programme covers about 400,000 farms per year, with 4000 extension staff, and helps farmers form common interest groups for marketing produce. In addition, the programme promotes the principles of human rights and democracy of participation, non-discrimination, transparency and accountability. Over the past six years, productivity has continued to grow remarkably, and many farmers have diversified with bananas, vegetables, dairy animals, fish ponds and beehives. Japhet Kiara says:

> *the programme has benefited hugely from the soil conservation programme, farmers' yields and incomes have increased, more resource-poor and vulnerable farmers are receiving farming technology information, and staff are motivated.*[3]

Elsewhere in Kenya, there are many local non-government groups who have been equally successful, such as the Community Mobilisation against Desertification and the Environmental Action Team. The social processes incorporate participatory learning methods, farmer-based research groups, strengthening community and village groups, and collaboration with government and non-government research and extension agencies. Many new farming techniques have been developed. The idea of double-dug beds is also being widely promoted by groups such as Manor House and the Association for Better Land Husbandry (ABLH). These involve investments in very small patches of the land, though some professional agriculturalists dismiss this as only gardening. Double-dug beds are combined with composts and animal manures to improve the soil. A considerable initial investment in labour is required, but the better water-holding capacity and higher organic content means that they are able to sustain vegetable growth long into the dry season. Once the investment is made, little more has to be done for the next two to three years. Many vegetable and fruit crops can be cultivated, including kale, onions, tomatoes, cabbages, passion fruit, pigeon peas, spinach, peppers, green beans and soya. Self-help groups have found that their family food security has improved substantially. Families are now finding that by working more on their own farms rather than selling labour to others, they are getting greater returns. Children have again been beneficiaries, as their health has improved through increased vegetable consumption and longer periods of available food. In the ABLH's work in twenty-six communities in eight districts, three-quarters of households are now free from hunger throughout the year, and the proportion of households having to buy vegetables has fallen from eight to just one out of ten. By 2005, Manor House had trained 70,000 farmers in how to create these double-dug beds.

For too long, agriculturalists have been sceptical about these methods, saying they need too much labour, are too traditional and have no impact on the rest of the farm. Yet you only have to speak to the women involved to find out what a difference they can make. In Kakamega, Joyce Odari has twelve raised beds on her farm. They are so productive that she now employs four young men from the village. She says: 'if you could do your whole farm with organic approaches, then I'd be a millionaire. The money now comes looking for me.' She is also aware of the wider benefits:

> *my aim is to conserve the forest, because the forest gives us rain. When we work our farms, we don't need to go to the forest. This farming will protect me and my community, as people now know they can feed themselves.*

Another farmer, Susan Wekesa, says she has 'moved [her] household from misery to a normal rich life. My small *shamba* is producing a surplus, which I sell for income [...] I can now face the future proudly.' She has just over a tenth of a hectare of land. Once again, the spin-off benefits are substantial, as giving women the means to improve their food production means that food gets into the mouths of children. They suffer fewer months of hunger, and so are less likely to miss school.

Similar approaches are being used across the drylands of West Africa. About 100 kilometres to the north of where I took my first dusty steps, water harvesting is turning barren desert lands green. Again, the technologies are not complex and costly, and are being used in the poorest of communities. There is an enduring myth in the literature – as numbers of people increase, so it is inevitable that the deserts encroach, and the lands become sandy and bare instead of green. But it is not always like this. It all began in the central plateau of Yatenga in Burkina Faso, when Yacouba Sawadogo decided to revive the traditional practice of planting pits for reviving abandoned land. These *zai* (or *tassa* in Hausa) are 20–30cm-deep holes dug in soils that have been sealed by a surface layer hardened by wind and water erosion. The holes are filled with manure or organic matter to promote termite activity and enhance infiltration. When it rains, water is channelled by simple stone bunds to the holes, which fill with water and into which are planted seeds of millet or sorghum. Normally, cereal yields even on good soils are precariously low, rarely exceeding 300kg per hectare in a bad year and 1000kg when the rains are good. Yet these formerly abandoned lands now produce between 500 and 1000kg per hectare where earlier there was nothing.[4]

These *zai* and *tassa* require hard work, and it is the lack of labour or capacity to pay for it that limits their rapid spread. However, several tens of thousands of farmers in both Yatenga and in Illéla in Niger have now reclaimed barren land. Some planting pits are used for trees, and another key Burkinabe innovator, Ousseni Zorome, has more than 2000 trees on his fields, where formerly there were only 10. Ousseni has also created a *zai* school, where farmers come together to share new ideas, and he already has 1000 members. Chris Reij of the Free University in Amsterdam found that the average family in Burkina Faso using these technologies had shifted from being short of food for six and a half months to producing a surplus of 150kg per year. There have also been considerable social impacts of these soil and water conservation methods, particularly in leading to a market for young day labourers who, rather than migrating each year, now earn money by building these structures.

The proper management of water is essential for agriculture. Too much or too little and crops and animals die. Carefully managed, though, and landscapes become productive. About one-fifth of the world's cropland is irrigated, allowing food to be produced in dry seasons when rainfall is in short supply but sunlight is abundant. Most farmers, though, are entirely dependent on rainfall, an input that is becoming increasingly erratic in the face of climate change. There is great scope for improvement and farmers in many developing countries are leading the way. Through better social organization, they are finding that shared management and cooperation can lead to greater returns for whole systems. But there may be an even more interesting twist to all this building-up of local capacity. Across the world, so many good things are happening at the local level, with communities utterly transformed and people's lives improved. But at the national and especially international levels, there seems so much indifference. On the one hand, leaders seem to find it hard to believe that poor people should not just stay poor, or think that they deserve to stay poor. On the other hand, it is these very same leaders who are moving the whole world into an ever more unsustainable state. Can these local groups do anything to shape the larger forces?

Back in northern India, in the uplands of Gujarat, Rajasthan and Madhya Pradesh, land degradation is also severe, soils poor and agricultural production so low that most families need someone working in the city to survive. Again, though, with the right approach and best sustainable practices, much is being done. The Indo-British Rainfed Farming project works with 230 local groups in 70 villages on water harvesting, tree planting and grazing land improvements. Grain yields of rice, wheat, pigeon peas and sorghum have doubled, and the increased fodder grass production from the terrace bunds is valued for livestock. The improved water retention has raised water tables by one metre over three to four years, meaning that an extra crop is now possible for many farmers, thus turning an unproductive season into a productive one. Women are again the major beneficiaries. P S Sodhi of Gram Vikas Trust in Udaipur puts it like this:

> *In these regions, women never had seen themselves at the front edge of doing things, taking decisions and dealing with financial transactions. The learning by doing approach of the project has given them much needed confidence, skills, importance and awareness.*

The wider benefits of a transformed agriculture are also evident, as:

> *the project has indirectly affected migration as people are gaining more income locally through the various enterprises carried out in the project. People are now thinking that they must diversify more into new strategies. There has also been a decline in drawing on resources from the forests.*

But perhaps more importantly:

> *people have also started to question the nature of democratic participation. They have also started to challenge the political systems – those who are in power or control power have little incentive to allow participatory institutions to develop. Yet in our villages, people are voicing their concerns, have overruled elites, and have even elected women as Sarpanchs, local leaders.*[5]

Perhaps just in time a new form of leadership will emerge from these local communities who have transformed their own lands, turning the brown to green. Or perhaps the world's indifference, and even downright opposition, will continue, and we will never know what could have been done to conquer poverty in ways that do not also destroy the world through over-consumption and the modernist progress myth.

11

Rewilding Agriculture

It would be easy to make the mistake of thinking that the separation between agriculture and nature began when the first seeds were sown ten thousand years ago. At a stroke, Neolithic hunter-gatherers set aside their spears and take up the axe to clear the forests and ploughs to till the fields. Then, the wilds become steadily pushed back as the agricultural frontier advanced. Domestication of plants and animals comes to dominate the world, as more than six billion of us today place relentless daily demands on food production systems. In truth, though, the separation of domesticated and wild was never this clear.

We now know that the wildernesses are not pristine and untouched by humans. Almost every ecosystem has been amended by people, as hundreds of plants at any given place contribute to food, housing, medicines, traps, poisons, fodder and weapons. People have set light to the grasslands to increase wild grass seed production, they have sown the seeds of wild grasses and have harvested and replanted wild bulbs, they have created forest islands by deliberately planted preferred trees. At the same time, most apparently agricultural communities have long relied on wild plants and animals to supplement their diets. In Ghana, a fifth of harvested food supply comes from the wild; in western Kenya, 100 species of wild plants are still collected, with half of households also deliberately maintaining wild species near their homes. In north-east Thailand, a half of all foods consumed are wild foods from paddy fields, and include fish, snakes, insects, mushrooms, fruits and vegetables. In the southwest of the US, 375 plant species have a variety of uses for native Americans. And in India, 150 to 200 species of plants are regularly collected for food, fodder, medicine and fuel.[1]

In industrialized countries, the use of wild plants and animals for food is now quite rare, but this is a recent phenomenon. Today, we have the supermarket; one or two generations ago, we relied on the hedgerow, woodland and marsh for many components of our diet. In the north-west of Scotland, for example, fulmars were the main staple for some communities for at least 1000 years, providing food, fertilizer, fuel, feathers, medicine and oil. Before the island was eventually abandoned, adults on St Kilda each ate about a hundred fulmars a year – the flesh variously described as salty, musty and oily. Elsewhere in the UK, song birds and bird's eggs were a regular part of the diet, as were rabbits. Today, we still collect blackberries for pies and sloes for gin, but this wild harvest is sadly becoming rarer.

Hunter-gatherers and nomadic pastoralists, too, rely on agricultural systems for some of their calories, either growing small patches of cereal or vegetables, or trading their produce with farming communities. When the landscape was large enough to accommodate both the farmed and non-farmed components, then these overlapping ways of life could easily coexist. But the last century has seen a massive expansion in agricultural intensity and extent. Driven by rapidly increasing numbers of people and their changing consumption patterns, food systems worldwide have come to be dominated by agriculture. It is the scale and speed of this expansion that now gives the impression that agriculture and the wild were always separate.

Modern industrialized farming has done two things. It has advanced its frontier into the forests, drylands, wetlands and mountains and it has intensified its modes of production to make the maximum use of as much of the land as possible. And it has worked spectacularly well. In the last half century, agricultural area has increased from 4.5 to 5 billion hectares, increasing annual world food production from about 1.8 to 3.9 billion tonnes. Over the same period, the number of chickens has increased fourfold to 16.4 billion, pigs twofold to 950 million, cattle and buffaloes by about a half to 1.5 billion, and sheep and goats by forty per cent to 1.8 billion. The key drivers of production intensity have grown rapidly too, with irrigation area doubling to 270 million hectares, tractors and other agricultural machinery more than doubling to 31 million in number, and fertilizer use up more than fourfold to 142 million tonnes per year.

But these changes in the scale and intensity of modern agricultural systems have not come without significant environmental costs. The sevenfold increase in nitrogen fertilizer use has led to substantial escapes of the nutrient to water and air and the disruption of many ecosystems, at worst leading to dead zones in some rivers and seas. Soil is eroded from fields to fill reservoirs and clog rivers; pesticides escape to cause harm to some wildlife and people; greenhouse gases contribute to climate change and ozone depletion; and even today forests are still coming under the bulldozer to make way for huge areas of rangeland and new fields. No one knows what wild plant and animal species are being lost in this haze of destruction.

That agriculture contributes significantly to some environmental problems is no longer in dispute. What remains to be seen is whether agriculture can survive without the nature it has so successfully removed, and whether current levels of food production can be maintained if we continue to accept these costly side effects as no more than regrettable. What are the prospects, then, of agriculture and biodiversity coexisting in the same landscapes? There are three possible levels of integration: biodiversity in the field that contributes a service to food production; integration of whole farms with internal mosaics of different land use; and whole landscapes in which ecological restoration can occur. All three have been a focus for recent efforts to make agriculture more sustainable.

What, then, do we now understand by today's concerns for agricultural sustainability? Many different expressions have come to be used to imply greater sustainability in some agricultural systems over prevailing ones (both pre-industrial and industrialized). These include biodynamic, community-based, ecoagriculture, ecological, environmentally sensitive, extensive, farm-fresh, free-range, low-input, organic, permaculture, sustainable and wise-use. We can say that systems high in sustainability can be taken to be those that aim to make the best use of environmental goods and services while not damaging these assets. The key principles for sustainability are:

- to integrate biological and ecological processes such as nutrient cycling, nitrogen fixation, soil regeneration, allelopathy, competition, predation and parasitism into food production processes;
- to minimize the use of those non-renewable inputs that cause harm to the environment or to the health of farmers and consumers;
- to make productive use of the knowledge and skills of farmers, so improving their self-reliance and substituting human capital for some costly external inputs; and
- to make productive use of people's collective capacities to work together to solve common agricultural and natural resource problems, such as for biodiversity, pest, watershed, irrigation, forest and credit management.

As a more sustainable agriculture seeks to make the best use of nature's goods and services, so technologies and practices must be locally adapted and fitted to place. These are most likely to emerge from new configurations of social capital, comprising relations of trust embodied in new social organizations and new horizontal and vertical partnerships between institutions, and human capital, comprising leadership, ingenuity, management skills and capacity to innovate. Agricultural systems with high levels of social and human assets are more able to innovate in the face of uncertainty. This suggests that there are likely to be many pathways towards agricultural sustainability, and further implies that no single configuration of technologies, inputs and ecological management is more likely to be widely applicable than another. There is no 'one size fits all' when it comes to sustainability.

A common, though erroneous, assumption about agricultural sustainability is that it implies a net reduction in input use, so making such systems essentially extensive (requiring more land to produce the same amount of food). Recent empirical evidence, however, shows that successful agricultural sustainability initiatives and projects arise from shifts in the factors of agricultural production (for example from use of fertilizers to nitrogen-fixing legumes; from pesticides to emphasis on natural enemies; from ploughing to zero-tillage). A better concept than extensive is one that centres on intensification of resources – making better use of existing resources (for example land, water and biodiversity) and technologies. The critical question centres on the type of intensification. Intensification using natural, social and human capital assets, combined with the use of best available technologies and inputs (best genotypes and best ecological management) that minimize or eliminate harm to the environment, can be termed sustainable intensification.[2]

What makes agriculture unique as an economic sector is that it directly affects many of the very capital assets on which it relies for success. Agricultural systems at all levels rely on the value of services flowing from all the assets that they influence. There are, though, some advantages and misgivings with the use of the term capital. On the one hand, capital implies an asset, and assets should be cared for, protected and accumulated over long periods. On the other hand, capital can imply easy measurability and transferability. Because the value of something can be assigned a monetary value, then it can appear not to matter if it is lost, as the required money could simply be allocated to purchase another asset, or to transfer it from elsewhere. But nature and its wider values are not so easily replaceable as a commodity. Nonetheless, as terms, natural, social and human capital are useful in helping to shape concepts around basic questions such as what agriculture is for and what system works best.[3]

As agricultural systems shape the very assets on which they rely for inputs, a vital feedback loop occurs from outcomes to inputs. Thus sustainable agricultural systems should have a positive effect on natural, social and human capital, while unsustainable ones feed back to deplete these assets, leaving fewer for future generations. For example, an agricultural system that erodes soil while producing food externalizes costs that others must bear. But one that sequesters carbon in soils through organic matter accumulation helps to mediate climate change. Similarly, a diverse agricultural system that enhances on-farm wildlife for pest control contributes to wider stocks of biodiversity; simplified modernized systems that eliminate wildlife do not. Agricultural systems that offer labour-absorption opportunities, through resource improvements or value-added activities, can boost local economies and help to reverse rural-to-urban migration patterns.

Agricultural sustainability emphasizes the potential benefits that arise from making the best use of both genotypes of crops and animals and their agroecological management. Agricultural sustainability does not, therefore, mean ruling out any technologies or practices on ideological grounds (for example genetically modified or organic crops) – provided they improve biological and/or economic productivity for farmers and do not cause undue harm to the environment. Agricultural sustainability thus emphasizes the potential dividends that can come from making the best use of the genotypes of crops and animals and the ecological conditions under which they are grown or raised. The outcome is a result of this genotype–ecology interaction. Agricultural sustainability suggests a focus on both genotype improvements through the full range of modern biological approaches, as well as improved understanding of the benefits of ecological and agronomic management, manipulation and redesign.[4]

But converting whole agroecosystems to more sustainable design is a complex task and generally requires a landscape or bioregional approach to both rural and urban restoration or management. An agroecosystem is a bounded system designed to produce food and fibre, yet it is also part of a wider landscape at which scale a number of ecosystem functions are important. For transitions towards sustainability, interactions need to be developed between agroecosystems and whole landscapes of other farms and non-farmed or wild habitats (for example wetlands, woods and riverine habitats), as well as social systems of food procurement. Mosaic landscapes with a variety of farmed and non-farmed habitats are known to be good for birds as well as farms. There are a range of resource-conserving technologies and practices that can be used to improve the stocks and use of natural capital in and around agroecosystems. These include:

- *integrated pest management*, which uses ecosystem resilience and diversity for pest, disease and weed control and seeks only to use pesticides when other options are ineffective;
- *integrated nutrient management*, which seeks both to balance the need to fix nitrogen within farm systems with the need to import inorganic and organic sources of nutrients and to reduce nutrient losses through erosion control;
- *conservation tillage*, which reduces the amount of tillage, sometimes to zero, so that soil can be conserved and available moisture used more efficiently;
- *agroforestry*, which incorporates multifunctional trees into agricultural systems, and collective management of nearby forest resources;

- *aquaculture and wetlands*, which incorporates fish, shrimps and other aquatic resources into farm systems, such as into irrigated rice fields and fish ponds, and so leads to increases in protein production;
- *water harvesting* in dryland areas, which can mean formerly abandoned and degraded lands can be cultivated and additional crops grown on small patches of irrigated land owing to better rainwater retention; and
- *livestock integration* into farming systems, of dairy cattle, pigs and poultry, for example, including using zero-grazing cut and carry systems.

Many of these individual technologies are also multifunctional. This implies that their adoption should mean favourable changes in several components of the farming system at the same time. For example, hedgerows and alley crops both encourage predators and act as windbreaks, so reducing soil erosion. Legumes introduced into rotations fix nitrogen; they also act as a break crop to prevent carry-over of pests and diseases. Grass contour strips slow surface water run-off, encourage percolation to groundwater and can be a source of fodder for livestock. Catch crops prevent soil erosion and leaching during critical periods and can also be ploughed in as a green manure. The incorporation of green manures not only provides a readily available source of nutrients for the growing crop but also increases soil organic matter and hence water retention capacity, further reducing susceptibility to erosion.

Although many of these resource-conserving technologies and practices are now being used, the total number of farmers using them worldwide is still relatively small. This is because their adoption is not a costless process. Farmers cannot cut their existing use of fertilizer or pesticides and hope to maintain outputs and profitability. They also cannot simply introduce a new productive element into their farming systems and hope it succeeds. These transition costs arise for several reasons. Farmers must first invest in learning. As recent and current policies have tended to promote specialized, non-adaptive systems with a lower innovation capacity, so farmers have to spend time learning about a greater diversity of practices and measures. Lack of information and management skills is, therefore, a major barrier to the adoption of sustainable agriculture. During the transition period, farmers must experiment more and so incur the costs of mistakes as well as of acquiring new knowledge and information.

The on-farm biological processes that make sustainable agroecosystems productive also take time to become established. These include the rebuilding of depleted natural buffers of predator stocks and wild host plants, increasing the levels of nutrients, developing microenvironments and positive interactions between them, and establishing trees. It has also been argued, however, that farmers adopting more sustainable agroecosystems are internalizing many of the agricultural externalities associated with intensive farming, and so could be compensated for effectively providing environmental goods and services. Providing such compensation or incentives is likely to increase the adoption of resource-conserving technologies.[5]

Periods of lower yields seem to be more apparent during conversions of indus-trialized agroecosystems. There is growing evidence to suggest that most pre-industrial and modernized farming systems in developing countries can make rapid transitions to more productive farming while protecting and even increasing the extent of the wild.

Modern farmers have come to depend on a great variety of insecticides, herbi-cides and fungicides to control the pests, weeds and diseases that threaten crop and animal productivity. Each year, farmers apply 2.5 billion kilograms of pesticides to their farms worldwide, with global annual sales in the early 21st century amounting to $25 billion, down from the $30 billion highs in the late 1990s. Now, though, many farmers are finding alternative methods for pest, disease and weed control. In some crops, this may mean the end of pesticides altogether, as cheaper and more environmentally-benign practices are found to be effective. Though integrated pest management dates back to the 1950s, a significant paradigm-shifting moment occurred in the early 1980s when Peter Kenmore and his colleagues in Southeast Asia found that pest attack on rice was directly proportional to the amount of pesti-cides used. In other words, more pesticides meant more pests. The reason was simple – pesticides were killing the natural enemies of insect pests, such as spiders and beetles. When these are eliminated from agro-ecosystems, then pests are able to expand in numbers very rapidly. This led to the launch of farmer field schools to teach farmers the benefits of biodiversity in fields. The outcomes in terms of human and social development have been remarkable, and farmer field schools are now being deployed in many parts of the world: by 2005, more than 4 million farmers had been trained in 175,000 field schools in 78 countries. The largest numbers of trained farmers are in Indonesia (1.1 million), Vietnam (930,000), Bangladesh (650,000), the Philippines (500,000), India (255,000), Egypt (210,000), China (130,000), Thailand (75,000), Nepal (57,000), Kenya (46,000) and Sri Lanka (45,000).[6]

Many countries are now reporting large reductions in pesticide use, and in no case has reduced pesticide use led to lower yields. There are even reports that many farmers are now able to grow rice entirely without pesticides: a quarter of field-school-trained farmers in Indonesia, a fifth to a third in the Mekong Delta of Vietnam and three-quarters in parts of the Philippines. The key to this success is biological diversity on farms. Pests and diseases like monocultures, as there is an abundance of food and no natural enemies to check their growth. In the end, they do not need to fear pesticides, as resistance inevitably develops within populations, and spreads rapidly unless farmers keep using new products. Moreover, when a harmful element is removed from an agricultural system, and biodiversity is managed to provide free pest-management services, then further options for redesign are possible. Traditionally, rice paddies were important sources of fish protein, and fish living in the fields helped in nutrient cycling and pest control. But most pesticides are toxic to fish, and their increased use from the 1960s eliminated beneficial fish from paddies. Take the pesticides away, though, and the fish can be reintroduced.

In Bangladesh, more than 31,000 farmer field schools have trained 650,000 farmers in more sustainable rice production methods. Some programmes also emphasize fish raising in paddy fields and vegetable cultivation on rice field dykes. Rice yields improve by a small amount, and costs of production fall owing to reduced pesticide use. Each hectare of paddy, though, yields up to 750kg of fish, a substantial increase in total system productivity for very poor farmers. One farmer said to Tim Robertson, former leader of the programme, 'our fields are singing again, after thirty years of silence'. It is the frogs that are singing – in diverse and healthy fields full of fish and rice. Arif Rashid of CARE suggests that tens of thousands of farmers have completely stopped using insecticides, and, as he says, 'we do not know how much this has spread to other farmers'. To him, farmers have crossed a frontier:

> *CARE was able to change the behaviour of participating farmers with regard to irrational use of fertilizers and unwise use of insecticides, and they now have an improved understanding of ecology. They now take decisions based on careful study of their farms.*

Once we start with the idea that diverse systems can provide enough food, particularly for farmers with few resources, then whole new fields of endeavour emerge. One of these is the science of semiochemicals, aromatic compounds given off by plants. Researchers from the International Centre for Insect Physiology and Ecology in Kenya and Rothamsted research centre in the UK have found that maize produces semiochemicals when fed upon by the stem borer. They also found that these same chemicals increase attack by parasitic wasps and that they are fortuitously also released by a variety of local grasses used for livestock fodder and soil erosion control. The interactions are complex. Napier and Sudan grass attract stem borers to lay their eggs on the grass instead of the maize. Another grass, molasses grass, and a legume, *Desmodium*, repel stem borers. Both Napier and molasses grass emit another chemical that summons the borers' natural enemies, so that pest meets predator. Furthermore, *Desmodium* not only fixes nitrogen but is allelopathic (toxic) to the parasitic witchweed, *Striga hermonthica*.

These redesigned and diverse maize fields were called *vutu sukuma* (push–pull in Swahili) by a popular radio programme. They clearly work, as by 2005 more than 4000 farmers in central and western Kenya had adopted maize, grass-strip and legume-intercropping systems and have at the same time more than doubled maize yields at a wide range of locations; farmers in neighbouring Tanzania and Uganda are now beginning to adopt the systems. The sad truth is that for thirty years, the official advice to maize growers in the tropics has been to create monocultures for modern varieties of maize and then apply pesticide and fertilizers to make them productive. Yet this very simplification eliminated vital and free pest management services produced by the grasses and legumes. *Vutu sukumu* systems are complex and diverse, and they are cheap as they do not rely on costly purchased inputs.[7]

The next level of integration of agriculture and wildlife is on whole farms, where mosaics can be encouraged for a variety of purposes. In many parts of Europe, important environmental goods and services have long been maintained by traditional farming systems.[8] These include the wood-pasture *dehesas* and *montados* of Spain and Portugal, the dry *maquis* and *garrigue* grasslands of France, the integrated crop–livestock systems of *tanya* in Hungary, *minifundia* in Portugal and *coltural promiscura* in Italy, the lowland mixed farms of Ireland, the pastoral systems in northern Sweden and Finland, and the permanent vine, olive, citrus and other tree crop systems of Mediterranean hills. In the UK, many woodlands are maintained on farms as cover for game birds. The value that farmers derive from shooting gives them a reason for accepting less than maximum possible food production from the land. Indeed, there is a close relationship between the amount of land devoted to woodland on farms and whether shooting occurs. For some, this remains a troubling dilemma. If shooting were not permitted, then many habitats would no longer have a financial reason to be conserved. They might be conserved for other reasons, just for the pleasure of seeing the wildlife, for example, but when farmers are under economic pressure, they need a good reason for looking after types of wildlife that provide no direct service to food production. Indeed, this wildlife takes from farming, as field edges have to be managed to allow weeds to survive as a source of food (seeds and the insects that live on the weeds) for the birds.

One clear January day, I accompany a group of shooters and beaters on a Norfolk farm renowned for its positive action to create favourable habitat for the extremely rare stone curlew. The easterly wind is raw, a lazy wind, says one beater, it goes straight through you rather than around, and the sky a hard eggshell blue above the pines and oaks. With whistles and calls, the beaters march through the woodland, driving the pheasants towards the four guns. Today is for male birds only, and the females and partridges are allowed to clatter by untouched. Gun dog spaniels and labradors race away to find the downed birds as the guns echo across the fields. I walk with the beaters too; 'what you up to then, boy?' they mutter. You can walk through an apparently empty woodland and be surprised at how much is present. Hares, deer and birds seem to sublime from the land to the air, and you wonder how they could possibly have been hidden. The beaters, in their own kinds of uniform, stoically without gloves and red raw in the wind, continue to move ahead. The guns, through, retreat for hot soup and sloe gin, both products of the local land. This microcosm of social history on the land, this sharpening of dilemmas about our relations with the wild, indicates simply that if we wish for agriculture and the wild to coexist, then we need their uses to be incorporated into a variety of values. And these may continue to appear contradictory. We look after something in order to shoot it later, but if we did not value the shooting, then the reasons for looking after it would disappear, and so would the conservation ethic.

A very different kind of diversification centres on the increasing diversion of land to wetlands. The draining of wetlands has long been a key strategy during agricultural intensification, yet their demise also meant the loss of important environmental services. It was not until the wetlands were gone that we noticed wader bird numbers declining and flood incidents increasing when water had nowhere to go. But now wetlands are returning. You approach the wide skies and green wetlands of Elmley Marshes through the almost post-industrial heartland of north Kent. The pull of London and the ease of transport on the Thames has left power stations, pylons, cranes, paper factories and crumbling swing bridges. A few minutes away, though, is a landscape of peace and tranquillity. Here, 1200 hectares have been farmed for the past thirty years by Philip Merricks for both rare waders and farm produce. On this spring afternoon, the sun warms the wet scrapes and rills, and lapwings and redshanks scuttle, some with young, or rise up in alarmed flight. The marshes themselves are open to the horizon. No ugly fences, only ditches to separate the store cattle and sheep.

There are some 15,000–20,000 visitors to the Elmley farm each year. It was the first working farm to be declared a National Nature Reserve, and visitors come to see the landscape and its birds. Each winter, some 30,000 wildfowl and waders stop over, filling the water and sky with their swirling presence. By spring, the lapwings and redshanks are breeding, along with oystercatchers and iconic avocets. The management has to be thoughtful and precise, as the birds need different microhabitats, including wet puddles and rills, scraped earth, low grass, taller grass in which to hide, and both dry and wet patches. Winter waterlogging attracts the wigeon and dunlin, and also slows spring grass growth, which allows the young lapwing to survive. Predators have to be removed too. If you want breeding waders, then the foxes and crows have to go. Herons, falcons and gulls will take chicks and eggs, but there is little that can be done about them. It all works too, as breeding wader numbers have increased tenfold on the farm in twenty years. Philip Merricks is proud of this remote and open landscape, and says it has 'an elusive and powerful charm. Our birds are our landscape'. And you only have to stop to listen to the constant fluting and mournful cries of the waders, mixed with the glorious rising and falling of skylarks, to realize what can be done to a landscape with intentionality. It will not entirely bend, but much can be done when the wild and agriculture are put together.

In some landscapes, though, there is much more to do to effect significant change. After the collapse of the Soviet Union at the beginning of the 1990s, many countries have been trying to find a way to cope with an era of post-collectivist farms and landscapes that need reinvention. One notable model is in central Armenia. You approach the Mera Eco-99 farm from under the distant gaze of snow-capped Mount Ararat, through the industrial wastelands of deserted fruit-processing factories with shattered windows. The road twists past relics of state-run farms and over wide irrigation channels flanked with rushes. Hoopoes flash over the scrubland and settle on the crumbling concrete remains of another building. This is what rural Armenia, a pocket-sized country of four million on the Eurasian border, now in its second decade of post-Soviet self-management, mostly looks like.

For much of the 20th century, this agricultural landscape was dominated by large collective farms and agro-industrial complexes. After independence in 1991, agricultural policy switched to small-scale farming, with some 300,000 small plots of land handed back to rural people. Yet about 30,000 hectares of land remain severely salinized, mainly because of past over-irrigation, but also because of the very low levels of organic matter in the light soils. The collective challenge is enormous – how to turn a degraded land with a new farm ownership structure that few people yet understand into a productive landscape? Despite best efforts to date, Armenia remains a net food importer. And this is where the twenty-hectare Mera farm could be an exemplar. Set in the middle of a wide valley on salty soils, the land was purchased seven years ago by Vardan Haykazyan and his colleagues with support from the World Council of Churches Armenia Inter-Church Charitable Round Table Foundation, Christian Aid, Interchurch Organisation for Development Co-operation (ICCO) and the Church of Norway. Their idea was to turn this wasteland dotted with low scrub into a diverse and productive farm. They had no local models to copy but had seen and read about farms elsewhere in the world that had intensified their use of locally available resources to create sustainable and productive farms.

From a distance, you cannot mistake the fact that something unusual is happening at the farm, as its poplars, tamarisk and acacia are the only trees apparent in the landscape. Closer up, you can see the orchard of apricots, now being rehabilitated. And now it is clear that this farm is doing much that is different. The farm manager shows the Russian olives, grape vines, and apple, pear, walnut and plum trees. Interspersed are a wide variety of vegetables, including onions, spicy greens, aubergines, cabbages, horseradish, carrots and beets. Patches of herbs – coriander, parsley, basil, sage and dill – indicate their attention to food culture. A couple of smaller fields contain wheat, maize and alfalfa. Cattle are kept for their manure and milk – cheese, sour cream and yoghurt are central to many meals. The key to agricultural success here lies in stabilizing the soils by adding organic matter, either animal or green manures. The trees also play a vital role in creating a new microclimate for the farm.

But where the farm also differs is in the two new fishponds that contain some 3000 rainbow trout. These have become a valuable source of income. But they are also the location for a touch of animal ingenuity that should make us all think more carefully about our place in the world. People at the farm have noticed more biodiversity since they were established, with more songbirds particularly, and also hedgehogs, frogs, water voles, and storks that come for the fish. But it is the red foxes that provide a surprise. Watch carefully at dusk, and you can see these animals creep up to the fishponds and dip their tails into the water to act as fishing rods. The foxes have learned that the fish immediately bite anything entering the water. When the fox feels a trout bites its tail, it then flips it out of the water for its evening meal. For the sake of the business, the foxes are discouraged, but everyone feels that it is a shame to stop such clever behaviour.

How, then, can this farm be so very different from all those around it? The answer lies partly in having access to new or different technologies and practices, partly in human vision and ingenuity. This is where all transformations begin. With an idea, and then hard work, and then demonstration to others that they can do it too. There is no reason why other farms in the valley should not do the same, although at the moment officials, farmers and consumers do not recognize that anything of value is occurring. But this could change with plans to develop Mera as an agritourism attraction. It is only a short ride from the heavily visited fourth-century cathedral at Echmiadzin, centre of the Armenian church, and people may come to appreciate a farm that is an oasis of distinctive locally produced foods.

Here, then, is a small and diverse farm, showing what is possible on formerly salinized soils. There is no reason why other farmers in the valley should not be doing something similar. As has been seen elsewhere in the world, particularly in developing countries, the deserts and apparent wastelands can be greened if people have the ideas, the strength of purpose and the capacity to work together. Another good example comes from China, where government officials have been much more proactive about ecological restoration. In the shadow of the Great Wall, Bei Guan village lies in the rolling hills and plains of Yanqing County and is the site for one of many remarkable experiments in the integration of sustainable agriculture and renewable energy production. It was selected by the Ministry of Agriculture as an ecological demonstration village as part of one of 150 counties across the country for implementation of integrated farming systems.

It has made the transition from monocultural maize cultivation to diverse vegetable, pig and poultry production. Each of the 350 households has a tiny plot of land, of about two *mu* (a seventh of a hectare), a pen for the livestock and a biogas digester. Ten types of vegetable are grown and sold directly to Beijing markets. The green wastes are fed to the animals, and their wastes in turn are channelled into the digester. This produces methane gas for cooking, lighting and heating, and the solids from the digester are used to fertilize the soil. Each farmer also uses plastic sheeting to create greenhouses from the end of August to May, thus extending production through the biting winter, when temperatures regularly fall to -30°C.

The advantages for local people and the environment are substantial – more income from the vegetables, better and more diverse food, reduced costs for fertilizers, reduced workload for women, and better living conditions in the house and kitchen. In Bei Guan, there is also a straw gasification plant that uses only maize husks to produce gas to supplement household production. Instead of burning husks in inefficient stoves, requiring five hundred baskets per day for the whole village, now just twenty are burned per day in the plant. As the village head, Lei Zheng Kuan, says:

> these have saved us a lot of time. Before, women had to rush back from the fields to collect wood or husks, and if it had been raining, the whole house would be full of smoke. Now it is so clean and easy.

The benefits of these systems are far reaching. The ministry promotes a variety of integrated models across the country, involving mixtures of biogas digesters, fruit and vegetable gardens, underground water tanks, solar greenhouses, solar stoves and heaters, and integrated pig and poultry systems. These are fitted to local conditions. As Wang Jiuchen, Director of the Division of Renewable Energy in Beijing, says 'if farmers do not participate in this ecological reconstruction, it will not work'. Whole integrated systems are now being developed across many regions of China, and altogether eight million households have digesters. The target for the coming decade is the construction of another one million digesters per year. As the systems of waste digestion and energy production are substituting for fuelwood, coal or inefficient crop-residue burning, the benefits for the natural environment are substantial – each digester saves the equivalent of one and a half tonnes of wood per year, or three to five *mu* of forest. Each year, these biogas digesters are effectively preventing six to seven million tonnes of carbon from being emitted to the atmosphere, a substantial benefit to us all.[9]

These small-scale models might not appear to have any relevance for modernized landscapes in industrialized countries. But could something more happen, beyond the on-farm conservation and nature reserve protection that is being increasingly encouraged? Could whole landscapes be transformed to rewild agriculture? One of the most compelling of Aldo Leopold's short essays is called 'Thinking like a mountain', in which he details the relationship between the wolf, deer and mountain. He recalls his own shooting of a mother wolf caring for a pack of tumbling cubs: 'in those days, we never heard of passing up a chance to kill a wolf'. But seeing the green light in its eyes extinguished, he comes to mourn their loss and his earlier lack of understanding, and goes on to describe the consequences of eliminating the wolves, for, without them, the deer expand too greatly in numbers and the mountain loses all its vegetation. In the end the whole system collapses.[10]

What prospects are there, then, to bring back some of the more iconic wild animals into industrialized landscapes? Rewilding has been described by Peter Taylor as 'putting a new soul in the landscape'. It aims to retrieve something lost, and perhaps even to create something quite new. Many of the animals and birds being proposed as possible reintroductions have long since disappeared from the memories of the people; bringing them back would change the land and change the people too. Some reintroductions have been relatively uncontroversial in the UK. The white-tailed eagle was eradicated in 1916, reintroductions attempted from 1959, and breeding successfully established in the Western Isles of Scotland from the mid-1980s. The great bustard is being reintroduced from Hungary to Salisbury Plain and has so far survived the predatory effects of foxes and motor cars. Tarpan and Konik horses have been brought in by several county wildlife trusts to help in the managed grazing of coastal marshes and reed beds. Chillingham cattle, relatives of ancient aurochs, have been brought back to some forests.[11]

But it is the next cohort of introductions that will excite controversy. Beavers have been proposed for release into habitats in Kent and Scotland, but hitherto rejected by some for fear that their escape would lead to habitat destruction – too many people still remember the coypu in Norfolk. Others are talking about elk –

could they be introduced as part of the Wicken Fen project to the northeast of Cambridge, as fragmented fens in the landscape are gradually linked by careful land purchase and consolidation? Wild boar are already present in four or five herds across southern England, and the policy question centres on whether they should be permitted to remain, or be hunted out. But the greatest of all controversy would come with predator introductions, particularly wolves, bear and lynx. Bear get a better press than wolves, but are rather low on any proposed lists. Lynx do not carry so much public concern and might be permitted one day.

Wolves, though, would be an extraordinary attraction if introduced into a landscape large enough to support active packs. I suspect many people would love to see them in the wild, while at the same time feeling the almost visceral fear that wolves seem to provoke. In Norway, some wolves have crossed the border from Sweden, provoking public concern, despite the fact that there are no records of wolves having attacked people, while dogs hospitalize 4000 people per year but are not subject to the same concern. Elsewhere in Europe, wolves are now in Poland, Germany, Slovenia, Italy, Switzerland, France, Romania, Ukraine and Russia. But these iconic animals would need whole landscapes to be devoted to them if they were to survive. The best example of such a project is at Oostvaarderplaasen in the Netherlands, a 5600 hectare reserve created on a reclaimed polder. There are no predators, but there is a herd of 300 Hech cattle and another of 200 Konik horses. The largest example of an unintentional project is the 4000-square-kilometre exclusion zone around the Chernobyl plant in northern Ukraine and southern Belarus.

What do all these rewilding ideas mean for agriculture? Some of this rewilding does mean the creation of completely separate habitats, but most implies an overlap, a sharing of the landscape for its various functions. I believe that it is possible to have food-producing systems that complement and enhance nature. More often than not, such nature will be in farms and fields. There is now growing confidence that we can indeed make the transition directly to sustainable and productive agricultural and food systems that both protect and use nature, although this will require some rethinking about the very idea of a farm, and its redefinition as an activity that does many things rather than just one. The new model farm both produces wholesome food that people want to buy and eat and contributes to the production of many environmental goods and services. It coexists with wildlife and links people to the land directly via the food they eat and places they know about and can enjoy visiting.

Part 4

People and the Land

Legible Landscapes

Modern society, in all its urbanized and industrialized form, is wonderfully sophisticated, but more disconnected from the natural world than ever before. Despite
many people expressing the value of connections through visits to the countryside and urban parks, and by the pleasure taken in their domestic pets and children's
stories full of animal characters, many urban dwellers seem now to be completely
cut off in their daily lives from green places and the wildness of the world. We
now do new things, have learned new skills and derive many of our pleasures in
new ways. But might something fundamental get lost when direct experience of
nature and the living world declines, leaving us to care less about the consequences
of modern economic progress? We may forget to ask, 'What happened here?', and
so stories about the land and our relations to it recede further from memory. When

the knowledge and stories go, so it becomes easier for others to damage or destroy the very places and resources created and valued over generations.

When the vast ice sheets of the Anglian glaciation retreated nearly half a million years ago, the meltwaters drained east and southeast to form the main river valleys of south Suffolk and north Essex. One river, the Stour, now forms the boundary between the two counties, and its rolling hills and tributaries form what is called Constable Country, a nationally designated Area of Outstanding Beauty. John Constable lived at Dedham, in the valley's lower reaches, and it is to Flatford Mill and Willy Lott's cottage that many thousands of visitors are attracted. Come a few kilometres upstream, though, and you find a quieter country, rich with the layers of history. At Horkesley lock, one of fifteen on the river, weeping willows flank the old millpond, and a dense patch of mixed woodland planted a decade ago by local schoolchildren hides the river. Forty to fifty years ago, otters disappeared from all these rivers, mainly because of persistent pesticides, destruction of riverine habitats and drowning in eel nets. Today, though, they are back and taking advantage of new holts built by the local countryside project. These animals are secretive and rarely seen, though they once were common.[1]

One winter's morning, we stand on the riverbank, watching the blood-red sun emerge from the mist above the hedgerows and ploughed fields. The cold seeps up from the ground as we wonder whether there are otters and their youngsters in the five-metre holt constructed from logs and sweeping perpendicular from the river to the safety of higher ground. In the mud of the riverbank, we find the distinctive five-toed paw prints, and can see paths padded down in the ground vegetation. As the sun climbs and shrinks, two swans circle and then approach along the river to clatter in a cloud of water into the millpond. We step back a few metres, and then, splash, and an otter is into the water, leaving a chain of bubbles as it sets off to hunt eels. It must have been waiting at the mouth of the holt while we talked of paw prints and sweet-smelling spraints. Later, as the cold has bitten deeply and the sun casts a golden glow across the trees and water, we see another line of bubbles as the otter returns. Once these animals were hunted by men and women in blue serge plus-fours, with horns and dogs, and the river ran red. Today, we feel touched, even though the animals themselves have cleverly escaped observation. Twenty years of effort have been put into otter reintroductions, and they are only just succeeding. Some people will be unhappy, worried that the fish and eels will be eaten out. But most of us will appreciate the changing story in the local river.[2]

Once this river was the only industrial route into the heart of the region. The Stour navigation from Sudbury to Manningtree was created by a 1705 Act of Parliament, and in Constable's time barges carried agricultural produce downriver to the sea, and then down to the Thames, returning with city night soil to put on the land. There were, of course, very few trees by the river, as horses had to pass easily with ropes attached to the barges. When the navigation fell into disuse by the 1920s, and was eventually abandoned in 1937, so trees were replanted. Now grey-green cricket willows line the riverbank, and it is a source of dismay among local people when they have to be chopped down for their valuable wood. But this is a very recent part of the story of this land.

Inland from the lock are the remains of a moated Roman settlement. Just ten kilometres north of Camoludonum, capital of Roman Britain, this would have been situated on a busy straight road striking into the heart of Trinovantes territory. With the better-known Iceni to the north, these Iron Age civilizations had been present in these river valleys since the first Neolithic farmers settled the region more than 4500 years before the Romans arrived. Their landscape signs are in the barrows, ring ditches, field marks and village remains dotted across the land. Looking down from the rafters above the nave of the flint church is the face of a green man, wreathed in oak leaves, a symbol of many woodsman and wildmen myths that remain from a mysterious past. Behind the church are the allotments, and by them a meadow, Little Lye, just restored for its wild flowers. The return of bee orchids was a source of great excitement, though last year each flower was nibbled off by muntjac deer. We like the presence of the deer, and we like the orchids too, but it seems the two might not be able to coexist in the same landscape. This year, though, we count 29 bee orchid plants, and celebrate their resilience.

Soon, though, you can rise out of the village by the pathway leading from the cemetery past a seemingly ancient wooden scout hut. This was donated by Miss Oates, sister of Captain Lawrence Oates, who famously went outside to his death on his 32nd birthday during the Scott polar expedition of 1912. If you climb from the mosaic fields of the floodplain, soon the paths and roads converge on sunken lanes. These are at least Anglo-Saxon in origin, some perhaps set out in the time of the seventh-century dynasty of Wuffinga. Centuries of cart wheels have eroded the clay tracks, leaving some deep below the surrounding fields. These green lanes are a world apart, warm and damp in mid-winter, cool in the heat of summer, where there is a permanent half-light, and partridges run in line when startled from the undergrowth, eventually lifting in a rattle of wings where the overhanging branches thin. The deepest lanes in the region are six to seven metres below field level, though most are at least two to three metres deep.

The lane leading into the hills is one of many St Edmunds' Ways in the area, created by pilgrims heading north to Bury St Edmunds. In the banks of these sunken lanes, deep in the twisted roots of pollarded oaks, are badger sets marked by sandy entrances. In spring, bluebells carpet the patches of woodland with a haze of purple light. Here there are also elms alongside the ancient oaks. Two of the patches of woodland are planted with match poplars, another industrial remnant in this landscape, as they no longer had economic value when matches could be sourced more cheaply from overseas. Walk these woodlands at dusk and you may see small herds of roe deer, or the more solitary muntjac. You will certainly hear tawny, barn and little owls, 'preaching desolation', as Ronald Blythe has put it, and possibly the wild calls of foxes too. What they may mean in this animated land is difficult to know. 'At best,' writes local poet Dave Charleston, 'earth only teaches you silence.'[3]

But watch carefully and you will see it is a route that passes under a rooks' daily flyway. Their gregarious kraas and tsaks mark their swirling easterly morning migration and westerly homeward return. A line of poplars contains a tree where I have twice seen a rooks' parliament. On the leafless branches, some thirty birds gather and perch, respectfully equidistant from one another. They face inwards, apparently unconcerned about a circling sparrowhawk, towards one or two birds in the middle of the tree, debating something unknowable to us. Incoming birds seem to receive a summary of proceedings, and then the parliament continues. This is an animated landscape of birds and animals, and within a few minutes you can feel far from the trappings of civilization.

Some have taken Constable's paintings of these hills and valleys to be of a quintessential English rural idyll, an unchanging landscape where people are tied to place and land. I prefer to think of them as snapshots of an economic as well as cultural landscape, geared mainly to producing food. Now we increasingly recognize that our land has many values and functions, and with care may be able to maintain some mystery and tranquillity as the urban continues to sprawl out into the rural. There is a constancy in this natural and historic landscape, with its cycles of life and death and rhythmic change. 'Round and round we all go,' writes Ronald Blyth in neighbouring Wormingford, 'the living, the departed, the abundance, the death, the planets, the prayers.' It is too easy to take our attachments to place for granted, and thereby forget to renew them. If we ask, 'What happened here?', as Keith Basso suggests, we may find the wisdom is tied to particular places – places that are shaped by thousands of years of human–nature interactions. Natural and social history is everywhere in this country, and some of the ancient memories can be unlocked by feeling the wind on our faces and hearing the alien language of birds.[4]

Alienation from nature has contributed to environmental problems in today's world. Until fairly recently in human history, our daily lives were intertwined with living things. Now we are increasingly suffering from an extinction of experience. David Suzuki says, 'we must find a new story', and Thomas Berry writes 'we are in between stories. The old story, the account of how we fit into it, is no longer effective.' Observation today can bring much needed respect, and, if we are lucky, we will find that animals, birds and places intercept us in our wanderings, helping to bring forth distinctive and personal stories of the land.[5]

This story and knowledge creation from local circumstances has been called ecological literacy. Some have also called it traditional knowledge, but this remains a problematic term. To many moderns, it implies a backward step, knowledge that is only quaint or superstitious, for which there should be no place in our modern world. Traditional, though, is best thought of not as a particular body of knowledge, but as the process of coming to knowing. Our lives involve the continuous writing and rewriting of own stories, by adjusting behaviour and by being shaped by local natures, and so our knowledges must be undergoing continuous revisions. Ecological or land literacy is not just what we know, but how we respond, how we let the natural world shape us and our cultures.[6]

An acquisition process such as this inevitably leads to greater diversity of cultures, languages and stories about land and nature because close observation of one set of local circumstances leads to divergence from those responding to another set of conditions. Here are the critical elements of knowledge for sustainability – its local legitimacy, its creation and recreation, its adaptiveness, and its embeddedness in social processes. This knowledge ties people to the land, and to one another. So when landscape is lost, it is a loss not just of a habitat or feature, but also of meaning for some people's lives. Such knowledges are often embedded in cultural and religious systems, giving them strong legitimacy. And this knowledge and understanding takes time to build, though it can be rapidly lost. On the subject of American geographies, author Barry Lopez writes:

> to come to a specific understanding [...] requires not only time but a kind of local expertise, an intimacy with a place few of us ever develop. There is no way round the former requirement: if you want to know you must take the time. It is not in books.[7]

Such expertise remains a central part of the lives of indigenous people. For hundreds of thousands of generations, hunter-gatherers with predominantly oral cultures survived natural selection despite the greater brawn and speed of other predators. Our large brains must have given us a great advantage, and our transmission of knowledge and capacity to learn new things helped us to survive. Remnants of these contexts remain among the six hundred or so hunter-gatherer peoples spread across the world, living today mostly in landscapes on the edges of agricultural heartlands. Some, such as the pygmy peoples of central Africa, live hemmed into small patches of forest; others, such as the peoples of the boreal north, still survive in a continuous circle around the world's northern polar and sub-polar regions.

In these predominantly oral cultures, the values of stories and relations with the land are important. These tell us something about what ecological literacy really is. It is not just knowing the names of things and their functional uses (or values), but placing ourselves as humans as an intimate part of an animate, information-rich, observant and talkative world. They do not see the world as inanimate, with natural resources to be exploited, gathered, shot and eaten. These things are done, but only in certain ways, and the world is respected and treated with care. Indigenous people believe that if they cause harm to nature, then they will themselves come to harm, whether it is speaking without respect of certain animals, or whether it is overfishing a lake or hunting out a certain type of animal. This is something that we in the industrialized world have lost, and perhaps need to remember. We have come to believe that harm to the world is inconsequential, or at the very least if something is lost then it can be replaced. We no longer think the consequences will come back to haunt us. When we stop listening and watching with care, our literacy about the world declines, and the landscapes no longer speak to us.[8]

For the Western Apache, says Keith Basso, wisdom sits in places, and landscapes are never culturally vacant. Animals, places and whole landscapes have meanings, sometimes sobering, sometimes uplifting, but always with a moral dimension. Ecological literacy is not just about knowing, it is about knowing what to do, and when to do the right thing. Places and things 'acquire the stamp of human events' or memorable times, and people wrap these into stories that can be myths, historical tales, sagas or just gossip. Every story begins and ends with the phrase 'it happened at...', and this anchoring of narrative to places means mention of a place evokes a particular story, which in turn carries a moral standard, and implication for certain types of social relations. Some Apache dialogues comprise only of a sequence of place names. After one such interaction, an elderly woman explained, 'we gave that woman a picture to work on in her mind. We didn't speak too much to her. We didn't hold her down.'

There is an assumed courtesy in not speaking too much, and in not demanding that the listener sees the world as the narrator wishes. Too many words smother the audience, and an effective storyteller seems to open up thinking, letting people travel in their minds. At the same time, stories are never definitive. They vary over time and are regularly changed in detail. One particular kind of story is designed to have strong consequences. These are fired like arrows and are intended to guide people over long periods of time. As a result, said one old woman, 'the land is always stalking people'. 'Stories make us live right', says another man. For the Apache, places look after people, and so themselves must be treated with respect. The names of places do not lie, but if younger generations do not know the places or the stories, then the names will no longer evoke respect and understanding.

Respect for the land and its plants and animals is a central principle for indigenous people. It derives from an ethic that people and animals have the same origins, and, as time is seen as circular rather than linear, those origins are both near and far. Many indigenous people believe in a high level of people–animal communication and so adopt an ethic of care, respect and humility. Say the Cree, recalls Fikret Berkes, 'all creatures are watching you. They know what you are doing. Animals are aware of your activities.' Animals, therefore, are seen to be in control of the hunt, and, if there is respect, 'the game will get to know you'. It will come to the hunter.[9]

This cosmology, or world view, is fundamentally different to that adopted by most of we moderns. We tend to see nature as separated from culture, to believe in the presence of untouched wildernesses, to see those in touch with the land as backward and to believe that we have control over nature. We no longer seem particularly worried if we cause harm or behave incorrectly. When the Innu of Labrador are successful in the hunt, they hang the bones of animals on tree branches as a sign of respect. But if they mistreat animals, they know this breaking of rules will be punished in some way. George Rich told us one story of his grandfather, Simeon, who was an expert hunter. As a young boy, he had watched two young men, both strong and noted hunters themselves, drive a caribou over a cliff to its death – an approach that is considered a cheap and improper way of treating caribou. Two months later, both mysteriously drowned in a lake, even though they could swim. Coincidence maybe, but no surprise to some local people.[10]

Fikret Berkes recounts a more recent story about the George River caribou herd. These had been abundant in the early part of the last century, then had fallen to very low numbers (perhaps just 5000 individuals) by the 1950s. As a result, many Cree by the 1980s had never seen a caribou, and the distinct knowledge of them only rested in the memories of elders. Oral history recorded the systems of the pre-1900 *maanikan* used to catch caribou, in which posts were placed like a fence over several kilometres, becoming narrower until the caribou were forced into a single file, where they would be corralled and killed.

But younger people had never had any experience of hunting caribou and when, by the 1980s, the George River herd had grown back to some 600,000 animals and re-entered Cree territory, the hunters at first engaged in a frenzy of shooting, letting wounded animals escape and not using all the meat. The elders said nothing at the time, but later told a story at a community meeting. They said that in the 1910s, a similar thing had happened to them, and the caribou had responded by going away for seventy years because of the hunters' lack of respect. The story had a profound effect on all the hunters present and led to the restoration of proper hunting ethics. The caribou did come back, and were shot and used with care.

Today, we moderns are like the young Cree, but without the wise elders to guide our behaviour. However, the disconnections may not be entirely profound, and there are many behaviours in which we engage that appear to contradict the rationality of the age. These are the many surviving relics of an animate world. Children see their world as one of magic trees and animated rocks, often creating their own stories about what the world is telling them.[11] Only later, as Ronald Blythe has noted, do they 'learn to stop thinking this way'. Another remnant of a former way of living is superstition. We apparently rational moderns are still extraordinarily superstitious, believing that our actions or even thoughts can influence events. We hang horse-shoes over doors and gather flints with holes for good luck. We seek to influence the likelihood of lightning striking by hanging mistletoe on houses, or believe that the hooting owl is an omen of death, as are bats that fly three times around a house. Sacred trees are planted near houses, and horses and dogs are believed to be able to see ghosts. Stormy petrels are believed to be souls of lost sailors and are seen to be the bringers of bad fortune, especially bad weather. The boom of the bittern was once taken to be an ill-omen, though today is a sound celebrated because of the bird's precarious recovery from close to extinction.

Much more common today, though, is the superstitious behaviour of support-ers of sports' teams. Almost every passionate fan of a football, cricket, baseball or basketball team will surely smile if asked, 'If your team wins one week, might you wear the same shirt, jumper or hat the next week? If you are watching an important match on the television, do you stay in the room or leave the room to create good luck, or stop bad luck? If you lose one week, will you do something different the next?' All to seek to influence something remote and untouchable. And we do this all the time, it seems to me, trying to create a favourable world. We try to shape the world by doing or thinking certain things, even though we know there is no known mechanism that can explain how this might happen, except perhaps the weirdness of quantum mechanics, where quarks do affect one another remotely.

It is normal to see the world as something that can be shaped by our individual actions and thoughts. Some things are obviously shaped – walk the same route through a meadow time and again, and a path will form, on which different grasses of a tougher nature will survive. The walking has shaped a little part of the world. But influencing whether your team will score in a match hundreds of miles away? Impossible, says the rationalist. Yet we do not shake off this reciprocity so easily. The landscape is intelligent, full of information, and when we are trained, we can interpret it – from the alarm call of a blackbird to the cough of a leopard in the dead of night.

We bring forth the world through our interactions with it. Our body is open and interactive – it might look like we have a clear boundary, where the skin ends and the rest of nature begins, but we give off gases and pheromones that send signals out to the world, and in return receive light and chemical signals. We are not so fixed as we think. If we are an emergent property of the world, we must in part depend on what we are interacting with. When we lose this reciprocity and interaction, or get something different, we must logically lose something inside ourselves. We also gain an unfortunate arrogance, that we are somehow chosen or special. And because we are special, we can do anything. We seek to inherit a position in the world that is separate and unique, rather than one that is humble and connected. This estrangement is a false economy. It looks good to some, but we will all regret it when the world endures and we do not.

Many stories about nature and our Earth are embedded in local languages. Language and land are part of people's identities, and both are under threat. There are between 5000 and 7000 oral languages spoken today, only about a half of which have more than 10,000 speakers. The rest, about 3400 languages, are spoken by only eight million people, about a tenth of one per cent of the world's population. The top ten spoken languages now comprise about half of the world's population. A great deal of linguistic diversity is thus maintained by a large number of small and dwindling communities. They, like their local ecologies and cultural traditions, are under threat. And here there is a vicious circle. As languages come under threat, so do the stories people tell about their environments. Local knowledge does not easily translate into majority languages, and moreover, as Luisa Maffi states, 'along with the dominant language usually comes a dominant cultural framework which begins to take over'.[12]

Thus we increasingly lack the capacity to describe changes to the environment and nature, even if we were able to observe them. Slowly, it all slips away. Gary Nabhan describes how the children of the Tohono O'odham of the Sonoran Desert in the southwest US are losing both a connection with the desert and with their language and culture. Even though they hear the language spoken at home, they are not exposed to traditional storytelling and are no longer able to name common plants and animals in O'odham – though they could easily name large animals of the African savanna seen on television.[13]

A good example of the language of the landscape is birdsong. This alien language is no more than background chatter to most of us, distinguished by only a few species that are wholly characteristic, such as cuckoos and owls. But walk in the woods early on a spring morning and the dawn chorus comes to life when you know who is saying what and why. It is as if a foreign country suddenly becomes known. That silvery liquid song in the dark is a robin, and when light comes, it is joined by the clear calls of blackbirds. Others soon join in. Birdsong is unlike learning another human language, as the very basis for rules about content and structure have to be learned and translated into our own language. Songs change through the year and across lifetimes of birds. The young learn from adults and initially have a less complex song. Unmated and paired sing differently, as do individual territory and colony birds, as do many birds during the course of the day. Many engage in subsong, such as the trisyllabic cooing of doves, a way of singing without opening their beaks. In addition, not all communication is by song, such as the drumming of snipe wings or the action of woodpeckers on wood. Birdsong is easier to remember when we 'translate' it into our own language: the 'teacher, teacher' of the great tit, the 'take two cows, David' of the wood pigeon or the 'a little bit of bread and no cheese' of the yellow hammer. We still, though, need to create our own lexicon of words to describe particular song, from the clicks, pops and whistles of starlings to the fluting, haunting calls of curlew on the open marsh.

At the lower end of our river valleys are the twisting estuaries, wide marshes and huge skies so distinctive of the North Sea coast. These marshes and mudflats are home in winter to huge numbers of migrating waders, ducks and geese. On a winter morning, with the sky slate-grey and the wind from the sea whipping up white horses, the flocks of knot and redshank twist and swirl, flowing like liquid onto the mud. Their calls echo across the wet pastures and dense reed beds. These same estuaries are also home to the oyster, raised and fished since the time of the Romans. Today, a dozen or so families still have the knowledge and desire to raise the two types of oyster, the native Colchester and rock oyster, and they continue traditions that can be traced back many generations. On a glassy summer morning, when the easterly sun turns the water to silver, with only solitary oystercatchers wheep-wheeping across the water, the green smack belonging to Richard Hayward noses into these secret creeks. Some oysters are raised at the centre of the river and then trawled up to the boat side. Others are set out on the mudflats and exposed by the tides twice a day. As long as consumers are willing to pay for the luxury of oysters, and as long as these families are willing to work in a traditional way, and as long as young people come into the industry, then all should be well. But what if the young people now have some other career in mind? What if this tradition is no longer seen as desirable? And if there are no oysters, who will care that the water quality is kept to a high standard, or that these marshes and creeks are managed in a way that encourages so many waders? What if we then lose the means to describe the land, and our ecological literacy declines?

The accumulated knowledge about nature is an important part of people's capacity to manage and conserve both wild and agricultural systems over long periods. This place-based knowledge has been transferred across generations and between communities as a key survival tool. It differs from modern knowledge by being dynamic, adaptive and locally derived. There are four levels of this ecological literacy: the names of living (plants, animals) and physical (soils, water, weather) components of ecosystems; the functions and uses of each component; the land and resource management systems and the social institutions that govern them; and the world views and cosmologies that guide the ethics of people in the system.

The importance of ecological literacy and its increasing demise has only recently been recognized. But it has substantial economic and environmental value, as it codes for and contributes to a wide range of ecosystem services and is an important component of conservation management systems that may be long-standing or only recently developed. Thus its loss may potentially inhibit our own development in the future. Within communities, there are known to be different levels of ecological literacy for men and women, for old and young, for groups engaged in land or marine management and those not, and for those with different amounts of time resident at one place. However, ecological literacy is now being lost or is no longer being transmitted from one generation to another at many locations. And when knowledge pools are lost, much like gene pools, it is impossible to regain the accumulation of observations over the short term. When we know less, we will be less inclined to engage with nature; as we engage less, so we will know less. Barry Lopez puts it like this:

> *If a society forgets or no longer cares where it lives, then anyone with the political power and the will to do so can manipulate the landscape to conform to certain social ideals or nostalgic visions. People may hardly notice that anything has happened.*

How much do we know, and how has it changed since modern cultures have emerged? A team from the University of Essex has been investigating levels of ecological literacy in both the UK and in India and Indonesia. Within Indonesia, in a study of five coastal villages, Sarah Pilgrim and Leanne Cullen found that villages with the lowest household income had the highest dependence on the natural resources of the coast and coral reefs, and also had the greatest knowledge of the names and uses of local plants and animals.[14] Across nations, the levels of ecological literacy are again inversely related to income (as measured by the human development index and gross domestic product) – the poorest know, and the richest have forgotten. This data suggests an extinction of experience – as people have become wealthier, and economies become less dependent on local natural resources, so knowledge is no longer required on a daily basis to survive. At the same time, there may be less knowledge transmission between generations, or simply substitution for other forms of knowledge, particularly among younger generations as a result of cosmopolitan jobs and formal schooling. This raises doubts as to the survival of ecological literacy into the future in the face of modern patterns of economic development.

In the study, older people recognize more species and their uses than younger people only in the UK; in India and Indonesia, there are no significant differences with age and knowledge saturation occurs earlier, though there is a slight downward drift with older memory loss. Acquisition of ecological literacy clearly continues through adulthood in the UK, while in India and Indonesia, accumulation appears to be rapid at a young age, probably resulting from high dependence on local natural marine and terrestrial resources. In the UK, there is no difference in the ecological literacy between women and men; in India, women know more about the health uses of plants, reflecting their primary household roles, whereas men know more about livestock and fodder uses. In Indonesia, men know more about birds, plants and animals than women, as they spend more time fishing, hunting or farming. Household roles and frequent resource interaction are important for ecological literacy, and both contribute to knowledge acquisition through experience.

Levels of resource dependence and interaction appear critical for ecoliteracy in traditional communities, but where a community has become industrialized and independent of natural goods and services, other factors come into play. These factors include increased experience by living in rural areas and increased visits to countryside locations. The longer a person lives in an area the more local knowledge they gain. Also word-of-mouth sources such as parents, friends and relatives are more prevalent in rural areas, making ecoliteracy higher than in urban areas, where ecological knowledge levels are poor and primarily dependent upon television and school books.

So now we know: ecological literacy is lower in richer communities and appears to have declined with increasing disconnection and livelihood independence from natural systems. As almost half the world's population is now urbanized, and almost all population growth set to occur in urban regions rather than rural, it is likely that levels of ecological literacy will continue to decline. Ecological literacy saturates at an earlier age in traditional communities compared with industrialized ones, and gender differences occur where women and men have different roles in household livelihoods, suggesting that ecological literacy is an emergent property of regular interaction with nature. These changes and differences in ecological literacy have important implications if the many ecosystem goods and services are to be retained and the terrestrial and marine habitats from which they derive are to receive public support for their protection, conservation and long-term sustainable management.

Increasing urbanization and levels of income seem to result in a loss of local ecological knowledge. Over time, people then become immune to species loss, and they no longer know the uses for wild plants or animals, often no longer even the names. However, the longer someone dwells at a certain location, the more they do come to know about local ecologies. Again, though, this depends on the availability of locally available habitats. Green space in the city may be green, and thus beneficial to mental health as an oasis is in a desert, but if it is only mown grass and city trees, then there are only limited opportunities to develop a range of knowledge. Disconnections also allow more damage to occur. As we know less, so we care less, and then the powerful can take over as there are no remaining defenders of the landscape. Second, disconnections threaten the fundamental basis of human nature and our current civilization itself. Human evolution has progressed through shaping and self-shaping, with humans and environments coevolving. In this process, we have brought forth a world, and evolved in one entirely different to that which exists today. If the world emerges from our interactions with it, what world are we now creating?

Television and other media now shape so much of what we know about the world, yet we are only a spectator rather than a participant. In the TV world, there will be lions in a programme about lions. In the real world, you may see nothing for long periods, and only be very lucky to see lions if you go looking for them. Simon Barnes, irreverent author of *How to be a Bad Birdwatcher*, asks, 'What if you were to turn on the TV for a programme about lions, and there weren't any?', and goes on to say that:

> *most wildlife watching is humdrum. Not dull – no, dear me, no. But you do need to find a different mindset if you want to get the hang of it. You need to make a mental adjustment.*

This mental adjustment may be crucial if we are to retain a level of land and ecological literacy essential to both the world's and our future. Participation with the wild can be profound, changing us forever. We should be giving every opportunity for these natural interactions to occur, rather than just with human-made artefacts. Robert Macfarlane perceptively notes that landscapes are 'imagined into existence [...] we do not see what is there, but largely what we think is there'. If we think nothing, then we are in trouble.[15]

13

Exclusion Zones

The mayor roars with laughter, refills the finger glasses with amber brandy from the mountains in the east and toasts his new town, carved from the deep forest. In a windowless booth of pine, more akin to a sauna than a roadside restaurant, cold soup, hot mustard and grilled pork accompany jokes about politics and people, and reflections on the more serious challenge of reviving Slavutych's economy. Volodymyr Udovychenko is civic leader of Ukraine's newest town, created in the aftermath of the Chernobyl nuclear accident, and one that is now struggling with the subsequent closure of the remaining reactors and loss of jobs. Later, back on the dark road, the great trees crowd against the roadside for a hundred kilometres or more, and trucks with swaying trailers lumber north towards Russia. Slavutych eventually appears like an oasis, with wide streets and bright sodium streetlights, a town of 20,000 people linked by sixty kilometres of the iron road to the Chernobyl complex to the west.

This project started in the 1970s, when the USSR built two nuclear plants on the banks of the meandering Dniepr River, with its wide flood plain of marshes and birch and pine forests, by the northern Ukraine border with Belarus and Russia. By 1983, two more reactors were completed, part of a grand plan to construct eight in all. But reactor four lasted only three years, and the remainder would never be built. On 26 April 1986, the catastrophic Chernobyl accident occurred, now known to be mostly a result of human error: some staff at the plant conduct a test to check the plant's capacity to continue to provide electrical power to the cooling system under conditions of a sudden loss of power. Unfortunately, they do not tell the operators of the nuclear part of the plant, and the combination of a series of unlikely events and decisions lead suddenly to an uncontrollable power surge, resulting in two violent explosions at 1.23 a.m. The 1000-tonne sealing cap is blown off the plant, the reactor is destroyed, and the melting of the fuel rods at 2000°C causes the graphite cooling rods themselves to catch fire. A plume of fissile material – gases, aerosols and six tonnes of fragmented fuel – reaches a kilometre into the sky, and leads eventually to the deposition of radioactive material across the whole of the northern hemisphere.

Firefighters are on the scene within minutes, but it takes 400 of them ten days to put out the graphite fire. They receive very high doses of radiation; 31 later die and another 237 suffer acute radiation sickness. Many thousands of liquidators are brought in to make the plant safe. They fly 1800 helicopter flights to drop lead, sand and dolomite on the reactor, they dig tunnels under the plant that are filled with concrete to prevent downward movement of molten material, and finally they build a sarcophagus around the whole plant. In seven months, 600,000 people work on the sarcophagus, some in the early days only being permitted to be present for a few hours before doses became too great. Twenty years later, the plant remains as it was, a menacing grey coffin thrown together as remotely as was feasible, leaking rainwater through a rusting roof, and subject now to an urgent plan to surround it in a new and more comprehensive sarcophagus.

The plume of radiation escaping from Chernobyl is first measured at Forsmark in Sweden a couple of days later, where the local response is first to assume that it has come from a local accident. Only then do authorities in the former Soviet Union break from institutional paralysis and begin to act to protect local people. An exclusion zone of 30-kilometre radius is created, and within two days all 49,000 people from the service town of Pripyat are evacuated in 1200 buses. A further 115,000 people are then evacuated from 76 rural settlements over the next ten days or so, and evacuees are settled in urban settlements to the south towards Kiev in Ukraine and to the north towards Minsk in Belarus. Some 15,000 cattle have to be slaughtered, and the exclusion zone of about 4000 square kilometres is cleared of all the social and economic activity of human civilization.[1]

This much is known as fact. Since then, Chernobyl has entered the psyche of people worldwide. An industrial disaster of the greatest possible magnitude. The incompetence of people and safety mechanisms. The health consequences borne not by political leaders and technocrats, but by common people. No wonder, then, that international political pressure led to the closure of all the remaining nuclear reactors by the end of the year 2000. But it is here that fact and fiction start to diverge. Chernobyl has now emerged as a site of ecological recovery in the almost complete absence of people. And neither are the health effects as expected – these are mostly social and psychological rather than caused directly by radiation. The acute effects were limited to the heroic firefighters, who, of course, had little personal choice at the time.

The lack of severe health effects is a surprise. Despite large-scale monitoring by the International Atomic Energy Authority and teams of domestic and international scientists, no chronic radiation effects have been observed in the general public of the three countries of Ukraine, Belarus and Russia. The occurrence of so-called 'late effects' has been confirmed, however, among young children exposed to iodine-131 and caesium-137 in the immediate aftermath of the accident: among the cohort of under five year olds, some 982 now have a very aggressive form of thyroid cancer. Other thyroid effects have also been found, but these are termed occult cases – they exist everywhere in general populations, and are only found when looked for. Among the liquidators, the main cause of death over the two decades has been smoking, and again no other radiation effects have been found. This is especially surprising, as increased leukaemia, congenital abnormalities and adverse pregnancy outcomes were all predicted. Of course, it is possible to find such cases among the population of exposed people, but they occur at a rate no higher than in the populations of average towns across Europe and North America, although there are confounding factors, as many people have sought to join the list of liquidators because of the financial advantages. At the same time, it is also to the financial advantage of individuals and towns to talk up the ill-health effects, as this leads not unreasonably to continued flows of financial welfare support.[2]

There have, on the other hand, been many severe social and psychological health problems arising from the forced evacuation of Pripyat and the rural villages of the exclusion zone. Your life is stable, the children are content at school, there is food in the shops, your extended family and friends are here, and, for the rural villagers, your ancestors have been buried in these soils for centuries. One day it all changes, with no warning. You see a plume of smoke from the plant a few kilometres away. You hear rumours, then the civic and military leaders start a panic. Everyone is to leave, immediately. Collect only what you can carry, hold tight to the children's hands, and jump on the bus. There is no preparation, no imagination of a new place, just the fear and pain of fleeing something you cannot see. Everything else is abandoned. Communities are broken up and social networks disrupted, and people are settled in rows of decrepit blocks of flats on the edges of what were to them nameless towns and cities. Many go on to suffer a victim mentality – they are shunned by recipient communities, yet dependent for welfare on distrusted authorities, whose support in turn comes unhelpfully to be called a 'coffin subsidy'.

The psychological effects are probably worse for the farming families of the rural villages, as they were resident in the region long before the reactors were built and had little to do with them on a daily basis. Within three to four months of the disaster, some rural people began to return, and now some 800 or so live permanently inside the exclusion zone. As they are technically illegals, they receive no official support from government agencies. But, interestingly, they have been found to be less stressed and anxious than those who stayed away. They are now all old, and gradually approaching their own end times.

Today, you approach the Ukrainian exclusion zone from the east by crossing the blue-green Dniepr marshes, and passing through a finger of Belarus. At the checkpoints, young immigration officers in light green uniforms and aggressively peaked caps check and stamp every piece of paper several times, and in the fullness of time let the car pass. Ahead, a roe deer scampers across the road, which then sweeps from the forests to cross the great cooling ponds, now home to giant two-metre catfish. The exclusion zone itself is now the subject of a unique experiment on what happens when people leave. When civilizations end, and people disperse or die off, what then happens to nature? What happens, too, to the few people who might survive?[3]

You come into the town of Pripyat along a street crowded with silver birches. This former town of 49,000 people is now an eyrie reminder of how civilization treads on thin ice. One day it is a vibrant city, the next it is abandoned. Today, there are only ghosts in the crumbling infrastructure. One day it will be completely overrun by nature, lost in the forests, perhaps to be discovered in the future by amazed archaeologists, as were Tikal, Machu Picchu and Angkor Wat. We park in the central square, a light wind rustling the birch and poplars, raising a worrisome dust on a day of sparkling sunshine and azure sky. Some street surfaces are clear and grey, as patrols do pass on occasions. But everywhere else, the green of trees, grass and flowering plants dominates.

In one meadow, grown up over paving stones, local scientist Igor Chernivsky and I count some forty species of plants in flower. Sergey Gachuk, of the Radioecology Laboratory in Slavutych, has recorded 226 species in Pripyat alone. Walking across the main square towards the grand steps and wide windows of the Palace of Culture, we see the clumped droppings of moose. In the old fountains, a reed bed has established, and red dragonflies and neon-blue mayflies flit across the water. Above, swifts swoop and chitter. We crunch over broken glass and into blocks of flats and official buildings. A case for a trumpet lies forlornly, a child's stuffed toy on the stairs. The temptation is to gather up some of the smaller items of this modern archaeology, a film strip or old pens, but then you remember they are likely to be hot, and so best remain. Memories are safe, but artefacts are likely not.

Silver birch has sprouted along the upper balcony of the Palace of Culture and is beginning to fill the spaces formerly taken by huge plate glass windows. There is something strange about the glass. It is all broken, and clearly not by the blast of the accident. Vandals must have later come to cause this damage – evidence perhaps of some latent desire on the part of we moderns to destroy our own civilization – acts that can be undertaken with impunity as there are no police or citizenry to stop them. A vandal's paradise. We push through a tall grass meadow to come upon a seemingly ancient theme park – rusty rides, peeling faded paint, rotten wood and a great ferris wheel with silent yellow cabins, bright against the sky. You turn around once, and then again, and there is only silence. Open spaces, concrete riding up where the roots of an apple tree are bursting out. The purples, reds, blues and yellows of flowers are everywhere.

We climb the 16 stories of the tallest block of flats, first fighting our way through thick vegetation to reach the hidden front porch. A door hangs on a broken hinge, and we crunch up the crumbling stairs, flakes of pale green paint covering every surface. Up we go, counting the floors and trying not to breathe too deeply for fear of inhaling the dust, until we find a ladder in a dark loft. The rusty door creaks, and then gives way, and we are on the roof. And here the view takes our breath away. On the east horizon, the River Pripyat and cooling ponds, the power plant complex standing tall beyond the town; on the other three horizons, the forests of pine, willow and birch stretch away. Before the accident, a fifth of the region was forested, now it is 80 per cent. This reminds me vividly of climbing the Mayan Temple of the Giant Jaguar at Tikal and emerging from the rainforest to gaze down on the tree tops full of howler and spider monkeys, stretching away in a sea of green to Belize and Mexico. Here, we look down on roads cramped by invading grass, trees sprouting through concrete. Rows of flats march into the distance, every one of them empty.

By day, you can see no wildlife save birds, but it is here. The city and its surrounds host wolves, boar, roe and red deer, and moose. Beavers, otters and mink are abundant in the rivers, and bear footprints can be found if you look carefully. Some 15 lynx have returned to the exclusion zone. Bats have invaded old trees and abandoned houses, badgers are abundant, and kestrels nest in abandoned window boxes. A total of 240 species of animals have been counted in the exclusion zone, most of which were present only in very low numbers before the desertion by the people. The wider region always had some wolves, for example, but now there are several packs numbering some 200 individuals, of which 90–100 are adults. The rare Przewalski's horse was introduced from the steppes and now number a herd of 70 individuals. On the Belarus side, the European bison has been introduced. The 1500 beaver and 7000 wild boar are already beginning to reshape the local ecosystems. Many rare birds have returned, including black storks, eagles, swans and owls. Sergey Gachuk indicates that there may be new relationships emerging between animals and people: 'It is very exciting. I think many animals have never now seen people and do not know what to make of us.' The animals are also less affected by radiation than expected. Small mammals in the hottest area, for example, show no signs of ill-health, although rodents brought in from clean areas and released do suffer ill-health. The local animals seem to have evolved in an intriguing way.

From horizon to horizon, the land is green. The city is tiny by comparison. After the accident, people had to leave in a day or two of utter chaos, but now all is serene.

And in this way civilization is abandoned. Will it be like this elsewhere in the world? What will it be like when our numbers fall, or when climate change affects the viability of some regions? Settlements will surely be abandoned, whole suburbs forgotten, towns where economic activity dries up left to nature. Perhaps Pripyat is the first of many to come during the next couple of centuries. Which, then, are doomed? We have never had to ask such questions. No civilization ever conceives of its own failure, of the likelihood of departure, of abandonment to nature. And we will have to face nature anew as it reinvades, and if whole ecosystems arrive, then they will bring predators too. Perhaps there will be no problems – but ask how people feel in India on the edge of national parks where tigers are now abundant, or in Boulder, Colorado, where mountain lions have reinvaded urban areas, or indeed the people of this exclusion zone, where wolves eat the domestic dogs as they are easy prey. Or perhaps by then we will have wreaked such harm on certain parts of nature that there will be little left to invade.

Later, we walk through villages hanging onto their own histories. After the accident, all the domestic animals were rounded up and shot, and the people trucked off to distant cities. Some came back, and strangely enough they seem happy. An 81 year old, Anastasia, her headscarf and blouse a riot of flower-design and smile of silver and gold, recalls her 60 years of marriage in this village. She was sad at first that only 20 people came back to the village – formerly of 2000 people – but now she says she feels fine. She has land, a pig and some cows, and friends. The children sometimes come up from the south, and they eat and sing songs. An old man and his wife, Vassily and Maria, were both born in the village more than 70 years ago; now they are its youngest residents. They sit under the shade of an apple tree by the empty road, and complain about the lack of transport. This gnarled man, stubble half-shorn, teeth at all angles, wears the blue serge jacket of peasants the world over. They like it here because it is home. They like to talk too, as no one ever comes this way except for those making occasional clumsy attempts to remove them.

We walk across a farm with Hannah, as she darts between potatoes and peas in brightly coloured slippers. She grows cabbages and carrots, maize and onions, red and white beets, squashes and courgettes, and spindly tomatoes. She has two pigs – one is to be killed at the New Year celebrations. All the villagers still gather plants and animals from the forests, and should leave the hot mushrooms and berries alone, but do not – they like them too much. They are approaching their own end times, and have come to terms with the patchy and invisible threat of radiation.

Though the children will not come back, and new people will not move here, these forgotten people seem happy and content, living where their identities have been shaped over centuries. But soon each village will steadily decline in numbers, until the last woman or man standing has it all to themselves. How will they feel? What will they do then? Move to another village, or simply wait? We walk into the abandoned wooden houses, with glassed-in verandas at the entrances, kitchens centred on great stoves attached to raised bed platforms to keep warm in winter.

Some windows are broken, but fewer than in Pripyat. A vine twists around a window, an ancient pear tree hangs branches across a roof, currant bushes run wild in the yard, a pigsty roof has collapsed, great banks of nettles thrive on nutrient-rich soils. The roofs of some buildings are made of flaky asbestos, probably more hazardous to health than the local sources of radiation. It is warm today, but in the middle of winter it will be bitterly cold, and people will huddle around their stoves and let their local vodka warm them from the inside. And they will count the winters away until they, too, are gone.

In most other parts of the world, our numbers are increasing, though economics is causing the abandonment of rural communities in the Mid-west of the US and in the Mediterranean countries of Europe. But this exclusion zone contains two exemplars of a modern parable that we may have to become more used to – the consequences of the sudden abandonment of a whole town or city, and the results of a slow death of villages, with the end times knocking hard on their doors. Will these people go gentle into the night, or will they, as Dylan Thomas urged, 'rage, rage against the dying of the light'?[4]

Civilizations do come and go; this much we know. But the curious thing is how little we know about precisely why. Indeed it is only recently (in modern human history) that the world has come to know of the existence of the moai carved heads of the remote Rapa Nui (Easter Island), of the temples of the Mayans lost in the rainforest, of the Inca ruins of Machu Picchu at altitudes that challenge most people's physiologies, of the Minoan ruins on Crete, of the Angkor Wat complex in Cambodia, and many others. Every one of these is subject to great scholarship and debate, and multiple (and often conflicting) reasons have been proposed for the ending of civilizations that lasted thousands of years. Yet the final truth is that we have collectively forgotten what happened to cause people to abandon great cultures that underpinned symbols of power and permanence. In no case did all the people die off or disappear, though there may have been great losses due to conflict or natural disaster. People simply stopped doing what they were doing and returned to a simpler lifestyle. And the knowledge of astronomers, mathematicians, linguists, storytellers, accountants, architects and engineers was lost, save for a few carvings and, very rarely, written material in books. What would future archaeologists make of our civilization today in the absence of all books and accessible hard drives? They would have to decipher a civilization from graffiti left on urban subways and railway buildings, which would tell little or nothing of the theories of relativity and quantum physics, of evolution or international institutions.[5]

There is, of course, a danger of this thinking becoming biased towards civilizations that have left substantial material artefacts. Many persistent and successful civilizations, particularly those of hunter-gatherers, however, have left nothing more or less than a well-managed environment, perhaps an even greater testimony to human intentionality and advance. In *Make Prayers to the Raven*, Richard Nelson indicates that the Koyukon people of central Alaska have created no monuments such as Stonehenge or Machu Picchu, but that 'their legacy is the vast land itself, enduring and effectively unchanged despite having supported human life for count-less centuries'.[6]

Norman Hammond begins his discourse on the Mayan civilization by noting that this is 'one of the most surprising civilizations in pre-Columbian America: it arose, flourished and vanished in a little under a thousand years'. Since American lawyer John Lloyd Stephens and English artist Frederick Catherwood returned from their expedition of 1839–1842 with surprising news of extraordinary temples in the forests of what is now Guatemala, Belize and the Yucatán of Mexico, interest in both the persistence and disappearance of the Mayans has been intense. The Petén rainforest of northern Guatemala is now one of the world's biodiversity hotspots, with 200 species of mammals and 500 species of birds. You walk across the forest floor in deep shadow, sunlight piercing the gaps in foliage as it does through the windows of great cathedrals, past giant buttresses eventually to reach the former city of Tikal.

Once I climbed a rusting, vertical ladder to stand at the top of a temple and watched a dark storm race across the trees and other temple tops to sting us with cold rain. If you thought this was just a great wilderness, you would be mistaken, for Tikal was at its height one of the greatest cities in the world. The Mayan Classic Period lasted from about AD 250 to 900, and it was in the Late Classic Period that there was a great expansion in temple and pyramid construction. By the ninth century, there were some 40,000–70,000 people living in Tikal, surpassed in size by probably only four or five other cities worldwide. For some unknown reasons, these great temples and cities were then abandoned, with the Post-Classic Period surviving until the destructive arrival of the Spanish in the 16th century.

For such a persistent civilization, the Mayans strangely lacked the wheel and metal, and did not domesticate livestock. They did have hieroglyphic writing, though, and bark paper and deerskin books, a mathematical system with the use of very large numbers, astronomy of a high order without optical instruments, a complex calen-dar, intensive agriculture and kitchen gardens, a game played with a rubber ball in a special court, specialized markets using chocolate beans as money, a pantheon of gods, and an emphasis on self-sacrifice and mutilation. The Mayans had no contact beyond Mesoamerica, and, as Norman Hammond comments, 'such knowledge is, unfortunately, a perishable thing, dying with the minds in which it lives or the books in which it is written'. Of course, the Mayans did not disappear; there are some two million Mayan speakers across Mesoamerica today. They simply stopped the practices and norms of one culture and deserted its urban centres to do something different.[7]

Many theories have been advanced to explain the collapse. Some are ecological: soils became exhausted, erosion filled the lakes, water supplies were harmed, weeds swamped the crops or wood became scarce. Others centre on disease or malnutri-tion: an epidemic swept the region or food ran out. Others still are social: internal conflict, disaffected peasantry, bloody revolution, external invasion, the emergence of cult groups or the collapse of administrative systems. The truth is, no one really knows, and a compelling story can be built around any one or more of these theories.

What is better known is that after the arrival of Ponce de Leon in 1513, and then Córdoba in 1517, and the founding of the Spanish capital of Mérida in 1542, the Spanish conquered the Mayans and terminated the Late Classic Period. To Mayan scholars, though, it clearly matters greatly why the earlier Classic Period came to a sudden halt.

For my purpose, I am more interested in the simple fact that civilizations do come to a halt, and that such an end may not be able to be predicted by members of the civilization concerned. We cannot be sure, but we may suppose that the Mayans at the height of their powers thought that things would go on forever. There would have been some signs (such as ours today of climate change, or biodiversity loss, or overfishing) but many would disbelieve their significance, or rather simply continue to believe in the paradigm that defines a civilization. If it is here, has persisted for a long time, is hugely successful, then why raise any doubts? Doubts are for disbelievers. Then one day, all changes, and later people are left to wonder quite what happened.

One of the Mayan books of *Chilam Bulam* contains this prescient poem:

> *Eat, eat, thou hast bread,*
> *Drink, drink, thou hast water;*
> *On that day, dust possesses the earth,*
> *On that day, a blight is on the face of the earth,*
> *On that day, a cloud rises,*
> *On that day, a mountain rises,*
> *On that day, a strong man seizes the land,*
> *On that day, things fall to ruin,*
> *On that day, the tender leaf is destroyed,*
> *On that day, the dying eyes are closed…*
> *And they are scattered afar in the forests.*[8]

How is our record today? The self-imposed exclusion zone at Chernobyl is matched on a smaller scale by the notorious building of a community on a toxic waste dump at Love Canal in New York in the 1970s and its later desertion. Many other just as toxic places, though, have tragically not been abandoned. Nature also sometimes plays it hard, as it did for the 12,000 islanders of Montserrat in 1995, when the Soufriere Hills above the capital of Plymouth began to emit steam, which gave way to pyroclastic flows in 1997 that buried the capital. Many people fled the country, and the population fell to less than 4000 people. Efforts continue to revive the economy and tempt people back. But around the volcano, the exclusion zone persists because of a high probability of further eruptions.

But one of the world's most notorious contemporary collapses has been caused directly by the actions of people and their failed policies and practices. It may again be a sign of worse to come, or it may simply be ignored as it is located deep in central Asia, a location far from the eyes of most of the world. This is the demise of the Aral Sea, a planned assassination, as John McNeill has put it. In the quest to increase cotton production, the world's fourth largest lake has been turned into a salty desert. In a series of extraordinary irrigation projects, water was diverted from two river systems, the Amu-Darja and Syr-Darja, to irrigate some eight million hectares of cotton fields from the 1960s to the 1990s. In 1960 water influx into the Aral Sea was 55 cubic kilometres per year. By 1980, it had fallen to 20 per cent of this, by the 1990s to 10 per cent. The Aral Sea is in a closed basin, and so the consequence was rapidly falling sea levels. These are now 15 metres lower than in 1960, and the sea covers half the area and contains only 30 per cent of the water. Salinity has risen threefold, and a thriving fish industry that once caught 40,000 tonnes per year is now extinct. The Muynak cannery is now maintained by airlifted frozen fish brought in from northern Russia. By the mid-1990s, the Muynak population had fallen from 40,000 to 12,000, and its future prospects are poor unless the sea can be restored.

The Aral Sea used to moderate the local climate, but now the summers are hotter and winters colder. Aerial salt has been carried by winds across 200km, reducing crop yields, corroding power lines and damaging concrete structures. Yet, in the name of progress, the President of the Turkmen Academy of Sciences, A Babayev, once said:

> *I belong to those scientists who consider that the drying up of the Aral Sea is far more advantageous than preserving it. [...] Cultivation of cotton alone will pay for the existing Aral Sea, with all its fisheries, shipping and other industries [...] the disappearance of the sea will not affect the region's landscape.*

He was horribly wrong, but fortunately by 2006 an $85 million World Bank project was beginning to raise the sea level of the northern sea, offering some prospects of ecological and possibly economic recovery.[9]

In Britain, we have our own exclusion zones, but they date so far back that their memory has been almost erased. In Scotland, the consequences of the Highland clearances of the 18th and 19th centuries so entered popular culture that they form a significant part of many people's identity. Yet, curiously, England's own clearances, which occurred several hundred year earlier, were then forgotten until the mid-20th century, when historians and archaeologists, led in particular by Maurice Beresford, began to document the lost or deserted villages of England. Despite the existence of extensive records for mediaeval English society, historians had come to believe that whole village depopulations were rare or, if they had occurred, it was only due to the Black Death – which had reduced the population of England and Wales from 3.8 million in 1348 to 2.1 million by the early 1400s.

In the later Middle Ages, into the 1500s and early 1600s, however, there are many records of the effects of forced depopulation. An inquiry of 1517 recorded that many people were evicted and made unemployed, being sent to 'idleness and misery', and some 1000 villagers 'left their houses weeping, and became unemployed and finally, we suppose, died in poverty and so ended their days'. In the Midland riots of 1697, rioters said they knew of 300 places depopulated, and many earlier Tudor writers indicated the importance of the phenomenon, though they often exaggerated fears that it was continuing. In 1770 Oliver Goldsmith revived concerns about dispossession by focusing on the effects of enclosure in his poem *The Deserted Village*, indicating that 'rural mirth and manners are no more'. But this was in the middle of the period of the great Enclosure Acts, when the government sanctioned 4500 Acts to enclose open field and heath, moor and commons enclosures between 1700 and 1845, and one over-romantic and exaggerated poem was to have little effect. Yet by the 19th and 20th centuries, writers and historians had come to accept that 'there is very little evidence of emptied villages in Britain'. The first edition of the six inch Ordnance Survey maps of Northamptonshire, for example, recorded none of the earthworks or deserted village sites now know to be common across the county.[10]

The phenomenon of England's deserted mediaeval villages indicates how easy it is for civilization to forget what it has done. It may also show how easily we will come to forget our current civilizations in the future. Beresford found that 'oblique references to vanished villages can be detected in the nooks and crannies' of many documents, and set about finding and documenting deserted mediaeval villages in the 1940s and 1950s. At first, he and his colleagues thought there may be a few hundred at most. By the end of several decades of research, they had found more than 3000 – each a village once complete, but then entirely deserted. Beresford indicated how difficult was his initial research:

> *no traveller comes easily to a lost village. [...] You must be friends to mud, to green lanes and unused footpaths, to rotting footbridges and broken stiles, to branches and to barbed wire. [...] It is so long since anyone wanted to come this way.*

What is quite extraordinary is that in our small and cramped island, now of 60 million people, we could so easily have lost 3000 villages.

The term deserted for these villages can seem to suggest that people left of their own volition. But this was not the case. It is also generally not true that the Black Death was a primary cause of desertion, as there were only a very few cases where every villager died. The main flood of depopulation occurred from 1440 to 1520 and was provoked by ruthless landlords wanting to remove people from the land. In some cases, these were owners of large homes wishing to have their view unencumbered by peasant houses, or to create deer parks. 'Many a lost village stands in the shadows of the Great House', says Beresford. In other cases, Cistercian monasteries had nearby villages removed to enhance their solitude. At some locations, villages were lost to coastal erosion, particularly on the east coast of Yorkshire, Norfolk and Suffolk. But by far the most common reason was the desire of landlords to convert mixed farmland to sheepwalks. Sheep were cheaper to manage, requiring less labour, and wool had become valuable. By 1500, there were three times as many sheep in Britain than people. Farming families were cast from the land, and it was turned over to grass. Ironically, it is the conversion to sheep pasture that meant many of the original field patterns and village remains survive to this day, as they have avoided the destructive effects of the plough.

Many of the villages remain hard to locate, as Beresford indicated, and when found are often lonely and mournful places. The greatest density is in the Midlands. For example, of the villages recorded in 1316, 72 of Northamptonshire's 392 (18 per cent) were deserted by 1334, with corresponding figures of 52 out of 348 (15 per cent) for Leicestershire and 91 out of 359 (25 per cent) for Oxfordshire. One example is Wormleighton in Warwickshire. Today's village of 150 people is on a Cotswolds' hilltop, amid dense trees around a sandstone manor house. You walk past the church into a sunken lane full of swaying white cow parsley, and then come upon a wide expanse of grassland stretching to the valley bottom, through which the Oxford canal was built in 1777. Wormleighton had thrived as a village for some 550 years after it was recorded in a charter of 956. In the Domesday Survey of 1086, it had a population of 250. But by 1499, the lord of the manor, William Cope, who had recently acquired the estate in his role as adviser to Henry VII, put 100 hectares to pasture, and dispatched some 85 families from the village. In 1506 John Spencer, a grazier from a nearby village, bought the estate and came to live here, later amassing sheep flocks of 20,000 animals and vast wealth.

The hillside today is covered with house platforms and the remains of crofts, set by a hollow-way, the former main street and a stream. The hollow-way was later converted into four fishponds, fed by a reservoir. This field is still called the Old Town locally. Standing by the canal, you can see the distinct patterns of ridge and furrow running in parallel away from the house remains. For more than 500 years, a village thrived here. Now sheep and lambs laze in the sunshine, skylarks hover with swirling song and chaffinches chatter from the hawthorn hedge. But there are no people. You could pass it on the canal and not realize it was a deserted village. You might say that half a millennium is a good record for any community, and it may be that our modern settlements will not last half that long. But here, the exclusion was down to a single cold-hearted landlord who simply wanted to make more money from sheep.

Wormleighton did survive in a new form, as new houses were built around the new manor and church. Most deserted villages, however, remain completely empty. A close examination of maps will show areas with surprisingly large gaps between settlements. Very often, this is where you will find a deserted village. One example is Sulby in Northants, situated to the east of Welford and its reservoir built in the early 1800s to keep the Grand Union Canal full of water – enough for 9000 locks. One spring morning, I walk across the reservoir boom, past a pair of pied wagtails, to the left ridge and furrow, sheep at the top and rushes in the bottom wetlands. Pink-footed geese circle and land in a chorus of indignant calls and splashes, and join Canada geese with goslings. The early morning sunlight turns the water to silver, and the easterly wind buffets and blows. Three grebes bob, and disappear, and reappear some distance away. For the moment, there is no feeling of any ghosts in the landscape, but they are here somewhere up the hill.

I walk through an oak and ash wood and, turning a corner, come face to face with a red fox. It stands, and I stand, we look at one another carefully. The world comes to a halt, and then, blink, it has disappeared among the bluebells and ragged robin. All that remains is the insistent alarm call of a watchful songbird. A couple of kilometres further, across wheat fields and on the top of a hill, are the earthwork remains of Sulby. In 1334 it had 31 houses, in 1377 some 89, but by 1428 only 4 and in 1721 just two. A steady death. End of story. The manor was sold in 1215 to Sulby Abbey, and it was they who later had the people removed.

The village site today is pasture, with cattle and black-faced sheep, a lamb hobbling horribly in the wind. A flock of rooks call from a nearby rookery. The village remains are barely discernable – if you did not know it was a village, you might think it was simply a bumpy field. This village was at its height 700 years ago. Where will we be in 700 years' time, I wonder? The hillside is covered with croft platforms and sunken roadways, with clumps of nettles. The rooks are insistent, and have probably been here hundreds of years. Standing by a disappointing single sycamore tree, on a platform eight to ten metres in size, you can begin to imagine children running between the wooden and unbaked mud houses, roofed with turf or straw, tumbling down the hillside, rolling and shouting, men strolling to the fields, women walking to the stream at the bottom to gather water. In winter, easterly winds would blow directly onto the houses, whistling through the eaves, and people would gather together around the fires to stay warm. One day, someone in the Abbey decided to change everything, and give the land to sheep. Perhaps the Black Death also helped to push this village to the edge.

And what of other sites? By the Grand Union Canal, the main highway snaking through central England for a century before the advent of the railway, is the village of Downton, long deserted too. Aerial pictures from the 1960s show the remains of croft and hollow-way earthworks, but then modern ploughing destroyed them all. Today, the village is under blue-grey wheat fields, edged by hedgerows of maple. Interestingly, there are more trees and hedgerows today compared with the landscape completely levelled after modern farming arrived. This day, a boom sprayer marches through cereal three fields away. If it comes to this field, that will be the end of the hovering skylarks and their hidden nests.

A few kilometres distant is Stanford, a village cleared for parkland by the owners of the nearby hall. Again, earthworks around a north–south sunken lane, still wet, with glorious oaks dotted across the field, and ridge and furrow in nearby fields. Once a thriving community paying considerable taxes, now sheep pasture. Or Fawcliffe, by a busy road, a chewed up and over-grazed pasture, deeply poached by cattle, with hawthorn following an ancient ridge line up over the hill.

Or Brauncetonbury and Wolfhamcote, twin deserted villages, leaving the isolated St Peter's Church as the only remaining part of the villages, long since abandoned for worship, the gravestones lost in deep grass. Both were enclosed and depopulated in 1501, some 500 or more years after being granted their charters, leaving a giant ridge and furrow open field, a kilometre or more in length, surrounded on one side by a canal and two others by railway viaducts (both themselves now abandoned). The field is marked only by a huge badger set in one corner, rarely visited, I imagine, as the badgers have chosen to construct their set upon a Victorian spoil, and all their burrow entrances are thick with hundreds of glass bottles dug up and deposited as waste. These villages persisted for half a millennium and were abandoned; the canal was cut and then abandoned a century later; two railway lines were constructed and then closed in the 1960s. It is a remote piece of countryside, where the wind bends the sheets of yellow buttercups.

Cublington in Buckinghamshire is similar to Wormleighton, a deserted community on the edge of the new village. The local folk myth is that the Black Death was the cause, but records show a substantial shrinking of arable lands before the 1340s. The site is marked by a small hill, called the beacon or castle mound locally, and now populated by a herd of curious Charolais cattle and a mad black horse. You can easily be drawn into underestimating these places – they are now just fields with earthworks on the edges of current civilization. But once they were part of the civilization, and local residents probably thought they would go one forever. I talk to a local couple about the site, still proud about having fought off plans for London's third airport in the 1970s, but there are no folk memories of any detail, or perceptions of ancient ghosts. It is probably too late for any of that – 664 years of grazing is long enough to forget a good deal.

Just after a cold dawn, I walk down through the five wide terraces of Harrington, the sun glistening in the heavy spring dew. Once a village, it was converted to create ornate gardens and fish ponds after the Knights Hospitallers of the Order of St John of Jerusalem, owners since 1232, lost the land in the dissolution, and it passed to the local lord. He enlarged the manor house, and descendants created splendid Italian-style ornamental gardens that in 1712 were thus acclaimed: 'for a descent of garden walks, there is nothing so remarkable as the walks of the garden on the northern front of the Rt Hon the Earl of Dysert's house at Harrington'. Apart from the ghosts of the villagers dispatched from this hillside, it is said that a Lady Jane Stanhope floats above the gardens at dusk, as she once argued with a gardener in the 1600s and killed him with a spade. At Church Charwelton, also in Northamptonshire, all that remains again is a church by a farmhouse a couple of kilometres from the nearest house. You pass through several gates to reach this remote spot, depopulated by two abbeys in the late 1400s. What we see here, in the warm evening sunlight at the end of the day, is a landscape transformed by the powerful, leaving only somewhere for the poor to worship and give thanks for what they have.[11]

What can we make of these exclusions and desertions? Perhaps just a certain humility would be enough, and a recognition that, as Thomas Hardy wrote, dynasties do pass. Philip Larkin's 1972 poem 'Going, going', though, lamented the disappearance of something valued about the country, and was characteristically gloomy about future prospects:

I thought it would last my time —
The sense that, beyond the town,
There would always be fields and farms [...]

And that will be England gone,
The shadows, the meadows, the lanes,
The guildhalls, the carved choirs.
There'll be books; it will linger on [...]

Most things are never meant. [...]
I just think it will happen, soon.

14

Life and Land on the North Atlantic Fringe

Make your way to the northwestern fringe of Europe or to the northwestern edge of the North Atlantic and you will find two landscapes that are today substantially emptier of people than in the not too distant past. The dominating impression in the first, the Highlands and Islands of Scotland, is of a largely empty landscape, one apparently too harsh for many people to make a living. The land is wet and boggy, raked by gales and frequent rain, and trees seem to survive only in hollows and valleys. Such an impression holds some truths, but look more closely at the land, dig down a little, and you will see it was not always this empty.

The Western Isles of Scotland are famed for their Neolithic stone circles and fortified towers and are home today to 164,000 sheep and 26,000 people, a third of whom live in the capital Stornoway on the island of Lewis. Turn seawards on north Lewis from Scaliscro at Little Loch Roag, towards the two seal colonies at the mouth of the loch, and you have to struggle across the waterlogged hillsides. In one of Britain's driest summers, our feet still sink to a calf's depth where clumps of sticky red sundew await unsuspecting insects. The sphagnum forms mounds of soft green and red moss, and clumps of rushes hide deeper pools. The whole landscape is alive with the sound of gurgling water. Later, we come to realize that we are rising and falling across abandoned croplands, remnants of raised lazy beds or *feannagan*. This hillside, which now appears fit for only sheep, and that at a stretch, is hiding a formerly cultivated landscape. A slope of fields, cleverly draining water between the ridges. Closer observation also shows us that this whole lochside was once dotted with houses. The deserted villages of Strome and Drovernish lie towards the head of the loch. Looking down on them from a rocky outcrop, it is possible to make out the stones of old houses and the brighter green of grasses growing on nutrient-enriched soil.

What happened to the people who once lived whole lives in these houses is now part of a story of heartless dispossession that reshaped a whole country and its landscapes. These houses were cleared in the 19th century by a distant landowner keen to reduce his costs. Sheep need only shepherds, whereas families require whole systems of reciprocal arrangements. Clear the people and all these obligations towards your tenants evaporate. No more warm dinners here, no more shared stories on a black winter's night or long summer's evening when the low light survives to midnight. The large landowner, with little respect for the culture and specificities of a place, can easily forget, even if it might trouble him for a day or two. Those people who are forced to resettle to other places – or, worse, to emigrate – are disadvantaged forever, and they never forget.

Standing by the loch's shore, an hour or so before a summer midnight, and the landscape shimmers in the long dusk. To the west, the hills are a sharp blue against a rose sky, the tallest of them now hidden in cloud. The water slaps against the stone pier, and a busy gun dog suddenly skitters through the rushes and over the stone walls, back again and away, leaving silence again. The water turns slate-grey as the colour drains from the sky. Now the land is all but empty and abandoned. I think back two centuries, when this place would have been enriched with crofts by the lochside, boats pulled up on the shore, the lazy murmur of night-time talk, and gentle rise of peat smoke from chimneys.

The Beaker people of 5000 years ago were the first to leave their spectacular marks on this land. Come twenty kilometres south of Carloway along the stony loch shore, and you will find the spectacular standing stones of Calanais. Here some fifty stones of up to three metres in height are set out in rings and radiating lines on a hilltop overlooking another sea loch. No one now knows why these stones were raised, nor much about the people of that time. We do know, however, that they were more numerous than now, that they were able to cultivate barley, and that many stones circles were constructed and are yet to be excavated. In some places, peat has accumulated and grown past the stones, leaving their tops barely prominent.

Later, iron age people from roughly 2000 years ago built stone towers known as *brochs*, of which several hundred remain in the Highlands and Islands. One of the best preserved stands more than six metres high on a hill overlooking the Atlantic sea lochs and single-storey crofts at Carloway on Lewis. This *broch*'s diameter is more than 14 metres and originally it stood more than 13 metres in height. No one is quite sure of their main function – was it protection, ostentation or an expression of power? Whatever the reasons, the multi-chambered structure with galleried hollow walls containing twisting walkways are a reminder of a successful yet mysterious culture.

Soon after came the Romans, who left little mark, and then, in the 800s, the Vikings, who made this part of their empire. The Hebridean islands were formally a part of Norway until 1266, when they came under Scottish jurisdiction. This remained weak, allowing the rise of the Lordship of the Isles in the 14th and 15th centuries, a semi-autonomous and wholly Gaelic principality. The Lordship was formally ended in the 1490s, but again formal control by the monarchy was not exercised. During the agricultural revolution of the 1700s and 1800s, land use and rights were transformed across the British Isles, as several thousand Acts of Parliament converted common fields and the so-called wastelands into enclosed farms. The Highlands and Islands were not immune to these revolutionary changes, but perhaps they were so distant from the seats of power and from curious media and commentators that the voices of the dispossessed were heard less. As a result, the eventual social change was even more notorious.

From the mid-1700s, the region's land use underwent a series of rapid fluctuations, in which those with power over the land, including landlord estate owners and even some owners of whole islands, forcibly moved tenant families with impunity so that they could maximize their own economic returns. Livelihoods were changed and dashed. The outcome of the kelp boom and bust, the establishment of crofts too small to be agriculturally self-sufficient, the adoption of sheep farming, and its later collapse – all this comprised what came to be known as the Highland Clearances. In the end, the people who had lived on this land for more than a hundred generations, who absorbed the Vikings after their period of rule, who had a distinctive Gaelic language and culture, were simply deemed excess to requirements. They were resettled, evicted, settled again, and finally put on ships to Canada and Australia.

The Clearances were partly driven by events on the European stage that made one local natural resource suddenly very valuable. In the 1790s, imports of Spanish barilla, the main source of industrial alkali for the soap and glass industries, were blocked by the war with France. The great kelp forests of the Atlantic shores then leapt in value. The kelp was harvested from the sea, brought ashore, dried, chopped and then burned in kilns to produce a brittle blue residue. Landowners with shorelines quickly found that returns on kelp exceeded the land rents received from farmers, provided they could get the labour. And this is how the crofting system came to be created. Areas of farmland of less than a hectare were laid out, deliberately too small to be self-sufficient, so that families would have to engage in other labouring activities to ensure a living. In this way, some ten thousand families in the Hebrides were diverted within a few years from solely relying on the land to kelping.[1]

As we know today, though, any community entirely dependent on the vagaries of distant markets is likely to be subject to sudden and unpredictable changes, and the losers always seem to be the small people. First, the price of wool rose so much that landlords began to see the opportunity for better returns from sheep than from local people and their rents. Then the Napoleonic wars ended and the bottom fell out of the kelp market as tariffs on imports were ended. For the landowners, forced resettlement was the obvious answer. The cheviot and blackface sheep brought to the region were called big sheep as they were quite unlike the wiry, black highland and Soay indigenous sheep. Numbers of these big sheep rose rapidly – in Inverness-shire, for example, they grew from 50,000 in 1800 to 600,000 fifty years later. One local estate worker in the islands wrote, 'families who had not been disturbed for four or five hundred years are turned out of house and home and their possessions given to the highest bidder'. The need for winter grazings for these new sheep was paramount, and the people were secondary. Another observer coldly noted in 1824 that 'if the country has any inhabitants at all, they must, to a trifle, be expelled'.

The list of clearances makes for grim reading today, and, as James Hunter reminds us, still 'loom large in the collective psychology of those of us who live today in the northern half of Scotland'. The first departures occurred in the early 1800s, with some 20,000 people leaving for Canada and America in 1803 alone. Whole districts were depopulated. In 1826 the owner of the island of Rum had almost all his crofters shipped to Canada, and in the 1840s Lord Macdonald forced 1300 people to leave North Uist. In Harris, at the southern end of the island of Lewis, the whole of the *machair* side of the island was cleared of people in the 1830s for sheep, and the communities of Sgaranta, na Burrgh and Seilibost were completely emptied. In the 1850s the Duke of Argyll shipped 600 people from Tiree to Canada, and the owner of Lewis, Sir James Matheson, had another 1770 tenants emigrate to Quebec. Another 400 families left Harris, 300 left Knoydart, and Macdonald shipped another 2500 people to Canada and Australia from his estates.

Most of these evictions were vigorously opposed by local people, and estate officers occasionally had to call on the armed forces for help. Others, though, went quietly, as years of extreme hunger and poverty appear to have reduced many people's capacity for resistance. And while it is true that emigration brought welcome escape for many, they also knew that ties to their home places were being cut forever. One new resident of Glengarry County in Ontario later wrote home to say:

we cannot help looking at our native spot with sympathy and feelings which cannot be described. Yet I have no hesitation in saying that [...] we are surely better off to be out of the reach of such unnatural tyranny.

But people would not forget, and still do not. Peggy MacCormack, another Canadian settler formerly of South Uist, lamented that:

the thought of those young days makes my old heart both glad and sad even at this distance of time. But the clearances came upon us, destroying all, turning our crofts into big farms for the stranger, and turning our joy into misery, our gladness into bitterness.

The narratives of the evictors betrays a disturbingly inhumane core with little sense of any guilt. An estate official (known as a factor) of Sutherland, one Patrick Sellar, also a lawyer, reflected on the relationship between himself and locals, saying it was 'not very different from that between the American colonizers and the aborigines of that country'. He called locals a 'parcel of beggars' who spoke a 'barbarous jargon' that had turned them into savages. Any change he could bring about was clearly then an improvement. About his massive Sutherland estate of some 400,000 hectares, he wrote:

Lord and Lady Stafford were pleased humanely to order a new arrangement of this country: that the interior should be possessed by cheviot shepherds and the people brought down to the coast and placed in lotts (or crofts) under the size of three arable acres, sufficient for the maintenance of an industrious family, but pinched enough to cause them to turn their attention to fishing. I presume to say that the proprietors humanely ordered this arrangement, because it surely was a most benevolent action to put these barbarous hordes into a position where they could better associate together, apply to industry, educate their children and advance in civilization.

In 1816 Sellar was put on trial for the culpable killing of two people he was attempting to evict. His counsel told the jury:

the question at issue involves the fate and progress of agriculture and even moral improvement in the county of Sutherland [...] it is a trial of strength between the abettors of anarchy and misrule as well as the laws of this land.

The jury deliberated for just fifteen minutes before declaring him innocent. Despite the later 1886 Crofters Act that followed the Napier Commission's inquiry into crofters' conditions, and which finally gave people some security of tenure, wider economic conditions continued to put these communities at a serious disadvantage. As James Hunter has put it, 'nowhere in the region was the crofter's lot an easy one', and testimony of the crofters themselves shows this to be true. Angus MacLellan said of life on South Uist:

> *we mostly lived on potatoes and fish. We used to have bread and tea in the morning, potatoes and fish for our midday meal, and porridge and milk for supper.*

Diets were supplemented with any rabbits, duck and seabirds that could be captured.

The population continued to fall through the 20th century. Tarasaigh is two miles off the coast of Harris, and is now empty. In the early 1800s there were three villages with 140 people, by 1881 only 55, and in 1974 the last family finally departed. The more distant island of St Kilda (or Hiort) has a similar history, though perhaps even tougher given its location in the middle of the Atlantic. It was abandoned in the 1930s, and now Soay sheep, gannets and fulmars have the run of the island's crofts, village streets and imposing cliffs. In the parish of Uig, northwest Lewis, there were 68 births, 4 marriages and 36 deaths in 1900. In 2000 there was just the one birth, no marriages and 8 deaths. The nearby village of Valtos had 331 people a century ago, today it has just 47.[2]

But then, perhaps surprisingly, something quite remarkable happened towards the end of the 20th century that has brought new hope to these communities. Land reform has started a revival of community ownership, and the formerly powerless have finally come to see some benefit. First, though, there is another story to tell – about the land to which many of the Highlanders emigrated during the Clearances. On the western edge of the islands, centuries of waves have crushed seashells and left spectacular white sandy beaches and calcareous grasslands called *machair*. When you stand on the shore, looking west into long surf or north towards the Faroes and the Arctic, you can see why visitors and residents alike are enchanted by the landscape's glorious colours. The *machair* itself supports a carpet of wild flowers, none able to dominate in the nutrient-poor conditions. There are the purples of orchids, golds of yellow-rattle, kidney vetch and buttercup, sky-blue of harebell and speedwell, piercing whites of aster and eye-bright, and blood reds of clover and vetchling. If you journey west from these sparkling land and seascapes, following the route of both the Vikings and later Canadian emigrants, you strike land on the Labrador coast after a journey of 5000 kilometres.[3]

The Canadian region of Labrador is slightly larger than Britain in area, but contains only 29,000 people. It is home to some 2300 indigenous Innu, and lately to settlers too. Most of the emigrants from the Highlands and Islands went to Quebec and Nova Scotia. Some, though, went to work for the Hudson Bay Company, as its outward bound ships regularly provisioned on Orkney before the Atlantic crossing. One of the company's outposts was established at North West River, just across the water from what is now the Innu settlement of Sheshatshiu. In a mournful echo of the clearances of Scotland, Labrador has seen its own nomadic people dispossessed and disconnected from their lands. This time, though, it is all too recent. The once hunting and trapping nomadic Innu have been settled since the 1960s in the name of civilization and modernization, and they are suffering because of it. Their numbers are small, just 20,000 on the whole of the Labrador and Quebec peninsula, and so their plight is barely noticed on a global scale.

The Innu's nomadic way of life has almost been extinguished since Labrador and Newfoundland joined the Canadian federation in 1949. The Innu homeland is called Nitassinan, a vast area of boreal forest which becomes taiga shield and eventually tundra in the far north. These slow growth boreal forests, in which a finger-sized black spruce can be one hundred years old, are rich with caribou, bear, beaver, otter and porcupine, and the lakes, rivers and seashore contain vast salmon and trout. The archaeological record shows that the Innu have been present for at least 8000 years, during which time no animals have become locally extinct because of their hunting and gathering. So what is the problem? If they are few, and the land is wide, why has there been such an effort towards assimilation?

The Innu were first contacted by fur traders of the Hudson Bay Company in the 1700s, and though they remained deep in the country throughout most of the year, they started to come to trading posts to buy sugar, tea, baking powder, flour and tobacco. They were famed for their hunting skills, but visiting explorers and commentators still saw them as inferior to the white settlers, with hunting itself seen as an impediment to advanced and civilized ways of living. This is a theme played out on all continents of the world at one time or another – troublesome tribes making a living in the wrong way, and encouraged, often harshly and certainly hastily, to drop the old ways for the new, so that they too can become part of the modern and civilized world.

During the 1950s and 1960s, the Innu of Labrador began to be settled in two communities on the Labrador shore, one at Utshimassits (Davis Inlet) in the north (later moved to Natuashish), the other at Sheshatshiu on the shore of Lake Melville in the south. Children had to attend school, so their families needed to be settled. Families also had to have a formal address to receive welfare payments. And above all, missionaries and priests made it clear that spiritual salvation would only come about if people were part of what was called a modern society. Politicians were under no illusion about what was best. Walter Rockwood, director of the Division of Northern Labrador Affairs, said in 1957:

> *one fact seems clear – civilization is on the northward march, and for the Eskimo and Indian there is no escape. The last bridges of isolation were destroyed with the coming of the airplane and the radio. The only course now open, for there can be no turning back, is for him as soon as may be to take his full place as a citizen of our society.*

Revealing his deeper values, he also said, 'unless a strong positive approach is adopted now there is a danger that the Indians will become loafers whose only aim is to extract more and more handouts from government'.[4]

Today, the Innu are indeed settled, but it does not feel like home to them. They visit the country when they can, very occasionally for periods of months, but more usually for weeks or just days. Mostly, though, they feel thoroughly disconnected from a lifestyle and its associated community arrangements that brought them across some 400 generations of life in what they call *nutshimit* – the country. Today, alcoholism is widespread, childhood mortality is high, life expectancy low, and type II diabetes affects many. Instead of active lifestyles eating country foods, dense in protein and light in fats, people are mostly inactive and consume modern junk food. Instead of meaning and self-identity, many feel they have little hope for the future. Mary May Adele is a thin elderly woman, and as she gazes wistfully out of a window, she says, 'it feels lonely here, when you look outside at the sky and the trees. Even though we are here in the village, we feel lonely.' Her husband continues, 'it was beautiful and happy before. Now I sit in my home, and I feel pain and feel sick. I feel very unhappy in the house.'

What has gone so very wrong? The key lies in understanding the nature of life in the country – the daily connectedness and respect for nature and the closeness of families and communities. When Innu look at the country, they do not just see trees and water. They see places with stories and locate specific events, they see ancestors and animal spirits wandering the land, they see the past and present intimately linked, and they feel nature tied together with them. But when civilization marched north, it saw only the economic value of lumber, of reservoirs for hydro-electricity, of nickel in the rocks and of the wildlife that needed protecting. This difference in values cannot be underestimated. For the Innu, to destroy one part of their connected system is eventually to undermine the whole. For outsiders, opportunities for exploitation abound, and they have been grasped with little worry about the severe consequences for people and the land.

The Innu say they always care for the country and the animals in it. They never took too much and have a tradition of sharing what was caught with other families in the camp. They hunted beaver, otter, porcupine, rabbit, caribou, fox, lynx, duck, goose, ptarmigan and partridge for food, and wolves and hares for fur. From the lakes and sea, they caught salmon, trout and seals. It is their view that the animals control the hunt, so when they are caught they are given respect by sharing the food and hanging the bones on trees. Animal spirits were like governments, as they permitted the hunting. Says Dominic Pokue, one old hunter, 'the animal spirits gave approval for the hunt'. They never shot more caribou than could be eaten, and when hunting beaver would always leave sufficient females in a river as breeding stock. When an area was hunted, they would then leave it fallow for at least two years before returning.

'In the old days', says Katnan Pastitchi, 'people did not find it difficult. We never used to be tired. We were strong and happy.' There were no skidoos, but pulling sledges did not feel like hard work. It was just part of life. Men were the hunters, women in charge of the camps. But they were seen as equals, each with their own sphere of activity and decision making. Katnan learned all she knows from her grandmother, and is still making clothing from caribou hide to this day. She eats wild food when she can get it, but her grandson, who lives in the same house, wants none of it. She laments the loss of a way of life.[5]

But in truth, these human communities and forest ecosystems have coevolved since the last ice age. What we now see is an emergent property of human intentionality, and not some untouched, or even idle, wilderness. And if this is the case, what are the consequences of removing the people? Ultimately, we recreate the wasteland inside us when we indirectly permit these disconnections to occur. Federal authorities, though, still see going to the country as something akin to summer camp, a place for recreation perhaps, whereas the Innu see it as a place for fundamental reconnection and maintenance of their identity.

Of course, it would be wrong to represent the country, the *nutshimit*, as idyllic. There was extreme hunger at times, outbreaks of measles, tuberculosis, jaundice and pneumonia. Sometimes flour, tea and sugar had to be looked after very carefully, along with ammunition and matches. Technologies are changing too – now people use motorized skidoos instead of pulling sledges by hand; they can cut fish holes in the ice with a drill rather than by hand. For some older people, some of whom can still remember hunters using spears, bows and arrows – some of this is already too much, another loss of cultural significance. For others, though, it is a way to ensure that links to the country can be maintained.[6]

One evening, having spent the day in a square canvas tent sheltering from torrential rain on Lake Melville's shore by the mouth of the Kenemau River, lying on sweet spruce boughs and sharing stories across a glowing stove, we travelled up river in search of a birch bark canoe built by Shushep and a group of his friends three years previously. We moor the boat and push first through low willow scrub, splashing across the marsh, past the piercing blue of flag irises, accompanied by a mist of black fly and midges. The ground becomes drier as we climb up a few metres, and the scrub gives way to humid silver birch and spruce forest. Pushing through the trees, we come upon an empty glade carpeted with the white stars of the frog-flower. There is no canoe. We stand in silence, looking sadly at the place where it should be. We can see the signs: three wooden posts in the ground for props, stumps of branches which had been cut for tent poles, another space where a tent had been pitched, the stripped bark of a birch taken for snowshoes as well as the canoe, a bleached otter skull hung from a branch in respect. We sense something deeply significant about this place, an underlying rhythm, a mysterious pulse from the land, and it makes us catch our breath.

With distant eyes, Shushep recalls how the canoe was built over three months in the summer, how a vibrant community of twenty families had lived together. Here were the tents, and over there was the canoe. There they killed a moose that strayed into the camp. Elsewhere, they hunted beaver, otter and caribou and gathered wild cloudberries. The place is full of stories and deep value. Yet sometime later, after they had gone, someone had walked into this place, found the canoe and, sensing nothing special nor respecting another's ownership, had made off with it. The best analogy I can think of is to imagine the reaction if someone were to walk into a grand cathedral in Europe on a quiet afternoon and conclude that as there was no one around, the space was idle, so any ornaments and paintings could be claimed and removed. We walk out of the trees on a curving path, past a second campsite, and there on the water's edge is a settler's new white summer cabin, complete with boardwalk, barbecue, solar panels and piles of freshly hewn logs.

This land is officially designated by law for Innu use alone, yet people are claiming this new frontier for their own. Shushep says, 'this is our land', yet he shows no explicit animosity. Perhaps he knows it is all too late. Or perhaps he is just more generous than we feel. We wonder what these people did with the canoe. We also speculate about what they think when they stand here, barbecuing a chicken or steak flown in from some distant farm-factory. Would they recognize any other significance in this place, apart from its value as a good place for a summer retreat with a glorious view of the lake? Would they have known that Innu stories are locked up in the land? Do they, indeed, care at all? We walk back along the shore, and cast off into the wide brown river, through the treacherous shifting shallows and into the lake proper to check the salmon nets. The dusk draws in, and the wind whips the white tops off the waves. The water is unforgiving, smacking hard on the side of the boat. Perhaps this lake is telling us to beware – for here, on a summer's evening, we have seen a snapshot of colonial history, and its resulting loss and gain, disconnectedness and despair. We continue on, looking forward to the distant warm tent.

The greatest concern for the Innu is that there is not much time left. The frontier is pushing northwards into their lands, areas are proposed as national parks, within which no hunting will be permitted, the older generation with all the knowledge of animals and plants will die, and the children will no longer understand the old ways. This loss of ecological literacy, this extinction of experience, is a loss to us all – partly because we can never know what is understood about these boreal forests and lakes, and partly because there is a lesson we all need to learn about the value of respect, care and stewardship of the land.

What else, then, can communities like the Innu and Scottish Islanders do? Not much, until they have a degree of local control over their land and its future. And this is precisely where there has been surprising progress in Scotland. After a century of steadily declining populations, economic hardship, and only the recent provision of electricity, water and sanitation, communities of local people have been allowed to buy whole estates, even whole islands. First, in 1992, crofters on the 8500-hectare North Assynt estate mounted a bid to buy the whole estate, and, against all the odds, succeeded. The change of government in the UK in 1997 led to greater regional devolution and more support for land reform of this type from the new Scottish Parliament. The 7085-hectare Knoydart estate was then acquired by local people in 1999, then Borne and Annishadder in Skye, the 3000-hectare island of Eigg, Melness in Sutherland, and Valtos in Lewis. In 2003 the 22,350-hectare estate of North Harris was sold, and in 2006 a community buyout was completed for the massive 37,650-

hectare South Uist estate, which includes Eriskay and part of Benbecula, together with 850 crofts.

As the numbers show, these are not small parcels of land, but whole landscapes. The island of Gigha is a good example. Just eleven kilometres long and two and a half wide, it had 700 inhabitants two centuries ago, but by 2000 the number had fallen to less than 100, with 80 per cent of the houses in disrepair. In March 2002 the Isle of Gigha Heritage Trust acquired the island from the previous laird, and a new spirit has emerged. Businesses have been created, housing repaired, a community-owned wind farm developed, and visitors are encouraged to come for the heritage and nature. Already the population has grown to 121. Willie McSporran, Chair of the Trust, said in 2004:

> *nobody can realize what a community like this had to suffer through bad lairdship. But whatever happens now, the island can never be sold again. Children living on the island can be secure that a laird will not come along and sell their homes for profit.*

The new owners, too, see the land in a different way. Iain Wilson, a Knoydart farmer, said:

> *we don't really own the land – nobody does. We are only stewards of it for as long as we are here. We, as a community [will] try to pass it on to the next generation in a slightly better state than that in which we received it.*[7]

Crofting is now seen as offering something special to many groups of people. It was never possible to survive on only a tiny patch of land, and in the past a crofter might also have been a fisherman, weaver or tradesman. Today, they might be a web-designer, teleworker, teacher or wildlife guide. Some people, it is true, do not like the idea of repopulation, especially if they have moved there precisely because the land is empty; but even if the population were doubled, the Western Isles would still be the least populated part of western Europe outside the Arctic and sub-Arctic of Scandinavia. With repopulation and occupation of the land and the country, can come identity and pride.

In Labrador, the Tshikapisk Foundation is developing plans to bring children out to the country on a regular basis and is working on getting the schools to change their calendar to allow families to get away at the right times of the year – spring and autumn – and not the long summer break imported from Europe. Others too are working on encouraging a healthy wild food culture and trying to find ways to maintain links to the country as part of a modern culture. Ecotourism would be a way to bring in visitors, whose money may help the local economy, but more importantly they might return home with a better understanding of the Innu than most moderns have. There will, of course, be no permanent return to a nomadic life, but the country and the land could again become the source of life and meaning for both young and old Innu.[8]

Who knows what these changes will bring, or whether they will happen quickly enough. What is clear, though, is that people who can make choices and decisions about the land on which they reside are able to think quite differently compared with those who feel they may be removed at any moment. They show that being in their country, and feeling a part of it, is something important to all people.

Part 5

The Future

Ecolution

In one of the most striking opening lines for a novel, the narrator of Flann O'Brien's *The Third Policeman* begins by explaining that not everyone knows how he had killed old Phillip Mathers, 'smashing his jaw in with my spade'. After many perambulations around the mythic Irish countryside, time comes full circle, and we learn how the main characters will be locked into a repetitive time-world that will go on forever. 'Is it about a bicycle?' asks the wide Sergeant Pluck with the violent red moustache, and tufted brows, and fat folds of skin. Indeed it is, for the bicycle is at the centre of the sergeant's theory about shaping and self-shaping, about how what we do affects ourselves, and about how our world affects us in return.

    'Michael Gilheny', says the Sergeant:

is nearly 60 years old by plain computation and he has spent no less than thirty-five years riding his bicycle over the rocky roadsteads and up and down the hills and into the deep ditches when the road goes astray in the stain of winter [...] If it wasn't that his bicycle was stolen every Monday, he would be sure to be more than half way now.

'Halfway to what?' asks the narrator. 'Halfway to being a bicycle himself,' answers the Sergeant. People who spend most of their natural life riding bicycles, is seems, get their personalities mixed up with the personalities of their bicycle as a result of the interchange of atoms in each of them. 'And you would be flabbergasted', he says, 'at the number of bicycles that are half-human almost man, half partaking of humanity.' The comedy is further explained by the number of men who lean against walls on the elbow, or stand propped by one foot at kerbstones. 'The behaviour of a bicycle that has a high content of humanity is very cunning and entirely remarkable,' concludes the Sergeant.[1]

One hundred and twenty years after Charles Darwin and Alfred Russel Wallace turned the world upside down, James Lovelock wondered, too, in his Gaia hypothesis, if the Earth had been shaped by life. Such Kuhnian paradigm shifts cause rapid differences to emerge. The new believers wonder why they did not think of it first; the old disbelievers think it all utter nonsense, and sit back and wait. Years can pass before the new comes to be accepted. Max Planck famously once said, 'a new paradigm is often accepted not because it convinces the majority of its opponents, but because it outlives them'. Gaia remains controversial, mainly because some have misrepresented it as suggesting the Earth itself is alive. This was never the intention, but it remains an appealing idea to some searching for a guiding hand. What Lovelock did say was that life helped to make the Earth a place where life could persist. It made its own bed, and it's a comfortable one. At an average current temperature of 13°C (until climate change fully takes hold), the Earth is very hospitable. Mars and Venus, by contrast, are thoroughly inhospitable, one bitterly cold and the other twice as hot as an average oven. Life maintains the Earth's biogeochemical cycles far from equilibrium, and this in turn helps to shape and influence the kinds of life that persist.

This makes the biosphere an emergent property of millions of years of interaction between life, the Earth and its environments. And we humans are part of this process too. Hominids emerged some 5 million years ago (our genus about 2.5 million years ago; our species about 160,000 years ago), and we have been shaped by hundreds of thousands of generations to arrive at where we are today, bicycles notwithstanding. To paraphrase Sartre, all our lives have led us to this very moment. And here is the link back to Darwin, whose shattering idea of evolution driven by natural selection recognized the mechanism by which the many forms of life have emerged, survived and diverged in their specific environments. It is now clear that individual organisms, populations and their species change their environments, often in ways that increase their chances of survival. Survival of the fittest also means survival of those that influence their environments in a favourable way, and can then pass on these capabilities to descendents.

At the same time as Darwin's *Origin of Species* was published, a monk in Austria was laying the foundations for modern genetics. Gregor Mendel's experiments with peas during the 1850s and 1860s clearly showed how characteristics, or traits, could be passed from one generation to another (though his work was not recognized until the early 20th century). A half century after this, Francis Crick, James Watson and the mostly forgotten Maurice Wilkins and Rosalind Franklin established the structure for DNA, which later allowed chromosome structure and gene expression to be determined. Another half century of huge collaborative efforts across laboratories in many countries have seen all the genes for a number of organisms fully mapped, including the 30,000 or so genes of humans. For a while, this appeared to suggest we are near to knowing everything about us and these other mapped organisms. But this is far from true. We know more, but also have gained insights into how little we still know.

Mapping and naming genes is like picking up the phone directory for your local town or city. Lots of names and numbers, structured in columns and helpfully all in alphabetical order. But from these lists alone, you can only guess about the structure and functioning of the city. You would need to ring up every person (or gene) and ask them what they do. You would then need to find out what causes that person to get up in the morning. What are their motivations? If it is a rainy day, will that person stay inside; if sunny, go to the beach? Will that person do something when another person (gene) in the phone book calls them and invites then over for tea, or was it to the pub? You may have one contact that calls every day, another only every five years. Today we have a pretty good gene phone book and have begun to realize that we understand so little about how they interact – both with other genes and with the environments that are internal and external to the organisms which carry them.

This idea about having genes that need to be switched on before they act is beginning to entail some modifications to how genetic and environmental processes are understood. We have all been taught (at least, we should have been) that traits are either dominant or recessive, that we have two copies carried on different strands of DNA, and that inheritance is a pretty predictable game. And for some traits, it is. For blood groups, you can have an A or B gene, which are both dominant, but rare. If you have neither, you are O. If you have one A and one O, you are A. Chimpanzees, by the way, are either A or O, and gorillas are all B types. Thus we can see that you or I have genes for a particular trait. In short, a gene (or both) determines the outcome. Again, this is a simple and powerful idea, but it leads to many popular misconceptions about genetic discoveries. The gene for cancer, we are told, has been discovered. Or for left-handedness, or aggression, or divorce. And this is where the story begins to break down. Most traits, or outcomes, are shaped in very complex ways, and these driving influences can be both other genes and their products, and signals in the internal and external environment. Genes do determine things, but they are in turn switched on and off by other things.

This, then, brings us to another enduring controversy: how much do genes or the environment affect who we are? Is it nature (genes) or nurture (environment or culture) that is mostly, or even solely, important? Like all supposedly handy dichotomies, the truth lies in elements of both, not one or the other. But the post-Darwin literature is often less forgiving. And this has led us into many difficult places. A century of polarized opinions seemed to explode in the mid-1970s with the publication of E O Wilson's *Sociobiology*, in which biological explanations were provided for many aspects of human behaviour and society. Many social scientists attacked Wilson, as did some evolutionary biologists. Part of the problem may have come from Wilson's provocative claim that the social sciences would eventually be subsumed into biology, as he indicated that a great deal of behaviour could be explained by biology alone. Even after the dust from this particular controversy has settled, there still remains a wide range of divergent views, from those who appear to reject any cultural explanation of human behaviour, to those memeticists who seek to provide evolutionary perspectives that are essentially cultural.[2]

Even within evolutionary fields there is considerable controversy, and it remains hard to identify the relative roles of genes, the environment and human cultures on hominid and human development. Speculation and prejudice are common, probably because who and what we are actually does mean a lot to most of us. Inevitably, ideas get misrepresented, either accidentally or deliberately, in ways that suit some people's prior political, religious or even scientific interests. It is hard, therefore, to separate out biological fact, or indeed portion out the relative roles for biology and culture (or nature and nurture) in human evolution and our arrival to this point. Moreover, a great deal of discomfort about using genetic explanations for some aspects of human behaviour has arisen in reaction to those in the 19th and 20th centuries who sought to use genetics to explain differences between races and between the rich and poor. To some, like Darwin's cousin, Francis Galton, this provided an opportunity to put all the differences between human groups down to heredity, and nothing to culture (through education or economic opportunity). Galton pioneered the study of twins, but also wanted to investigate 'the practicability of supplementing inefficient human stock by better strains', as Matt Ridley has explained. These led to a position that suggests you have a set of genes passed to you, that these determine all that you are, and that there is no role for choice (or free will). The slippery slide to eugenics had begun.

If evolutionary perspectives seem to explain so much about human behaviour and society, why are so many people hostile to these ideas – from the creationists and believers in intelligent design to the social scientists concerned about past uses of evolutionary theory to support certain political ideologies? Creationists cannot believe that the complexity we see in the world could have emerged as a result of evolution over millennia. And their opinions seem to be winning in some places – the 'new ignorance', as Steve Jones calls it. In the US, surveys seem to indicate that 40–50 per cent of people during the 1990s and early 2000s believed God created humans in their current form less than 10,000 years ago, 30–40 per cent believed humans developed over millions of years, but that God still guided the process, and only about 10 per cent believed humans developed from less advanced forms of life, with God having no part in the process. Of course, many people believe in one thing and act in contradictory ways. How many evolutionary sceptics, we might wonder, are quite content to have a flu jab that requires evolutionary understanding to develop and redevelop as the flu virus itself rapidly evolves? As Steve Jones also says, evolutionary stories are all around us, from dog and pigeon breeds to HIV – a retrovirus that is bad at making exact copies of itself, 'which is one reason why it does so well'.[3]

One reason for these large numbers of evolution deniers (about a hundred million people in the US alone) is the enduring problem that evolution can appear to have direction. Things go from simple to complex, from worse to better, and at the end of the line, whether evolved or designed, are the humans (who are obviously the best). We should be very careful about the naturalistic fallacy of 'what is should be'. What we see now in the world, in human society, is not what should have happened. Nor is it the best, just because it is now. It is what emerged. As far as humans go, Neanderthals had an advanced and complex society, and then disappeared. As for past civilizations, some 40 major ones have come and gone, lasting on average for 900 years, each of which probably thought itself to be the best just before the candles guttered out.

After Darwin, the concept of evolution as a linear and progressive force became widely adopted and remains with us today. Jean Lamarck erroneously believed in the inheritance of acquired characteristics and suggested that species strove to evolve greater complexity, and that thus the pinnacle of evolution had to be humans. Later, social Darwinism came to suggest that nature was more important than nurture, and that the development of individuals from birth to death (ontogeny) reflected closely the evolutionary development of species (phylogeny). Such ideas of progression (implying that the later is better, the more complex the cleverer), were later applied to human societies. Lewis Henry Morgan's *Ancient Society*, published in 1877, suggested seven stages of human cultural evolution, beginning with lower savagery and progressing through barbarism eventually to reach civilization. The idea was that all human societies did share a common ancestor, but that some groups (or races) were now higher on the ladder than others. Such ideas fitted very well with prevailing views about the superiority of European and North American culture, and again came to be widely accepted (though of course still hotly contested by many).

Setting aside the extreme religious views, the central problems that many people have with evolution and genetics centre on questions of instinct and free will (which, in the light of what we now know about genes, are probably false assumptions anyway). Ethologists like Nikolaas Tinbergen and Konrad Lorenz showed clearly that many animals and birds responded to cues in very predictable and deterministic ways. Instinct, it would appear, was critical. But instinct implies no thought – it is something an animal, or you, do, driven only by your genes. This is already troubling, especially to those who base their philosophical and political ideas on those of, among others, John Stuart Mill, who indicated that the mind at birth was empty and is gradually filled as we experience the world, implying that we have the ability to choose these experiences and so shape our own lives.

Before E O Wilson, others took a similar line, such as Desmond Morris in *The Naked Ape*, whose hugely popular book suggested that modern humans were shaped in the Stone Age, and that most of our behaviour was explained by reference to those conditions. This has wide resonance, but Morris also treated humans as if current culture played second fiddle to genes. The problem, as in so much of the history of evolutionary thought, is that some people cannot resist slipping into language that says what they believe is right and wrong, or better and worse, rather than explaining what happened, or might occur in the future. Evolution does not have a directing hand, or a determined pathway. It is about adaptation to environments, changing environments to make them more suitable and the survival of those genes (and the organisms that carry them) that are best able to do these things.[4]

As we shall see, genes play a fundamental role in shaping who and what we are, but they do not act in a vacuum. They take their signals from the environment, which once was predominantly ecological but now is cultural too, and these signals switch them on and off. What we are is actually an emergent property of both genes and ecological-social environments, and thus we do have choice. We cannot bend our genes to our intentionality, at least not personally, but we can and do affect the environment which indirectly presses our genetic buttons. Thus, as Kevin Laland and Gillian Brown say, 'using evolutionary theory is not the same as taking a genetic determinist viewpoint'. Indeed, says Richard Dawkins, 'the bogey of genetic determinism needs to be laid to rest'.[5]

Decades of binary controversy over either nature or nurture should now lead us to the sensible conclusion that neither alone is explanatory. Both are important. This will annoy both those who have come to believe that culture is predominant and those who would believe that genetics can explain all. It is not my intention here to review all the science behind the many different strands of evolutionary theory (including sociobiology, evolutionary psychology, human behavioural ecology, memetics, gene–culture coevolution and evolutionary anthropology). But what is common to all is the idea that hominids evolved over millions of years, that we spent a long time becoming adapted to environments of our ancestors (as are all organisms), that many complex aspects of culture emerged fairly recently (50,000 to 100,000 years ago), and that the ecological and social environment played a role in influencing which genes succeeded and were passed to later generations.[6]

The controversy over how much genes or the environment affect who we are is curious, as we pretty well accept the fact that genes are units of inheritance. Genes determine a great deal, but strangely we do not seem to find this a comfort. The problem centres on questions of free will, which we would all like to think we have. I am free to choose what I think or like, I am free to be happy or sad, or to choose one person or food over another. I can choose, in other words, my own future. It is not, though, that simple. Genes shape those choices, as we do our environments, which once had antelopes in them, but now have supermarkets and fast food outlets. And how much free will do we actually have when it comes to buying food? Are we not subliminally influenced by advertising anyway? Do the stores not seek to influence your choices in subtle ways? Of course they do. The average American child will have seen 360,000 TV advertisements and 200,000 violent acts by the age of 18.[7]

Both genetic determinism and the idea of being born with a blank slate are wrong. None of the commonly used binary oppositions – genes or environment, nature or nurture, innate or acquired, individuals or culture – are alone correct. The problem is that false insights into these questions has led to the expression of many political and social prejudices, and in the hands of tyrannical leaders allowed many atrocities to be justified. Some believed they could and should create a master race (as if the environment did not matter), others that they could rewrite human nature if social circumstances were changed (as if genes did not matter), though most, it is true, have not occupied such extreme territory. The worries about genetic determinism, though, are centred on false ideas about genetics. As Matt Ridley has rightly put it, genes are not gods. Just because you or I have a particular gene does not mean it will necessarily be expressed (it may sit quietly doing nothing); equally, if we lack a certain gene, it does not mean we will lack a trait or characteristic (another gene may step in and do the job instead). As Ridley rightly says:

genes spend just as much of their time responding to our actions as they do causing them. Genes do not constrain human freedom, they enable it.

The central dogma of genetics has long been that information flows out of the gene, not back to it. Experience (the environment) does not change gene sequences (DNA), otherwise Lamarck would be correct. But information does flow back to genes to affect their expression. Genes are switched on and off by signals from the environment. These signals can be transcription factors (themselves encoded by genes) that bind to the promoter sequences of genes, or a range of other molecules, such as proteins, that transmit external environmental cues into some form of internal signal. For example, the 17CREB genes are part of the mechanism of learning and memory. If one of them does not work, then long-term memory cannot form. These genes alter the connections between nerves and are switched on when the brain lays down new memories. If you create no new memories, then these genes will not be used. The act of learning turns on these genes, and learning is affected by what we do as whole organisms in our environments.

Each of us carries our own phone-book set of genes, but not all of them are expressed in a lifetime. It depends on the external and internal signals that switch genes on and off. One example is the changing of skin colour. Over time, pale-skinned people living in environments with plenty of sunshine will become dark skinned. This is not because they acquire this characteristic and then pass it on to their children. It is because melanin production in the skin is very sensitive to exposure to sunlight. Sunlight switches on genes that individuals might have carried for their lifetime without expression (had they stayed out of the sun). Descendents have the same sets of genes, but they are switched on early in life, producing darker skin. Over time, whole populations living in sunny places will become dark skinned.

Philosopher Daniel Dennett has called the concern about genes and free will 'the panic that lies underneath the surface'.[8] Are we fully responsible for our actions? We may more often come to hear the cry 'it's not my fault, it's the fault of my genes'. Indeed, this has already happened in the US, where in 1994 the lawyers for a convicted murderer, Stephen Mobley, argued in his appeal that he came from a long line of criminals, and that he committed murder because his genes made him do it. In short, he wanted to pretend he had no free will. This raises more fundamental philosophical questions. People generally want to be responsible, want to have the choices to avoid a behaviour that may be coded for by a particular set of genes. Yet knowing about how genes and the environment interact could actually increase free will, not constrain it further, as some people worry. Ridley argues that 'knowing you have an instinct makes it possible that you will decide to override that instinct'. When we know that certain genes are associated with certain kinds of behaviour, it does not mean that someone with that gene is locked into a certain and inevitable pathway. They still have choices. We rewrite ourselves as we grow.

Organisms do not evolve in a static environment. They are constantly changing it, and therefore changing the course of their own evolution. This is what Kevin Laland and John Odling-Smee have called 'niche construction'. Organisms modify the environment and so modify the sources of natural selection too (often to make them more favourable). All organisms constantly interact with their local environments, and so change them over time. Earthworms change the structure and chemical composition of soils by dragging leaves and other organic matter into the soil, thus mixing organic with inorganic materials. Thus 'contemporary earthworms live in worlds that have been partly niche-constructed by many generations of ancestors'. Other niche modification examples include elephants that uproot whole trees, open canopies, create parkland and recycle the herbage through their bodies, which in turn reduces the incidence of fires. Hippos create close-cropped riverside grasslands, and as large browsers trample vegetation and keep the understorey open. Wild boar create open ground and aid tree germination, and beavers form riverside water meadows and coppice willows. Thousands of spectacled eider duck assemble on the Arctic Sea during winter, keeping the sea ice open through their continuous movement on the surface, so allowing them to dive down 60 metres to get food throughout the winter.[9]

The idea of niche construction is similar to Dawkins' idea of the extended phenotype. Genes build environmental states beyond the organism to increase their chance of survival. Some extended phenotypes can be inherited, if the environment is changed, and benefit future generations, which then continue to maintain the environment in a favourable state. Ecological inheritance does not depend on just biological replicators (genes) but on the persistence of physical changes too. Organisms modify environmental resources. They effectively try to change their worlds to make them more favourable to their own survival. Laland and Odling-Smee suggest that organisms shape environments as surely as environments shape organisms, with the result that 'evolution is transformed from a linear to a cyclic process'.

But Odling-Smee and Laland also suggest another concept – that of negative niche construction, when organisms destroy their habitats. Could we humans be driving ourselves to extinction by harming the very environments in which we evolved so successfully? It is now an increasingly common conception that humans are well adapted to the ancestral Pleistocene environment, but not particularly to the industrialized environment. But this is only partly correct. Foundations were indeed laid in the Pleistocene, but evolution has been working since then. We have also been modifying the later environments, and these must have been having an effect on us too. Niche construction also suggests that the initial environment of savannahs was in the first place shaped by hominids. We did not simply evolve in one environment, and then stop. We continued to change. Sergeant Pluck would certainly agree.

Time, though, is a key factor. We spent many thousands of generations in the savannahs before moving out across the world some 100,000 years ago, and so many design solutions of that time could be expected to have persisted to today. During most of our history, natural selection was the key determinant of who survived to pass on their genes – presumably those of us who jumped the furthest when the scimitar-toothed cat leapt, or those who knew where to find or catch food. Later, more complex components of culture came to play an important role, with the richest and most powerful having the resources to ensure their progeny survived best. Only recently, however, has culture come to dominate, and built a new environment that is increasingly hostile to the genes we carry.

For most of our time, in other words, we have survived in a world rich in biological diversity. We have, of course, been part of this diversity, shaping it and being shaped in return. We change the environment – burn the grasses to prevent scrub encroachment, channel the water to trees, collect the fish with care – and it shapes us. The natural environment is not a fixed entity that does not change over time. We amend it, and the environment affects which of us will survive. But if the shaping is harmful, does this mean we eventually harm ourselves? Are humans now, by causing massive species extinctions and changing the global climate, actually threatening the survival of modern civilization? And it would be good to know now, as it might still be possible to do something about it.

Ancestral humans did clearly play a significant role in reducing biological diversity before this generation's extraordinary extinctions. We hunted the mammoths to extinction in Europe, the ground sloths in the Americas and the slow-moving ground marsupials in Australia. But nothing compares with today's losses – called by many the sixth great extinction. The previous five were all caused by global geological or climatic catastrophes. This one is being provoked by humans alone.

One question might be, then, 'Are we still evolving?' Many would like to believe that human evolution stopped some 50,000 years ago, before races and groups diverged. But recent research on single nucleotide polymorphisms (SNPs) has shown that many versions of the same gene (called alleles) have evolved during the past 10,000 years. Genes known to be evolving include those for skin colour, skeletal development, hair formation, food metabolism (especially leptin control) and susceptibility to Alzheimer's disease. Bruce Lahn of the University of Chicago discovered a gene called microcephalin that emerged 14,000–60,000 years ago and is carried by 70 per cent of us, and another, ASPM, which is carried by a quarter of the world's population, even though it emerged only 500–14,000 years ago. If we are still evolving, then this may paint a different picture for how the future may unfold.

Another example is language acquisition. On chromosome 7, the forkhead box P2 gene (or FOXP2) codes for a transcription factor (switch for other genes) which, when broken, leads to severe language impairment. FOXP2 is necessary for the development of normal grammatical and speaking ability. In all mammals (including mice, chimps and humans), the gene is the same. But since humans and chimpanzees split, there have been two very small changes to the protein products. One mutation substitutes a serine molecule for an arginine at the 325th (of 715) position in the protein. The mutation appeared about 200,000 years ago, and was so successful that it quickly came to dominate in all human populations. Humans and higher apes use completely different parts of the brain to produce calls compared with those that humans now use for language, and this language centre is on the left side of the brain in a part of the motor region used for gestures.

A variety of other human traits have emerged as a result of recent evolution. These include the increase in myopia following the invention of spectacles, the spread of the ability to digest milk sugars after the invention of dairy farming, and the extension of our physical abilities without having to get bigger muscles after the invention of stone tools. We are now changing our environments even more, and these changes will inevitably have some influence on future human evolution. This raises a variety of interesting questions. What types of environments shape which genes? Which environments are better for us, and which worse? What is the effect of certain environments on our health? Moreover, what is it to be human, when so many of our genes are shared in identical fashion with other organisms? For example, the difference between two humans is 0.1 per cent of the genome (3 million base pairs); it is 1.5 per cent between a human and a chimpanzee (45 million base pairs). Humans and chimpanzees have some 30,000 genes, with only 450 differences. We also now know that the genetic variation between human populations is small compared with the differences within populations.

A good reason to be humble about our hominid status is the striking uniformity across species when it comes to genes. Humans share 3000 of our 30,000 genes with the fruit fly and round worm. We also share 1000 genes with unicellular yeast, and 500 with bacteria (these are universal to all living things, as they mediate DNA, RNA and protein links). Many of our genes and development pathways are thus shared with other organisms. For example, the hox (homeotic) genes lay down the body plan, and work in identical fashion in flies, frogs and fish as well as us. As they are shared widely across species, the clear evolutionary implication is that these organisms share a common ancestor. We now know that one gene can do different jobs at different times, and different genes can do the same job. Thus the presence or absence of a particular gene does not guarantee the presence or absence of a particular trait. It may do; it may not. It will depend on transcription factors, and how they switch genes on and off. The Eve gene in fruit flies is switched on ten times in a fly's lifetime. It has 8 promoters, and each promoter requires 10–15 transcription factors to switch it on. Thus a small number of genes can interact in very complex ways to do different jobs.

How, then, do some of these interactions occur? It is now known that early activities can change us for life. The behaviour of mother rats can influences the expression of genes in their offspring. If young pups are not licked and groomed, then methyl groups are added to the DNA of a receptor gene expressed in the hippocampus of the brain. This gene normally helps to mediate responses to stress, but when methylated, rat pups produce higher levels of stress hormones and are less confident in new environments. The effects last for life. Moshe Szyf and colleagues at McGill University in Montreal found that a common amino acid and food supplement, L-methionine, has a similar effect in adults: it methylates the gene, and makes people more stressed.[10] In theory it should be possible to find compounds that demethylate, though the problem is that most such compounds do many jobs, and it may be very difficult to predict wider and unintended effects (methylation is not all bad – it helps to shut down human endogenous retroviruses that are inserted into our genes). Equally, we may find that a walk in the country acts in an equally good way to reduce stress.

Sarah Hrdy at University of California at Davis believes that the way modern adults are rearing their children is likely to have long-term emotional effects.[11] Society may be becoming less empathetic, especially as fewer people live in extended families. It is known, for example, that men who spend time with infants have lower testosterone levels. Without families or mixed communities, this natural control over high-octane behaviour is lost. In one-year-old children, the higher the testosterone level, the less eye contact is made by the baby with the mother. Females seem to have more interest than males in faces, and this gradually forms into a preference for social relationships. There are also other predictors. The more testosterone in the womb, the longer the ring finger of the embryo, as the hox genes that control the growth of genitals also control digit size. Men with long ring fingers have a greater risk of autism, dyslexia, stammering and immune dysfunction and have more sons. But men with very short fingers are at greater risk of heart disease and infertility. Like all of these types of correlation, though, it is very difficult to be clear about causality.

Some genes are also known to shape components of personality. The gene for brain-derived necrotrophic factor (BDNF) is on chromosome 11 and is a short gene of 1335 base pairs. The protein it produces encourages the growth of neurons in the brain. In three-quarters of humans, the 192nd letter is G; in a quarter, it is A.

The G causes a methionine amino acid to be put in the 66th position on the protein; the A puts in valine instead. As we all have two copies of each gene, there are three kinds of people: met–met, who are likely to be the least neurotic, met–val, who tend to be intermediate, and val–val, who are the most neurotic. But, again, it does not mean we are stuck with these labels with no choice. We can still decide to behave in different ways. Owen Flanagan of Duke University has found that Buddhists who practice meditation have significantly increased activity in their left prefrontal lobes, indicating positive emotions and good mood (the right prefrontal lobe is for negative emotions).[12] But Buddhists are not born happy. They develop the characteristic by learning and practised behaviour. Buddhist training also seems to change the way the brain responds to other stimuli. As a result of their distinct pasts, they are much less likely to be shocked, surprised or angry.

As knowledge of gene function increases, many new questions are raised about environmental influences. It is now known that weight is partially heritable: the correlation in weight between identical twins is 80 per cent, against only 43 per cent between fraternal twins. Thus, given the same access to food, some people will put on more weight than others. Food shortages during pregnancy change the likelihood of the embryo suffering from obesity in later life. A poorly nourished embryo is born expecting to live in a state of food deprivation throughout its life. Its metabolism is geared to being small and is good for hoarding calories and avoiding excessive exercise. If this individual finds itself with plenty of food all the time, then it responds by growing rapidly, putting on weight and straining its heart. If there is famine in the first two trimesters, then babies with normal birth weight themselves give birth to small babies. On the savannah and other locations where food is sometimes scarce, they survive. In cities populated with junk food outlets, they will not.

Genes and the environment shape IQ too. In studies of 350 pairs of twins, it was found that virtually all the IQ variability among the poorest group was accounted for by the environment and not genetic type. Among the richest, the opposite was true. Thus raising the safety net of the poorest does more to equalize opportunity than reducing inequality among the middle classes. Ironically, too, the more equal we make society and the environment, in other words the less wealth and background matter, the more genes define differences between us.[13]

Ever since the earliest hominids stepped into the savannahs, some 250,000–350,000 generations ago, a dance of genetics and culture has determined which genes have survived to reach us today. In some circumstances, the fittest have survived – those that caused their bodies to run the furthest when prey needed chasing down. In others, the richest or most powerful survived – those with the resources to ensure their progeny survived best. It is the poorest who are more likely to suffer high levels of infant mortality; it is the richest who are more likely to pay their way out of a problem – buying clean water rather than relying on sewage-contaminated ponds. The balance between biology and culture changes through human history, but will it change again? What will the future bring? There are two certainties: environmental destruction will continue for some time, perhaps the whole of this century, and, at the same time, medical and biological technology will transform us internally, perhaps even bringing mergers with silicon technology to produce new cyborgs. We may bring on an age of destruction and an age of isolation at the same time.[14]

When great civilizations fall, for whatever reasons, who among their people are most likely to survive? No longer does a particular bundle of cultural values or symbols of economic power guarantee survival. Indeed, those most likely to survive will be making a living without relying on the large infrastructure and institutions of a dominant civilization. They will survive if they can grow and collect their own food, if they have families and neighbours who can work collectively, if they have the knowledge and skills to make a local livelihood. But is the inevitable outcome of our current civilization to charge towards the precipice with our eyes closed, damaging the very environments that produced us? Will modern globalized society become number 41 on the list of departed civilizations? Or might there come another phase in human history, where we recognize the critical importance of the environment in making us who we are, and appreciate that harm to this world harms us too? Such a new phase may rely equally and intelligently on a mix of evolutionary and environmentally sensitive cultural influences. But is there any possibility of a further phase of human history centred on survival of the greenest, a process we might call 'ecolution'?

For ecolution to happen, it is going to take some pretty big leaps of imagination. We will need to recognize that green places are important to us, and then look after them. We will need to be more humble about ourselves, and step off the comfortable plinths. 'There is nothing', as Laland and Brown have put it, 'about natural selection that supports a progression of population towards an end goal or higher state.' We will have to have a sensible adult debate about genetics and free will. And we will have to ask some tough questions about what it is we want to sustain. As David Orr asks, do we wish to preserve an 'intimate relation with nature or total mastery'? Do we want to preserve an ever richer world, but one that can only become richer by converting natural resources to monetary values, and also by increasing the gap between the poorest and richest? Or is their another way?

Natural selection produces diversity, but only because a variety of environments or conditions means that a range of genes are required. If the environment becomes a monoculture, then inevitably a more limited set of genes will be selected. Monocultures are not just bad because they are not diverse. They undermine the fundamental nature of the biological world itself. Today's industrialized processes have often come to mean a desire for homogenization. Yet a diversity of environments, or opportunities, drives evolution, so not only are we destroying species through habitat destruction, we are undermining the likelihood of the persistence of the world as we know it. Evolution increases information content and increases intelligence. Will ecolution continue these processes after our current age of destruction – of biodiversity, of nature, of languages and communities, of stories? Good communities are places where imagination grows and memories persist. Does imagination, like intelligence, grow over time? And has it now stopped growing in the modern age? Has, in other words, normal evolution been put on hold (while we destroy and are destroyed)?

The key to ecolution is imagination, knowledge and interest; the same thing, time after time, no longer keeps us interested, and we become bored. The modern homogenized world has reduced our understanding of the natural world, our daily connections, our capacities and desires to care. It is true that we develop other interests – and there is nothing inherently wrong in these, whether electronic games or films, or celebrity goings-on; the problem only emerges if we come to think of these as a replacement for the real world, and that there is no other reality that matters anymore. Diversity of places (and their associated memories) is good, as it provokes imagination and desire and provides stability at the same time. It makes us think about how to solve new problems, how to understand things. After all, we all have genes passed on from a group of hominids that left the savannahs of Africa and dispersed across the world – discovering new environments, learning sufficiently rapidly to prevent consumption by larger predators and changing the world to suit us.

Evidence suggests that we have some innate connections to nature, and also to diverse environments. When, then, do we lose heart and interest? When we no longer feel we can influence the future. When we have a repetitive and boring job, or when the commute to work is the same, day after day. We then yearn for something else, something new, an escape. Why do we go to different places for our holidays and in our leisure time? Why do we wish to visit the big city when we grow up in the country? Why do we wish to follow our relatives to another country? Of course, finance and opportunity play a role. That cities have streets paved with gold is an enduring component of many myths and stories. And when we do not move, then we do something else to keep up the interest and provoke imagination – we tell stories and create myths. We make the world more interesting by telling stories, which may carry important messages, but which most importantly seem to make our lives have more meaning. They are fuel for our minds. And without this, we are diminished, and our mental well-being suffers. We need mysteries and questions, as memories link the present to the past, compressing time into space. But a monoscape has no mysteries and no memories.

If we no longer have a big story that matters, we may no longer care. Despite great scientific consensus on the harm being caused to our planet, there is extraordinarily little macro-political or economic imperative that something fundamental might need to change. Why is this? Is it so easy to ignore the evidence or bodies of opinion on the effects of pollution or harm to the environment in the name of economic need or greed? We are going to need, at the very least, a better story. Increasing disconnections from nature mean more urbanization and fewer rural communities, a more corporate world and less community spirit, more speed and less time, more simple solutions that do not recognize the world's complexity and diversity. As disconnections increase, we must in the end suffer a personal loss – in emotional well-being and in common identity. This will create a positive feedback, especially if we collectively do not realize why we face physical and mental ill-health. It is difficult enough to specify the effects of increased ultraviolet light on the skin because of diminished atmospheric ozone. But what about the effects of living by a forest compared with a concrete-dominated urban landscape? Or walking to work along a leafy lane versus a daily commute inside a half tonne of metal on rubber wheels? And so things will get worse, not better, unless we tell a different story and act differently, every one of us.

A phase of ecolution is now required, in which the value of cultural diversity is reaffirmed and the value of biological diversity is recognized and increased. But will this lead to the survival of the greenest – or simply once again the richest (or even the most environmentally destructive)? A preserved, green world has more opportunities for emotional well-being for the people in it – and different people like different environments, from the tundra to tropical rainforests, from the savannahs to the sands (and theatres, cafes and concert halls). If we lose these environments, then we lose the opportunity to express some of our genes, and thus these will decrease in frequency over time. And we will change. An environmentally impoverished world will be a post-human world. As the poet Gary Snyder says:

> *how could we **be** were it not for this planet that provided our very shape? The land gave us a stride, and the lake a dive [...] We should be thankful for that.*[15]

Ecolution, then, suggests the need to recognize the tightly coupled nature of ecological and social systems, and to develop new opportunities for creative self-organization for enduring with this world. Our condition is linked to that of the planet. Now they are both in crisis, on a collision course, with the potential for destruction of biodiversity, cultures and life on this planet as we know it. In an imagined post-industrial world, human populations will fall, perhaps to as low as half of our current numbers. Many pressures will then have been lifted. But can we make it across this century, possibly the most critical of all human history?

Put simply, we collectively have the choice. Our genes are saying nothing. T S Eliot said that 'humankind cannot bear very much reality'.[16] Our genes are at the mercy of the environment, as Matt Ridley points out. What kind of natural and social environments will we now create – ones that are harmful to us and our genes, or ones in which we can coevolve and survive?

16

Liberation

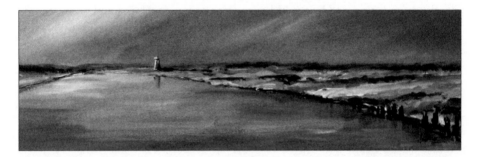

At the lowest point of a dry world, the dense air takes on a liquidity that makes this landscape of ochre hills and strange blue sea look as though it should belong to another planet. A fine dust blows off the desert scrub of the Judean Hills, populated only by mostly ignored and disdained nomads. The Dead Sea, almost supersaturated with salt and famously buoyant, is some 400 metres below sea level, and, with all the extra air to pass through, harmful ultraviolet light is almost entirely filtered out. This is a place rich with memories and abundant recorded history, but also one of conflict. This is desert, and water is contested, as is much of the land. The River Jordan flows from the Sea of Galilee to the Dead Sea, with Jordan and its capital Amman to the east and Israel and the West Bank to the west. Some 90 per cent of the water is now removed from both banks, with untreated sewage pumped back in its place.

For 75,000 years, the Dead Sea has remained stable, but now the sea level is falling dramatically at almost a metre a year. The area of the sea has shrunk by a third. At Masada, Herod's boat could moor by the base of the hill fort; today it rises 300 metres above the desert, and you have to climb high into the sandy ruins to see the distant shimmering sea. There are grand plans to pipe water from the Red Sea, but this will be costly, and there are ecological concerns about introducing sea water to the Dead Sea. In this remarkable place, you can see vividly the results of our inability to look after the planet, of our uniquely blind incapacity to work together to solve common problems.

Half way down the west coast of the sea are the caves of Qumran, where the Dead Sea scrolls were found in 1947. And a kilometre south is a type of place that lives in all our dreams, something mythical and alluring, something hopeful, but which is often no more than mirage. Here is an oasis known as both Enot Tzukim and En Fashha – the springs of the cliffs, of the fissure. A century ago, archaeologists with the Palestinian Exploration Fund leant out of a boat to paint a red line on the cliffs to mark the water level. Today, this line is about four metres above the cliff base, and the sea itself is more than a kilometre away, across dangerous mudflats and yawning sinkholes. The springs, though, have created a still point in this dusty and contested world.

You step across a sharp boundary, from one side desert, all dust and sand and heat, into another that is cool and green. Here are tamarisk, giant reeds and date palms. The clear water trickles over stones and into wide ponds. Fish flit in the shadows, and everywhere there is the chatter of birdsong. There are heron and kingfisher, and, attracted by the lush green vegetation, antelopes and porcupine, as well as predatory caracals, hyena and leopard. When you stand in an oasis, breathing in the damp air and listening to a world animated by water, you know why all oases will always be places of magic. 'These shady groves allure us,' says André Gide, with their 'mirage of permanent springs'. You also know why we bring them forth into our imagination when they are not there. These are places we want to exist. These are places that bring meaning and connection to some distant memories, perhaps from a time when we would like to think we had a lighter touch on this delicate land.[1]

My early years were spent on the Sahara's southern edge at Maiduguri, once a shore town but now distant from Lake Chad, once also the centre of the great Bornu and Hausa civilizations, and the supposed source of the Nile for mediaeval Europeans. Received memories speak of low dugouts paddling through the reeds, and of floating islands of thick vegetation moved by elephants. Lake Chad has shrunk too, like the Dead and Aral seas. What I remember, though, is the light and colour of the sub-desert, which is on your skin forever. Red laterite soils, gritty eyes, flat-topped acacia and the expansive sands of dry river beds. My earliest memory is of the rarity of water – lying in a cot in a room with blue walls, the enveloping sense of damp air, and the deluge of rain drumming on the corrugated iron roof through the night. Later memories are of an animated land, of a lion met in the bush, of cobras in the house, of an ocelot in the roof space, of giant grasscutter rats out back, of the aviary of songbirds, and of my pet Patas monkey, More. At nightfall, when the sky rapidly fades to pitch black, the great fruit bats brought their own mystery as they acrobatically swooped in utter silence.

On our return to England, we lived in a tall house that overlooked the North Sea. This seaside town laid down other elemental memories that remain vivid today. The aroma of malt at the nearby brewery, fresh-brewed bread at the bakers, the salty tang of the fishmongers. Most important was the sea. My brother and I grew up by the desert, and here our bedrooms looked east into a sun that rose out of the sea, as if every day was summer, turning the water to molten shimmering silver. We would run across the promenade and down the cliff path, and swim and run and throw stones, and climb on the groynes and pier, and feel the dry salt crisp on our skins. As Eva Salzman says, 'once visited, you take the smell of the sea with you everywhere, for the rest of your life'. The colour of the desert stays in you forever too, but the sea in the dazzling morning light, again under seemingly endless blue skies, becomes another sensation that endures.[2]

I wonder now why some memories survive and others do not. Those that do persist help to shape us, giving meaning and identity. Many other important events, though, do not survive. I cannot say whether it is these elemental memories that are most likely to survive. But it does seem that it is a smell, a cast of light, a snatch of music, a colour of a flower, a shape of a hill that can unlock certain memories, accelerating us back to another time in an instant. What happens, we may again wonder, when people engage less with the land and nature and do not have the chance to create such memories? In later times, there will be no unlocking of doors. No time travel. No buffering of today by yesterday, of contemporary knowledge by earlier understandings. Lose the memories and we create a world that forgets how it came about, and then we come too easily to believe that we are at the pinnacle of a long line of irreversible biological, technological and economic progress. If we lose touch with this animated world, we come easily to believe a myth that we have absolute control. Full steam ahead, and do not worry about the hidden reefs, icebergs or dangerous shallows. This 'faith in progress', as Hugh Brody has put it, 'is itself a kind of religion'.[3]

Time is a strange thing. We always seem to want more of it. We consider the prospect of living longer desirable, or at least that living shorter is a failure or loss. But time flies when we're enjoying something, which seems so very unfair, and goes agonizingly slowly when we're bored or unhappy. Old people feel the years flash by, but the days can drag. We take on busy jobs in which there is never enough time, and often describe it as a rat race, another animal metaphor. Then we wish we had spent more time watching and contemplating the world. Some of us do this well; to many it comes late in life. In his calendar of life in rural Essex and Suffolk, *Word from Wormingford*, Ronnie Blythe describes sitting with a 96-year-old neighbour in a car, which is 'parked by a great field where the wheat is so new and what we remember is so old'.[4]

Biologists believe we have three types of timekeeping. Circadian rhythms control our sleep and wakefulness, and are remarkably accurate. Millisecond timing is a feature of our motor tasks, the muscle movements and flows of chemical and electron signals in our nervous systems. Interval timing, on the other hand, is how we consciously perceive the passage of time, and it is here that we seem to have more control than we thought. Sequential time can be arrested and stretched, something athletes try to do when they get in the zone. Others meditate or pray to do the same. Others find time stretching to the point of stopping when they immerse themselves in the natural world. This has been called flow, the complete absorption in an activity. When we are in this flow zone, we stop being conscious, and find it a welcome release.[5]

T S Eliot's poem *The Four Quartets* takes circular time as its central theme. Eliot says we have a restlessness, and that where there is motion there is time. The timeless would therefore be free of motion, but this is not death. This is our dance with the world, the centre of a turning wheel. Linear time is a straight line, a fundamental concept to we moderns. The horizon (a circle) demarks an area of space. But linear time encloses no space. Circular time encloses space. David Abram observes, 'our future probably relies on us seeing time, and progress, in a new way. We are doing different things, not necessarily better things.' Cyclical time has the same shape as space. In Inuit, the term *uvatiarru* is translated as both long ago and in the future.[6]

We all seem to seek still points in our lives, but are they getting harder to recognize, and thus possibly even more important, at least for their scarcity value? There cannot be many people on this planet who own a camera and have not taken a photograph of a sunset, where past and present are gathered. Nature teaches us about the circularity of life, of the inevitability of things happening again. The wheat and barley will be gold in summer, and the poplar leaves will rustle even if the air seems quite still; in autumn clouds of gulls will follow the plough; in spring the leaves will appear from bare soil as if by magic again. 'And it will go onwards the same', as Thomas Hardy predicted, 'though dynasties pass'. Eliot begins his poem with:

> *Time present and time past*
> *Are both perhaps present in time future,*
> *And time future contained in the past,*
> *If all time is eternally present.*

Is our liberation to come from a recognition that we are only one civilization among many, and that those before came and went with little hint of these approaching end times? Like Eliot's dancers, they are either under the sea or under the hill. And yet we race forward, without really stopping to contemplate what we are doing to the planet and thus ourselves. Thankfully, many now accept that environmental harm is something undesirable, that it would be good if it stopped (though often only if we can carry on doing what we do now). But it is not just some abstract environment that is being harmed. It is us. We are tightly coupled to this world, we helped to shape it, and it us. We harm one, and the other will inevitably be harmed too. Of course, we can develop technological solutions, many of which will be quite brilliant and unforeseen, but will they lead us to have less stressed and happier lives, to be able to have enough food to feed our families, to reduce the need for chemical intervention to stay mentally stable? There will be many advances, but we may not be any happier.[7]

There is another component of time – the number of occasions that humans have passed on their genes to descendent generations. Since the first hominids emerged, this has probably happened some 250,000–300,000 times (at roughly 20 years per generation). For all but 600 of those generations, all our ancestors were hunter-gatherers. Lately, we developed agriculture, and then cities, and forty major civilizations came and went. And now our industrialized world, say six to eight generations in length, seems to be our only choice. Put human history into one week, starting Monday, and this modern world emerges about three seconds before midnight on the Sunday. But no one suggests that we should return to being hunter-gatherers. Indeed, one of the basic tenets of modern civilization is to disdain such ways of life and the people who keep to them. They are seen to be backward, primitive, stone-aged, unsophisticated, and would best be served by entering wholeheartedly into the modern world. But why are we so convinced that this is the right thing to do? What is there to fear from permitting indigenous groups, whether Innu, Hadza, Mbuti or Sami, to continue their ways of life? I suspect it is something to do with a deep fear that they are right in many ways, and we moderns are wrong, and the sooner we remove the evidence, the sooner we can forget this truth.

In our collaboration with the Algonkian Innu of Labrador, Colin Samson and I have identified some components of hunter-gatherer lifestyles that could help we moderns find a new form of liberation today. Both the physical activity and nutrition transitions have so far led to greater imprisonment for we moderns. A change in each could help to save us and the world (if only it were that easy). Hunter-gatherers eat wholesome foods and have varied diets, though often suffer periods of acute shortage. Moderns have adopted diets high in refined sugars and saturated fats, and these are leading to rapidly increasing incidence of obesity, cancers and type II diabetes. Hunter-gatherers engage in regular physical activity, usually in intense periods, but these are interspersed with periods of rest and social engagement. Moderns are increasingly sedentary, and physical activity is increasingly only linked to periods of leisure, and so needs to be part of positive lifestyle decisions. For hunter-gatherers, interactions with nature are a central part of livelihoods that respond to changing seasons and places. Moderns, by contrast, are increasingly disconnected from nature, certainly for survival needs, though some engage in lots of ecotourism to make up for it. Hunter-gatherers spend lots of time in social interactions, as their success depends on cooperation, trust and emotional support. There is no loneliness in hunter-gatherer communities. But in modern communities, social interaction and social capital are replaced by individual activities and passive entertainment, and families are increasingly atomized. There is also time for conviviality and storytelling among hunter-gatherers, with knowledge about the land valued and passed on. But we moderns get our stories from the television (which is controlled by the few) and have too little time to create personal memories.

Perhaps these are all self-evident truths. We may recognize the remnants, even desire them, but simply find them unattainable. But there may, too, be things that have slipped our minds. We have forgotten that the countryside is not only animated, but is also full of the signs of history. It is full of stories, which we now erase in the rush to get foods from farms to our plates. We have forgotten that we and the rest of life created this land, and it shaped us. We have forgotten that memories count for much in our own identities. We have forgotten about the constancy of the natural world, and that wildness need not be destroyed by people living there.

Gary Snyder talks of the need for a reinhabitation of the wild. I would say we need a reinhabitation of all of nature – the urban, the farmed and the wild. Wilderness ideas have, of course, created their own troublesome dichotomies, helping further to separate humans from nature. In truth, almost all of the world has been shaped by human interactions with it, and only later did the assumption of *terra nullius* come to be applied to land that colonists wanted to be empty (so that they could move there without feeling guilty). Chief Luther Standing Bear said in 1933 of the Lakota lands, 'we did not think of the great open plains, the beautiful rolling hills, the winding streams with tangled growth, as wild'. The wilderness idea, as Baird Callicott has put it, 'ignores the historic presence and effects of people on practically all the world's ecosystems'.[8]

Gary Nabhan makes a telling comparison[9] of two Tohono O'odham (formerly known as Papago) oases 50km apart, one in the US and the other in Mexico. At the US site, authorities designated A'el Waipia as a bird sanctuary in 1957 (because of the importance of the wildlife) and stopped all cultivation by local people. In Mexico, though, Kiitowak has always been farmed in a traditional way. After 30 years, studies had shown that the Mexican oasis supported 65 species of birds, whereas only 32 remained at the US site. One resident of Kiitowak said:

> *when people live and work in a place, and plant their seeds and water their trees, then birds go to live with them. They like those places. There's plenty to eat and that's when we are friends to them.*

Nabhan suggests that the whole desert ecosystem is influenced and shaped by local people. It is only those from the outside with preconceptions about what is correct who make the mistakes.

There is great interest today in ecological restoration, which could bring a double benefit of environmental healing and deeper understanding.[10] So even though so much is going wrong, what are the prospects for recovery? At the local level, there has been remarkable progress in the past couple of decades across a huge range of countries. Wetlands have been recreated, hay meadows protected, woodlands planted, degraded lands turned green, rice fields reinhabited by helpful insects, rare birds brought back from the edge of extinction, urban wastelands turned into vibrant gardens and small farms made a success. At national levels, too, there is much to celebrate in positive policies. The Chinese Three North Shelterbelt Development Programme, also known as the Great Green Wall, has planted millions of trees across the southern edge of the Gobi and Takliman deserts, a 2500km line of green which can be seen from space and which will eventually cover 35 million hectares. The Brazilians of Santa Caterina have helped small farmers into groups that have led to ecological recovery across large parts of the state. The Australian Landcare movement has changed both rural and urban people's thinking about the land, increasing pride in what they can do collectively. The Kenyans have a huge programme of participatory extension working with farmers and local groups. Maybe the Aral Sea will fill up, too, now that efforts are being made to undo past errors. Though this list could go on, however, it is still true that much of what is good has happened despite policies rather than because of them. What would happen if we could scale up the many efforts at ecological restoration and regeneration for the whole world?

Acts of ecological recovery can bring forth a new world, but it will take time for the memories to be laid down. Chris Baines, creator of so much green in the urban setting, says, 'we may make a forest look as good as the original. But it won't sound as good, and won't smell as good, and it won't have the ghosts in it.' Of course, they will come in time. But you rather suspect not when it comes to the faked nature of plastic trees in the atriums and halls of modern shopping malls.[11]

Places become meaningful when there is a story. Things take on different meanings because of the context. Not just the thing itself, but its history and memories. The celebration of a goal in football (a goal is a goal) is quite different if you have already won, if it is a consolation as your team has already lost, or if it is the winning goal scored against all the odds. The real world comprises not context-less objects, but an 'intertwined matrix', as David Abram has put it. Things, including bodies, are creative, are shape-shifters. All we have done in recent times is to remove the stories, turning places and food into simple commodities. But places do acquire the stamp of human events. As Keith Basso says, 'places are as much a part of us as we are a part of them'. In oral cultures, spoken words are everything. They are used to mix facts and metaphors, to tell stories, to engage both the storyteller and listeners. They imagine the land. It is an act of creation. It is also time travel. Effective narrators, says Basso, open up thinking, and travel in their minds to the places where things happened and will happen.[12]

Hugh Brody observes, 'to know this particular territory is to prosper; neither the land nor the knowledge of the land can be replaced'.[13] But the polar and sub-polar north is a big land. The taiga spreads 13,000 kilometres in a belt through Canada and Alaska and then through Russia and around to northern Scandinavia. There are some ten million square kilometres of land still mostly populated by hunters, gatherers and trappers. In northern Canada, there is a 4000km continuous line of hunter-gatherer communities from east to west, a line that crosses just two roads and meets no major towns. We once travelled 200km by skidoo into central Labrador, a trifle on the grand scale, but far enough to sense a land that does not bend to human intentionality. When the gales blow, you barely dare leave the tent all day. When the animals permit, you have porcupine, ptarmigan or caribou on the stove. When the fish choose, they will bite on a line dropped through a couple of metres of snow and ice. When the sun shines, you can make a lot of distance, until the surface snow melts in the afternoon, and claws at the tracks or simply gives way to the tread of feet.

How often does the weather intervene in our lives? In centrally heated or air-conditioned houses, the outside cannot get in. No more scraping off the ice from the inside of windows in winter; no more nights bathed in sweat. No sweet smell of honeysuckle on the night breeze, or song of the nightingale, or buzz of cicadas and ghostly calls of owls. In creating the comfortable life of a space station, we also cut ourselves off yet more. 'I hear', says Ronnie Blythe of his four-hundred-year-old farm house:

> *an orchestrated sound of wind in trees, Bernhard ploughing, birdsong, far cries from the sports field, water flowing, walls scratching and creaking, old clocks on their rounds, much rustling.*[14]

An animated landscape is always changing, dynamic and unpredictable day by day, though the longer rhythms of the seasons and years can be predicted. This all requires observation and respect. But today, we interact almost solely with other people and human-made artefacts, 'a precarious situation, given our age-old reciprocity with the many voiced landscape,' says David Abram. Could you give a friend instructions on how to get to your house using only natural features of the landscape? In the Inuktitut language of the Inuit, Hugh Brody describes how there is no hierarchy of people or rights to use land. There is no demarcation between humans and animals, and individuals are left to make decisions for themselves. *Atiq* describes the web of relationships that links individuals to everything else in the world, including their ancestors.

Claude Lévi-Strauss has suggested we need a new kind of ecological civicism, a new ethic, a sacred ecology, as Fikret Berkes has put it. Paul Shepard thought we had progressed far in ecological thinking, but not far enough in ecological being. Sooner or later, we have to reinhabit the land. And thus care for it, and ourselves, better. As Baird Callicott says:

> *can't we be good citizens [...] and envision and work to create an eminently liveable, systemic, post-industrialized technological society well-adapted to and at peace and in harmony with its organic environment?*[15]

Not much to ask. And the answer is, of course, yes. We can. But will we make it happen soon enough? Will it take serious scaremongering to wake us all up? Or will appeals to place and memory, reconnections to nature, and reminders of what makes us happy and content be enough? Will there ever be the progressive policies put in place, or will we have to wait for major ecological disasters to occur first? Will there be the investments in science and technology that could help?

In short, do you think things from here will get better or worse? If we think they'll get better, we may sit back and do little. If worse, we may just give up (or even, like some extremists, think this actually is the way to salvation). In recovery programmes, people are told to take it day by day, and not get too far ahead of themselves. We need the vision of an animated connected world, where people matter and where nature matters, and where we develop a new interconnected ethic.

We will have to consume less, or with a light touch on the land, and at least ensure that consumption does not drive natural resources to extinction. We might also need to spend more time not doing much. In 'The abundance of less', Andy Couturier describes his relationship with Nakamura, a Japanese artisan in the mountains of Shikoku, who shows that frugality does not mean deprivation. On a rainy day, Nakamura says, 'sometimes I carve woodblocks or read, but mostly, when I have nothing to do, I just stare at the fire [...] Doing nothing all day – it's difficult at first.' Couturier adds:

> *perhaps such a life – very little production, very little consumption – might be an important part of the solution to the world ecological crisis.*[16]

We will need to become more native to our places. We then need the millions of small day-by-day actions of billions of people that will in the end add up to something. When something works, we need to pass it on, whispering truths; when it doesn't work, we'll need to be angry, resolute, persuasive and resilient. In such a new engagement and dance, we may yet survive.

Notes

Chapter 1 – Becoming Green
PAGES 3–7

1   For details of the emergence of life, and in particular the chlorophyll molecule, see Broda (1975) and Björn (1976).
2   See James Lovelock's *The Ages of Gaia* (1995) for a clear summary of the Gaia hypothesis, and the more recent *Revenge of Gaia* (2005), and Stephen Harding's *Animate Earth* (2005) for updates on theories and evidence.

Chapter 2 – Birch Bark and Blue Sky
PAGES 9–26

1   The E O Wilson quote comes from Wilson (2002). For details of species losses and their importance for survival, see IUCN's 'Red list of threatened species' (2006) and the Millennium Ecosystem Assessment's comprehensive summary of ecosystem services and their values (MEA, 2005). See also Daily (1997) for a summary of nature's services. Bill Adams' *Future Nature* (1996) contains an excellent overview of conservation challenges. For a classic account of the land ethic, see Aldo Leopold's *A Sand County Almanac* (1949). In truth, no one knows how many species there are, even how clearly to define a species. 'What indeed is a species in the first place?' asks Steve Jones (1999). There are, for example, 17,500 recognized species of butterfly, and 100,000 subspecies. Richard Dawkins (2003) describes the curious case of a ring species, the herring gull/lesser blackbacked gull. In Britain, they are distinct species with quite different colours. But if you follow the herring gull westwards across North America, Alaska, Siberia and back, they become more like lesser blackbacked gulls. At every stage of the ring, the birds can interbreed, but not in Europe, where they appear to be separate species.
2   The David Rothenberg and Wandee Pryor quote on progress and evolution is in *Writing the Future* (2004), and John Gray's comment about going on forever is in *Heresies* (2004).
3   For more on Neanderthals, see Arsuaga (2003) and Fernández-Armesto (2004).
4   Two very good books summarize the rise and fall of civilizations – Haywood (2005) and McEvedy (1980). Jared Diamond's *Collapse* (2005) documents some cases in greater detail, and the excellent *Sustainability or Collapse* by Costanza et al (2007) clarifies the many reasons for collapse. See also John McNeill's *Something New Under the Sun*.
5   The David Ehrenfeld quote is in Ehrenfeld (2005) and his classic text on humanism, *The Arrogance of Humanism*, was published in 1981.

6 David Orr's comments on the time for reason running short are from Orr (2005). For a scary view of fossil fuel depletion, see James Kunstler's *The Long Emergency* (2005). See also Costanza et al (2007).

7 The various data on consumption patterns and levels are drawn from L Brown (2004); WRI (2006); Myers and Kent (2004). William Rees first came up with the idea of ecological footprints (see Rees W, 2003; Rees et al, 1996), and Wackernagel et al (2004) have developed the use of the term 'global hectares' to show how natural resources are appropriated. There are many websites now devoted to calculating and comparing ecological footprints. See also Bell (2004) for a discussion of the consumption treadmill. There are various very good texts on consumption behaviour and happiness, including Frank (1999); Schwartz (2004); Kasser (2002); Nettle (2005).

8 See Norman Myers and Jennifer Kent's *The New Consumers* (2004) for details of the growing influence of affluence on the world's economy and environment. Also see Myers and Kent (2003). It is vital to economic growth that people are made to feel dissatisfied with what they have got. Growth needs discontented people (Porritt, 2005). If we say enough is enough, then we begin to change the world.

9 Veblen (1899), also quoted in Bell (2004).

10 These paragraphs draw on Schwartz (2004) and Frank (1999). The observation about lottery winners and accident victims, and who are the happier one year on, comes from a paper by Brickman et al (1978). Ostir et al (2001) describe the effects of emotional well-being on health.

11 The David Suzuki quote is in his *Sacred Balance* (1997). For a very good paper on memories and ghosts, see Bell (1997 and 2004).

12 Niels Röling's story about the Chinese farm worker is from Röling (2005).

13 Martin Rees's book on the 21st century is *Our Final Century* (Rees M, 2003), containing the data on the number of people killed in the last century in conflict. John Gray covers this topic well in *Straw Dogs*. Rees's book is also my source for the Arthur C Clarke remark.

14 Bill McKibben's comments about the lake are from his persuasive *The End of Nature* (2003).

15 The John Gray quote on inherited faith is from *Heresies* (2004).

16 This paragraph draws on Bell (2004) and Nettle (2005).

17 Gray's quote on progress condemning idleness is in *Straw Dogs* (2002). Jay Gershuny's studies on busyness are in Gershuny (2005).

18 The Sahlins quote is from Sahlins (2003). For more on hunter-gatherer lifestyles and workload, see the classic *Man the Hunter* by Lee and DeVore, Hugh Brody's *Maps and Dreams* (1981) and *The Other Side of Eden* (2000), and Lee and Daly's *The Cambridge Encyclopedia of Hunters and Gatherers* (1999). There are 5000–8000 indigenous groups across the world, numbering some 600 million people (Stevens, 1997). See Paul Shepard (1998) for a discussion of the Pleistocene hypothesis.

19 T S Eliot's *Four Quartets* can be found in many books of his poems. Two good analyses of the poem can be found in Blamires (1969) and Bergsten (1973).

20 The famous 1798 essay by Thomas Malthus is 'An essay on the principles of population'. The UN Population Division publishes many assessments of population trends and forecasts (e.g. UN, 2004, 2005a, b). In their predictions of population to 2300, the high scenario is now extremely unlikely, yet it is based on only 2.35 high children per woman, and would yield world population of 36 billion by 2300.

21 The John Caldwell quote is from the UN (2004) report. The 'low scenario' implies that most countries of the world come to adopt low fertility patterns. Decivilization is a term coined by Timothy Garton Ash (in Porritt, 2005).

22   See Wilson (1984) and Kellert and Wilson (1993).

23   Felipe Fernández-Armesto in *So You Think You're Human?* discusses our relations with the wild and the consequences of creating separate categories.

24   More on big cats can be found in Taylor (2005).

25   Transhumanism is discussed by Joan Maloof (2004), and various perspectives on the role of genes and the environment in human evolution can be found in Jones (1999), Ridley (2003), Pinker (2002) and Laland and Brown (2005).

26   The impulse for mass slaughter has not necessarily changed since earlier times (early civilizations could be just as bloody). But modern technologies have certainly increased the scope and scale of tyranny.

27   The Dee Brown quote on Native American groups is from *Bury My Heart at Wounded Knee* (1970).

28   The modern story of Las Vegas is in Mike Davis's *Dead Cities* (2002).

29   The James Lovelock quote is in Michael McCarthy's interview with him for *The Independent* newspaper, published on 16 January 2006. There are those, it seems, who welcome the idea of end times, as they believe in the prophesies in the Book of Revelation. They are thus content with the idea of environmental destruction, as it hastens the arrival of the apocalypse, and the predicted one thousand years of peace that are predicted to follow (see Porritt, 2005).

Chapter 3 – A Room with a Green View
PAGES 27–38

1   Many features of the natural and built environment are known to affect our behaviour and actual mental states (see Tuan, 1977; Freeman, 1984; Kellert and Wilson, 1993; Tall, 1996; Frumkin, 2002, 2003; Maller et al, 2002; Pretty, 2004; Pretty et al, 2003, 2004 and 2005a, c). See also Kals et al (1999).

2   The five categories of factors that appear to shape our reasons for engaging with nature and green space were developed from the following University of Essex research: CRN research (Pretty et al, 2005a) – 263 subjects; Environment Agency research (Peacock et al, 2005) – 92 participants; Dedham Vale research (1999) – 212 people; Gateshead research (2001) – 877 people; Jaywick (1999) – 270 people; Hythe, Colchester (2000) – 308 people; Highwoods (1999) – 370 people; St Anne's, Colchester (2000) – 662 people; sub-total 3054. Further research on 2154 adults, see Tabbush and O'Brien (2004) – 123 participants; and National Trust MORI poll (2004) – 2031 adults), which confirm these findings.

3   The 'biophilia hypothesis' is explained in Wilson (1984) and Kellert and Wilson (1993). See also White and Heerwagen (1998). The number of miles walked by Wordsworth is reported by Jeremy Burchardt (2002). The Cowper, Bacon and John Stuart Mill quotes are all in Thomas (1983). The effect of nature on well-being is summarized in Pretty et al (2004 and 2005a, c); Pretty (2004). References of detailed studies include Moore (1981); Ulrich (1984 and 1999); Tennessen and Cimprich (1995); Larsen et al (1998); Kaplan (2001); Kuo and Sullivan (2001); Diette et al (2003); Cooper-Marcus and Barnes (1999); Hayashi et al (1999); Whitehouse et al (2001); Hartig et al (1991 and 2003); Fredrickson and Anderson (1999); Frumkin (2001 and 2005); Williams and Harvey (2001); Herzog et al (2002). The opposite of biophilic is biophobic. Many people have innate negative reactions to heights, small spaces, snakes and spiders, rats and mice, bats, and blood. The heritability of the aversion to snakes and spiders is about 30 per cent and is usually triggered early in life (Wilson, 2002).

4   Studies showing the effect of the view from the window include those by Tennessen and Cimprich (1995); Larsen et al (1998); Parsons et al (1998); Kaplan (2001); Laumann et al (2003); Verderber and Reuman (1987); Heerwagen and Orians (1993); Ulrich (1993).

5   Frances Kuo's research in Chicago is written up in Kuo et al (1998); Taylor et al (1998 and 2001) and Kuo and Sullivan (2001). Aquaria are good for health too (DeSchriver and Riddick, 1990).

6   See Peiser and Schwann, 1993; Wood and Handley, 1999; Luttik, 2000; Lange and Schaeffer, 2001; Luther and Gruehn, 2001; Lindsey et al, 2004. The Cabe Space (2006) study of ten locations in England shows that properties with park views are 12 per cent more valuable than those at the same location with no views: building nothing increases land values if open green space is created (Savills, 2006). Nature drives also seem to have an immunizing effect against future stresses that might arise during the day (Parsons et al, 1998). The classic prison and hospital studies were by Moore (1981) and Ulrich (1984). Howie Frumkin's quote is in Frumkin (2001).

7   There have been a variety of studies using photographs to investigate the effects of different scenes on cognition and emotions (Coughlin and Goldstein, 1970; Shafer and Richards, 1974; Sorte, 1975; Russell and Mehrabian, 1976). For example, in a comparison of videos of different roadside corridors on a virtual drive to work, the urban drive was more stressful and drives through nature were more protective against stresses that subsequently arose during the working day (Parsons et al, 1998). Most studies of this type have used still photographs, mainly comparing urban with rural scenes (Honeyman, 1992; Purcell and Lamb, 1998; Staats and Hartig, 2004), and all have consistently shown reduced stress and improved mental well-being in the presence of nature scenes. Relatively few studies have investigated the effects of exposure to different scenes on physiological measures such as heart rate and blood pressure (Ulrich, 1981; Hartig et al, 2003; Laumann et al, 2003) and none has analysed the potential synergistic effects of physical activity.

8   Nancy Wells and Gary Evans' research is in Wells (2000) and Wells and Evans (2003).

9   Terry Hartig's research is in Hartig et al (1991 and 2003) and Staats and Hartig (2004). Older people who walk in green places live longer (Eden Alternative, 2002; Takano et al, 2002).

10   The effects of plants inside homes and offices is analysed by Lewis (1992); Randall et al (1992); Ulrich and Parsons (1992); and Larsen et al (1998).

11   Gardens and nature in hospital environments appear to enhance mood, reduce stress and improve the overall appreciation of the health care provider and quality of care (Nightingale, 1860; Lindheim and Syme, 1983; Ulrich, 1984; Cooper-Marcus and Barnes, 1995 and 1999; Gerlach-Spriggs et al, 1998; Whitehouse et al, 2001). The children's hospital in California study was by Whitehouse et al (2001). Allotment data is in Burchardt (2002), and the survey of allotment gardeners was by NSALG (1993).

12   The survey of New York community gardens was by Armstrong (2000); see also Jane Weissman's (1995a and b) earlier detailed studies of Green Thumb urban gardeners in New York City.

13   Horticulture therapy is discussed by Lewis (1992); Ulrich (1999); Sempkirk et al (2002); Frumkin (2001).

14   Forest Schools in the UK are being developed by the Forest Education Initiative, whose partners are BTCV, the Field Studies Council, the Forestry Commission, the Forest Industries Development Council, Groundwork, the Timber Trade Federation, The Tree Council and the Woodland Trust. For more, see www.foresteducation.org/about_fei.php. See also woodland schools in the US (www.woodlandschool.org). See also BTCV's green gym at www.btcv.org/greengym, and Reynolds' evaluation (Reynolds, 2002).

15 The benefits of national parks and lately of adventure therapy are discussed by Muir (1911); Thoreau (1837–1853); Williams (1994); Williams and Harvey (2001); Herzog et al (2002). The adventure therapy studies quoted are by Kaplan (1995); Fredrickson and Anderson (1999); Williams and Harvey (2001); and Herzog et al (2002).

Chapter 4 – Unhealthy Places
PAGES 39–51

1 The spread of depression and stress-related illness is reviewed in WHO (2001). For more on mental health problems in the UK, see Sainsbury Centre for Mental Health (2005); HSE (2004); Mind (2005). For summaries of the status of the nation's health, see Wanless (2002 and 2004). See Goodwin (2000) for an overview of the value to health of a 'glass half full' attitude.

2 See Nettle (2005) for more on what happiness is and what drug solutions are increasingly favoured.

3 Activity also enhances mental health, fosters healthy muscles and bones, and helps maintain health and independence in older adults: see North et al (1990); Camacho et al (1991); Pate et al (1995); CDC (1996); Scully et al (1998); DCMS (2002 and 2004); DoH (2004a); Lim and Taylor (2005). Declining rates of physical activity are described in Brownson et al (2005).

4 For the value of open and communal space in urban areas, see Newman (1972 and 1980); Freeman (1984 and 1998); Halpern (1995); Kaplan et al (1998). Urban form affects physical activity levels (see Dalgard and Tambs, 1997; Owen et al, 2000; Berrigan and Troiano, 2002; Handy et al, 2002; Boslaugh et al, 2004; Braza et al, 2004; Owen et al, 2004; Rutt and Coleman, 2005; Sallis et al, 2006). Joel Garreau's *Edge City* (1992) describes the emergence of a new type of urban-suburban phenomenon in the US.

5 This paragraph draws on Kahn and Kellert (2002) and Brechin et al (2002).

6 For studies of open space and mental ill-health in Japan, Scandinavia and the Netherlands, see Takano et al (2002); de Vries et al (2003); Grahn and Stigsdotter (2003). Open space affects levels of activity (Craig et al, 2002).

7 Open space is important for children: see Kaplan and Kaplan (1989); Kahn and Kellert (2002); Bingley and Milligan (2004); Fjørtoft (1999); Taylor et al (2001). Children spend less time outdoors today than they used to (Orr, 2006). See also Richard Louv's *Last Child in the Woods* (2006).

8 For the Dagenham story, see Freeman (1998); for US slum clearance, see Halpern (1995); Newman (1972).

9 See Frumkin et al (2004) and Frumkin (2005) for comprehensive analyses of the effects of urban sprawl. See also Lewis and Booth (1994) and Davis (2004) for unhealthy cities.

10 The research of Frances Kuo and colleagues can be found in Kuo et al (1998) and de Vries et al (2003).

11 The analysis of the effects of distance from green space is by Grahn and Stigsdotter (2003).

12 The Stegner quote is from Metzner (2000), the Hugh Freeman from Freeman (1984). Gary Snyder discusses reinhabitation in *A Place in Space* (1995).

13 Reviews of identity and nature are in Fox (1995) and Milton (2002). See also Arne Naess (1989 and 1992) for more on deep ecology.

14 The Maslow experiment is recorded in Maslow and Mintz (1972).

15 The Yi-Fu Tuan quote is from Tuan (1977), as is the Kronberg castle story. Mike Bell's paper on the ghosts of place was published in 1997. See Gallagher (1994) and Lippard (1997) for accounts of the importance of place.

16 Places are created and imagined by us: see Kaplan and Kaplan (1989) and Macfarlane's superb *Mountains of the Mind* (2003). Robert Harrison's book about the dead is *The Dominion of the Dead* (2003).

17 See Cernea (1999) for a review of resettlement programmes. See the World Commission on Dams report (2002) for a summary of the effects of dams on resettlement. Some 45,000 dams were built in the 20th century in 140 countries.

18 The average American is said to move 14 times in a lifetime (Tall, 1996).

19 Regarding Terrence Lee of St Andrews University and the term 'chronic environmental stress disorder', see Bonnes et al (2003).

20 For urban tree planting projects, see Austin and Kaplan (2003); for trees as FHOs (fixed hazardous objects), see Sommer, 2003 (in Clayton and Opotow, 2003). See also National Urban Forestry Unit (2002a and b).

21 The garden stories are in Ryan and Grese (2005) and Lynch and Brusi (2005), both part of Peggy Barlett's excellent book *Urban Place* (2005).

22 A wide range of adventure therapy programmes are discussed in Hobbs and Shelton (1972); Jerstad and Stelzer (1973); Berman and Anton (1988); Moyer (1988); Davis-Berman and Berman (1989); Kaplan and Talbot (1993); Warady (1994); Hyer et al (1996); Martin (1996); Bennett et al (1998); Fredrickson and Anderson (1999); Williams (1999); Stys (2001); Williams and Harvey (2001); Hayashi (2002); Johnson (2002); Michalski et al (2003).

23 For evaluations of the effects of wilderness therapy programmes, see Russell (2002). The longer the time that people spend, or the more often they return, the more fond they grow of places – see Richards and Smith (2003).

24 The excellent report on the effects of the English National Forest is by Morris and Urry (2005). See also Tabbush and O'Brien (2003).

25 Green care – see Hassink (2003); Braastad (2005).

26 The Gary Snyder quote is in *The Practice of the Wild* (1990).

Chapter 5 – Where the Wild Things Were
PAGES 55–68

1 Neanderthals are now known to have evolved from a completely different lineage to *Homo sapiens*. They had a complex and rich culture, but lacked some adaptive capacity that the new hominids had, and so did not survive (see, for example, Krings et al, 1997). For more on the peopling of Britain, see Slack and Ward (2002), and on humans as a species, see Deacon (1978).

2 The date for dog domestication from wolves is still uncertain – see Savolainen et al (2002) and Leonard et al (2002) for genetic data that suggests an early date. For a discussion on how animal domestication led to a more utilitarian relationship with animals, see Philo and Wilbert (2000) and Buller (2004). For a comprehensive historical account of relations with nature in Europe, see Thomas (1983). Stephen Budiansky (1998) addresses the human–animal dualism or continuity debate.

3 In the UK, of the remaining wild mammals, only hedgehogs, hares, squirrels and bats number more than a million each, followed by 800,000 feral cats, 500,000 roe deer, 450,000 each of stoats and weasels, 360,000 red deer, 250,000 each of badgers and red fox, 100,000 fallow deer and 74,000 otters. In addition, there are 93,000 grey seals and 35,000 common seals in our seas and estuaries. See Macdonald and Baker (2006) for a summary of the state of British mammals. Species loss data for the US are from Bergman (2003).

4   Domestic livestock numbers worldwide are from the FAOSTAT database of the Food and Agriculture Organization of the United Nations (http://faostat.fao.org/) and are as follows: in 2004 there were 1324 million cattle, 952 million pigs, 1011 million sheep and 759 million goats. The countries with the most cattle, pigs, sheep and goats are China (920 million), India (382 million), Brazil (248 million), the US (162 million) and Australia and Sudan (125 million each). China has the most chickens (3.97 billion), followed by the US (1.97 billion), Brazil (1.1 billion) and India (425 million). The UK has 162 million cattle, pigs and sheep and 170 million chickens.

5   The Gary Snyder quote is from *The Practice of the Wild* (1990).

6   The Harold Herzog paper on types of mice is from 1988. The Keith Thomas summary is from *Man and the Natural World* (1983). One of the best accounts of the animals we know as pets is by James Serpell (1986).

7   Charles Bergman's *Wild Echoes* (2003) gives a range of excellent accounts of species on the brink of extinction in the US.

8   The hedgehog controversy in the Western Isles of Scotland is covered in various ways by Reeve (1998), Morris (1998), Jackson and Green (2000), Jackson (2001), and factsheets from Scottish Natural Heritage and the Scottish Executive (SNH et al, 2002). In early 2007, the Scottish authorities decided to stop hedgehog culling, and adopt instead a policy of relocation. Hedgehogs are not the only example of introduced 'alien' species causing severe ecological problems on islands. Feral cats have been introduced in the past to many islands to control rodents and rabbits, but often with devastating effects on other island fauna: at least 33 bird species are known to have become extinct because of cats (Nogales et al, 2004). On Kergulen Island (sub-Antarctic) cats killed 1.2 million seabirds a year in the 1970s; on Ascension Island, the sooty tern was reduced from one million pairs in the 1940s to 150,000 in the 1990s; and on Marion Island (sub-Antarctic), cats kill 450,000 seabirds a year. Cat eradication is being attempted on several islands, but has only so far been successful on very small islands of less than five square kilometres.

9   Uist Hedgehog Rescue argues that the waders do indeed come first and that something must be done to control hedgehog numbers – the objection is that killing them is unnecessary. See www.uhr.org.uk.

10 For a very good review of tiger numbers, see Stephen Mills's *Tiger* (2004). The most famous books about fearsome predators (leopards and tigers) in India were by Jim Corbett – *The Man-Eaters of Kumaon* (1946) and *The Man-Eating Leopard of Rudraprayag* (1989). Some data reported by David Quammen suggest that deaths in British India in the 19th and early 20th centuries were extraordinarily high: 800 people killed by tigers in 1877, 851 in 1910 and 1603 in 1922.

11 David Quammen's *Monster of God* (2004) is an excellent account of our relations with a range of predators. Shark attack data is kept by the Florida Museum of Natural History in their International Shark Attack File, see www.flmnh.ufl.edu/fish. Val Plumwood's article 'Being prey' (1996) is about a 1985 crocodile attack in Kakadu National Park in Australia. It describes in graphic details what is means to be prey. One part of her incredulity during the attack was the feeling 'this can't be happening to me, I'm a human being, I am more than food'.

12 For books on wolves, see Barry Lopez (1978), Karen Jones (2004) and Charles Bergman (2003). Robert Busch's *The Wolf Almanac* (1995) is a comprehensive study of wolf biology and management. The European wolf situation is discussed in Buller (2004) and the Nowegian context specifically by Skoga and Krange (2003). Perceptions of wolves in Wisconsin are discussed by Naughton-Treves et al (2003). The Leo Cottemoir quote is from Jones (2004).

13 For an account of rewilding, see Taylor (2005) and the *Ecos* (2006) special issue on reintroductions, volume 27(1). See also Donlan (2005) and Donlan et al (2006) for US perspectives on rewilding and the Wildland Network (www.wildland-network.org.uk) and Tooth and Claw (www.toothandclaw.org.uk) for the UK. Reintroductions do take a long time to work, though. Sea eagles were first introduced to Rum in 1975; the first young were observed in 1985 and there were 10 young in 1997 and 100 in 2000.

Chapter 6 – Hunters and the Hunted
PAGES 69–83

1   The use of wild foods is much more extensive than many people realize. These are reviewed in *The Hidden Harvest* (Scoones et al, 1992) and in the excellent *Flora Britannica* by Richard Mabey (1996) and *Birds Britannica* by Mark Cocker and Richard Mabey (2005).

2   One of the most comprehensive collections on the diversity of human cultures and their connectedness with nature and the land is Darrell Posey's seven-hundred-page volume *Cultural and Spiritual Values of Biodiversity* (1999). Containing contributions from nearly three hundred authors from across the world, these highlight 'the central importance of cultural and spiritual values in an appreciation and preservation of all life'. These voices of the Earth demonstrate the widespread intimate connectivity that people have to nature, and their mutual respect and understanding. In Australia, Henrietta Fourmile of the Polidingi Tribe says, 'Not only is it the land and soil that forms our connections with the Earth but also our entire life-cycle touches most of our surroundings. The fact that our people hunt and gather these particular species on the land means emphasis is placed on maintaining their presence in the future. [...] What is sometimes called "wildlife" in Australia isn't wild; rather it's something that we have always maintained and will continue gathering.' Pera of the Bakalaharil tribe in Botswana points to their attitudes in using and sustaining wild resources: 'Some of our food is from the wild – like fruits and some of our meat [...] We are happy to conserve, but some conservationists come and say that preservation means that we cannot use the animals at all. To us, preservation means to use, but with love, so that you can use again tomorrow and the following year.' Johan Mathis Turi of the Saami reflects on the mutual shaping in the Norwegian Arctic: 'The reindeer is the centre of nature as a whole and I feel I hunt whatever nature gives. Our lives have remained around the reindeer and this is how we have managed the new times so well. It is difficult for me to pick out specific details or particular incidences as explanations for what has happened because my daily life, my nature, is so comprehensive. It includes everything. We say *lotwantua*, which means everything is included.' A similar perspective is put by Gamaillie Kilukishah, an Inuit from northern Canada who, in translation by Meeka Mike, says, 'You must be in constant contact with the land and the animals and the plants.' When Gamaillie was growing up, he was taught to respect animals in such a way as to survive from them. At the same time, he was taught to treat them as kindly as you would another fellow person.

3   The Richard Nelson quote on personal ecology is from the Nelson chapter in Petersen (1996). Richard Nelson's superb *Make Prayers to the Raven* (1983) is quoted in various places in this chapter, including from pages 14, 200 and 225. Nelson's balanced study of hunting, *Heart and Blood* (1987), is also quoted (pp96–97).

4   It is important, though, to be careful about generalizations that all indigenous groups have always looked after their food resources carefully. There have been major extinction episodes of megafauna on a number of continents driven by hominids (Flannery, 1997; Holdaway, 1999).

5　The point about being in control of the hunt is made by Terry Tempest Williams (1996). See Lee and Daly for a summary of hunter-gatherer groups across the world. See also Fikret Berkes's *Sacred Ecology* (1999) for an excellent account of the Cree of north-east Canada, and his edited volume *Breaking Ice* (Berkes et al, 2005) for a perspective on coastal and ocean resources of the Canadian north. Sheldrake (2003) has a discussion of the widespread belief amongst hunters that some animals can detect their intentions at a distance. Some wildlife photographers notice a similar phenomenon – they see their best pictures when they do not have a camera.

6　A summary of the concepts of the wilderness can be found in *Agri-Culture* (Pretty, 2002). The classic text remains Roderick Nash's *Wilderness and the American Mind* (1973). See also Callicott and Nelson (1998); Callicott et al (2000); Muir (1992); and Thoreau (1902).

7　Keith Thomas (1983) reviews the changes in animal welfare legislation in the UK. There are many different views on animal welfare that are not discussed in this book. See for example Tester (1991) and Noske (1989).

8　From Abbey (1996), one of a number of quotations in this chapter from David Petersen's *A Hunter's Heart*.

9　From Wallace (1996).

10　From Rudner (1996).

11　See Nuttall (1998).

12　Oldfield et al (2003) conducted the study that found landowners who both hunt and maintain game-bird stocks conserve seven per cent of their farms as woodland, whereas those who do neither keep less than one per cent as woodland.

13　Woods (1996) and McGuane (1996), both in *A Hunter's Heart*.

14　The previous page draws heavily on *A Hunter's Heart* (Petersen, 1996; Williams, 1996; Fergus, 1996; Bodio, 1996; Causey, 1996). The Cleveland Amory quote comes from the same book.

15　Deer in the US are discussed with great depth and understanding by Richard Nelson in *Heart and Blood* (1987). It is very difficult to say accurately how many deer there are in the UK and US. They are difficult to find, even for experienced stalkers. Richard Prior (2000) says, 'forget about trying to count roe deer accurately – it is a waste of time'. For UK deer, see Alastair Ward (2005) and Piran White et al *Economic Impact of Deer* (2005) and Defra's 'Deer action plan' (2005). Data on traffic accidents involving deer at www.deercollisions.co.uk and discussed in White et al (2005).

16　From Madson (1996).

17　The humans as prey hypothesis is contained in Hart and Sussman's *Man the Hunted* (2004). The authors show that predators played a significant role in our social and cognitive evolution. It always paid to have friends and allies.

18　A range of books cover the role of mountain lions as predators of humans in recent American history, including those by Hansen (1992), Bolgiano (1995) and Barron (2004). Jim Corbett's classic texts are the 1946 *Man Eaters of Kumaon* and *The Man-Eating Leopard of Rudraprayag* (1989).

19　The quote from the woman whose daughter was attacked by a mountain lion is in Barron (2004).

20　The Barry Lopez quote is from *Arctic Dreams* (1986).

Chapter 7 – Animal Magic
PAGES 85–95

1   The white horses of the UK are described in full at www.wiltshirewhitehorses.org.uk and
    www.berkshirehistory.com/archaeology/white_horse.html. The Uffington White Horse is at
    grid reference 302866. Barry Lopez's stone horse is beautifully described in *Crossing Open
    Ground* (1988).

2   For more on big cats in the UK, see Taylor (2005); Harpur (2006); Sieveking (2003). See also
    www.britishbigcats.org and www.toothandclaw.org.uk. The British Association for Nature
    Conservationists (BANC) discusses big cats at occasional conferences, and articles are
    published in their journal, *Ecos*. One contemporary problem is that we erroneously think we
    know the land, and so find it hard to believe that strange animals may be hiding there. Try
    this thought experiment: the UK is 24 million hectares in size, or 240,000 square kilometres.
    Imagine you walked across 1 kilometre squares, with a view to the right and to the left of
    500 metres. You could walk 10km a day and it would take you 65 years to cross every square
    in the UK. Our land is unknowable; we can know places, yet we wrongly believe we know it
    all.

3   On pets: pet keeping is not a modern practice – there were one million dogs kept as pets in
    UK in 1800 (Thomas, 1983). Data on households keeping pets are from the American
    Veterinary Medical Association; Beck and Meyers (1996); Fawcett and Gulone (2001).
    Research showing the health benefits to owners of pets includes Siegel (1990); Anderson et
    al (1994); Katcher and Wilkins (1993); Friedmann and Thomas (1995). For more on pets, see
    Schoen (2001) and Serpell (1996).

4   The named bears of Victorian Britain are from Thomas (1983).

5   The survey of the top fifty things people wanted to do before they died was conducted by
    the BBC in mid-2003.

6   The value of the Great Barrier Reef is from Bulbeck (2004).

7   See Bill Adams's (1996) *Future Nature* for an account of conservation thinking and practice.

8   This behaviour is not restricted to developing countries. Recently Dudley Zoo in the UK
    began to find its wallabies dying overnight, often of severe injuries. At first, keepers
    thoughts it was urban foxes, until the view from the CCTV showed that it was a group of
    young boys regularly breaking into the zoo to torture and kill the wallabies. Why would these
    young boys do this? Is it control, expression of power, boredom, or recognition that the
    animals somehow did not matter?

9   See Stephen Budiansky's 1997 *The Nature of Horses*. For more on Suffolk Punches, see
    Suffolk Horse Society, Woodbridge, Suffolk, www.suffolkhorsesociety.org.uk. See also
    George Ewart Evans' *The Horse and the Furrow* (1960) and *Horse Power and Magic* (1979). It is
    interesting to note that breeders of Suffolk Punches were also involved in other now rare
    Suffolk animals, such as Red Poll cattle, Suffolk sheep and Large Black pigs. The loss of
    horses from the landscape was clearly not a simple replacement with efficient machines.
    Horses regularly themselves suffered from grass sickness, a disease even today not fully
    understood, and their numbers had not recovered after the huge losses in the First World
    War. Reliable machinery thus helped to replace relatively unreliable horses. See George
    Ewart Evans (1979) for the quote about horses at Hollesley Bay open prison.

10 The allusion is to the remark 'land includes us' from a Western Apache woman in David
    Abram's *The Spell of the Sensuous* (1996).

Chapter 8 – The Fatta and the Lan'
PAGES 99–111

1   See Kroeber (1957) and Blackburn and Anderson (1993) for comprehensive accounts of Native Americans in California.

2   John Steinbeck's *Of Mice and Men* was first published in 1937.

3   Barry Popkin's nutrition transition is described in his 1998 and 1999 papers.

4   Diet and physical activity as critical determinants of well-being are described in CDC (1996); Ferro-Luzzi and James (2000); DCMS (2002).

5   Vegetable consumption in the UK – the bottom income decile in the UK spends 25 per cent of income on food, yet consumes only 120g of fruit and vegetables per day, providing 43mg of vitamin C. The top income decile spends 6 per cent of income on food and consumes 300g of fruit and vegetables per day, providing 81mg of vitamin C. National Food Survey data is from Defra (2002a and b).

6   The data on amounts of calories in fast food are from Percy Schlosser's *Fast Food Nation* (2002) and Marion Nestle's *Food Politics* (2003).

7   The contents and consequences of wild foods are from Samson and Pretty (2006) and Winston (2002).

8   A discussion on the famine hypothesis can be found in Matt Ridley's *Nature via Nurture* (2003). See also Motluk (2004).

9   Schlosser (2002) gives the details of ownership of fast food outlets by a limited number of companies. The daily consumption of one soft drink above energy needs by a child would add a massive 50kg of body weight over a ten-year period (Ebbeling et al, 2002).

10 The WHO position on food is well presented in Aileen Robertson et al *Food and Health in Europe* (2004). Discussions on the consequences of eating more meat can be found in books by Lester Brown (2004) and Colin Tudge (2004).

11 Modern meat lacks many of the nutrients and vitamins of wild meat and is higher in saturated fats (first analysed by Crawford, 1968). A similar trend appears to have occurred in fruit and vegetables. One study of 20 fruits and vegetables found that calcium, magnesium, sodium and copper content of vegetables fell between the 1930s and 1980s, and potassium, iron, magnesium and copper content had fallen in fruit. Water content had increased in all (Mayer, 1997).

12 On diet-related illness and public health consequences, see Ferro-Luzzi and James, 2000; Astrup, 2001; Eurodiet, 2001. The strongest association between diet and cancer is provided by the positive relationship between the consumption of vegetables and fruit and a reduction in the risk of cancers of the digestive and respiratory tracts. Low fibre content, vitamin and mineral insufficiency, high meat consumption and excessive alcohol intake have also been implicated as risk factors for cancer (Doll, 1992; Riboli and Norat, 2001; Key et al, 2002; Lang and Heasman, 2004).

13 The outnumbering of the hungry by the obese is described in WHO (1998 and 2002).

14 Body mass index is not the only measure of overweight or obesity. Waist circumference is another measure of body fat. In the US, male waists have expanded between 1960 and 2000 by 9.9cm, female ones by 23.2cm (Okuson et al, 2004). In the UK, female waists expanded from 70 to 86cm between 1950 and the early 2000s. Data on BMI in the US are recorded by the Centers for Disease Control and Prevention (see CDC, 2005; see also Hedley et al, 2004). Data in the UK are kept by the DoH (2004b and 2006). The Department of Health (2006) now estimates that there will be 12 million adults and 1 million children obese by 2010. Obesity levels in China are described in Xu et al (2005).

15 One epidemiological study has suggested that being in the overweight category may protect against mortality, yet also that being obese does increase mortality (Flegal et al, 2002). Quotations come from Campos (2006).

16 An adult 50 years ago did the equivalent of a marathon each week more exercise than the average adult today (NAO, 2001). There are important trade-offs. The average evening meal 50 years ago took two and a half hours to prepare; today it is less than 10 minutes. Women have greatly benefited from this release – yet if they spend this saved time on the sofa watching television, they may be physically worse off.

17 The public health consequences have only recently begun to be widely accepted (DCMS, 2002). Data on cycling and walking comes from the DOT National Travel Survey (2001) and DoH (2004a, b).

18 The CDC (1996) report of the Surgeon General was one of the first to document alarming declines in physical activity and consequent effects on ill-health. In the US, 13.5 million people have CHD, and 1.5 million suffer the effects in any year; 8 million people have type II diabetes; 95,000 people are newly diagnosed with colon cancer each year; 250,000 people suffer hip fractures each year; 50 million people have high blood pressure; 60 million adults are obese with a BMI > 30kgm^{-2}; 9 million young people (15 per cent of all those aged 6–19) are overweight; and 77 per cent of adults do not eat the recommended 5 or more servings of fruit and vegetables per day.

19 Data from Department of Health (2006).

20 Changes in hours spent watching TV come from Sport England (2000). The amount of time spent outdoors by children is from Orr (2002).

21 The role of leptins is in Friedman and Halaas (1998) and Speakman et al (2002). The value of omega-3 fats are described in Hibbelin (1998). Like vitamins, omega-3 essential fatty acids must be obtained from the diet. They are more prevalent in oil-rich fish, such as mackerel, herring, salmon, sardine and tuna, than in low fat fish like cod and haddock. On physical activity and psychological well-being, see Berger (1996); Scully et al (1998); Biddle et al (2000).

22 See Benton (2002); Benton and Nabb (2003); Benton et al (2001); see also www.foodandmood.org.

23 The value of physical activity for well-being is in many places (see Paffenbarger et al, 1993; Berlin and Colditz, 1990; Bacon et al, 2004). The Department of Health quote is from DoH (2004a).

24 The classic report that shows that people think they do more exercise than they actually do is by Allied Dunbar (1992). Declining rates of physical activity are in Brownson et al (2005).

25 The costs of diet and physical activity are analysed in Kenkel and Manning (1999) and NIH (2002), and the benefits of progressive policies are in Puska (2000), Lang and Heasman (2004) and Robertson et al (2004).

26 The benefits of successful policies in Finland are described in Vuori et al (2004). See also Winter (2003) on the benefits of localism.

Chapter 9 – Little Houses on the Prairie
PAGES 113–124

1 All Thomas Jefferson quotes are from Peterson (1970, p23 and p63) and from Yarbrough (1998, pp63–68). It is worth noting that there are many contradictions in the stance taken by Jefferson. At his time, much of America, especially in the South, relied on slavery for its

agricultural labour. In addition, Native Americans had been removed from their lands to allow the new settlers to forge their own freedoms and independence. Much later than Jefferson, between 1872 and 1874, 3.4 million buffalo were killed on the plains, and General Sheridan famously said, 'let them kill, skin and sell until the buffalo is exterminated, as it is the only way to bring lasting peace and allow civilization to advance' (in Brown, 1970).

2　The Wallace Stegner quote is from *Wolf Willow* (1962).

3　Wes Jackson's piece about Matland is drawn from his 1994 book, *Becoming Native to this Place*. In some states, such as North Dakota, there are already signs of what severe rural depopulation can bring. Only settled in the late 19th and early 20th centuries, 90 per cent of rural towns now have fewer than 3000 people each, and shops, gas stations and churches have closed with so few people to maintain them. See Wendell Berry's *The Unsettling of America* (1977) for still one of the best and clearest analyses of what has gone so very wrong.

4　Like many such processes, they tend to be very successful in their early years of implementation, but then fade as the years pass. There are also concerns about good participatory programmes being only adopted in name when spread across communities. The participation challenges in Brazil are discussed by Luiz Carlos Mior (2005) and Julia Guivant (2002). One problem was that extension agents were brought in to develop participatory methods, but were withdrawn when the funding for the project ended. This then threatened the sustainability of the practices adopted by some farmers. The Brazilian case from Santa Caterina is further developed in de Freitas (1999) and Pinheiro et al (2002). See also Sciallaba and Hattam (2002).

5　The organic jobs survey was conducted out by Rachel Hine, James Morison and Jules Pretty and published in Morison et al (2005). Among other things, this found a clear inverse relationship between farm size and full time equivalent jobs per 100 hectares on each of the 1143 farms surveyed. In other words, small farms employ more people per area of land than large farms.

6　David Kline's book is *Great Possessions* (1990). For an overview of Amish culture, see Kraybill (2001).

7　For more on collaborative CSAs in the US, see Bregendahl and Flora (2006).

Chapter 10 – The Shadow of the Rain
PAGES 125–137

1　When people are organized in groups, then they are more likely to sustain activities after project completion (see, for example, de los Reyes and Jopillo, 1986; Cernea, 1991; Uphoff, 1993; Pretty, 1995a, b; Narayan and Pritchett, 1996; Röling and Wagemakers, 1997; Bunch and López, 1999; Pretty and Smith, 2004).

2　For a summary of social capital principles, see Pretty and Ward, 2001. For the main social capital literature of the past, see Tonnies (1887); Kropotkin (1902); Jacobs (1961); Bourdieu (1986); Coleman (1988 and 1990); Putnam (1993 and 1995); Uphoff (1998). For more on trust, see Gambetta (1988); Fukuyama (1995). For more on reciprocity, see Coleman (1990); Putnam (1993); Platteau (1997). For more on rights and responsibilities, see Taylor (1982); Colins and Chippendale (1991); Etzioni (1995). For more on connectedness, see Uphoff (1993); Flora (1998); Grootaert (1998); Woolcock (1998); Barrett et al (2001). For more on the problem of free-riders, see Grootaert (1998); Dasgupta and Serageldin (2000); Ostrom et al (2002). For a study of the effects on social capital on health, see Pevalin and Rose (2003). Social capital and the commons is discussed in Ostrom (1990), Baland and Platteau (1998) and Dasgupta and Sergeldin (1998). The creation of social capital is covered by Flora and Flora (1996), and the effects on food networks in Ireland is in Sage (2003).

3   The Swedish government in the form of Sida has approved in 2006 phase two of the Kenyan National Agriculture and Livestock Extension Programme (NALEP), whose coverage is expected to reach a total of 580,000 farmers each year. The programme will also cover arid and semi-arid areas to support community initiatives to diversify livelihoods in order to cope with the increased frequency of prolonged droughts.

4   The West African examples of water harvesting are described by Chris Reij (1996), Hassame et al (2000) and Kabore and Reij (2004). For a summary of the effects on both yields and environmental resources of 286 projects in 57 countries, see Pretty et al (2003c and 2006). Chambers et al (1989) is still an excellent summary of the benefits of putting farmers first, and Robert Chambers' *Ideas for Development* (2005) is a clear and helpful update. See also Ellis (2000). The role of sustainable agriculture in sequestering carbon in India and China is analysed in Pretty et al (2002).

5   All quotations on this page were recorded by the author.

Chapter 11 – Rewilding Agriculture
PAGES 139–152

1   Many of these wild plants used by rural people are, in truth, not entirely wild. They will have been looked after and managed by human populations for centuries. Though not strictly domesticated, they are also not strictly wild.

2   For references on the costs of agricultural and food system externalities, see Crissman et al (1998); Subak (1999); Pretty et al (2000 and 2001); Norse et al (2001); Buttel (2003); Tegtmeier and Duffy (2004); Sherwood et al (2005b); Pretty and Waibel (2005). For the cost of food miles, see Pretty et al (2005b). For an overview of agriculture and pollution, see Conway and Pretty (1991).

3   For a discussion on the terminology of capitals, see Ted Benton (1998).

4   Systems high in sustainability can be taken to be those that aim to make the best use of environmental goods and services while not damaging these assets (see Altieri, 1995; Pretty, 1995b, 1998 and 2005; Conway, 1997; Hinchcliffe et al, 1999; NRC, 2000; Li Wenhua, 2001; Jackson and Jackson, 2002; Tilman et al, 2002; Uphoff, 2002; McNeely and Scherr, 2003; Clements and Shrestha, 2004; Swift et al, 2004; Tomich et al, 2004; Gliessman, 1998, 2004 and 2005; MEA, 2005).

5   For more on policies to incentivize the production of environmental services, see Dobbs and Pretty (2004). Baumol and Oates (1988) is an enduring and useful summary of environmental policymaking.

6   The best summary of the effects of farmer field schools is by Braun et al (2005). For more on farmer field schools, see Eveleens et al (1996); Heong et al (1999); Gallagher et al (2005); Uphoff (2002). Feder et al (2004) present a contrary view on farmer field schools. Herren et al (2005) provide a good summary of moves towards zero pesticide use in Africa.

7   For the semiochemicals research and outcomes, see Pickett (1999); Khan et al (2000); Hassanali et al (2007). The push–pull strategy involves trapping pests on highly susceptible trap plants (pull) and driving them away from the crop using a repellent intercrop (push). The forage grasses *Pennisetum purpureum* (Napier grass) and *Sorghum vulgare sudanense* (Sudan grass) attract greater oviposition by stem borers (*Chilo* spp) than in cultivated maize. The non-host forage plants, *Melinis minutiflora* (molasses grass) and *Desmodium uncinatum* (silver

leaf) repel female stalk borers. Intercropping with molasses and Sudan grass increases parasitism, particularly by the larval parasitoid, *Cotesia sesamiae*, and the pupal parasitoid *Denticbasmis busseolae*. *Melinis* contains several physiologically active compounds. Two of these inhibit oviposition (egg laying) in *Chilo*, even at low concentrations. Molasses grass also emits a chemical, (*E*)-4,8-dimethyl-1,3,7-nonatriene, which summons the borers' natural enemies. Napier grass also has its own defence mechanism against stem borers: when the larvae enter the stem, the plant produces a gum-like substance that kills the pest. Finally, intercropping maize with the fodder legumes *Desmodium uncinatum* (silver leaf) and *D. intortum* (green leaf) reduces infestation by the parasitic weed, *Striga hermonthica,* by a factor of 40 compared to maize monocrop.

8   Traditional European systems are described in Bignall and McCracken (1996) and IEEP and WWF (1994). See also Terwan et al (2004) for a visual summary of agrarian landscapes across Europe and North America.

9   Chinese integrated farming systems are comprehensively described in Li Wenhua (2001).

10   This paragraph draws on Leopold (1949).

11   The Peter Taylor quote is from his *Beyond Conservation* (2005). See also Donlan (2005) and Donlan et al (2006) for updates on Pleistocene rewilding opportunities in North America. For more on rewilding options in the UK, see the Wildland Network at www.wildland-network.org.uk and Tooth and Claw, a group promoting predators, at www.toothandclaw.org.uk.

Chapter 12 – Legible Landscapes
PAGES 155–166

1   The opening section of this chapter also appears as part of the Victoria and Albert Museum's Memory Map project, a joint venture with the University of Essex and developed by Marina Warner.

2   Otter hunting is described in Matless et al (2005).

3   Dave Charleston's line is from his book *Nothing Better To Do* (1999). The Ronald Blythe quote is from *Word from Wormingford* (1997). See also Blythe's *A Year at Bottengoms Farm* (2006) for more on the rhythms of life in the Essex and Suffolk borders. The green man myth is described in Anderson (1990).

4   This paragraph draws on Blythe (1997) and Basso (1996).

5   The extinction of experience is described by Pyle (2001, 2003). The two quotes about stories are from Suzuki (1997) and Berry (1999). See also Okri (1996) on storytelling and Worster (1993) on the ecological imagination.

6   For ecological literacy, see David Orr (1993). Traditional ecological knowledge (TEK) is more than just ecological literacy, as it is a knowledge–practice–belief complex that includes institutions (Berkes, 1999; Berkes et al, 2005). The importance of ecological knowledge is covered in Pierotti and Wildcat (2000); Olsson and Folke (2001); Olsson et al (2004); and Folke (2004).

7   The Barry Lopez quote is from the essay 'American geographies' in *Crossing Open Ground* (1988). The classic study of landscape and memory is Schama (1996). See also Nabhan (1982).

8   In oral cultures, stories are accessed bit by bit, not all at one time. But passing them on to others is no longer common (Watt, 2004).

9   Preceding paragraphs on indigenous people and their views of an animate Earth draw on Keith Basso's *Wisdom Sits in Places* (1996) and Fikret Berkes' *Sacred Ecology* (1999). See also Stephen Harding (2005) for an overview, and David Peat's *Blackfoot Physics* (1996).

10   George Rich was interviewed in 2004 by Colin Samson and me.

11   For more on children and nature, see Kahn and Kellert (2002); Nabhan and Trimble (1994).

12   Of the 5000–7000 oral languages persisting worldwide, 32 per cent are in Asia, 30 per cent in Africa, 19 per cent in the Pacific, 15 per cent in the Americas and 3 per cent in Europe. See Maffi (1999, 2006).

13   For more on the Tohono O'odham, see the work of Ofelia Zepeda at the University of Arizona on reinvigorating the language and its links to the land, http://home.nau.edu/environment/gary_nabhan.asp. See also Nabhan (2001) and Nabhan and St Antoine (1993). The Tohono O'Odham abandoned the old term for their culture, Papago ('bean eaters'), in the 1980s.

14   See Pilgrim (2006), Pilgrim et al (2007a and b). This research found an inverse relationship between wealth/development and ecoliteracy, also that knowledge saturation occurs early in life in India and Indonesia, but is lower in the UK and grows over time. The Barry Lopez quote is from Lopez (1998).

15   The Robert Macfarlane quote is from the excellent *Mountains of the Mind* (2003).

Chapter 13 – Exclusion Zones
PAGES 167–181

1   For a summary of the science behind the Chernobyl accident and its consequences, see publications by the International Radioecology Laboratory in Slavutych, Ukraine (original material is mostly in Russian).

2   See the UN-OCHA/WHO (2002) report on the human consequences of the accident, and the clear and comprehensive report by the OECD's Nuclear Energy Agency (2002) of ten years of radiological and health change. There are many scare stories about the extreme effects on health of the accident, but these are not backed up by the scientific and epidemiological evidence.

3   A summary of the following account appeared in the *BBC Wildlife Magazine* (Pretty, 2006). An excellent summary of the emergence of what now amounts to a wildlife reserve is Baker and Chesser (2000).

4   The Dylan Thomas quote is from his 1937 poem, 'Do not go gentle into that good night'.

5   For more on ancient civilizations, see the *Penguin History of Ancient Civilisations* by Haywood (2005) and Colin McEvedy's *Penguin Atlas of African History* (1980). The latter fills in many of the gaps for a continent often forgotten by history books.

6   Richard Nelson's quote about the Koyukon is from Nelson (1983).

7   The two references on the Maya are Hammond (1994) and Coe (1980). See also Vernon Scarborough's excellent account (Scarborough, 2007).

8   The poem from the Mayan *Chilam Bulam* is from Coe (1980, p142).

9   Jared Diamond's *Collapse* (2005) contains several case studies of civilization collapse. John McNeill's *Something New Under the Sun* (2000) contains a good account of the Aral Sea disaster, as does Precoda (1991).

10   The deserted mediaeval villages (DMVs) of England were researched by Maurice Beresford and his colleagues, and the best references include Beresford (1954), Beresford and Hurst (1979), Beresford and St Joseph (1979), Allison et al (1966), Hurst (1972), Dyer (1982) and

Rowley and Wood (1982). Many prominent historians of the early 20th century thought DMVs did not exist (e.g. Bradley, 1918, in Beresford, 1954). As late as 1946, the distinguished historian Sir Alfred Clapham said, 'deserted villages are singularly rare in England' (in Rowley and Wood, 1982). Various quotes are from Beresford (1954). See E P Thompson's *Whigs and Hunters* for a summary of the effects of enclosure on English rural life in the 18th century.

11 Northamptonshire material is in Allison et al (1966). The grazier Spencer moved to Althorp in Northamptonshire in 1508; Diana, Princess of Wales, was one of his descendents. The quote about the gardens at Harrington is from an interpretation board at the site. Thorpe (1965) contains the detailed description of the changes in Wormleighton in Warwickshire (grid reference 443542). Grid references for the other villages mentioned are as follows: Sulby in Northants (653815), Downton (615802), Harrington (772802), Church Charwelton (545555), Cublington (834223).

Chapter 14 – Life and Land on the North Atlantic Fringe
PAGES 183–194

1 The emergence of the crofting system in Scotland is described by James Hunter (1976, 1999 and 2005a). For two excellent summaries of crofting and its history, see Hunter's inaugural lecture for the University of the Highlands and Islands Centre for History (2006) and his 2nd Angus Macleod Memorial Lecture (2005b).

2 Various quotes are from publications by Hunter (1976, pp22, 93; 1999, pp218, 254). The Sellar case is from Hunter (1976, p218). Life on South Uist is described by Angus MacLellan (2002). The losses on Harris are described by Bill Lawson (2002).

3 Many of the Highland settlers from Lewis ended up in the Eastern Townships of Quebec, particularly between Bury and Lingwick. Settlers came from Lewis in 1838, and then from Skye and the Uists. Even in the late 1890s, the Lewis community made up a third of the population of the Eastern Townships, concentrated in an area between St Francis River and Lake Megantic.

4 Colin Samson (2003) details the history of the Innu. See also Samson et al (1999); Innu Nation (1993, 1995 and 1996); Henriksen (1973 and 1993); Loring (1998); Loring and Ashini (2002). Berkes et al (1994 and 1995) describe similar changes for the Cree. See also Fikret Berkes' *Sacred Ecology* (1999). The Walter Rockwood quotes are from Samson (2003, p18).

5 The interviews with Mary May Adele and Dominc Pokue were in July 2003, the one with Katnan Pastitchi in April 2006. All were translated by Basile Panashue. For more on health, food and the country for polar and sub-Arctic and other native peoples, see Usher (1976); Andrew and Sarsfield (1984); Mackey and Orr (1987); Wein et al (1991 and 1996); Young (1994); Loney (1995); Delormier and Kuhnlein (1999); Eaton and Eaton (1999); Adelson (2000); Boothroyd et al (2001); McGrath-Hanna et al (2003); Story et al (2003); US Commission on Civil Rights (2004). For more on indigenous people and conservation, see Alcorn (1993); Berkes et al (2000); Gadgil et al (1993 and 2000); Ghimire and Pimbert (1997); Nuttall (1998); and Turner et al (2000). See Samson and Pretty (2006) for a summary of the nutrition and activity transition undergone by the Innu. References to initiatives for making improvements to the lives of indigenous people include Morice (1976); Lavalée et al (1994); Marquardt and Caulfield (1996); Stevens (1997); Veitayaki (1997); Kishigami (2000); Pars et al (2001); Kirmayer et al (2003).

6　The return to the settlement after some time spent in the country can be demoralizing. These are supposed symbols of modernity and success. Instead, people feel dislocated, undervalued and lack meaning to their lives. We felt this painfully one summer when returning from camp across Lake Melville. We escaped the clutches of a sudden storm by eventually beaching our small boat on a welcome sandy spit. We unloaded our bags and three foot salmon and trout, and walked the eleven kilometres around a series of bays back to what some call civilization. For those intent on meeting flight deadlines, it was a relief to get back. For the Innu in the party, it progressively got worse as we came nearer. A deep gloom descended as we walked along the dirt track leading into the back of the village. A group of kids leant against bikes, morosely watching our progress back to gaol. Our companions had escaped, but were now consigning themselves back inside. Mary Adele Andrews says, 'on the land, we are ourselves. In the settlement, we are lost. This was the way they made our minds weak.' And Hugh Brody comments that in settlements of this type, he heard 'from person to person […] a quiet, understated dismay'.

7　The quote from Willie McSporran was in *The Independent*, 31 July 2004, p16. The Iain Wilson quote is in Hunter (1999, p379).

8　The activities of the Tshikapisk Foundation can be seen at www.tshikapisk.ca.

Chapter 15 – Ecolution
PAGES 197–211

1　Flann O'Brien's *The Third Policeman* was published in 1967.

2　E O Wilson's *Sociobiology* was published in 1975. For the best review and update of *On the Origin of Species*, see Steve Jones' *Almost Like a Whale* (1999). Matt Ridley's *Genome* (1999) and *Nature via Nurture* (2003) are extremely well-written accounts of genetics and the environment. See also Rutter (2005). David Rothenberg and Wandee Pryor's *Writing the Field* (2004) contains a series of clear contemporary accounts of evolution. For a very good summary of evolutionary sub-theories of human behaviours, see Kevin Laland and Gillian Brown's *Sense and Nonsense* (2005) and Laland and Brown (2006). There are many books by Richard Dawkins that are worth exploring, not least his set of essays in *A Devil's Chaplain* (2003).

3　For more on intelligent design, see a good summary in the *New Scientist* (2005). See also Steve Jones (1999).

4　Desmond Morris's *The Naked Ape* was published in 1967, with a new edition appearing in 2005.

5　See Laland and Brown (2005) and Dawkins (2003).

6　It is worth noting that many other apes and primates have elements of culture, and so it can be argued that such components have been important in all hominid history. It is also true that many aspects of learned culture (e.g. tool use) long pre-date *Homo sapiens*. In some sense, therefore, adaptation to ancestral environments is misleading. It is evolution of flexible adaptability that is important.

7　The statistic about TV advertisements seen by American children is in Orr (2002). As David Orr says, 'capitalism works best when children stay indoors in malls and in front of televisions or computer screens. It loses its access to the minds of the young when then discover pleasures that cannot be bought.'

8　The quote from Daniel Dennett is in Laland and Brown (2005).

9　For a discussion about niche construction, see Odling-Smee et al (1996, 2003) and Laland and Odling-Smee (2003).

10 The effects of methylation of DNA are in Weaver et al (2004).

11 The natural controls on testosterone levels are described in Hrdy et al (2005).

12 Owen Flanagan's research is discussed in Ridley (1999). See also Flanagan (1991, 2004).

13 The twins research is discussed in Ridley (1999) and Laland and Brown (2005).

14 For a robust discussion on modern cyborgs, and the possible route to a cyborg society of the future, see Kevin Warwick (2004). Warwick says, 'history is littered with species of one type or another that were once extremely powerful but are no longer with us'. Are we already dependent on machines, and what would happen if they were taken away? There are already many machines that make decisions for us each day – think of computers in the car, email servers, climate control in offices and homes, coffee machines, traffic lights, energy supply, telephones, satellite navigation, and the restocking of supermarkets.

15 The Gary Snyder quote is from Snyder (1990, p31).

16 The T S Eliot quote is from his poem 'Four quartets' (1935–1942).

Chapter 16 – Liberation
PAGES 213–221

1 The André Gide quote is from *Fruits of the Earth* (1897).

2 The quote is from Salzman (2004).

3 Quote from Brody (2000).

4 Quote from Blythe (1997).

5 In recent years, the emergence of the Slow Food and Slow Cities movements have shown the attractiveness to many of trying to change the passage of time, of slowing lives, ultimately to reject the myth we have a linear time. The national example of the emergence of a slow food system is Cuba (see Funes et al, 2002). The concept of flow is discussed in Nettle (2005). Some of the world can be left to pure experience. Richard Nelson describes how this can affect us: 'time expands and I am suspended in the clear reality of the moment' (Nelson, 1987, in Halpern, 1987). Repetition and ritual can come in many forms. It is not just the monk chanting on a cold morning, but gathering the kids and off to school every day (Snyder, 1990). 'Such a round of chores is not a set of difficulties we hope to escape from [...] that will put us on a path – it is our path'.

6 In 1950 Dorothy Less called Native American perception of space a non-linear codification of reality. Space is not linked by geometric straight lines, it bends and warps according to experience, and to what happened there and is part of memory. Neither space nor time is linear (in Shepard, 1998).

7 The Thomas Hardy quote is from the poem 'In time of "The Breaking of Nations"' (1915). For a discussion of Eliot's *Four Quartets*, see Blamires (1969) and Bergsten (1973). Eliot's poem indicates that you can only know and explain a time and place with reference to past and future: what has happened and what will occur (Blamires, 1969). But Eliot is also bleak. In East Coker, it is clear that, throughout life, we are lost in a dark wood, on the edge of a mire, our foothold is insecure, and there is the threat of lurking monsters. In the rose garden in Burnt Norton, Eliot suggests distant images of laughing children and leaves and memories and unidentified figures and empty ponds and dry concrete and glittering sunlight. The eternal rose garden is many symbolic things as well as a garden. It is full of memories, and it is also a moment. History is a pattern of timeless moments. 'For us', says Eliot, 'there is only trying. The rest is not our business' (in Bergsten, 1973).

8 Both the Chief Standing Bear and Baird Callicott quotes are in Callicott and Nelson (1998) *The Great New Wilderness Debate.*

9   In Callicott and Nelson (1998).

10   For ecological restoration, see Jordan (2003) and Higgs (2003). For ecological redesign, see David Orr's *Design on the Edge* (2006) and *The Last Refuge* (2004).

11   The Chris Baines quote is from Jordan.

12   David Abram's quote is from his *The Spell of the Sensuous* (1996), and Keith Basso's quote is from his *Wisdom Sits in Places* (1996).

13   The Hugh Brody quote is from his *The Other Side of Eden* (2000).

14   The Ronald Blythe quote is from *Word from Wormingford* (1997).

15   The various quotes and comments are from Berkes (1999), Shepard (1998), Lévi-Strauss (cited in Callicott and Nelson, 1998) and Callicott (1998).

16   Andy Couturier's essay, 'The abundance of less', is in Rothenberg and Pryor (2004).

References

Abbey E (1996) 'Blood sport', in Petersen D (ed) *A Hunter's Heart*, Henry Holt, New York

Abram D (1996) *The Spell of the Sensuous*, Vintage Books, New York

Adams W M (1996) *Future Nature: A Vision for Conservation*, Earthscan, London

Adelson N (2000) *Being Alive Well: Health and the Politics of Cree Well-Being*, University of Toronto Press, Toronto

Alcorn J B (1993) 'Indigenous peoples and conservation', *Conservation Biology* 7, pp424–426

Allied Dunbar (1992) *Fitness Survey*, Allied Dunbar, London

Allison K J, Beresford M W and Hunt J G (1966) *The Deserted Villages of Northamptonshire*, Leicester University Press, Leicester

Altieri M A (1995) *Agroecology: The Science of Sustainable Agriculture*, Westview Press, Boulder, CO

Anderson W P, Reid C M and Jennings G L (1994) 'Pet ownership and risk factors for cardiovascular disease', *Medical Journal Australia* 157, pp298–301

Anderson W (1990) *Green Man*, Compass Books, Fakenham

Andrew B and Sarsfield P (1984) 'Innu health: The role of self-determination', in Fortune R (ed) *Circumpolar Health '84: Proceedings of the Sixth International Symposium on Circumpolar Health*, University of Washington Press, Seattle, WA, pp 428–430

Armstrong D (2000) 'A survey of community gardens in upstate New York: Implications for health promotion and community development', *Health and Place* 6(4), pp319–327

Arsuaga J L (2003) *The Neanderthal's Necklace: In Search of the First Thinkers*, Arrow, London

Astrup A (2001) 'Healthy lifestyles in Europe: Prevention of obesity and type II diabetes by diet and physical activity', *Public Health Nutrition* 4, pp499–515

Austin M E and Kaplan R (2003) 'Identity, involvement and expertise in the inner city: Some benefits of tree planting projects', in Clayton S and Opotow S (eds) *Identity and the Natural Environment*, MIT Press, Boston, MA

Bacon S L, Sherwood A, Hinderliter A and Blumenthal J A (2004) 'Effects of exercise, diet and weight loss on high blood pressure', *Sports Medicine* 34, pp307–316

Baker R J and Chesser R K (2000) 'The Chernobyl nuclear disaster and subsequent creation of a nature preserve', *Environmental Toxicology and Chemistry* 19(5), pp1231–1232

Baland J-M and Platteau J-P (1998) 'Division of the commons', *American Journal of Agricultural Economics* 80, pp644–650

Balmford A, Clegg L, Coulson T and Taylor J (2002) 'Why conservationists should heed Pokémon', *Science* 295, p2367

Barlett P (ed) (2005) *Urban Place*, MIT Press, Cambridge, MA

Barnes S (2004) *How to be a Bad Birdwatcher*, Short Books, London

Barrett C, Brandon K, Gibson C and Gjertsen H (2001) 'Conserving tropical biodiversity amid weak institutions', *BioScience* 51(6), pp497–502

Barron D (2004) *Beast in the Garden*, W W Norton, New York

Basso, K (1996) *Wisdom Sits in Places: Landscape and Language among the Western Apache*, University of New Mexico Press, Albuquerque, NM

Baumol W J and Oates W E (1988) *The Theory of Environmental Policy*, Cambridge University Press, Cambridge, UK

Beck A M and Meyers N M (1996) 'Health enhancement and companion animal ownership', *Annual Review of Public Health* 17, pp247–257

Bell M M (1997) 'The ghosts of place', *Theory and Society* 26, pp813–836

Bell M M (2004) *An Invitation to Environmental Sociology*, 2nd edn, Pine Forge Press, Thousand Oaks, CA

Bennett L, Cardone S and Jarczyk J (1998) 'Effects of a therapeutic camping program on addiction recovery: The Algonquin Haymarket relapse prevention program', *Journal of Substance Abuse Treatment* 15, pp469–474

Benton D and Nabb S (2003) 'Carbohydrate, memory and mood', *Nutrition Reviews* 61(5), pp561–567

Benton D, Slater O and Donohoe R T (2001) 'The influence of breakfast and a snack on psychological functioning', *Physiology and Behaviour* 74, pp559–571

Benton D (2002) 'Carbohydrate ingestion, blood glucose and mood', *Neuroscience and Biobehavioural Reviews* 26, pp293–308

Benton T (1998) 'Sustainable development and the accumulation of capital: Reconciling the irreconcilable?', in Dobson A (ed) *Fairness and Futurity*, Oxford University Press, Oxford

Beresford M W (1954) *The Lost Villages of England*, Lutterworth Press, London

Beresford M W and Hurst J (1979) *Deserted Medieval Villages*, St Martin's Press, New York

Beresford M W and St Joseph J K S (1979) *Medieval England: An Aerial Survey*, Cambridge University Press, Cambridge, UK

Berger B G (1996) 'Psychological benefits of an active lifestyle: What we know and what we need to know', *Quest* 48, pp330–353

Bergman C (2003) *Wild Echoes*, University of Illinois Press, Urbana and Chicago, IL

Bergsten S (1973) *Time and Eternity*, Humanities Press, New York

Berkes F (1999) *Sacred Ecology*, Taylor and Francis, Philadelphia, PA

Berkes F, George P J, Preston R J, Hughes A, Turner J and Cummins B D (1994) 'Wildlife harvesting and sustainable regional native economy in the Hudson and James Bay lowland, Ontario', *Arctic* 47(4), pp350–360

Berkes F, Hughes A, George P J, Preston R J, Cummins B D and Turner J (1995) 'The persistence of Aboriginal land use: Fish and wildlife harvest areas in the Hudson and James Bay lowland, Ontario', *Arctic* 48(1), pp81–93

Berkes F, Colding J and Folke C (2000) 'Rediscovery of traditional ecological knowledge as adaptive management', *Ecological Applications* 10, pp1251–1262

Berkes F, Huebert R, Fast H, Manseau M and Diduck A (2005) *Breaking Ice, Renewable Resource and Ocean Management in the Canadian North*, University of Calgary Press, Calgary

Berlin J A and Colditz G A (1990) 'A meta analysis of physical activity in the prevention of coronary heart disease', *American Journal of Epidemiology* 132, pp612–628

Berman D S and Anton M T (1988) 'A wilderness therapy program as an alternative to adolescent psychiatric hospitalisation', *Residential Treatment for Children and Youth* (the official journal of the American Association of Children's Residential Centers) 5, pp41–53

Berrigan D and Troiano R P (2002) 'The association between urban form and physical activity in US adults', *American Journal of Preventive Medicine* 23, pp74–79

Berry T (1999) *The Great Work*, Bell Tower, New York

Berry W (1977) *The Unsettling of America*, Sierra Club Books, San Francisco, CA

Biddle S J H, Fox K R and Boutcher S H (eds) (2000) *Physical activity and Psychological Well-Being*, Routledge, London

Bignall E M and McCracken D I (1996) 'Low-intensity farming systems in the conservation of the countryside', *Journal of Applied Ecology* 33, pp413–424

Bingley A and Milligan C (2004) *Climbing Trees and Building Dens: Mental Health and Well-being in Young Adults and the Long-term Effects of Childhood Play Experience*, Institute for Health Research, Lancaster University, Lancaster

Björn L O (1976) *Light and Life*, Hodder and Stoughton, London

Blackburn T and Anderson K (eds) (1993) *Before the Wilderness: Environmental Management by Native Californians*, Ballena Press, Menlo Park, CA

Blamires H (1969) *Word Unheard, A Guide through Eliot's Four Quartets*, Methuen, London

Blythe R (1997) *Word from Wormingford*, Penguin, London

Blythe R (2006) *A Year at Bottengoms Farm*, Canterbury Press, Norwich

Bodio S (1996) 'Passion, gifts, rages', in Petersen D (ed) *A Hunter's Heart*, Henry Holt, New York

Bolgiano C (1995) *Mountain Lion: An Unnatural History of Pumas and People*, Stackpole Books, Mechanicsburg, PA

Bonnes M, Lee T and Bonaiuto M (eds) (2003) *Psychological Theories for Environmental Issues*, Ashgate, Aldershot

Boothroyd L J, Kirmayer L J, Spreng S, Malus M and Hodgins S (2001) 'Completed suicides among the Inuit of northern Quebec, 1982–1996: A case control study', *Canadian Medical Association Journal* 165, pp749–755

Bourdieu P (1986) 'The forms of capital', in Richardson J (ed) *Handbook of Theory and Research for the Sociology of Education*, Greenwood Press, Westport, CT

Boslaugh S E, Luke D A, Brownson R C, Nalied K S and Kreuter M W (2004) 'Perception of neighborhood environment for physical activity: Is it "who you are" or "where you live"?' *Journal of Urban Health* 81(4), pp671–681

Braastad B (2005) 'Green care in agriculture, COST action proposal', Norwegian University of Life Sciences, Ås, Norway

Braun A, Jiggins J, Röling N, Van den Berg H and Snijders P (2005) *A Global Survey and Review of Farmer Field School Experiences*, International Livestock Research Institute, Addis Ababa

Braza M, Shoemaker W and Seeley A (2004) 'Neighborhood design and rates of walking and biking to elementary school in 34 Californian communities', *American Journal of Health Promotion* 19(2), pp128–136

Brechin S R, Wilshusen P R, Fortwanglers and West P C (2002) 'Beyond the square wheel', *Society and Natural Resources* 15, pp41–64

Bregendahl C and Flora C B (2006) *The Role of Collaborative Community Supported Agriculture: Lessons from Iowa*, North Central Regional Center for Rural Development, Iowa State University, Ames, IA

Brickman P, Coates D and Janoff-Bulman R (1978) 'Lottery winners and accident victims', *Journal of Personality and Social Psychology* 36, pp917–927

Broda E (1975) *The Evolution of the Bioenergetic Processes*, Pergamon Press, Oxford

Brody H (1981) *Maps and Dreams*, Pantheon, New York

Brody H (2000) *The Other Side of Eden*, Faber and Faber, London

Brown D (1970) *Bury My Heart at Wounded Knee*, Vintage, London

Brown D (2004) *The American West*, Pocket Books, London

Brown L (2004) *Outgrowing the Earth*, W W Norton, New York

Brownson R C, Boehmer T K and Luke D A (2005) 'Declining rates of physical activity in the US: What are the contributors?' *Annual Review of Public Health* 26, pp421–443

Budiansky S (1997) *The Nature of Horses*, Phoenix, London

Budiansky S (1998) *If a Lion Could Talk*, Phoenix, London

Bulbeck C (2005) *Facing the Wild*, Earthscan, London

Buller H (2004) 'Where the wild things are: The evolving iconography of rural fauna', *Journal of Rural Studies* 20(2), pp131–141

Bunch R and López G (1999) 'Soil recuperation in Central America', in Hinchcliffe F, Thompson J, Pretty J N, Guijt I and Shah P (eds) *Fertile Ground: The Impact of Participatory Watershed Management*, Intermediate Technology Publications, London, pp32–41

Burchardt J (2002) *Paradise Lost*, I B Tauris and Co, London

Busch R (1995) *The Wolf Almanac*, Lyons Press, Guilford, CT

Buttel F H (2003) 'Internalising the societal costs of agricultural production', *Plant Physiology* 133, pp1656–1665

Callicott J B (1998) 'The wilderness idea revisited', in Callicott J B and Nelson M P (eds) *The Great New Wilderness Debate*, University of Georgia Press, Athens, GA and London

Callicott J B and Nelson M P (eds) (1998) *The Great New Wilderness Debate*, University of Georgia Press, Athens, GA and London

Callicott J B, Crowder L B and Mumford K (2000) 'Normative concepts in conservation biology: Reply to Willers and Hunter', *Conservation Biology* 14, pp575–578

Camacho T C, Roberts R E, Lazarus N B, Kaplan G A and Cohen R D (1991) 'Physical activity and depression: Evidence from the Alameda County study', *American Journal of Epidemiology* 134, pp220–231

Campos P (2006) *The Diet Myth*, Gotham Books, New York

Causey A (1996) 'Is hunting ethical?' in Petersen D (ed) *A Hunter's Heart*, Henry Holt, New York

CDC (Centers for Disease Control and Prevention) (1996) *Physical Activity and Health*, A Report of the Surgeon General, Washington, DC

CDC (2005) *Prevalence of Overweight and Obesity Amongst Adults: United States 1999–2002*, Washington, DC

Cernea M M (1991) *Putting People First*, 2nd edn, Oxford University Press, Oxford

Cernea M M (1999) *The Economics of Involuntary Resettlement*, World Bank, Washington, DC

Chambers R (2005) *Ideas for Development*, Earthscan, London

Chambers R, Pacey A and Thrupp L A (eds) (1989) *Farmer First: Farmer Innovation and Agricultural Research*, IT Publications, London

Charleston D (1999) *Nothing Better To Do*, Jardine Press, Lower Raydon, Suffolk

Clayton S and Opotow S (eds) (2003) *Identity and the Natural Environment*, MIT Press, Boston, MA

Clements D and Shrestha A (2004) *New Dimensions in Agroecology*, Food Products Press, Binghampton, NY

Cocker M and Mabey R (2005) *Birds Britannica*, Chatto and Windus, London

Coe M D (1980) *The Maya*, Thames and Hudson, London

Coleman J (1988) 'Social capital and the creation of human capital', *American Journal of Sociology* 94, supplement, ppS95–S120

Coleman J (1990) *Foundations of Social Theory*, Harvard University Press, Cambridge, MA

Colins C J and Chippendale P J (1991) *New Wisdom: The Nature of Social Reality*, Acorn Publications, Sunnybank, Queensland

Conway G R (1997) *The Doubly Green Revolution*, Penguin, London

Conway G R and Pretty J N (1991) *Unwelcome Harvest: Agriculture and Pollution*, Earthscan, London

Cooper-Marcus C and Barnes M (1995) *Gardens in Healthcare Facilities: Uses, Therapeutic Benefits and Design Recommendations*, The Centre for Health Design, Martinez, CA

Cooper-Marcus C and Barnes M (1999) *Healing Gardens: Therapeutic Benefits and Design*

Recommendations, John Wiley and Sons, New York

Corbett J (1946) *Man Eaters of Kumaon*, Oxford University Press, New York

Corbett J (1989) *The Man-Eating Leopard of Rudraprayag*, Oxford University Press, New Delhi

Costanza R, Graumlich L J and Steffen W (2007) *Sustainability or Collapse*, MIT Press, Cambridge, MA

Coughlin RE and Goldstein KA (1970) 'The extent of agreement among observers on environmental attractiveness', Regional Science Research Institute Discussion Paper Series, no 37, Regional Science Research Institute, Philadelphia, PA

Couturier A (2004) 'The abundance of less', in Rothenberg D and Pryor W J (eds) *Writing the Future*, MIT Press, Cambridge, MA

Craig C L, Brownson R C, Cragg S E and Dunn A L (2002) 'Exploring the effect of the environment on physical activity: A study examining walking to work', *American Journal of Preventive Medicine* 23, pp36–43

Crawford M A (1968) 'Fatty acid ratios in free-living and domestic animals: Possible implications for atheroma', *Lancet* 1(7556), June 22, pp1329–1333

Crissman C C, Antle J M and Capalbo S M (eds) (1998) *Economic, Environmental and Health Tradeoffs in Agriculture: Pesticides and the Sustainability of Andean Potato Production*, CIP, Lima and Kluwer, Boston, MA

Daily G (ed) (1997) *Nature's Services: Societal Dependence on Natural Ecosystems*, Island Press, Washington, DC

Dalgard O S and Tambs K (1997) 'Urban environment and mental health: A longitudinal study', *British Journal of Psychiatry* 171, pp530–536

Dasgupta P and Serageldin I (eds) (2000) *Social Capital: A Multiperspective Approach*, World Bank, Washington, DC

Davis M (2004) *Dead Cities*, The New Press, New York

Davis-Berman J and Berman D S (1989) 'The wilderness therapy programme: An empirical study of its effects with adolescents in an outpatient setting', *Journal of Contemporary Psychotherapy* 19, pp271–281

Dawkins R (2003) *A Devil's Chaplain*, Phoenix Press, London

DCMS (2002) 'Game plan: A strategy for delivering government's sport and physical activity objectives', Department of Culture, Media and Sport and Cabinet Office, London

Deacon T (1978) *The Symbolic Species*, Penguin, London

Defra (2002a) 'National food survey (2000)', Department of Environment, Food and Rural Affairs, London

Defra (2002b) 'Expenditure and food survey (2001)', Department of Environment, Food and Rural Affairs, London

Defra (2005) 'Deer action plan', Department of Environment, Food and Rural Affairs, London

de Freitas H (1999) 'Transforming microcatchments in Santa Caterina, Brazil', in Hinchcliffe F, Thompson J, Pretty J, Guijt I and Shah P (eds) *Fertile Ground: The Impacts of Participatory Watershed Development*, IT Publications, London

Delormier T and Kuhnlein H (1999) 'Dietary characteristics of eastern James Bay Cree women', *Arctic* 52(2), pp182–187

de los Reyes R and Jopillo S G (1986) *An Evaluation of the Philippines Participatory Communal Irrigation Program*, Institute of Philippine Culture, Quezon City

Department for Culture, Media and Sport (2004) 'Sporting Britain', Department for Culture, Media and Sport, London

Department for Transport (2001) 'National travel survey, 1999–2001 update', Department for Transport, London

Department of Health (2004a) 'At least five a week: Evidence on the impact of physical activity and its relationship to health', report from the Chief Medical Officer, Department of Health, London

Department of Health (2004b) 'Choosing health: Making healthy choices easier', Department of Health, London

Department of Health (2006) 'Forecast for obesity to 2010', Department of Health, London

DeSchriver M M and Riddick C C (1990) 'Effects of watching aquariums on elders' stress', *Anthrozoos* 4, pp44–48

de Vries S, Verheij R A, Groenewegen P P and Spreeuwenberg P (2003) 'Natural environments – Healthy environments? An exploratory analysis of the relationship between greenspace and health', *Environment and Planning A* 35, pp1717–1731,

Diamond J (2005) *Collapse: How Societies Choose to Fail or Survive*, Allen Lane, London

Diette G B, Lechtzin N, Haponil E, Devrotes A and Rubin H R (2003) 'Distraction theory with nature sights and sounds reduces pain during flexible bronchoscopy', *Chest* 123, pp941–948

Dobbs T and Pretty J N (2004) 'Agri-environmental stewardship schemes and "multifunctionality"', *Review of Agricultural Economics* 26(2), pp220–237

Doll R (1992) 'The cancers of life', *Cancer Research* 52, pp2024–2029

Donlan J (2005) 'Re-wilding North America', *Nature* 436, pp913–914

Donlan C J, Berger J, Bock C E, Burney D A, Estes J A, Foreman D, Martin P S, Roemer G W, Smith F A and Greene H W (2006) 'Pleistocene rewilding: An optimistic agenda for twenty-first century conservation', *The American Naturalist* 168(5)

Dyer C (1982) 'Deserted medieval villages in the West Midlands', *Economic History Review* 35, pp19–34

Eaton S B and Eaton S B III (1999) 'Hunter-gatherers and human health', in Lee R and Daly R (eds) *The Cambridge Encyclopedia of Hunters and Gatherers*, Cambridge University Press, Cambridge, UK, pp449–456

Ebbeling C B, Pawlak D B and Ludwig D S (2002) 'Childhood obesity: Public health crisis, common sense cure', *Lancet* 360(9311), pp473–482

Ecos (2006) Special issue of *Ecos* journal on reintroductions, British Association of Nature Conservationists, Gloucester, www.banc.org.uk

Eden Alternative (2002) 'Eden alternative green house project', at www.edenalt.com/

Ehrenfield D (1981) *The Arrogance of Humanism*, Oxford University Press, New York

Ehrenfield D (2005) 'The environmental limits to globalization', *Conservation Biology* 19(2), pp318–326

Ellis F (2000) *Rural Livelihoods and Diversity in Developing Countries*, Oxford University Press, Oxford

Etzioni A (1995) *The Spirit of Community*, Fontana Press, London

Eurodiet (2001) 'The Eurodiet reports and proceedings', *Public Health Nutrition Special Issue* 4.2(A), pp265–436

Evans G E (1960) *The Horse and the Furrow*, Faber and Faber, London

Evans G E (1979) *Horse Power and Magic*, Faber and Faber, London

Eveleens K G, Chisholm R, van de Fliert E, Kato M, Thi Nhat P and Schmidt P (1996) 'Mid term review of Phase III report – The FAO Intercountry Programme for the Development and Application of Integrated Pest Management Control in Rice in South and South East Asia', GCP/RAS/145-147/NET-AUL-SWI, FAO, Rome

Fawcett N R and Gulone E (2001) 'Cute and cuddly and a whole lot more', *Behaviour and Change* 18, pp124–133

Feder G, Murgai R and Quizon J B (2004) 'Sending farmers back to school: The impact of farmer field schools in Indonesia', *Review of Agricultural Economics* 26(1), pp45–62

Fergus J (1996) 'From a hunter's road', in Petersen D (ed) *A Hunter's Heart*, Henry Holt, New York

Fernández-Armesto F (2004) *So You Think You're Human?* Oxford University Press, Oxford

Ferro Luzzi A and James P (2000) 'European diet and public health: The continuing challenge', Eurodiet final report, Brussels

Fjørtoft I (1999) 'The natural environment as a playground for children: The impact of outdoor play activities in pre-primary school children', in *Proceedings of OMEP's 22nd World Congress and 50th Anniversary on the Child's Right to Care, Play and Education*, Copenhagen

Flanagan O (1991) *The Science of the Mind*, MIT Press, Cambridge, MA

Flanagan O (2004) *Dreaming Souls: Sleep, Dreams, and the Evolution of the Conscious Mind*, Oxford University Press, New York

Flannery T F (1997) *The Future Eaters*, Reed New Holland, Sydney

Flegal K M, Carroll M D, Ogden C L and Johnson C L (2002) 'Prevalence and trends in obesity among US adults 1999–2000', *Journal of the American Medical Association* 288, pp1723–1727

Flora C B and Flora J L (1996) 'Creating social capital', in Vitek W and Jackson W (eds) *Rooted in the Land: Essays on Community and Place*, Yale University Press, New Haven, CT and London, pp217–225

Flora J L (1998)' Social capital and communities of place', *Rural Sociology* 63, pp481–506

Folke C (2004) 'Traditional knowledge in social-ecological systems', *Ecology and Society* 9(3), p7

Forster E M (1908) *A Room with a View*, Edward Arnold, London

Fox W (1995) *Toward a Transpersonal Ecology*, State University of New York Press, New York

Frank R H (1999) *Luxury Fever*, Princeton University Press, Princeton, NJ

Fredrickson L M and Anderson D H (1999) 'A qualitative exploration of the wilderness experience as a source of spiritual inspiration', *Journal of Environmental Psychology* 19, pp21–39

Freeman H (1984) (ed) *Mental Health and the Environment*, Churchill Livingstone, London

Freeman H (1998) 'Healthy environments', in *Encyclopedia of Mental Health*, Academic Press, London

Friedman J M and Halaas J L (1998) 'Leptin and the regulation of body weight in mammals', *Nature* 395, pp763–770

Friedmann E and Thomas S A (1995) 'Pet ownership, social support, and one-year survival after acute myocardial infarction in the cardiac arrhythmia suppression trial (CAST)', *The American Journal of Cardiology* 76, pp1213–1217

Frumkin H (2001) 'Beyond toxicity: Human health and the natural environment', *American Journal of Preventative Medicine* 20(3), pp47–53

Frumkin, H (2002) 'Urban sprawl and public health', *Public Health Reports* 117, pp201–217

Frumkin H (2003) 'Healthy places: Exploring the evidence', *American Journal of Public Health* 93, pp1451–1456

Frumkin H (ed) (2005) *Environmental Health: From Global to Local*, Jossey-Bass, San Francisco, CA

Frumkin H, Frank L and Jackson R (2004) *Urban Sprawl and Public Health*, MIT Press, Cambridge, MA

Fukuyama F (1995) *Trust: The Social Values and the Creation of Prosperity*, Free Press, New York

Funes F, Garcia L, Bourque M, Perez N and Rosset P (eds) (2002) *Sustainable Agriculture and Resistance*, Food First Books, Oakland, CA

Gadgil M, Berkes F and Folke C (1993) 'Indigenous knowledge for biodiversity conservation', *Ambio* 22, pp151–156

Gadgil M, Seshagiri Rao PR, Utkarsh G, Pramod P, Chhatre A and members of the People's Biodiversity Initiative (2000) 'New meanings for old knowledge: The people's biodiversity registers program', *Ecological Applications* 10, pp1307–1317

Gallagher K, Ooi P, Mew T, Borromeo E, Kenmore P and Ketelaar J-W (2005) 'Ecological basis for low-toxicity integrated pest management (IPM) in rice and vegetables', in Pretty J (ed) *The Pesticide Detox*, Earthscan, London

Gallagher W (1994) *The Power of Place*, Harper Perennial, New York

Gambetta D (ed) (1988) *Trust: Making and Breaking Cooperative Relations*, Blackwell, Oxford

Garreau J (1992) *Edge City, Life on the New Frontier*, Anchor Books, New York

Gerlach-Spriggs N, Kaufman R E and Warner S B (1998) *Restorative Gardens: The Healing Landscape*, Yale University Press, New Haven, CT

Gershuny J (2005) 'Busyness as a badge of honour', Institute of Economic and Social Research Working Paper 2005–09, University of Essex, Colchester

Ghimire K B and Pimbert M P (1997) *Social Change and Conservation: Environmental Politics and Impacts of National Parks and Protected Areas*, Earthscan, London

Gide A (1897 [1970]) *Fruits of the Earth*, Penguin, Harmondsworth

Gliessman S R (1998) *Agroecology: Ecological Processes in Sustainable Agriculture*, CRC Press, Boca Raton, FL

Gliessman S R (2004) 'Integrating agroecological processes into cropping systems research', in Clements D and Shrestha A (eds) *New Dimensions in Agroecology*, Food Products Press, Binghampton, NY

Gliessman S R (2005) 'Agroecology and agroecosystems', in Pretty J (ed) *The Earthscan Reader in Sustainable Agriculture*, Earthscan, London

Goodwin J S (2000) 'Glass half full attitude promotes health in old age', *Journal of the American Geriatrics Society* 48, pp473–478

Grahn P and Stigsdotter U A (2003) 'Landscape planning and stress', *Urban Forestry and Urban Greening* 2, pp1–18

Gray J (2002) *Straw Dogs*, Granta Books, London

Gray J (2004) *Heresies, Against Progress and Other Illusions*, Granta, London

Grootaert C (1998) *Social Capital: The Missing Link*, World Bank Social Capital Initiative Working Paper No 5, World Bank, Washington, DC

Guivant J (2002) 'Gender and land rights in Brazil', UNRISD Working Paper, Geneva

Halpern D (1987) *On Nature: Essays on Nature, Landscape and Natural History*, North Point Press, New York

Halpern D (1995) *Mental Health and the Built Environment – More than Bricks and Mortar*, Taylor and Francis, Bristol

Hammond N (1994) *Ancient Mayan Civilisation*, Rutgers University Press, Piscataway, NJ

Handy S L, Boarnet M G, Ewing R and Killingsworth R E (2002) 'How the built environment affects physical activity: Views from urban planning', *American Journal of Preventive Medicine* 23, pp64–73

Hansen K (1992) *Cougar: American Lion*, Northland Publishing, Flagstaff, AZ

Harding S (2005) *Animate Earth*, Green Books, Devon

Harpur M (2006) *Mystery Big Cats*, Heart of Albion Press, Loughborough

Harrison R P (2003) *The Dominion of the Dead*, University of Chicago Press, Chicago, IL and London

Hart D and Sussman R (2004) *Man the Hunted: Primates, Predators and Human Evolution*, Westview Press, Boulder, CO

Hartig T, Evans G W, Jamner L D, Davis D S and Garling T (2003) 'Tracking restoration in natural and urban field settings', *Journal of Environmental Psychology* 23, pp109–123

Hartig T, Mang M and Evans G W (1991) 'Restorative effects of natural environment experiences', *Environment and Behaviour* 23, pp3–26

Hassame A, Martin P and Reij C (2000) *Water Harvesting, Land Rehabilitation and Household Food Security in Niger*, International Fund for Agricultural Development, Rome

Hassanali A, Herren H, Khan Z R and Pickett J A (2007) 'Integrated pest management', *Philosophical Transactions of the Royal Society of London B* (in press)

Hassink J (2003) 'Combining agricultural production and care for persons with disabilities: A new role of agriculture and farm animals', Wageningen University, Wageningen, The Netherlands

Hayashi A (2002) 'Finding the voice of Japanese wilderness', *International Journal of Wilderness* 8, pp34–37

Hayashi T, Tsumura K, Suematsu C, Okada K, Fujii S and Endo G (1999) 'Walking to work and the risk for hypertension in men: The Osaka health survey', *Annals Internal Medicine* 130, pp21–26

Haywood J (2005) *The Penguin Historical Atlas of Ancient Civilisations*, Penguin, London

Hedley A A, Ogden C L, Johnson C L, Carroll M D, Curtis L R and Flegel K M (2004) 'Overweight and obesity among US children, adolescents and adults 1999–2002', *Journal of the American Medical Association* 291, pp2847–2850

Heerwagen J H and Orians G H (1993) 'Humans, habitats and aesthetics', in Kellert S R and Wilson E O (eds) *The Biophilia Hypothesis*, Island Press, Washington, DC

Henriksen G (1973) *Hunters in the Barrens: The Naskapi on the Edge of the White Man's World*, Institute of Social and Economic Research Press, St John's, Newfoundland

Henriksen G (1993) 'Report on the social and economic development of the Innu community of Davis Inlet to the economic recovery commission', Government of Newfoundland and Labrador, St John's, Newfoundland

Heong K L, Escalada M M, Huan N H and Mai V (1999) 'Use of communication media in changing rice farmers' pest management in the Mekong Delta, Vietnam', *Crop Management* 17(5), pp413–425

Herren H, Schulthess F and Knapp M (2005) 'Towards zero-pesticide use in tropical agroecosytems', in Pretty J (ed) *The Pesticide Detox*, Earthscan, London

Herzog H A (1988) 'The moral status of mice', *American Psychology* 43(6), pp473–474

Herzog T, Chen H C and Primeau J S (2002) 'Perception of the restorative potential of natural and other settings', *Journal of Environmental Psychology* 22, pp295–306

Hibbelin J (1998) 'Fish consumption and depression', *Lancet* 351, p1212

Higgs E (2003) *Nature by Design*, MIT Press, Cambridge, MA

Hinchcliffe F, Thompson J, Pretty J, Guijt I and Shah P (eds) (1999) *Fertile Ground: The Impacts of Participatory Watershed Development*, IT Publications, London

Hobbs T R and Shelton G C (1972) 'Therapeutic camping for emotionally disturbed adolescents', *Hospital and Community Psychiatry* 23, pp298–301

Holdaway R N (1999) 'Introduced predators and avifaunal extinction in New Zealand', in MacPhee R D E (ed) *Extinctions in New Time*, Kluwer, New York

Honeyman M C (1992) 'Vegetation and stress: A comparison study of varying amounts of vegetation in countryside and urban scenes', in Relf D (ed) *The Role of Horticulture in Human Well-Being and Social Development: A National Symposium*, Timber Press, Portland, OR, pp143–145

Hrdy S B, Carter CS and Ahnert L (2005) *Attachment and Bonding*, MIT Press, Cambridge, MA

HSE (2004) 'Health and safety statistics highlights', at www.hse.gov.uk

Hunter J (1976) *The Making of the Crofting Community*, Mainstream, Edinburgh

Hunter J (1999) *Last of the Free: A Millennial History of the Highlands and Islands of Scotland*, Mainstream, Edinburgh and London

Hunter J (2005a) *Scottish Exodus*, Mainstream, Edinburgh

Hunter J (2005b) 'Moorland without crofters', 2nd Angus Macleod Memorial Lecture, Pairc School, Gravir, Isle of Lewis, 18 October

Hunter J (2006) 'History: Its key place in our future', inaugural lecture, University of Highlands and Islands Centre for History, Inverness, 19 May

Hurst J G (1972) 'The changing medieval village in England', in Ucko P J, Trigham R and Doubleday G W (eds) *Man, Settlement and Urbanism*, Duckworth, London

Hyer L, Boyd S, Scurfield R, Smith D and Burke J (1996) 'Effects of outward bound experience as an adjunct to inpatient PTSD treatment of war veterans', *Journal of Clinical Psychology* 52, pp263–278

IEEP and WWF (1994) *The Nature of Farming, Low Intensity Systems in Nine European Countries*, Institute for European Environmental Policy, London and World Wide Fund for Nature, Geneva

Innu Nation and Mushuau Innu Band Council (1993) *Gathering Voices: Discovering our Past, Present and Future*, Innu Nation Office, Sheshatshiu, Labrador

Innu Nation and Mushuau Innu Band Council (1995) *Gathering Voices: Finding Strength to Help Our Children*, Douglas and McIntyre, Vancouver

Innu Nation (1996) *Between a Rock and a Hard Place*, Innu Nation, Sheshatshiu

IUCN (2006) 'Red list of threatened species', at www.iucnredlist.org

Jackson D B and Green R E (2000) 'The importance of the introduced hedgehog as a predator of eggs of waders on Machair in South Uist, Scotland', *Biological Conservation* 93, pp333–348

Jackson D B (2001) 'Experimental removal of introduced hedgehogs improves wader nest success in the Western Isles, Scotland', *Journal of Applied Ecology* 38, pp802–812

Jackson D L and Jackson L L (2002) *The Farm as Natural Habitat*, Island Press, Washington, DC

Jackson W (1994) *Becoming Native to this Place*, University Press of Kentucky, Lexington, KY

Jacobs J (1961) *The Life and Death of Great American Cities*, Random House, London

Jerstad L and Stelzer J (1973) 'Adventure experiences as treatment for residential mental patients', *Therapeutic Recreation Journal* 7, pp8–11

Johnson B (2002) 'On the spiritual benefits of wilderness', *International Journal of Wilderness* 8, pp28–32

Jones K (2004) *Wolf Mountains*, University of Calgary Press, Calgary

Jones S (1999) *Almost Like a Whale*, Doubleday, London

Jordan W R III (2003) *The Sunflower Forest*, University of California Press, Berkeley, CA

Kabore D and Reij C (2004) 'The emergence and spreading of an improved traditional soil and water conservation practice in Burkina Faso', Environment and Production Technology Division Paper 114, International Food Policy Research Institute, Washington, DC

Kahn P H and Kellert S R (2002) *Children and Nature: Psychological, Sociocultural and Evolutionary Investigations*, MIT Press, Cambridge, MA

Kals E, Schumacher D and Montada L (1999) 'Emotional affinity toward nature as a motivational basis to protect nature', *Environment and Behaviour* 31, pp178–202

Kaplan R (2001) 'The nature of the view from home: Psychological benefits', *Environment and Behaviour* 33, pp507–542

Kaplan R and Kaplan S (1989) *The Experience of Nature: A Psychological Perspective*, Cambridge University Press, Cambridge, UK

Kaplan R, Kaplan S and Ryan R L (1998) *With People in Mind, Design and Management of Everyday Nature*, Island Press, Washington, DC

Kaplan S (1995) 'The restorative benefits of nature: Toward an integrated framework', *Environment and Behaviour* 33, pp480–506

Kaplan S and Talbot J F (1983) 'Psychological benefits of a wilderness experience', in Altman I A and Wohlwill J F (eds) *Human Behaviour and Environment*, Plenum, New York, pp163–203

Kasser T (2002) *The High Price of Materialism*, MIT Press, Cambridge, MA

Katcher A and Wilkins G G (1993) 'Dialogue with animals: Its nature and culture', in Kellert S R and Wilson E O (eds) *The Biophilia Hypothesis*, Island Press, Washington, DC

Kellert S R and Wilson E O (1993) (eds) *The Biophilia Hypothesis*, Island Press, Washington, DC

Kenkel D S and Manning W (1999) 'Economic evaluation of nutrition policy, or, There's no such thing as a free lunch', *Food Policy* 24, pp145–162

Key T J, Allen N E, Spencer E A and Travis R C (2002) 'The effect of diet on risk of cancer', *Lancet* 360, pp861–868

Khan Z R, Pickett J A, van den Berg J and Woodcock C M (2000) 'Exploiting chemical ecology and species diversity: Stem borer and *Striga* control for maize in Africa', *Pest Management Science* 56(1), pp1–6

Kirmayer L, Simpson C and Cargo M (2003) 'Healing traditions: Culture, community and mental health promotion with Canadian Aboriginal peoples', *Australasian Psychiatry* 11, supplement, ppS15–S23

Kishigami N (2000) 'Contemporary Inuit food sharing and hunter support program of Nunavik, Canada', in Wenzel G, Hovelstrud-Broda G and Kishigami N (eds) *The Social Economy of Sharing: Resource Allocation and Modern Hunter-Gatherers*, Senri Ethnological Series No 53, National Museum of Ethnology, Osaka, Japan

Kline D (1990) *Great Possessions*, Wooster Book Company, Wooster, OH

Kraybill D B (2001) *The Riddle of Amish Culture*, 2nd edn, Johns Hopkins Press, Baltimore, MD

Krings M, Stone A, Schmitz R W, Kawanitzki H, Stoneking M and Paabo S (1997) 'Neanderthal DNA sequences and the origin of modern humans', *Cell* 90, pp19–30

Kroeber A L (1957) *Handbook of the Indians of California*, Dover Publications, Mineola, NY

Kropotkin P (1902) *Mutual Aid*, Extending Horizon Books, Boston, MA (1955 edition)

Kunstler J H (2005) *The Long Emergency*, Atlantic Books, London

Kuo F E and Sullivan W C (2001) 'Environment and crime in the inner city: Does vegetation reduce crime?' *Environment and Behaviour* 33, pp343–367

Kuo F E, Bacaicoa M and Sullivan W S (1998) 'Transforming inner-city landscapes: Trees, sense of safety and preference', *Environment and Behaviour* 30, pp28–59

Laland K N and Brown G R (2005) *Sense and Nonsense*, Oxford University Press, Oxford

Laland K N and Brown G R (2006) 'Niche construction, human behaviour and the adaptive-lag hypothesis', *Evolutionary Anthropology* 15, pp95–104

Laland K N and Odling-Smee J (2003) 'Life's little builders', *New Scientist* (15 November), pp43–45

Lang T and Heasman M (2004) *Food Wars*, Earthscan, London

Lange E and Schaeffer P (2001) 'A comment on the market value of a room with a view', *Landscape and Urban Planning* 55, pp113–120

Larsen L, Adams J, Deal B, Kweon B-S and Tyler E (1998) 'Plants in the workplace: The effects of plant density on productivity, attitudes and perceptions', *Environment and Behaviour* 30, pp261–281

Laumann K, Garling T and Stormark K M (2003) 'Selective attention and heart rate responses to natural and urban environments', *Journal of Environmental Psychology* 23, pp125–134

Lavalée C, Robinson E and Valverde C (1994) 'Promoting physical activity in a Cree community', *Arctic Medical Research* 53, supplement 2, pp197–203

Lawson B (2002) *Harris in History and Legend*, John Donald, Edinburgh

Lee R B and Daly R (eds) (1999) *The Cambridge Encyclopedia of Hunters and Gatherers*, Cambridge University Press, Cambridge, UK

Lee R B and DeVore (1968) *Man the Hunter*, Aldine, Chicago, IL

Leonard J A, Wayne R K, Wheeler J, Valadez R, Guillen S and Vila C (2002) 'Ancient DNA evidence for old world origin of new world dogs', *Science* 298, pp1613–1616

Leopold A (1949) *A Sand County Almanac and Sketches Here and There*, Oxford University Press, London and New York (1974 edition)

Lewis C A (1992) 'Effects of plants and gardening in creating interpersonal and community well-being', in Relf D (ed) *The Role of Horticulture in Human Well-Being and Social Development, A National Symposium*, Timber Press, Portland, OR, pp55–65

Lewis G and Booth M (1994) 'Are cities bad for your mental health?' *Psychological Medicine* 24, pp913–915

Li Wenhua (2001) *Agro-Ecological Farming Systems in China*, Man and the Biosphere Series Volume 26, UNESCO, Paris

Lim K and Taylor L (2005) 'Factors associated with physical activity among older people – A population-based study', *Preventive Medicine* 40(1), pp33–40

Lindheim R and Syme S L (1983) 'Environments, people and health', *Annual Review of Public Health* 4, pp335–339

Lindsey G, Man J, Payton S and Dickson K (2004) 'Property values, recreation values and urban greenways', *Journal of Park and Recreation Administration* 22(3), pp69–90

Lippard L R (1997) *The Lure of the Local*, New Press, New York

Loney M (1995) 'Social problems, community trauma and hydro project impacts', *Canadian Journal of Native Studies* 15(2), pp231–254

Lopez B (1978) *Of Wolves and Men*, Simon and Schuster, New York

Lopez B (1986) *Arctic Dreams*, Harvill, London,

Lopez B (1988) *Crossing Open Ground*, Picador, London

Lopez B (1998) *About this Life*, Harvill, London

Loring S (1998) 'Stubborn independence: An essay on the Innu and archaeology', in Smith P J and Mitchell D (eds) *Bringing Back the Past: Historical Perspectives on Canadian Archaeology*, Mercury Series, Archaeological Survey of Canada Paper 158, Canadian Museum of Civilization, Hull, Quebec, pp259–276

Loring S and Ashini D (2000) 'Past and present pathways: Innu cultural heritage in the twenty-first century', in Smith C and Ward G (eds) *Indigenous Cultures in an Interconnected World*, Allen and Unwin, St Leonards, NSW, pp167–200

Louv R (2005) *Last Child in the Woods*, Algonquin Press, Chapel Hill

Lovelock J (1995) *The Ages of Gaia*, Oxford University Press, Oxford

Lovelock J (2005) *The Revenge of Gaia*, Allen Lane, London

Luther M and Gruehn D (2001) 'Putting a price on urban green spaces', *Landscape Design* 303, pp23–25

Luttik J (2000) 'The value of trees, water and open space as reflected by house prices in the Netherlands', *Landscape and Urban Planning* 48, pp161–167

Lynch B D and Brusi R (2005) 'Nature, memory and nation: New York's Latino gardens and casitas', in Barlett P (ed) *Urban Place*, MIT Press, Cambridge, MA

Mabey R (1996) *Flora Britannica*, Sinclair Stevenson, London

Macdonald D and Baker S (2006) *The State of Britain's Mammals (2006)*, Mammals Trust, London

Macfarlane R (2003) *Mountains of the Mind*, Granta, London

Mackey M G A and Orr R D (1987) 'An evaluation of household country food use in Makkovik, Labrador, July 1980–June 1981', *Arctic* 40(1), pp60–65

MacLellan A (2002) *The Furrow Behind Me*, translated by John Lorne Campbell, Berlinn, Edinburgh

Madson J (1996) 'Why men hunt', in Petersen D (ed) *A Hunter's Heart*, Henry Holt, New York

Maffi L (1999) 'Linguistic diversity', in Posey D (ed) (1999) *Cultural and Spiritual Values of*

Biodiversity, IT Publications and UNEP, London

Maffi L (2006) 'Language: A resource for nature', in Pretty J (ed) *Environment*, Vol 1 of 4, Sage, London, pp157–174

Maller C, Townsend M, Brown P and St Leger L (2002) *Healthy Parks Healthy People: The Health Benefits of Contact with Nature in a Park Context*, Deakin University and Parks Victoria, Melbourne, Australia

Maloof J (2004) 'De-evolution and transhumanism', in Rothenberg D and Pryor W J (eds) *Writing the Future*, MIT Press, Cambridge, MA

Malthus T (1798) *An Essay on the Principles of Population*, J Johnson, St Paul's Churchyard, London

Marquardt O and Caulfield R (1996) 'Development of west Greenlandic markets for country foods since the 18th century', *Arctic* 49(2), pp107–119

Martin P (1996) 'New perspectives of self, nature and others', *Australian Journal of Outdoor Education* 1, pp3–9

Maslow A H and Mintz N L (1972) 'Effects of aesthetic surroundings', in Gutman R (ed) *People and Buildings*, Basic Books, New York

Matless D, Merchant P and Watkins (2005) 'Animal landscapes: Otters and wildfowl in England, 1945–1970', *Transactions of the Institute of British Geography* 30, pp191–205

Mayer A M (1997) 'Historical changes in the mineral content of fruits and vegetables', *British Food Journal* 99, pp207–211

McEvedy C (1980) *The Penguin Atlas of African History*, Penguin, London

McGrath-Hanna N, Greene D, Tavernier R and Bult-Ito A (2003) 'Diet and mental health in the Arctic: Is diet an important risk factor for mental health in circumpolar peoples? A review', *International Journal of Circumpolar Health* 62(3), pp228–241

McGuane T (1996) 'The heart of the game', in Petersen D (ed) *A Hunter's Heart*, Henry Holt, New York

McKibben B (2003) *The End of Nature*, Bloomsbury, London

McNeely J A and Scherr S J (2003) *Ecoagriculture*, Island Press, Washington, DC

McNeill J (2000) *Something New Under the Sun*, Penguin, London

MEA (Millennium Ecosystem Assessment) (2005) *Ecosystems and Well-Being, Vol 1: Current State and Trends*, Millennium Ecosystem Assessment, Island Press, London,

MEA (2006) *Ecosystems and Human Well-Being*, Island Press, Washington, DC

Metzner R (2000) *Green Psychology, Transforming Our Relationship to the Earth*, Park Street Press, Rochester, VT

Michalski J H, Mishna F, Worthington C and Cummings R (2003) 'A multi-method impact evaluation of a therapeutic summer camp program', *Child and Adolescent Social Work Journal* 20, pp53–76

Mills S (2004) *Tiger*, BBC Books, London

Milton K (2002) *Loving Nature: Towards an Ecology of Emotion*, Routledge, London

Mind (2005) *Stress and Mental Health in the Workplace*, London

Mior L C (2005) *Agricultores Familiares, Agroindústrias e Redes de Desenvolvimento Rural*, Federal University of Santa Caterina, Florianopolis, Brazil

Moore E O (1981) 'A prison environment's effect on health care service demands', *Journal of Environmental Systems* 11, pp17–34

Morice R D (1976) 'Woman dancing dreaming: Psychosocial benefits of the Aboriginal Outstation Movement, *Medical Journal of Australia* 225–26, pp939–42

Morison J, Hine R and Pretty J (2005) 'Survey and analysis of labour on organic farms in the UK and Republic of Ireland', *International Journal of Agricultural Sustainability* 3(1), pp24–43

Morris D (2005) *The Naked Ape*, new edition, Vintage, London

Morris P A (1998) 'Hedgehog rehabilitation in perspective', *Veterinary Record* 143, pp633–636

Morris J and Urry J (2005) *Growing Places*, Centre for Mobility Research, Department of Sociology, Lancaster University, Lancaster

Motluk A (2004) 'Life sentence', *New Scientist* 30, October, p47

Moyer J A (1988) 'Bannock bereavement retreat: A camping experience for surviving children', *The American Journal of Hospice Care* 5, pp26–30

Muir J (1911) *My First Summer in the Sierra*, Houghton Mifflin, Boston, MA (reprinted in 1988 by Canongate Classics, Edinburgh)

Muir J (1992) *The Eight Wilderness-Discovery Books*, Diaden Books, London and Seattle

Myers N and Kent J (2003) 'New consumers: The influence of affluence on the environment', *Proceedings of the National Academy of Sciences* 100, pp4963–4968

Myers N and Kent J (2004) *The New Consumers*, Island Press, Washington, DC

Nabhan G (1982) *The Desert Smells Like Rain*, North Point Press, San Francisco, CA

Nabhan G P (2000) 'Interspecific relationships affecting endangered species recognised by O'odham and Comcáac cultures', *Ecological Applications* 10, pp1288–1295

Nabhan G P and St Antoine S (1993) 'The loss of floral and faunal story: The extinction of experience', in Kellert S R and Wilson E O (eds) *The Biophilia Hypothesis*, Island Press, Washington, DC

Nabhan G P and Trimble S (1994) *The Geography of Childhood*, Beacon Press, Boston, MA

Naess A (1989) *Ecology, Community and Lifestyle: Outline of an Ecosophy*, Cambridge University Press, Cambridge, UK

Naess A (1992) 'Deep ecology and ultimate premises', *Society and Nature* 1(2), pp108–119

NAO (National Audit Office) (2001) *Tackling Obesity in England*, Stationary Office, London

Narayan D and Pritchett L (1996) *Cents and Sociability: Household Income and Social Capital in Rural Tanzania*, Policy Research Working Paper 1796, World Bank, Washington, DC

Nash R (1973) *Wilderness and the American Mind*, Yale University Press, New Haven, CT

National Urban Forestry Unit (2002a) *Greenspace and Healthy Living*, The Comedy Store, Manchester

National Urban Forestry Unit (2002b) *Urban Forestry in Practice: Hospital Greenspace as an Aid to Healthcare*, Wolverhampton

Naughton-Treves L, Grossberg R and Treves A (2003) 'Paying for tolerance: Rural citizens' attitudes toward wolf depradation and competition', *Conservation Biology* 17(6), pp1500–1511

Nelson R (1983) *Make Prayers to the Raven*, University of Chicago Press, Chicago, IL

Nelson R (1987) *Heart and Blood, Living with Deer*, Vintage, New York

Nelson R (1996) 'Finding common ground', in Petersen D (ed) *A Hunter's Heart*, Henry Holt, New York

Nestle M (2003) *Food Politics: How the Food Industry Influences Nutrition and Health*, University of California Press, Berkeley, CA

Nettle D (2005) *Happiness*, Oxford University Press, Oxford

Newman O (1972) *Defensible Space*, Macmillan, New York

Newman O (1980) *Community of Interest*, Anchor Books, New York

New Scientist (2005) 'A skeptic's guide to intelligent design', 9 July, pp10–11

Nightingale F (1860, revised 1996) *Notes on Nursing (Revised with Additions)*, Balliere Tindall, London

NIH (National Institute of Diabetes and Digestive and Kidney Diseases of the National Institutes of Health) (2002) 'Prevalence statistics related to overweight and obesity', National Institutes of Health, Washington, DC

Nogales M, Martín A, Tershy B R, Donlan C J, Veitch D, Puerta N, Wood B and Alonso J (2004) 'A review of feral cat eradication on islands', *Conservation Biology* 18(2), pp310–319

Norse D, Li Ji, Jin Leshan and Zhang Zheng (2001) *Environmental Costs of Rice Production in China*, Aileen Press, Bethesda

North T C, McCullagh P and Tran Z V (1990) 'The effects of exercise on depression', *Exercise and Sport Sciences Reviews* 18, pp379–415

Noske B (1989) *Humans and Other Animals*, Pluto Press, London

NRC (2000) *Our Common Journey: Transition Towards Sustainability*, National Research Council, National Academy Press, Washington, DC

NSALG (National Society of Allotment and Leisure Gardeners) (1993) 'National survey of allotment gardens', London

Nuttall M (1998) *Protecting the Arctic: Indigenous Peoples and Cultural Survival*, Routledge, Abingdon

O'Brien F (1967) *The Third Policeman*, Picador, London

Odling-Smee F J, Laland K N and Feldman M W (1996) 'Niche construction', *The American Naturalist* 147, pp641–648

Odling-Smee F J, Laland K N and Feldman M W (2003) *Niche Construction: The Neglected Process in Evolution*, Princeton University Press, Princeton, NJ

OECD Nuclear Energy Agency (2002) *Chernobyl: Assessment of Radiological and Health Impact, Ten Years On*, Vienna

Okri B (1996) 'Joys of Story Telling', in *Birds of Heaven*, Penguin, Harmondsworth

Okuson I S, Chandra K M, Boon A, Boltri J M, Choi S T, Parish D C and Dever G E A (2004) 'Abdominal adiposity in US adults, 1960–2000', *Preventive Medicine* 39, pp197–206

Oldfield T E E, Smith R J, Harrup S R and Leader-Williams N (2003) 'Field sports and conservation in the UK', *Nature* 423, pp531–533

Olsson P and Folke P (2001) 'Local ecological knowledge and institutional dynamics for ecosystem management: A study of Lake Racken watershed, Sweden', *Ecosystems* 4, pp85–104

Olsson P, Folke C and Hahn T (2004) 'Social-ecological transformation for ecosystem management: The development of adaptive co-management of a wetland landscape in southern Sweden', *Ecology and Society* 9(2), available from www.ecologyandsociety.org/vol9/iss4/art2/

Orr D W (2002) 'Political economy and the ecology of childhood', in Kahn P H and Kellert S R (eds) *Children and Nature: Psychological, Sociocultural, and Evolutionary Investigations*, MIT Press, Cambridge, MA, pp279–304

Orr D W (1993) *Ecological Literacy*, SUNY Press, New York

Orr D W (2004) *The Last Refuge*, Island Press, Washington, DC

Orr D W (2005) *The Right to Life*, Oberlin College, Oberlin, OH

Orr D W (2006) *Design on the Edge*, MIT Press, Cambridge, MA

Ostir G V, Markides K S, Peek M K and Goodwin J S (2001) 'The association between emotional well-being and the incidence of stroke in older adults', *Psychosomatic Medicine* 63, pp210–215

Ostrom E, Dietz T, Dosãak N, Stern P C, Stonich S and Weber E U (eds) (2002) *The Drama of the Commons*, National Academy Press, Washington, DC

Ostrom E (1990) *Governing the Commons: The Evolution of Institutions for Collective Action*, Cambridge University Press, New York

Owen N, Leslie E, Salmon J and Fotheringham M J (2000) 'Environmental determinants of physical activity and sedentary behaviour', *Exercise and Sport Sciences Reviews* 28, pp153–158

Owen N, Humpel N, Leslie E, Bauman A and Sallis J (2004) 'Understanding environmental influences on walking', *American Journal of Preventative Medicine* 27(1), pp67–76

Paffenbarger R S J, Hyde R T, Wing A L, Lee I-M, Jung D L and Kampert J B (1993) 'The association of changes in physical activity level and other lifestyle characteristics with mortality among men', *New England Journal of Medicine* 328, pp538–545

Pars T, Osler M and Bjerregaard P (2001) 'Contemporary use of traditional and imported food among Greenlandic Inuit', *Arctic* 54(1), pp22–31

Parsons R, Tassinary L G, Ulrich R S, Hebl R S and Grossman-Alexander M (1998) 'The view from the road: Implications for stress recovery and immunization', *Journal of Environmental Psychology* 18, pp113–140

Pate R R, Pratt M, Blair S N, Haskell W L, Macera C A, Bouchard C, Buchner D, Ettinger W, Heath G W, King A C, Kriska A, Leon A S, Marcus B H, Morris J, Paffenbarger R S, Patrick K, Pollock M L, Rippe J M, Sallis J and Wilmore J H (1995) 'Physical activity and public health: A recommendation from the Centers for Disease Control and Prevention and the American College of Sports Medicine', *Journal of the American Medical Association* 273, pp402–407

Peacock J, Hine R, Willis G, Griffin M and Pretty J (2005) 'The physical and mental health benefits of environmental improvements at two sites in London and Welshpool', report for the Environment Agency, CES, University of Essex, Colchester

Peat F D (1996) *Blackfoot Physics: A Journey into the Native American Universe*, Fourth Estate, London

Peiser R B and Schwann G M (1993) 'The private value of public open space within subdivisions', *Journal of Architectural and Planning Research* 10 (summer), pp91–104

Petersen D (ed) (1996) *A Hunter's Heart*, Henry Holt, New York

Peterson M D (1970) *Thomas Jefferson and the New Nation*, Oxford University Press, New York

Pevalin D J and Rose D (2003) *Social Capital for Health – Investigating the Links Between Social Capital and Health Using the British Household Panel Survey*, University of Essex, Colchester

Philo C and Wilbert C (2000) *Animal Spaces, Beastly Places*, Routledge, London

Pickett J A (1999) 'Pest control that helps control weeds at the same time', *BBSRC Business*, April

Pierotti R and Wildcat D (2000) 'Traditional ecological knowledge: The third alternative (commentary)', *Ecological Applications* 10, pp1333–1340

Pilgrim S E (2006) 'A cross-cultural study into local ecological knowledge', PhD thesis, University of Essex, Colchester UK

Pilgrim S, Smith D J and Pretty J (2007a) 'A cross-regional quantitative assessment of the factors affecting ecoliteracy: Implications for conservation policy and practice', *Ecological Applications* (in press)

Pilgrim S, Cullen L, Smith D J and Pretty J (2007b) 'Hidden harvest or hidden revenue', *Indian Journal of Traditional Knowledge* 6(1), pp150–159

Pinheiro S, Cardoso A M, Turnes V, Schmidt W, Brito R and Guzzati M (2002) 'Sustainable rural life and agroecology, Santa Caterina State, Brazil', in Sciallaba N El H and Hattam C (eds) *Organic Agriculture, Environment and Food Security*, FAO, Rome

Pinker S (2002) *The Blank Slate*, Penguin, London

Platteau J-P (1997) 'Mutual insurance as an elusive concept in traditional communities', *Journal of Development Studies* 33(6), pp764–796

Plumwood V (1996) 'Being prey', in Rothenberg D and Ulvaeus M (eds) *The New Earth Reader: The Best of Terra Nova*, MIT Press, Cambridge, MA, pp76–91

Popkin B M (1998) 'The nutrition transition and its health implications in lower-income countries', *Public Health Nutrition* 1(1), pp5–21

Popkin B M (1999) 'Urbanisation, lifestyle changes and the nutrition transition', *World Development* 27, pp1905–1916

Porritt J (2005) *Capitalism as if the World Matters*, Earthscan, London

Posey D (ed) (1999) *Cultural and Spiritual Values of Biodiversity*, IT Publications and UNEP, London

Precoda N (1991) 'Requiem for the Aral Sea', *Ambio* 20(3–4), pp109–114

Pretty J N (1995a) 'Participatory learning for sustainable agriculture', *World Development* 23(8), pp1247–1263

Pretty J (1995b) *Regenerating Agriculture: Policies and Practice for Sustainability and Self-Reliance*, Earthscan, London

Pretty J (1998) *The Living Land*, Earthscan, London

Pretty J (2002) *Agri-Culture: Reconnecting People, Land and Nature,* Earthscan, London

Pretty J (2004) 'How nature contributes to mental and physical health', *Spirituality and Health International* 5(2), pp68–78

Pretty J (ed) (2005) *The Pesticide Detox*, Earthscan, London

Pretty J (2006) 'A tale of two cities', *BBC Wildlife Magazine*, vol 24, no 1, pp52–55

Pretty J and Smith D J (2004) 'Social capital in biodiversity conservation and management', *Conservation Biology* 18, pp631–638

Pretty J and Waibel H (2005) 'Paying the price: The full cost of pesticides', in Pretty J (ed) *The Pesticide Detox*, Earthscan, London

Pretty J and Ward H (2001) 'Social capital and the environment', *World Development* 29(2), pp209–227

Pretty J, Brett C, Gee D, Hine R, Mason C F, Morison J I L, Raven H, Rayment M and van der Bijl G (2000) 'An assessment of the total external costs of UK agriculture', *Agricultural Systems* 65(2), pp113–136

Pretty J, Brett C, Gee D, Hine R E, Mason C F, Morison J I L, Rayment M, van der Bijl G and Dobbs T (2001) 'Policy challenges and priorities for internalising the externalities of agriculture', *Journal of Environment, Planning and Management* 44(2), pp263–283

Pretty J, Ball A S, Li Xiaoyun and Ravindranath N H (2002) 'The role of sustainable agriculture and renewable resource management in reducing greenhouse gas emissions and increasing sinks in China and India', *Philosophical Transactions of the Royal Society of London, A* 360, pp1741–1761

Pretty J, Griffin M, Sellens M and Pretty C J (2003a) 'Green exercise: Complementary roles of nature, exercise and diet in physical and emotional well-being and implications for public health policy', CES Occasional Paper 2003-1, University of Essex, Colchester

Pretty J, Mason C F, Nedwell D B and Hine R E (2003b) 'Environmental costs of freshwater eutrophication in England and Wales', *Environmental Science and Technology* 37(2), pp201–208

Pretty J, Morison J I L and Hine R E (2003c) 'Reducing food poverty by increasing agricultural sustainability in developing countries', *Agriculture, Ecosystems, Environment* 95(1), pp217–234

Pretty J, Griffin M and Sellens M (2004) 'Is nature good for you?' *Ecos* 24, pp2–9

Pretty J, Griffin M, Peacock J, Hine R, Sellens M and South N (2005a) *A Countryside for Health and Well-Being: The Physical and Mental Health Benefits of Green Exercise*, Countryside Recreation Network, Sheffield

Pretty J, Lang T, Ball A and Morison J (2005b) 'Farm costs and food miles: An assessment of the full cost of the weekly food basket', *Food Policy* 30(1), pp1–20

Pretty J, Peacock J, Sellens M and Griffin M (2005c) 'The mental and physical health outcomes of green exercise', *International Journal of Environmental Health Research* 15, pp319–337

Pretty J, Noble A, Bossio D, Dixon J, Hine R E, Penning de Vries F W and Morison J I L (2006) 'Resource conserving agriculture increases yields in developing countries', *Environmental Science and Technology* 40(4), pp1114–1119

Prior R (2000) *Roe Deer: Management and Stalking*, Swan Hill Press, Shrewsbury

Purcell A T and Lamb R J (1998) 'Preference and naturalness: An ecological approach', *Landscape and Urban Planning* 42, pp57–66

Puska P (2000) 'Nutrition and mortality: The Finnish experience', *Acta Cardiologica* 55, pp213–220

Putnam R D, with Leonardi R and Nanetti R Y (1993) *Making Democracy Work: Civic Traditions in Modern Italy*, Princeton University Press, Princeton, NJ

Putnam R (1995) 'Bowling alone: America's declining social capital', *Journal of Democracy* 6(1), pp65–78

Pyle R M (2001) 'The rise and fall of natural history: How a science grew that eclipsed direct experience', *Orion* 20, pp17–23

Pyle R M (2003) 'Nature matrix: Reconnecting people and nature', *Oryx* 37, pp206–214

Quammen D (2004) *Monster of God*, Hutchinson, London

Randall K, Shoemaker C A, Relf D and Geller S E (1992) 'Effects of plantscapes in an office environment on worker satisfaction', in Relf D (ed) *The Role of Horticulture in Human Well-Being and Social Development: A National Symposium* (proceedings), Timber Press, Portland, OR, pp106–109

Rees M (2003) *Our Final Century*, Arrow Books, London

Rees W, Wackernagel M and Testemae P (1996) *Our Ecological Footprint, Reducing Human Impact on the Earth*, New Society, Gabriola, Canada

Rees W (2003) 'Ecological footprints', *Nature* 421, p898

Reeve N J (1998) 'Survival and welfare of hedgehogs after releases back into the wild', *Animal Welfare* 7, pp189–202

Reij C (1996) 'Evolution et impacts des techiques de conservation des eaux et des sols', Centre for Development Cooperation Services, Vrije Univeriseit, Amsterdam

Reynolds V (2002) *Well-being Comes Naturally: An Evaluation of the BTCV Green Gym at Portslade, East Sussex*, Report 17, School of Health Care, Oxford Brookes University, Oxford

Riboli E and Norat T (2001) 'Cancer prevention and diet: Opportunities in Europe', *Public Health Nutrition* 4, pp473–484

Richards K and Smith B (eds) (2003) *Therapy Within Adventure*, proceedings of the Second International Conference, University of Augsburg, Zeil, Germany

Ridley M (1999) *Genome*, Fourth Estate, London

Ridley M (2003) *Nature via Nurture*, Fourth Estate, London

Robertson A, Tirado C, Lobstein T, Jermini M, Knai C, Jensen J H, Ferro-Luzzi A and James W P T (2004) *Food and Health in Europe*, WHO, Copenhagen

Röling N G and Wagemakers M A E (eds) (1997) *Facilitating Sustainable Agriculture*, Cambridge University Press, Cambridge, UK

Röling N (2005) 'From causes to reasons: The human dimensions of agricultural sustainability', *International Journal of Agricultural Sustainability* 1(1), pp73–88

Rothenberg D and Pryor W J (eds) (2004) *Writing the Future*, MIT Press, Cambridge, MA

Rowley T and Wood J (1982) *Deserted Medieval Villages*, Shire Archaeology, Princes Risborough, UK

Rudner R (1996) 'The call of the climb', in Petersen D (ed) *A Hunter's Heart*, Henry Holt, New York

Russell J A and Mehrabian A (1976) 'Some behavioural effects of the physical environment', in Wapner S, Cohen S B and Kaplan B (eds) *Experiencing the Environment*, Plenum, New York

Russell K C (2002) 'A longitudinal assessment of outcomes in outdoor behavioural healthcare', Technical Report 28, Idaho Forest, Wildlife and Range Experimental Station, Moscow, ID

Rutt C D and Coleman K J (2005) 'The impact of the built environment on walking as a leisure-time activity along the US/Mexico border', *Journal of Physical Activity and Health* 3, pp257–271

Rutter M (2005) *Genes and Behaviour, Nature–Nurture Interplay Explained*, Routledge, London

Ryan R L and Grese R E (2005) 'Urban volunteers and the environment: Forest and prairie restoration', in Barlett P (ed) *Urban Place*, MIT Press, Cambridge, MA

Sage C (2003) 'Social embeddedness and relations of regard: Alternative good food networks in South West Ireland', *Journal of Rural Studies* 19, pp47–60

Sahlins M (2003) *Stone Age Economics*, 2nd edn, Routledge, London

Sainsbury Centre for Mental Health (2005) *The Economic and Social Costs of Mental Illness*, London

Sallis J F, Bauman A and Pratt M (1998) 'Environmental and policy interventions to promote physical activity', *American Journal of Preventive Medicine* 15, pp379–397

Salzman E (2004) 'From Broken Island', in Rothenberg D and Pryor W J (eds) *Writing the Future*, MIT Press, Cambridge, MA

Samson C (2003) *A Way of Life That Does Not Exist: Canada and the Extinguishment of the Innu*, Verso, London

Samson C and Pretty J (2006) 'Environmental and health benefits of hunting lifestyles and diets for the Innu of Labrador', *Food Policy* 31(6), pp528–553

Samson C, Wilson J and Mazower J (1999) *Canada's Tibet: The Killing of the Innu*, Survival International, London

Savills Residential Research (2006) *How Building Nothing Can Increase Land Value*, London

Savolainen P, Zhang Y-P, Luo J, Lundberg J and Leitner T (2002) 'Genetic evidence for an East Asian origin of domestic dogs', *Science* 298, pp1610–1613

Scarborough V (2007) 'The rise and fall of the ancient Maya' in Costanza R, Graumlich L J and Steffen W (2007) *Sustainability or Collapse*, MIT Press, Cambridge, MA, pp51–60

Schama S (1996) *Landscape and Memory*, Fontana Press, London

Schlosser P (2002) *Fast Food Nation*, Penguin, London

Schoen A M (2001) *Kindred Spirits*, Broadway Books, New York

Schwartz B (2004) *The Paradox of Choice*, Harper, New York

Sciallaba N El H and Hattam C (2002) *Organic Agriculture, Environment and Food Security*, FAO, Rome

Scoones I, Melnyk M and Pretty J (1992) *The Hidden Harvest: Wild Foods and Agricultural Systems, A Literature Review and Annotated Bibliography*, IIED, London

Scully D, Kremer J, Meade M M, Graham R and Dudgeon K (1998) 'Physical exercise and psychological wellbeing: A critical review', *British Journal of Sports Medicine* 32, pp111–120

Sempkirk J, Aldridge J and Becker S (2002) *Social and Therapeutic Horticulture: Evidence and Messages from Research*, Report Evidence Issue 6, Loughborough University, Thrive and CCFR (Centre for Child and Family Research), Loughborough University

Sendak M (1963) *Where the Wild Things Are*, Red Fox, London

Serpell J (1996) *In the Company of Animals*, Cambridge University Press, Cambridge, UK

Shafer E L and Richards T A (1974) 'A comparison of viewer reactions to outdoor scenes and photographs of those scenes', USDA Forest Service Research Paper NE-302, Northeastern Forest Experiment Station, Upper Darby, PA

Sheldrake R (2003) *The Sense of Being Stared At*, Arrow Books, London

Shepard P (1998) *Coming Home to the Pleistocene*, Island Press, Washington, DC

Sherwood S, Cole D, Crissman C and Paredes M (2005) 'Transforming potato systems in the Andes', in Pretty J (ed) *The Pesticide Detox*, Earthscan, London

Siegel J (1990) 'Stressful life events and use of physician services among the elderly: The moderating effect of pet ownership', *Journal of Personality and Social Psychology* 58, pp1081–1086

Sieveking P (2003) 'Alien big cats in Britain', *Fortean Times* 167

Skoga K and Krange P (2003) 'A wolf at the gate: The anti-carnivore alliance and the symbolic construction of community', *Sociologica Ruralis* 43(3), pp309–325

Slack P and Ward R (2002) *The Peopling of Britain, The Shaping of a Human Landscape*, Oxford University Press, Oxford

SNH/Scottish Executive/RSPB (2002) Uist Wader Project Factsheets 1–8

Snyder G (1990) *The Practice of the Wild*, Shoemaker Hoard, Washington, DC

Snyder G (1995) *A Place in Space*, Counterpoint, New York

Sommer R (2003) 'Trees and human identity', in Clayton S and Opotow S (eds) *Identity and the Natural Environment*, MIT Press, Boston, MA

Sorte G (1975) 'Methods for presenting planned environment', *Man–Environment Systems* 5, pp148–154

Speakman J R, Stribbs R J and Mercer J G (2002) 'Does body weight play a role in regulation of food intake?' *Proceedings of the Nutrition Society* 61, pp1–15

Sport England (2002) *Addressing the Health Agenda*, Sport England, London

Staats H and Hartig T (2004) 'Alone or with a friend: A social context for psychological restoration and environmental preferences', *Journal of Environmental Psychology* 24, pp199–211

Stegner W (1962) *Wolf Willow*, Penguin, London

Steinbeck J (1937) *Of Mice and Men*, Covici Friede, New York

Stevens S (ed) (1997) *Conservation through Cultural Survival*, Island Press, Washington, DC

Story M, Stevens J, Himes J, Rock B H, Ethelbah B and Davis S (2003) 'Obesity in American Indian children: Prevalence, consequences and prevention', *Preventive Medicine* 37, supplement 1, ppS3–S12

Stys Y (2001) *Wilderness Therapy*, University of Ottawa, Ottawa

Subak S (1999) 'Global environmental costs of beef production', *Ecological Economics* 30, pp79–91

Suzuki D (1997) *Sacred Balance*, Bantam Books, London

Swift M J, Izac A-M N and van Noordwijk M (2004) 'Biodiversity and ecosystem services in agricultural landscapes – Are we asking the right questions?', *Agriculture, Ecosystems and Environment* 104, pp113–134

Tabbush P M and O'Brien E A (2003) *Health and Well-being: Trees, Woodlands and Natural Spaces*, Forestry Commission, Edinburgh

Takano T, Nakamura K and Watanabe M (2002) 'Urban residential environments and senior citizens' longevity in megacity areas: The importance of walkable green spaces', *Journal of Epidemiology and Community Health* 56, pp913–918

Tall D (1996) 'Dwelling; making peace with space and place', in Vitek W and Jackson W (eds) *Rooted in the Land: Essays on Community and Place*, Yale University Press, New Haven, CT and London

Taylor A F, Wiley A, Kuo F E and Sullivan W C (1998) 'Growing up in the inner city: Green spaces as places to grow', *Environment and Behaviour* 30, pp3–27

Taylor A F, Kuo F E and Sullivan W C (2001) 'Coping with ADD: The surprising connection to green play settings', *Environment and Behaviour* 33, pp54–77

Taylor M (1982) *Community, Anarchy and Liberty*, Cambridge University Press, Cambridge, UK

Taylor P (2005) *Beyond Conservation: A Wildland Strategy*, Earthscan, London

Tegtmeier E M and Duffy M D (2004) 'External costs of agricultural production in the United States', *International Journal of Agricultural Sustainability* 2, pp155–175

Tennessen C M and Cimprich B (1995) 'Views to nature: Effects on attention', *Journal of Environmental Psychology* 15, pp77–85

Terwan P, Ritchie M, van der Weijden W, Verschuur G and Joannides J (2004) *Values of Agrarian Landscapes across Europe and North America*, Reed Business Information, Doetinchem

Tester K (1991) *Animals and Society*, Routledge, London

Thomas K (1983) *Man and the Natural World*, Penguin, London

Thompson E P (1975) *Whigs and Hunters*, Penguin, Harmondsworth

Thoreau H D (1837–1853) *The Writings of H D Thoreau Volumes 1–6* (published 1981 to 2000), Princeton University Press, Princeton, NJ

Thoreau H D (1902) *Walden or Life in the Woods*, Henry Frowde and Oxford University Press, London, New York and Toronto

Thorpe H (1965) 'The Lord and the landscape', *Transactions of the Birmingham Archaeological Society* LXXX, pp38–77

Tilman D, Cassman K G, Matson P A, Naylor R and Polasky S (2002) 'Agricultural sustainability and intensive production practices', *Nature* 418, pp671–677

Tomich T P, Chomitz K, Francisco H, Izac A-M N, Murdiyarso D, Ratner B D, Thomas D E and van Noordwijk M (2004) 'Policy analysis and environmental problems at different scales: Asking the right questions', *Agriculture, Ecosystems and Environment* 104, pp5–18

Tönnies F (1887) *Gemienschaft und Gessellschaft*, Routledge and Kegan Paul, London

Tuan Y-F (1977) *Sense and Place*, University of Minnesota Press, Minneapolis, MN

Tudge C (2004) *So Shall We Reap*, Penguin, London

Turner N J, Ignace M B and Ignace R (2000) 'Traditional ecological knowledge and wisdom of aboriginal peoples in British Columbia', *Ecological Applications* 10, pp1275–1287

Ulrich R S (1981) 'Natural versus urban scenes: Some psychophysiological effects', *Environment and Behaviour* 13, pp523–556

Ulrich R S (1984) 'View through a window may influence recovery from surgery', *Science* 224, pp420–421

Ulrich R S (1993) 'Biophilia, biophobia and natural landscapes', in Kellert S R and Wilson E O (eds) *The Biophilia Hypothesis*, Island Press, Washington, DC

Ulrich R S (1999) 'Effects of gardens on health outcomes: Theory and research', in Cooper Marcus C and Marni B (eds) *Healing Gardens, Therapeutic Benefits and Design Recommendations*, John Wiley and Sons, New York, pp27–86

Ulrich R S and Parsons R (1992) 'Influences of passive experiences with plants on individual well-being and health', in Relf D (ed) *The Role of Horticulture in Human Well-Being and Social Development: A National Symposium*, Timber Press, Portland, OR, pp93–105

UN (2004) 'World population to 2300', New York

UN (2005a) 'Long-range world population projections: Based on the 1998 revision', UN Population Division, New York

UN (2005b) 'World population prospects, the 2004 revision', UN Population Division, New York

UN-OCHO/WHO (2002) 'The human consequences of the Chernobyl nuclear accident', United Nations and WHO, Copenhagen

Uphoff N (1993) 'Grassroots organisations and NGO in rural development: Opportunity with diminishing stakes and expanding markets', *World Development* 21(4), pp607–622

Uphoff N (1998) 'Understanding social capital: Learning from the analysis and experience of participation', in Dasgupta P and Serageldin I (eds) *Social Capital: A Multiperspective Approach*, World Bank, Washington, DC

Uphoff N (ed) (2002) *Agroecological Innovations*, Earthscan, London

US Commission on Civil Rights (2004) 'Broken promises: Evaluating the Native American health care system', Office of the General Counsel, Washington, DC

Usher P J (1976) 'Evaluating country food in the northern native economy', *Arctic* 29(2), pp105–120

Veblen T (1899) *The Theory of the Leisure Class*, Macmillan, New York

Veitayaki J (1997) 'Traditional marine resource management practices used in the Pacific Islands: An agenda for change', *Ocean and Coastal Management* 37, pp123–136

Verderber S and Reuman D (1987) 'Windows, views and health status in hospital therapeutic environments', *Journal of Architectural and Planning Research* 4, pp120–133

Vuori I, Lankenau B and Pratt M (2004) 'Physical activity policy and program development: The experience of Finland', Public Health Reports 119, pp331–345

Wackernagel M, White S and Moran D (2004) 'Using ecological footprint accounts: From analysis to applications', *International Journal of Environment and Sustainable Development*, vol 3, no 3–4, pp293–315

Wallace G N (1996) 'Dealing with death', in Petersen D (ed) *A Hunter's Heart*, Henry Holt, New York

Wanless D (2002) *Securing Our Future Health: Taking a Long-Term View*, HM Treasury, London

Wanless D (2004) *Securing Good Health for the Whole Population*, HM Treasury, London

Warady B A (1994) 'Therapeutic camping for children with end-stage renal disease', *Pediatric Nephrology* 8, pp387–390

Ward A (2005) 'Expanding ranges of wild and feral deer in Great Britain', *Mammal Review* 35, pp165–173

Warwick K (2004) 'Intelligent robots or cyborgs', in Rothenberg D and Pryor W J (eds) *Writing the Future*, MIT Press, Cambridge, MA

Watt E T (2004) *Don't Let the Sun Step Over You*, University of Arizona Press, Tuscon AZ

Weaver I C G, Cervoni N, Champagne F A, D'Alessio A C, Sharma S, Seckl J R, Dymov S, Szyf M and Meaney M J (2004) 'Epigenetic programming by maternal behaviour', *Nature Neuroscience* 7, pp847–854

Wein E, Henderson Sabry J and Evers F T (1991) 'Food consumption patterns and use of country foods by Native Canadians near Wood Buffalo National Park, Canada', *Arctic* 44(3), pp196–205

Wein E, Freeman M and Makus J (1996) 'Use and preference for traditional foods among the Belcher Island Inuit', *Arctic* 49(3), pp256–264

Weissman J (ed) (1995a) *City Farmers: Tales from the Field*, Parks and Recreation, City of New York, New York

Weissman J (ed) (1995b) *Tales from the Field, Stories by Green Thumb Gardeners*, Parks and Recreations, City of New York, New York

Wells N and Evans G (2003) 'Nearby nature: A buffer of life stress among rural children', *Environment and Behaviour* 35, pp311–330

Wells N (2000) 'At home with nature: Effects of "greenness" on children's cognitive functioning', *Environment and Behaviour* 32, pp775–795

White P, Smart J C R, Bohm M, Langbein J and ward A I (2005) *Economic Impact of Deer*, Forestry Commission and English Nature, Peterborough

White R and Heerwagen J (1998) 'Nature and mental health: Biophilia and biophobia', in Lundberg A (ed) *The Environment and Mental Health: A Guide for Clinicians*, Lawrence Erlbaum Associates, Mahwah, NJ, pp175–192

Whitehouse S, Varni J W, Seid M, Cooper-Marcus C, Ensberg M J, Jacobs J R and Mehlenbeck R S (2001) 'Evaluating a children's hospital garden environment: Utilisation and consumer satisfaction', *Journal of Environmental Psychology* 21, pp301–314

WHO (1998) *Obesity: Preventing and Managing the Global Epidemic*, WHO, Geneva

WHO (2001) *World Health Report*, World Health Organization, Geneva

WHO (2002) *World Health Report*, World Health Organization, Geneva

Williams A (1999) *Therapeutic Landscapes: The Dynamic Between Place and Wellness*, University Press of America, Lanham, MD

Williams K and Harvey D (2001) 'Transcendent experience in forest environments', *Journal of Environmental Psychology* 21, pp249–260

Williams T T (1996) 'Deerskin', in Petersen D (ed) *A Hunter's Heart*, Henry Holt, New York

Wilson E O (1975) *Sociobiology*, Belknap Press, Cambridge, MA

Wilson E O (1984) *Biophilia – The Human Bond with Other Species*, Harvard University Press, Cambridge, MA

Wilson E O (2002) *The Future of Life*, Abacus, London

Winston R (2002) *Human Instinct*, Bantam, London

REFERENCES

Winter M (2003) 'Embeddedness, the new food economy and defensive localism', *Journal of Rural Studies* 19, pp23–32

Wood R and Handley J (1999) 'Urban waterfront regeneration in the Mersey Basin, north west England', *Journal of Environmental Planning and Management* 42(4), pp565–580

Woods B (1996) 'The hunting problem', in Petersen D (ed) *A Hunter's Heart*, Henry Holt, New York

Woolcock, M (1998) 'Social capital and economic development', *Theory and Society* 27, pp151–208

World Commission on Dams (2002) *Dams and Development*, London

Worster D (1993) *The Wealth of Nature: Environmental History and the Ecological Imagination*, Oxford University Press, New York

WRI (2006) World Resources Institute Statistics, at www.wri.org

Xu F, Yin X-M, Zhang M, Leslie E, Ware R and Owen N (2005) 'Family average income and body mass index above the healthy weight range among urban and rural residents in regional mainland China', *Public Health Nutrition* 8(1), pp47–56

Yarbrough J M (1998) *American Virtues: Thomas Jefferson on the Character of Free People*, University Press of Kansas, Lawrence, KS

Young T K (1994) *The Health of Native Americans*, Oxford University Press, New York

INDEX